ANN DILLON

FOR THOSE OF US WAITING ON THAT DAY!

A Daily Devotional for Christians that are Grieving

WESTBOW
PRESS®
A DIVISION OF THOMAS NELSON
& ZONDERVAN

Scripture taken from the Holy Bible, NEW INTERNATIONAL VERSION®. Copyright © 1973, 1978, 1984 by Biblica, Inc. All rights reserved worldwide. Used by permission. NEW INTERNATIONAL VERSION® and NIV® are registered trademarks of Biblica, Inc. Use of either trademark for the offering of goods or services requires the prior written consent of Biblica US, Inc.

Scripture quotations taken from the Holy Bible, New Living Translation, Copyright © 1996, 2004. Used by permission of Tyndale House Publishers, Inc., Wheaton, Illinois 60189. All rights reserved.

Scripture quotations taken from the New American Standard Bible®, Copyright © 1960, 1962, 1963, 1968, 1971, 1972, 1973, 1975, 1977, 1995 by The Lockman Foundation. Used by permission. (www.Lockman.org)

WestBow Press books may be ordered through booksellers or by contacting:

WestBow Press
A Division of Thomas Nelson & Zondervan
1663 Liberty Drive
Bloomington, IN 47403
www.westbowpress.com
1 (866) 928-1240

Because of the dynamic nature of the Internet, any web addresses or links contained in this book may have changed since publication and may no longer be valid. The views expressed in this work are solely those of the author and do not necessarily reflect the views of the publisher, and the publisher hereby disclaims any responsibility for them.

Any people depicted in stock imagery provided by Thinkstock are models, and such images are being used for illustrative purposes only. Certain stock imagery © Thinkstock.

ISBN: 978-1-4908-8916-0 (sc)
ISBN: 978-1-4908-8917-7 (hc)
ISBN: 978-1-4908-8915-3 (e)

Library of Congress Control Number: 2015911143

Print information available on the last page.

WestBow Press rev. date: 02/10/2017

Thank you to those who shared their grief and the verses of comfort while waiting on that day to be reunited with the following loved ones: Keith Bryan, our cousin; Cleo Pettit, my wonderful brother-in-law's sweet mother; Sue Picus, our family friend whom we called aunt; Kenny Don Pettit; Phyllis Roberson; Grant McKoy; Bethany Wood; Oliver A. McElroy; Roy Garvin; Randy Glenn; Cleo Bowen; Shelly Copeland and Gonzalo Martinez.

Thank you to Tan Flippin for undertaking the tedious task of editing this book. Thank you for this labor of love for Don. I appreciate you so much.

Thank you to my church family and friends. You have been such a blessing to pray, contact me, the cards and emails. To Bro. Chet Haney, Jeff Harp, Barbara Cassidy, Ron and Martha and our Sunday School class: thank you.

Thank you to my clients who were with me before Don went Home and continued on with me, lifting us in prayer, being patient, and allowing my tears. You know who you are. Thank you.

Thank you Connie Seymour; Karla McDonald for walking with me; Pastor Scott for checking on us; Gloria Camp for crying with me; Dillon Enderby for the beautiful poems and affirmation of Don's and my love for eternity; Debi Mattocks for your encouragement of the continuity of relationships; and Penny Andrews (and Greg Andrews for sharing your wife and your help) for your constant walking with me with tears, prayers, Bible study, encouragement and for calling me your eternal friend. I look forward to the day we all celebrate in eternity.

Thank you to my family. God has blessed our family beyond measure. I look forward to the day we all worship God together in eternity. Jim and Carmen Bryan, thanks for your prayers; Our son-in-law Joel Williams, a blessing; Teresa, Carson, and Lanny Pettit, I don't know what I would have done without your being right there all the time. Thank you. Mom; you have so many whom you love in Heaven, yet you still give tirelessly here. Thank you for your example. To our beautiful daughters, Melody and Michelle, Dad and I thanked God for you every day. You are both a true blessing. We will all be reunited someday in eternity.

Dedicated with love to the two godly men in my life. They have preceded us to Heaven. They are an example to all of godly men, faithful to our Lord. Dad, "Bro. Bob Bryan," and Don, the love of my life, my soul mate, I long to be reunited with you in eternity, to worship our Lord together again.

I am waiting on that day. Come, Lord Jesus. Come!

This book was written out of my own need to seek God during my time of profound and deep sorrow. I was seeking God diligently and reading the Bible, several devotionals, and a number of Christian books. All were helpful but when I read the devotionals, there were so many times that they did not address specifically the relentless pain, sorrow and anxiety that come with grief. I hope and pray that if you are in that same place, God speaks to you through this book. Grief is universal but we each experience it in a very personal and unique way. In the forward to *A Grief Observed* by C.S. Lewis, his step-son wrote, "The greater the love the greater the grief, the stronger the faith, the more mightily Satan storms the fortress."[1] If you don't feel God, if He seems very distant or silent, remember those words. The doubt is from the enemy. Keep reading, keep praying, and keep seeking God. He is there and, trust me, there were and are many times I didn't feel Him.

I feel God has helped me see that I must keep an eternal perspective. Heaven is our true Home. Our sovereign, loving God has an eternal plan. We must look at this life through an eternal lens. As believers we journey Home. Death does not end the relationships of believers. Keep that in mind. Two books I highly recommend are *Heaven* by Randy Alcorn and *Heaven Revealed* by Paul Enns. I read and re-read them. I also encourage you to read the books from which I have quoted, especially if you find comfort in the words of the author.

As you do these devotionals, I recommend that you get a journal and write in it every day as you read. Memorize the scriptures used and other scriptures that God lays on your heart. Quote them even if you are not feeling God at the moment; journal them when you don't know anything else to write. I also created a play list on my iPhone of songs to listen to while I journaled and read. The songs that were of particular help to me were: "I can Only Imagine" by Mercy Me; "Homesick" by Mercy Me; "Broken Hallelujah" by Mandisa; "Watching

---

[1]   C.S. Lewis, *A Grief Observed* (New York: Harper Collins EBook, 2009), Location 133.

Over You" by Comfort Manyame; Steven Curtis Chapman's album: *Beauty Will Rise*; "Praise you in the Storm" by Casting Crowns; "How Great is Our God" and "I Will Rise" by Chris Tomlin.

Find the ones that speak to you and listen to the words as you seek God.

After I had written this book and while it was being edited, I discovered another book and song that I highly recommend. *Revelations: A Survivor's Story of Faith, Hope and the Coming Kingdom* by Nicole DiCenzio is an excellent book. And the song "SEE You in a Little While" by Steven Curtis Chapman is amazing.

My story:

I am a licensed professional counselor. I have done grief counseling for a number of years. I have cried with and for my clients as they hurt; I have prayed for them. But even with all of the experience, I was not prepared for my own journey.

I was blessed with a very strong Christian background. My parents raised us in a very loving and Christian home. My Dad was a Methodist minister, my mom a stay-at-home mom who earned extra money babysitting. I have a brother and sister. A cousin came to live with us, making us a family of six. We didn't have much money growing up, but we had a lot of love. In one of the small east Texas towns where we moved I met my future husband, Don. Even in high school he was a strong Christian. He and friends had started a devotional group that met each morning before school. We married after high school, and my parents became his parents, my family his family. God blessed us with two beautiful daughters.

In December 2009, my very godly father went home to be with the Lord. He had battled with COPD and then in August 2009 was diagnosed with lung cancer. He stayed strong and was a witness even in the hospital as he was hooked to all kinds of tubes. He was passing out cards that said, "Dear Friend, I have everything under control. Love, Jesus." We made trips to the hospital in the middle of the night as the COPD advanced. And though he suffered, his faith never wavered. His loving family surrounded him as he passed into our Heavenly Father's arms.

Then in November 2011, my godly husband, my soul mate, the love of my life, the man I had been with since I was fourteen years old, the man I married at eighteen and with whom I had two beautiful daughters with, the man with whom I am truly one in every sense of the word—spiritually, physically and emotionally—suddenly and without warning went Home to be with the Lord. Don was the epitome of a healthy man. He had a physical that summer and the doctor was amazed at his good health. At fifty-nine he rode his bicycle thirty to seventy miles a week. He rode in bicycle rallies that were a hundred miles long. He worked out, ate right, took vitamins, did all the things we are supposed to do. We called him superman. Yet he was humble and would say, "More like superman on kryptonite." We were packed to go out of town for a family weekend at our cabin in the woods. He said, "I am going to work out in the back, take a shower, and finish packing." We were looking forward to getting away. We talked about our trip. I was busy in the front part of the house, we would say something occasionally, and then I asked him something and he didn't answer. I stepped to the back room, and he was on the floor and gone. I called 9-1-1; my sister, brother-in-law, and nephew who live next door were there immediately and did CPR; but we knew he was already Home. Doctors called the heart attack a "widow maker."

Whatever your loss, whether it was sudden or expected, whether it was someone young or someone who lived many years, loss is never easy to experience. The pain and sorrow are overwhelming and relentless.

The Bible tells us that as Christians, we immediately go to be with our Lord. While you are planning the funeral, while you are still in shock, while you are asking why, your loved one is Home. While you are thinking this can't be happening, thinking surely you will wake up and find yourself in a horrid nightmare, while you are unable to sleep, eat, and breathe, your loved one is at Home and is surrounded by the glory of our Lord. You have emotions flooding your system. The pain overwhelms you; you can barely move. Your loved one dwells in perfect peace and love. Try to imagine your loved ones in Jesus' arms. I know it is hard to even think right now but as you close your eyes, try to picture their joy in seeing Jesus. Their joy in seeing loved ones that have gone before.

In his book *Heaven,* Randy Alcorn does a good job of explaining the intermediate Heaven and the eternal Heaven. The Bible lets us know we immediately go to be with our Lord (2 Corinthians 5:8-9; Philippians 1:23; Luke 23:43). But it also shows us that the eternal plan is a New Heaven and a New Earth. All of creation is looking forward to that day. All of the events of our lives are moving toward that goal. Life and death do not make sense if this life is all there is, but this life and this world is not all there is. We have an eternal destination. Your loved one arrived there before you.

My Dad, aware of the short time, told us that for his service, he wanted God to be glorified. He wanted Dr. Clara Reed, the District Superintendent of the Methodist churches in the Sherman-McKinney area, to do his service. She did a phenomenal job. She said, "We will do a Homegoing celebration." I have chosen to refer to our loved ones' departure as Homegoing. I want you to stay focused on the fact that they are at Home, our true Home. I have also chosen to capitalize Heaven like Randy Alcorn did in *Heaven* because Heaven is a real place, a destination. I have chosen to capitalize pronouns in reference to our Lord unless it is a direct quote. There are several times I have inserted a _____ with the hope you will put your own loved one's name there. I have also used some scriptural passages more than once because there is more to say about them than I can say in one day's devotional. When you are dealing with grief, you may find you are in a fog. So I think it also helps to view the same scripture different days. We need scriptural reinforcement, that reminder, to keep us focused on His Word. I have asked questions at the end of each day's devotional. I find that asking for your participation seems to help you think more. Every seventh day is a day of reflection of the ones before. I find that I need to ponder and meditate on those things that I read and, hopefully, taking a day for that will help you. I wrote this book for those who are grieving the loss of a Christian loved one. I use the words "Christian," "believing loved ones" and "redeemed." But I also know that there are some of you who may have had a young child called Home. We know Jesus loves children. (Mathew 18:2-4,10; 19:13-14; 21:16; Luke 18:16). Randy Alcorn does an excellent job of talking about babies and children in his book *Heaven*. He asks, "But what about infants, small children, and those that are mentally handicapped or have died too young to believe in Christ?"[2] He uses the above scriptures. He also quotes Luke 1:15 to explain how John the Baptist was filled with the Holy Spirit in his mother's womb. He goes on to write, "Because of such passages, I believe God in his mercy and his special love for children covers them with Christ's blood.... Perhaps in Heaven many people will meet their children who were aborted or their children who died in miscarriages.... Many parents will be reunited with children who died at an early age. Perhaps these children will grab our hands, and show us around the present Heaven. Then one day, after the final resurrection, we'll enjoy each other's company on the New Earth and experience its wonders together."[3] Every book I read on Heaven seems to agree and I have never thought differently. After all, family and the love of children is the nature of God.

I pray that these devotions help you keep your mind and heart focused on God and His eternal plan for those of us who accept Him as our Savior. Even though the pain will still be there, I pray you keep an eternal perspective. Please feel free to contact me for prayer or anything you may want to share as we journey Home together. You may contact me at adillon@cableone.net. Blessings, Ann Dillon

---

[2]   Randy Alcorn, *Heaven* (Carol Stream, IL: Tyndale House, 2004), 354.
[3]   Ibid., 356.

DAY 1

You saw me before I was born. Every day of my life was recorded in your book; every moment was laid out before a single day had passed. (Psalm 139:16, NLT)

God has an eternal plan. Our days are recorded before we are born. We have a Homegoing date already established. It may seem way too soon for us that our loved one has gone before us. We had many more plans here. But God is in control and this world is not all there is. I know that there are times it may not seem like He is in control. After all, how much sense does this loss make? Why? Why would He take _____?

There are some answers that we will not understand this side of Heaven. But God sees His children and their Homegoing is precious in His sight. Their days were written and ordained before they were born. The appointed time for our loved one to go Home has happened. If you are reading this book and have lost a child, I can imagine that you are truly wondering about the short time you had with your precious child. Perhaps you had a miscarriage and never held your child; remember this verse says, "You saw me before I was born." I don't know the answer to why some have very few days. There is much we do not understand; we have to trust Him at this point. No matter the age of the person who has gone Home, we were not ready and we are hurting. Our loved ones are not; they are safely in the arms of Our Lord. You may feel like I do: Then take me too, Lord. Let me go with him. Our days are written in the book as well. Your loved one has gone on before you to our Heavenly destination, to our Lord.

As I journaled one day early on, I felt as if God impressed on me to think of Don on a trip ahead of me. Our believing loved ones have gone ahead of us. Your ticket has been bought, though; the price paid. God knows your arrival date; you don't. For now, rest in Him here and seek His will. Know in God's timing we will someday see Jesus face to face. We will see Him fully; we will understand, and the time we are in now will all make sense in light of eternity. We will be reunited with our loved one. God is in control. There is an eternal plan. Trust Him even when you don't feel Him. Say, "Jesus, I trust you even if I don't feel you and I don't understand." We are waiting on that day!

What are your thoughts and feelings on this verse? How do you feel about the statement, "We have a Homegoing date already established?"

1

DAY 2

You don't let me sleep. I am too distressed even to pray. (Psalm 77:4, NLT)

Read Psalm 77:2, 7-9. The psalmist is very honest about not feeling God. He is crying out for God to not turn His back on him. If that is what you are feeling, journal that very thought just as the psalmist does. Sometimes it feels like God has shut the door at the time you need Him the most. I don't know why that is. Maybe it is because we are in such a panic ourselves that we wouldn't hear Him if He shouted. The silence is deafening and the darkness overwhelming. He is there, even if you don't feel Him.

There were so many nights that I felt like if I lay down, I could not breathe. Nights were excruciating. The man I loved whom I had slept with for over thirty-eight years was not at my side. Maybe you have lost a spouse and have that empty bedside; maybe a child that you long to hold and help fall asleep. If you are too distressed to pray, tell God how you feel. Remind yourself He is there even if you cannot feel Him. Write in your journal; call your prayer warriors and ask that they pray you feel God's presence. Listen to your music and breathe. God is the same God who has always been there for you. Sometimes we shut the door not meaning to do so. But He is there. As you talk to Him, imagine yourself at His feet, His hand on you. He loves you. Ask Him to surround you with His presence. C.S. Lewis experienced this same thing when his wife, Helen, died. In his book *A Grief Observed*, he wrote, "But to go to Him when your need is desperate, when all other help is vain, and what do you find? A door slammed in your face and a sound of bolting and double bolting on the inside."[4] But sometime later he also wrote:

And so, perhaps, with God I have gradually been coming to feel that the door is no longer shut and bolted. Was it my own frantic need that slammed it in my face? The time when there is nothing at all in your soul except a cry for help may be just the time when God can't give it; you are like the drowning man who can't be helped because he clutches and grabs, perhaps your own reiterated cries deafen you to the voice you hoped to hear.[5]

People have always called out to God from the beginning of time and will continue to do so…just like this moment in your life and until Christ comes again. You are not alone. We are not alone; God hears us even if we can't feel Him.

Are you having trouble sleeping? Write what happens when you try to sleep. What are your thoughts and feelings on C.S. Lewis' statements?

---

[4]   C.S., Lewis, *A Grief Observed* (New York: Harper Collins EBook, 2009), Location 201.
[5]   Ibid., Location 509.

DAY 3

Precious in the sight of the Lord is death of His faithful saints. (Psalm 116:15, NIV)

In God's sight, our going Home as a believer is precious. Because of the Fall, we will all see death unless we are still alive when Jesus comes back. But because of Jesus' sacrifice on the cross and His resurrection, death is not the end. We go to be with our Lord and Savior and our Homegoing is precious in His sight; He cares about each one of us. He welcomes us Home.

Joseph Stowell writes, "Heaven is where we are completely released from every consequence of the Fall and where we are finally restored to an eternal, unhindered relationship with God."[6] Tony Evans writes, "The world puts a period after death, but from God's standpoint death is only a pause so brief it's not even worth trying to measure. Paul says that at the resurrection our bodies shall be changed "in the twinkling of an eye" (1 Corinthians 15:52); that's how fast you and I will be in eternity when we die. Death is a conjunction, followed by a destination."[7] As Christians, we know that our loved one is with our Savior, but our temporary loss is still so very painful. As we constantly struggle through the pain we must try to try focus on the eternal perspective. Death, until Christ comes again, is the doorway to Heaven. We are not ready, but God is ready and planned for each one of us; our death is precious in His sight. Our passing from this life to the next is a precious moment. We too will make that journey. We will be welcomed into our Lord's presence, and we will be reunited with our loved one.

You may feel like you are being punished; after all you are hurting. You are the one left. You may feel like God is punishing you by taking someone you love so much. But, of course, He is not. The death of our loved one is precious in His sight. Death is not a punishment for you. It is a Homegoing for our loved ones.

What are your thoughts and feelings on this verse? What are your thoughts on the quotes?

---

[6] Taken from *Eternity* © 2006 by Joseph M. Stowell, and used by permission of Discovery House Publishers, Grand Rapids, MI 49501. All rights reserved. P.56.

[7] Tony Evans, *Tony Evans Speaks Out On Heaven and Hell* (Chicago, IL: Moody, 2000), 9.

DAY 4

A person's days are determined;
you have decreed the number of his months
and have set limits he cannot exceed. (Job 14:5, NIV)

Much like the verse in Psalms that states our days were recorded before we were born, this verse allows us to see we have an appointed time. I kept reminding myself of this when Don went Home so suddenly. He was in perfect health one minute, and we were planning a trip out of town. The next he was with our Lord. Nothing made sense and I could not wrap my brain around the nightmare I was living. But I have to remind myself even now: God is sovereign, and Don's days were recorded and appointed. I wish his life here had not ended so soon. But I have to trust God and I am immensely thankful for the days we had here and the days we will have together in eternity.

One reason Paul Enns' book *Heaven Revealed* was so special to me was his story was so similar to mine. I had already thought so many of the things he had written. I completely understand these words of his, "I still believe that God has appointed the days for Helen and the days for me. I just wished He had appointed more days for her. I am lonely—very lonely—without her, and no one else can fill that void."[8] He also writes:

God directs our lives, all the details, event after event, year after year, and then at precisely the right time, He takes us home. God determines the number of days we spend on earth. They are different for each of us. Some live longer lives, some shorter. Then, at the end of our days, he receives us home, into the brilliance of His Heavenly home.[9]

Shelley Copeland, a beautiful godly woman bravely fought cancer with her loving husband and children by her side. But she wanted all to know, "Cancer is never going to beat me, I am only going when the good Lord is ready for me at my appointed time." And when God did call her Home, her husband Steve and her children made sure that was known to all. Like my Dad, Shelley glorified God in her life, her sickness and her Homegoing. God was glorified in Don's life and Homegoing. Now as we walk Home we too will glorify God.

Our days are decreed and we cannot exceed them. Even though we want our loved one here with us, Like Paul Enns writes, "At this moment our loved one is in His brilliance of His Heavenly home." We must remember we will have an eternity with our loved ones to worship God. We are waiting on that day!

What are your thoughts and feelings on this verse and Paul Enns' words?

---

8   Paul Enns, *Heaven Revealed* (Chicago, IL: Moody, 2011), 14.
9   Ibid., 48.

4

DAY 5

To You, Lord I call: you are my Rock do not turn a deaf ear to me. For if you remain silent I will be like those who go down to the pit. (Psalm 28:1, NIV)

There are a number of scriptures throughout the devotional that deal with not hearing God. I think it is important to know that we are not alone in the seeming silence. With grief all is magnified. When someone we love is taken from this Earth to Heaven, our world falls apart. We cry out to God, our source of strength and comfort, and often we can't feel Him. Our prayers seem to go unanswered. Our loved one's absence is screaming at us, and we can't get our bearing; even God seems far away. The pain threatens to consume us. The pain within is screaming and feels like an abyss of sorrow and emptiness. And where is God? He is there; God is not turning a deaf ear.

A friend gave me a blanket on which she had written scripture verses. About the time she gave it to me, another friend wrote me that her ladies' group had prayer blankets and she would go "face down" in prayer for me. I took my new blanket and made it my prayer blanket. Although I pray sitting up, lying down, walking, and rocking, I find special comfort in the prayer blanket. I wanted some beam of light to encompass me, a magnificent voice to boom from Heaven. I wanted Heaven to open up and I wanted to see Jesus. I desperately wanted to hear from God. I didn't get the booming voice or the Heavens parting but I could find a moment of peace as I lay face down crying out to God. In my frantic state of mind, I found it hard to hold to those moments of peace. But there were moments I felt a peace. If you find yourself having those moments, even though rare, of feeling God's peace, try to write down those feelings so you can remember them later. Watch for those moments.

In her book *Discerning the Voice of God*, Priscilla Shirer writes, "Is God only God when we see Him speaking or see Him moving?"[10] We know He is the same God that we have always believed in and trusted. Now is the time to remind yourself by writing down those moments and by asking, "What do I know?" "What do I believe?" "What has always been true?"

Do you feel like God has turned a deaf ear to you? If so, write down things He has done in the past. Write what you believe to be true and have always believed to be true. Try creating a prayer blanket and find a special place to pray.

---

[10]   Priscilla Shirer, *Discerning the Voice of God* (Chicago IL: Moody, 2007), 148.

DAY 6

He sent them to the Lord to ask, "Are you the one who was to come, or should we expect someone else?" (Luke 7:19, NIV)

John the Baptist had announced the coming of the Christ and he had baptized Jesus, but now in prison, he had doubts. Your world has been shattered; you may not feel God and not feeling God can lead to doubt. "Where are you, God? Are you even there?" Just know that if John the Baptist doubted, Jesus can understand your doubts too. Jesus will meet you where you are. Let Him know your doubts, your fears. He knows your heart; He knows you are hurting.

Where would you go? He has always been in your life since the moment you first believed. Journal times in your life when you have felt Him. Remind yourself of those times in your life when you know God was working in your life. Look at the markers in your life and remind yourself He is present. He has always been with you. I don't understand right now, but I know He is with me. I don't want to be anywhere but in His love. Jerry Sittser, in his book for grief, *A Grace Disguised*, writes:

Loss may call the existence of God into question. Pain seems to conceal Him from us, making it hard for us to believe that there could be a God in the midst of our suffering. In our pain we are tempted to reject God, yet for some reason we hesitate to take that course of action. So we ponder and we pray. We moved toward God, then away from Him. We wrestle in our souls to believe. Finally we choose God, and in the choosing we learn that He has already chosen us and has already been drawing us to Him.[11]

My sister lives next door to me and our families have gotten used to popping back and forth. One night after Don went Home, she came over to be with me. She gently reminded me of the times we had felt God's hand moving in the past. She reminded me of the times when we would sit around and talk about what God was doing. When you don't feel God, you lose sight of those things. Ironically, Teresa, Don and I had just gone through a study at church by Henry Blackaby. During that study, we had been encouraged to write down "markers" in our life when we had felt God. I had tried to remind myself of these times. Grief and the doubt can blind you to those markers in the past. Try to remember those times and write them down now.

Are you having doubts? If so, write those down and say them aloud to God. Ask Him to help you with your unbelief. Write down the times in the past when you knew God was with you.

---

[11] Jerry Sittser, *A Grace Disguised: Expanded Edition* (Grand Rapids, MI: Zondervan, 2004), 160.

DAY 7 REFLECTION

As you look back over the last six days, what stands out? Read over the Bible verses again. The verses we looked at deal with a determined day to go Home, God's look at death, not feeling God, and doubt. Is there one topic that seems to resonate with you more? If so, read those devotions again. Meditate on the words and ask God to give you insight.

When we can hold to the truth that God has appointed our days, it allows us to keep the eternal plan in perspective, even though we may not understand. We can rest in His sovereignty and know that God does see death differently. The world sees death as the end. But God knows that when He calls His children Home, they are safe with Him and they are more alive than ever.

We can find comfort when we see people in the Bible just like us struggle to hear God. We tend to think of Bible figures as having their life all together and not struggling as we do. But clearly there were many times when they wondered why God did not answer them or why they didn't feel God. We are not alone in that feeling. How wonderful that God allowed us, in His inspired Word, to read of others who did not hear Him. God allows us to see that we are not alone. We can also find comfort when we realize that even John the Baptist doubted. John was so anointed that he leapt in the womb. He was confident in God when he baptized Jesus, but later felt alone and far from God. He had to wonder if he had gotten it all wrong. Take comfort in each of these events knowing we are not alone; God has an eternal plan. He does not view death as the end; He knows death is the doorway to His presence. Spend this time reflecting and reviewing. Be sure to write down or underline the quotes and the thoughts that seem to speak to you the most. You may want to go back to them several times throughout the year—and even beyond the year.

DAY 8

Simon Peter replied, "Lord, to whom would we go? You have the words that give eternal life. We believe, and we know you are the Holy One of God." (John 6:68-69, NLT)

John 6:68-69 is one of my favorite verses. When I would cry out and not feel God, when I would go back to the ever-present question of why, when the doubts hit me, I would quote this verse. Jesus is the answer; He is sovereign. Jesus has the words to eternal life. Our situation, our loss doesn't change who He is and always has been. Our loved one is in His presence.

A very good book on grief is *Hope for the Brokenhearted* by Dr. John Luke Terveen. He writes, "The sense of separation and loss of relationship cut deeply, and we naturally recoil. This tests our faith for in the face of death, submission to Father God—placing all that we are in his loving hands—requires total trust."[12] We have to remain in His Word and seeking Him. And quoting scriptures was one way that helped me to do just that. By quoting this scripture, I remind myself that, despite the pain and sorrow, He is with me. It is almost easy to slip into despair and to think, "I don't feel God; so what if He isn't there? What if what I have always believed isn't true?" But then what? Was I going to suddenly decide to become an atheist? Of course not! That certainly would not bring hope. Many followers had turned away from Jesus, so Jesus asked His disciples if they were going too. Peter's response was, "Lord, to whom would we go?" That is the question you need to ask yourself.

Mandisa's song "Broken Hallelujah" sums up the pain and praise:

> Oh Father, You have given
> Much more than I deserve
> And I have felt Your hand of blessing
> On me at every turn
>
> How could I doubt Your goodness
> Your wisdom, Your grace
> So Lord hear my heart
> In this painful place[13]

His hand has been—and still is—on you. Jesus is our only hope.

Try committing this verse to memory and repeating it aloud when you are doubting. What are your thoughts and feelings on the verse and quote?

---

[12] John Luke Terveen, *Hope for the Brokenhearted* (Colorado Springs, CO: Victor, 2006), 119.

[13] Mandisa, "Broken Hallelujah." *Freedom.* Sparrow, 2009.

DAY 9

Immediately the boy's father exclaimed, "I do believe, help me overcome my unbelief." (Mark 9:24, NIV)

In his book *A Grief Observed*, C.S. Lewis writes, "You never know how much you really believe anything until its truth or falsehood becomes a matter of life and death to you."[14] How true that statement is. We can talk about our faith; we can talk about Heaven, but when someone you love is now in Heaven or if you are facing death yourself, it becomes a stark reality. Your beliefs become a matter of life and death to you. Your beliefs are center stage and your faith is center stage. Is what you always believed right? Can you hold to that?

Sometimes when we are doing everything we know to seek Him, the doubts still hit us. Like the father of the boy, you believe; but you need help overcoming the doubt. Ask Jesus to help you with the doubts. Write down things in your past that have been answers to prayers—times when you felt God's presence. You might want to write affirmations of your faith. I believe that God created the Earth; I believe that Jesus died on the cross for our sins and was resurrected that we might have life; I believe the Holy Spirit lives within us; I believe in eternal life; I believe in Heaven; I believe Jesus is coming again and there will be a bodily resurrection; I believe I will be reunited with my loved one and we will live eternally in the presence of God. I believe. I believe. Write it, say it, and listen to the music you have selected that helps remind you. When the doubts hit, say, "I believe." In Steven Curtis Chapman's song "Faithful" these lines ring so true:

> I am broken, I am bleeding,
> I'm scared and I'm confused,
> but You are faithful.
> Yes You are faithful.
> I am weary, unbelieving.
> God please help my unbelief!

The last lines of the song finish with a beautiful affirmation:

> And with everything inside of me,
> I am choosing to believe You're faithful.[15]

What are your thoughts and feelings on today's Scripture and quotes?

---

[14]   C. S. Lewis, *A Grief Observed* (New York: Harper Collins EBook, 2009), Location 15.
[15]   Steven Curtis Chapman, "Faithful." *Beauty Will Rise*. Sparrow, 2009.

DAY 10

Read 2 Corinthians 5:1-10

So we are always confident, even though we know that as long as we live in these bodies we are not at home with the Lord. For we live by believing and not by seeing. (2 Corinthians 5:6-7, NLT)

We are so caught up in our life here that we easily lose sight that our true Home is Heaven. I keep saying, "I want my life back." But I know our life in this world is all temporary and we are just passing through. Our life will continue in eternity, only it will be perfect. The relationships we have here, the life choices and actions will all impact eternity. What I want is my true Home, the life eternal that God has planned. Our believing loved ones have gone to their true Home. We will join them. We are passing through. We have this confidence and as long as we are here, we are not at Home. And we accept this through faith and not by seeing.

In his book *The Bible and the Future*, Anthony Hoekema states, "In terms of the imagery of II Corinthians 5:6-8, our present life is actually a being away from the Lord, a kind of pilgrimage. Death for the Christian, however, is a homecoming. It is the end of his pilgrimage; it is his return to his true home."[16]

Because Dad was a Methodist minister, we probably moved more than some people. Even after we left home, wherever Mom and Dad lived became home even if we had never lived there. Why? Because home was with those we loved. And our true Home is with those we love. First, it is with our Lord and Savior. He established families and home. He is the author of Love. He is love. He has prepared a place for us. So our true Home is with Him. Our believing loved ones have made that trip Home and because it is Home, we will join them. Christian families worship God when they are together; they give God the praise and glory for their relationships. We will once again worship our Lord as a family in our true Home. We are waiting on that day!

What are your thoughts and feelings about this verse? How hard is it right now for you to live by believing and not by seeing?

---

[16]   Anthony A. Hoekema, *The Bible and the Future* (Grand Rapids, MI: Eerdmans), 108.

10

DAY 11

The Lord will rescue me from every evil attack and will bring me safely to his heavenly kingdom. To him be glory forever and ever. Amen. (2 Timothy 4:18, NIV)

Read this passage carefully. It states: "rescue me from every evil attack and bring me safely to his *heavenly kingdom*" (emphasis mine). It would be easy to think, "You did not rescue my loved one." But His promise is to bring him safely into His heavenly kingdom. We live in a fallen world; we are in a spiritual battle. Protection against the evil one is to bring us into God's presence safely—into His heavenly kingdom safely. Home is where our protection lies. As Paul Enns writes,

Paul's promise concludes the Lord 'will bring me safely to His heavenly kingdom.' The phrase 'will bring me safely' (soesi) means the Lord will save Paul and rescue him from the troubles of this earth by bringing him home to heaven. Paul was so excited at the prospect of his safe and certain arrival in heaven that he burst into a doxology: 'to Him be the glory forever and ever. Amen.' As believers we have no need to fear death. Christ Himself assures us of a safe arrival home in heaven![17]

When we read scriptures like this, they help to remind us that the true healing, the true rescue, the true life is yet to come. In Heaven, in His kingdom we receive the true healing, the true safety, and the life eternal. Life is hard to imagine without the struggles, without the spiritual warfare. Just think: right now our loved ones are free from the onslaught of the evil one. They are truly rescued and safe. And while you remember and think on that, be aware that you still live in the fallen world, that your sorrow, your vulnerability at this moment to spiritual warfare makes you a target. But we have the promise that God will keep us safe, that He will bring us Home. And we have the assurance that the battle has already been won.

What are your thoughts and feelings on this verse? What are your thoughts and feelings about the statement that the Lord will save Paul and rescue him from the troubles of this Earth by bringing him home to Heaven?

---

[17]   Paul Enns, *Heaven Revealed* (Chicago, IL: Moody, 2011), 47.

DAY 12

His intent was that now, through the church, the manifold wisdom of God should be made known to the rulers and authorities in the heavenly realms, according to his eternal purpose that he accomplished in Christ Jesus our Lord. (Ephesians 3:10-11, NIV)

His intent, according to His eternal purpose, is accomplished through Christ Jesus our Lord. God has an eternal plan. The rulers and authorities in the heavenly realms know this plan; we know this, and others will discover this. When we are ready to collapse because our world has collapsed, we have to remind ourselves that there is a plan. There is a plan, and even though we don't understand or see why, our loved one's going Home is all a part of that plan. But remember, there is more to come, so much more. If we lose sight of the fact more is to come then our sorrow becomes all the more painful.

Anthony Hoekema writes that the Christian view:

Sees history as a fulfillment of God's purpose and as moving toward His goal. For the writers of the Bible, history is not a meaningless series of recurring cycles but a vehicle whereby God realizes his purposes with man and the cosmos. The idea that history is moving toward divinely established goals, and the future is to be seen as the fulfillment of promises made in the past, is the unique contribution of the prophets of Israel.[18]

I pray continually and I pray for all of you reading this devotion, that God will teach you how to have an eternal perspective. I know how painful that is right now.

There were—and are—so many days I wanted to go to sleep and not wake up. I kept thinking, "I cannot handle this one more minute; much less one more day." I still cannot imagine another minute or day without the man I share everything with. Don and I are truly one in every sense. We shared everything. We finished each other other's thoughts and sentences. The thought of another second without him is unbearable. The only way to put one foot in front of the other is to depend on God and to recognize there is an eternal plan. This world is not all there is. Our hope is Jesus Christ our Lord and His eternal purpose. Our God is in control. We are waiting on that day!

How does focusing on God's eternal purpose help you right now?

---

[18]   Anthony A. Hoekema, *The Bible and the Future* (Grand Rapids, MI: Eerdmans), 25.

DAY 13

Do not let your hearts be troubled. You believe in God; believe also in me. My Father's house has many rooms; if that were not so, would I have told you that I am going there to prepare a place for you? And if I go and prepare a place for you, I will come back and take you to be with me that you also may be where I am. You know the way to the place where I am going. (John 14:1-4, NIV)

Jesus left to prepare a place for us. Our loved ones left to be with Jesus. And someday Jesus will come back and take us all to be with Him. The picture here is of a large dwelling with rooms for us all. Many people have speculated about what the dwelling might look like. But what we know is, we will be with Jesus. Your believing loved one already is. I would love a glimpse of Heaven. I would love to see just for a moment what Dad and Don are seeing. But I have to know that Jesus prepared a place for us, so it will be perfect. And I have to trust Him. There is a place prepared. Jesus said, "Don't let your hearts be troubled." We have to believe Him, trust Him. He says He would not have told us He was preparing a place for us if it were not true. Joseph Stowell writes, "Christ made it clear that He came to earth to take us to Heaven to be with Him. Heaven is truly our home."[19]

Jesus knew we would have times of troubles and sorrows. His own disciples were about to face their most difficult time and He was preparing them. He knows your heart is hurting. He reminds them and us. There is a plan. He has it under control. We know the way. We have eternity to be with Jesus and worship Him with our loved ones. Jesus knew His disciples, those that loved Him, would mourn. People are sometimes hard on the disciples because they scattered after the crucifixion. But you and I know how debilitating this grief is. We know these disciples had spent every day with Jesus. They loved Him and then He was crucified. Their grief would be overwhelming. Jesus knew all of this; He was preparing them so they would look back on this conversation with Him and remember what He said. He speaks to all of us. He has prepared a place for us, for your loved one who is in His presence now and for you who will be with Him someday. You will be reunited with your loved one. Jesus knows your heart. He has a plan. Trust Him. We are waiting on that day!

Had you ever thought about how hard it must have been for the disciples in their grief? How do Jesus' words to the disciples comfort you in your grief?

---

[19]   Taken from *Eternity*, © *2006* by Joseph M. Stowell, and used by permission of Discovery House Publishers, Grand Rapids, MI. All rights reserved. P.75.

DAY 14 REFLECTION

Look back over the last six days. Was there one particular day that seemed to speak to you more? This week, we looked at verses that spoke about doubt, our true Home, spiritual warfare, the eternal plan, and anxiety. The doubt can create the anxiety; the doubt grows if you cannot feel God. It can become overwhelming. In general, the emotions associated with grief are overwhelming. If we recognize the normalcy of these emotions, remember even the disciples were overwhelmed with grief, and try to have things in place that help us hold on to Jesus, the anxiety will subside. Only in trusting Jesus can that happen. We could turn to other unhealthy sources, but the pain would only magnify.

I found the verse, "To whom shall we go God?" particularly helpful when the anxiety would overtake me and I would wonder where God was. This verse reminds me that He is the same God I have always worshiped. There is no hope anywhere else. Quoting these scriptures isn't something we do once and then stop; quoting Scripture must be continual and our first impulse. Then as we quote those things that help us, we focus on the eternal plan. We focus on God's goodness and His love. Go back over the questions at the end of each day. What questions did you reflect on the most? What might you need to reflect on more today? Pick at least one verse to say aloud right now.

DAY 15

Very truly I tell you, you will weep and mourn while the world rejoices. You will grieve, but your grief will turn to joy. So with you: Now is your time of grief, but I will see you again and you will rejoice, and no one will take away your joy. (John 16:20,22, NIV)

Jesus was preparing His disciples because He knew they would mourn. He knew their world would feel like it had collapsed; they would doubt; they would weep. So Jesus affirms there is a time of grief. He tells them that now is their time of grief. He understands. But Jesus also encourages them with, "I will see you again and you will rejoice, and no one will take away your joy."

We will see Jesus when He takes us Home either through death or through His coming again. When we do, we will rejoice that the time of grief will be over. When we are rejoicing to see Jesus and be with Him, we will also be rejoicing to be reunited with our loved ones. I cannot imagine what it was like when our loved ones saw Jesus. I tried to imagine what that was like for Dad and Don. I listened to the song "I Can Only Imagine" by Mercy Me and tried to imagine how glorious that moment must be for them. And so it will be with us.

I was sitting in our church after Don went Home, tears streaming as I listened to the words of the songs. As the choir left the loft, a friend in the choir came up and took my face in her hands. She quoted this verse to me several times and said, "You will see Jesus; you will see Don; you will rejoice again." Then she left just as quickly as she had appeared. We go to a Baptist church, which we love, but someone going out of the way in that manner is an unusual occurrence for our church. I don't know if anyone else who was not sitting on the same pew noticed her, but at that moment, I felt like God had spoken through her. I found great comfort in her words. You will see Jesus; you will see your loved one and you will rejoice. We are waiting on that day!

Meditate on the words of Jesus. How do Jesus' words help you now?

DAY 16

So we fix our eyes not on what is seen, but on what is unseen, since what is seen is temporary, but what is unseen is eternal. (2 Corinthians 4:18, NIV)

Everything we see is temporary. There is an unseen realm; there is an eternal plan. We become very involved in this life, but this is not all there is. How do you fix your eyes on what you can't see? We go back to God's Word. We know what assurances God has given us; we hold to the conviction that He is faithful. We keep our spiritual eyes on the hope of eternity. God is eternal; Heaven is eternal. When we receive Christ as our Savior, we are promised an eternity with Him. That eternity is what we hope for, that eternal relationship with Jesus. To keep an eternal perspective, we have to remind ourselves that this world and temporary stay is not all there is. We have an eternity to spend with our loved one and to worship our Lord. As you meditate on this scripture, ask God to show you how to fix your eyes on what is not seen.

A day before Don's funeral I was sitting on our porch reminding myself to breathe, crying, and praying. We built our house thirty-two years ago. Everything I saw me reminded me of Don and I together. The house our children grew up in, the trees and landscaping we did together. I cried out, "Everything I see is us." The devotion I read later that day included this scripture. I had cried out with what I see; God was reminding me that what I see is temporary. Even though we will live again on the New Earth, all I was looking at right then was temporary. What I could not see was the eternal. Philip Yancey reminds us:

Jesus introduced a new way of thinking, raising sights to a life that extends into eternity and involves unseen worlds we have not the capacity to detect. He came to establish an alternate community centered on values from that invisible world, 'on earth as it is in heaven.' Seen in that light, the kingdom of heaven prescribes a way of life that promotes what matters most and lasts longest.[20]

We are waiting on that day!

What are your thoughts and feelings about this verse? Are you having trouble focusing on what is not seen? How does it comfort you to think of an unseen realm?

---

[20]   Philip Yancey, *Rumors of Another World*, (Grand Rapids, MI: Zondervan, 2003), 201.

DAY 17

Faith is the assurance of things hoped for, the conviction of things not seen. (Hebrews 11:1, NASB)

Now faith is confidence in what we hope for and assurance about what we do not see (Hebrews 11:1, NIV).

Faith is the confidence that what we hope for will actually happen; it gives us assurance about things we cannot see (Hebrews 11:1, NLT).

Sometimes reading verses in different translations of the Bible helps to get a better perspective. As you read each one of these translations, digest these words. In his book *Disappointment with God*, Philip Yancey writes, "Somehow that faith was what God valued, and it soon became clear that faith was the best way for humans to express love to God."[21] We accepted Christ by faith. We are believers through faith. We have the hope of Jesus and the resurrection. We have the conviction that, though we do not see Heaven, Heaven is very real.

I like Philip Yancey's definition of faith: "Faith means believing in advance what will only make sense in reverse."[22] He goes on to say, "The kind of faith God values seems to develop best when everything fuzzes over, when God stays silent, when the fog rolls in."[23]Right now, fog is a good description of what you are experiencing. You go through the motions of life and at times you don't remember what you have said or done. The fog can be intense. But your faith is still there to hold to, even though it may feel as though God is silent. Even though your pain and sorrow are relentless, you have your faith. Remind yourself of all that you know and believe.

God is the same yesterday, today, and tomorrow. The same God who saved you, whom you accepted by faith, is still that same God. Our faith is rock solid. God is rock solid. Your loved one is now getting to experience the fruits of his or her faith. He is seeing the things for which he hoped and the things for which he had conviction. She is Home and she finally sees what she has hoped to see all along.

Read this verse in different translations. Does one speak to you more? What are your thoughts on Philip Yancey's definition of faith?

---

21 Philip, Yancey, *Disappointment With God*, (Grand Rapids, MI: Zondervan, 1992), 71.
22 Ibid., 224.
23 Ibid., 228.

DAY 18

The Lord is near to the brokenhearted and saves those who are crushed in spirit. (Psalm 34:18, NASB)

"Brokenhearted and crushed in spirit" certainly describes how a grieving person feels. As we pray, "Lord, I may not feel you, but I know you are near," we hold to that promise. But right now, you are brokenhearted and crushed in spirit. God knew there would be times we would feel that way. Otherwise, God would not have allowed these words in the Bible. David, a man after God's own heart, felt brokenhearted and his spirit felt crushed.

Jerry Sittser writes, "Catastrophic loss by definition precludes recovery. It will transform us or destroy us but it will never leave us the same... Sorrow never entirely leaves the soul of those that have suffered a severe loss, if anything it may keep going deeper."[24] You have suffered a loss and you will never be the same. People say your life will get back to normal. But what is normal? Your life will not be the same as it was. A part of you is gone from this Earth. You are hurt and you are crushed. Don't let people rush you through your grief or make you feel like you "should not" feel a certain way. God does understand and He has not left you. He is near you even though you don't feel Him. He will be with you as you take this journey, and He will bring you Home. And then you will see Jesus face to face. You will be reunited with your loved one. You will see how God worked in your life and how near He was. For now, you have to believe that He is near. And He will not and does not leave you. Listen to these words of Steven Curtis Chapman's song "I will Trust You":

> You are my God, and I'll trust You
> And with every breath I take
> And for every day that breaks
> I will trust You
> I will trust You
> And when nothing is making sense
> Even then I will say again[25]

What are your thoughts and feelings on this verse? What are your thoughts on Jerry Sittser's words? Have you felt the emotions in Steven Curtis Chapman's song?

---

[24] Jerry Sittser, *A Grace Disguised: Expanded Edition* (Grand Rapids, MI: Zondervan, 2004), 73.
[25] Steven Curtis Chapman, "I Will Trust You." *Beauty Will Rise*. Sparrow, 2009.

DAY 19

Do not be anxious about anything, but in every situation, by prayer and petition, with thanksgiving, present your requests to God. And the peace of God, which transcends all understanding, will guard your hearts and your minds in Christ Jesus. (Philippians 4:6-7, NIV)

God has built in us a mechanism that allows us to respond to a threat. Our body has emotional and physical responses which allow us to flee, freeze, or fight. Sometimes we get stuck in these responses and, as a result, experience anxiety. When you have lost a loved one, anxiety is a common response. I sometimes ask clients who are dealing with anxiety, "What is the worst thing that can happen?" But in our cases, the worst did happen and then what do you do? Your body becomes stuck in a response mode. You can't eat: you can't seem to breathe; your heart is racing; you are scared; you may feel sick; and the list goes on.

There are no words that help right now. Christ is the only answer that will help you. Remember, regardless of what happens, He is in control. Usually, anxiety is worsened when we feel we have no control. But we can remember Jesus is in control.

One practical thing to remember is to breathe. In order to breathe therapeutically, breathe in through your nose, imagining a balloon in your abdomen; as you inhale through your nose, your abdomen should move out; hold it and exhale slowly through your mouth. As you exhale, drop your shoulders and imagine your whole body as a balloon. Do this several times. You are most likely holding your breath, and when you do, the anxiety is even worse. I had to remind myself over and over to breathe.

The answer to anxiety is the sovereignty of God, the peace of God. These verses in Philippians remind us what to do. Pray, petition, thank God for His love, for what He gave you in the person you love who is now with Him. Let Jesus know you cannot do this on your own. He already knows you cannot do it on your own but this is for you to remind yourself and to draw close to Him. Focus on His Holiness and His love. I know in the deepest darkness everything is hard to do. But it is in the darkness you most need to cry out to Jesus. When you feel the anxiety, it is a good time to journal and quote scripture too. Ask Him to let you feel His peace and assurance and then look for Him to answer.

What are your thoughts and feelings on this verse? If you are experiencing anxiety, try deep breathing and praying thanksgiving; write about how you feel when you do that. List things for which you are thankful. Write this verse out and quote it.

DAY 20

Good people pass away; the godly often die before their time. But no one seems to care or wonder why. No one seems to understand that God is protecting them from the evil to come. For those who follow godly paths will rest in peace when they die. (Isaiah 57:1-2, NLT)

Our youngest daughter, Michelle, had been reading Isaiah when her Dad went Home. The above verse in Isaiah was the first verse that came to her and it was of great comfort to her. We do not understand why certain people are taken sooner than others. When you are really hurting, there isn't any explanation that stops the pain. The person you love is not here right now and it hurts. But understand that God has a plan when He does take the devout, and we do not always know why. But He is sovereign.

   We have to trust that when He takes us Home, it is what is best. And our loved one does find rest. He finds rest in our Lord, rest from pain, and rest from the spiritual warfare. She finds rest in God's glory. It does not make sense to us why God would take someone who lives for Him from this Earth. It does not make sense to us when He takes someone young. We do not see down the road. We trust Him because He loves us, and He loves the ones we love. He is in control. Someday we will see so much more, but for now, we trust Him. Steven Curtis Chapman wrote these words when his six-year-old daughter was killed in a car accident:

> This is not how it should be
> This is not how it could be
> This is how it is
> And our God is in control
>
> This is not how it will be
> When we finally will see
> We'll see with our own eyes
> He was always in control
>
> And we'll sing holy, holy, holy is our God
> And we will finally really understand what it means
>
> So we'll sing holy, holy, holy is our God
> While we're waiting for that day[26]

His words give voice to how I feel. We are waiting on that day.

Write your thoughts on the verses and powerful lyrics of the song.

---

[26]   Steven Curtis Chapman, "Our God Is In Control." *Beauty Will Rise*. Sparrow, 2009.

DAY 21 REFLECTION

Read over the last six days. Reflect on the verses and devotionals that seemed to speak to you the most. We looked at verses that spoke of Jesus preparing His disciples to mourn, but also assuring them they would rejoice again. I know looking forward to the day that my mourning turns to joy brings me comfort.

We are reminded that there is an unseen world. We are to fix our eyes on the unseen. Our faith is the conviction of things not seen. I like Philip Yancey's definition of faith. It helps to remember that all we see is temporary, that there is an entire unseen world. We tend to only focus on what we see. I continually pray God teaches me how to focus on the unseen.

We read in Psalm 34 that God is near to the brokenhearted, which certainly describes us. I also spent some time on the psychological aspects of anxiety. Anxiety is such an overwhelming feeling and understanding where it comes from can be helpful. Do not underestimate just learning to deep breathe. But then hold to what we know is the true healing of anxiety—resting in God's sovereignty and His peace.

Finally, we look at verses that speak of the godly going Home young. Verses that brought our daughter comfort. What helped you the most? Pick one or more verses to reflect on and memorize and record your thoughts. Remember, today is for reflection; don't hurry, but digest those verses and words through the week. You may have found one day to be more comforting at the time, but as you reflect, God may open another verse to meet the need of today and the days to come as we wait on that glorious day that we see Jesus and are reunited with our loved ones.

DAY 22

But they were looking for a better place, a heavenly homeland. That is why God is not ashamed to be called their God, for he has prepared a city for them. (Hebrews 11:16, NLT)

We are to be looking for a better place, a heavenly homeland. Our loved one is in Heaven. Hebrew 11 is called the "Hall of Faith" because it includes a list of people throughout the Old Testament who lived by faith. This list includes Abel, Enoch, Noah, Abraham, Isaac, Jacob, Sarah, Joseph, Moses' parents, Moses, Rahab, and many more. The author of Hebrews tells us these people of faith were looking beyond where they were and what was happening, and looking for a better place, a heavenly homeland.

I like the way Joni Erickson expresses Heaven, "Heaven is your journey's end, you life's goal, your purpose for going on. If Heaven is the home of your spirit, the rest for your soul, the repository of every spiritual investment on earth, then it must grip your heart. And your heart must grip heaven by faith."[27] Since before the beginning of man, God has had a plan that included our heavenly Home with Him in eternity. By faith, we know this to be true. All of these people we have read about in the Bible were real people who had faith and died, but knew to look toward a better place, a heavenly homeland.

Heaven is much more real to us now. One of our own is now in that heavenly place. So by faith we know that even though we are in pain now, we will be there with them someday in that city God has prepared. We are waiting on that day!

What are your thoughts and feelings on this verse? What are your thoughts on Joni Erikson's words?

---

[27] Joni Eareckson Tada, *Heaven: Your Real Home* (Grand Rapids, MI: Zondervan, 1995), 23.

DAY 23

Jesus said to her, "I am the resurrection and the life. The one who believes in me will live, even though they die." (John 11:25, NIV)

Jerry Sittser writes, "No miracle can ultimately save us from it (death). A miracle is therefore only a temporary solution. We really need more than a miracle—we need a resurrection to make life eternally new. We long for a life in which death is finally and ultimately defeated."[28] We do long for death to be defeated and that is what Jesus is promising us in this verse. Unless we are here when He comes again, all of us will die, but we have this promise. Jesus is the resurrection and the life. Those of us who believe in Him will live even though we pass through death. You have this promise for your believing loved one.

Because of the resurrection and the life and the eternity we all look forward to, we will once again be reunited with our loved one. And when we do, there will be no more death. We will live in Jesus' glorious presence. Some of you may have prayed for a miracle. And sometimes there are miracles. But everyone Jesus healed eventually died. Ultimately the true healing comes in Heaven. Ultimately all those who believe in Him live and are healed. But that healing may not come until Heaven.

My dad, who struggled to breathe with COPD, will never struggle again. Dad is healed now. We wanted him healed here, but we will be with him again in Heaven. We will see Dad breathe and live again. And when we do, there will never again be the pain of disease and death. This healing is the ultimate healing and it will be forever. Even though we die here, we will live with Jesus. We have an eternity with our loves ones to worship Jesus! We are waiting on that day!

What does this verse say to you? What are your thoughts about how true healing happens in Heaven?

---

[28] Jerry Sittser, *A Grace Disguised: Expanded Edition* (Grand Rapids, MI: Zondervan, 2004), 164.

DAY 24

Then Jesus told him, "Because you have seen me, you have believed; blessed are those who have not seen and yet have believed." (John 20:29, NIV)

Jesus' statement is powerful because He is making it not just for those at that time who wouldn't see Him, but for all of us who have come since. Jesus said, "Blessed are those who have not seen and yet have believed"; that is us. Jesus knew there would be countless generations that would not have seen. Our belief is based on faith. And through grief, belief can be shaken. You have not seen Jesus, yet you believe. And when our world feels ripped apart, we might question our belief.

We live in a very visual world. We are entertained by a constant flow of the visual: TV, movies, and the internet. Many of us can access the internet from our phone. Bored? We whip out the phone or IPad or whatever we have and "look" at something. So what do we "look" at now? We can't visually see or hold our loved one. Our loved one's absence becomes excruciatingly painful. His physical absence is glaring, and we can't see Jesus either. And if we can't feel Jesus either, the seeming absence can create a panic. We may wonder where God is now. But we have to remember that Jesus is with us, and even though we can't see Him, we do believe. You have believed in Him, and as a believer you have trusted Jesus as your Savior. You didn't see Jesus when you made the decision to receive Him as your Savior, but yet you believed. Your loved one trusted Him and now he sees Jesus face to face. We are all waiting on that day; we will see Jesus face to face.

Don often did his morning devotion on our back patio. Don loved the outdoors. And he would sit out on the patio, drink his coffee, and read and pray. My sister and her family live next door to us. After Don went Home, my brother-in-law, Lanny, reminded me, "Ann, Don has been preparing for this day his whole life." He was right. Don had been and he is now seeing Jesus face to face and in His glory. I miss him so very much; I cannot wait to be with him again. But for now, I hold to my belief and even though I can't see Jesus, I still believe. I know I will see Jesus someday. I am waiting on that day!

How does this verse speak to you? Write some of the things you are missing most about your loved one.

DAY 25

I say to you that many will come from the east and the west, and will take their places at the feast with Abraham, Isaac and Jacob in the kingdom of heaven. (Matthew 8:11, NIV)

We know that Heaven will be glorious. We know we will see Jesus; we know that to be in His presence will be unbelievable. We also know that when we have someone leave before us, we suddenly stop just thinking about Heaven as a someday thing; it becomes so very real. And for a lot of us, that desire to know that the relationships will still be there is huge. We hold to the continuity of our lives. In *Heaven Revealed*, Paul Enns writes:

Scripture is also clear that there will be recognizable reunion with family members immediately at death. When Abraham died, 'he was gathered to his people.' The picture is further illuminated in Matthew 8:11 with Abraham reclining in the kingdom with Isaac and Jacob—his son and grandson. Family reunion! For believers, death brings a joyful reunion with believing family members. What a prospect![29]

Those who have not had someone they love with all their heart go before them may not fully understand how important this concept of continuity is. But for those of us who have, it is immensely comforting. You want to know you are going to be with the one you love.

Debi, a close friend, said, "I believe the soul connections are for all eternity and that we know our loved ones as we do now only, perfect and with no baggage. I can't believe that God made us where attachment and connection are so important just to tear them away. Death is a thing. It does not have the power to break those soul/spiritual connections." We worship God here with those we love; we will continue to worship with them in Heaven. God is the One who gives us these amazing relationships here. We hold on to that clear picture of continuity, and look forward to that reunion.

I have a digital frame with pictures that continually remind me of our family and our love. Many of those pictures are taken around a table eating. Jesus used a picture of a meal, a family meal, to describe one aspect of Heaven. He could have said Abraham, Moses and Elijah but instead He said the names of a family. Jesus named father, son and grandson. Clearly family is important in the Kingdom of God. Family, feasting, and, best of all, Jesus is the one who is the head of this feast. How glorious is that? We are waiting on that day!

What are your thoughts and feelings on this verse in light of it being a family reunion? How does a family reunion comfort you?

---

[29]   Paul Enns, *Heaven Revealed* (Chicago, IL: Moody, 2011), 43.

DAY 26

Since you have been raised to new life with Christ, set your sights on the realities of heaven, where Christ sits in the place of honor at God's right hand. Think about the things of heaven, not the things of earth. For you died to this life, and your real life is hidden with Christ in God. (Colossians 3:1-3, NLT)

Colossians 3:1-3 is a much-quoted verse for me. We are told to set our sights on Heaven. The NASB translates it, "keep seeking the things above"; vs. 3 "set your mind on things above." The NIV translates verse 2 as "set your hearts on things above"; vs. 3 "set your minds on things above." This verse is for all of us who are believers but who sometimes get so busy in our daily lives that we may forget to keep our hearts and minds focused on Heaven. I know I did. I thought about Heaven and wondered what it was like. Don and I talked about it a lot, especially after Dad went Home. But I don't think I gave it the focus I needed to until suddenly everything changed.

Greg Laurie writes, "But when Christopher died unexpectedly and went to heaven, I became far hungrier for knowledge of where he now lives."[30] I read twenty-six books on Heaven in the first nine months, and three of them were written by authors who had a loved one called to Heaven. I became obsessed on learning more about Heaven. Why? I think Greg Laurie does a good job of explaining that. He tells how in his thirty-five years of ministry he had preached on Heaven, life after death, and counseled scores of people who had lost loved ones. But he says when it happened to him, it was a whole new world. He goes on to say, "My desire to be in heaven is greater now than ever before, and heaven is more real to me now than any time I can remember. Why? Because I have an investment there now."[31] Greg's words resonate with me. I have an investment in Heaven even more now. You have an investment in Heaven now. We will visit this passage again. Much can be said about these verses. Books have been written about this verse. The more I focus on Heaven, the more comfort I feel.

What does this verse say to you? How do you feel about Greg Laurie's statement?

---

[30] Greg Laurie, *Hope for Hurting Hearts* (Dana Point, CA: Kerygma, 2008), 87.
[31] Ibid., 42.

DAY 27

Be of sober spirit, be on the alert. Your adversary, the devil, prowls around like a roaring lion, seeking someone to devour. (1 Peter 5:8, NASB)

In the foreword to *A Grief Observed* by C.S. Lewis, his step-son wrote, "The greater the love, the greater the grief, the stronger the faith, the more mightily Satan storms the fortress."[32] Dr. John Luke Terveen writes, "The loss of a loved one often ushers in a dangerous time of spiritual warfare. Faith is severely tested. Such grievous loss frequently stresses relationships."[33]

Satan prowls around looking for someone to devour. You are at your most vulnerable right now. Your world has been devastated and you are an open, raw wound. It is very important to draw close to God, even though you may not feel Him. Because we are vulnerable, it is important to surround ourselves with things that help us focus on God. Create a playlist or buy a CD; have those songs that minister to you readily available. I enjoy music, but I am the only one in our family who never had to have music on. But when sorrow hit, I created two playlists, and I would listen to those songs I listed in the foreword of this book over and over. Most of the songs I suggest seem to be written by someone who knew that pain and drew near to God.

The testimonies of others will help you. You can quote scripture. Have the verses that speak to you and say them out loud, even if you are not "feeling" them. Call someone to pray with you. Read the Bible; find those passages that help you concentrate on Heaven, on God's love, holiness, and sovereignty. I have quoted books on Heaven and grief throughout this book, check those out that seem to help you. Immerse yourself in God's Word. Satan will attack your relationships and your faith. If you are having strained relationships, get help. See your pastor or a counselor who is a Christian and can help you. Remember that we may grieve differently. The other person is not the enemy. The devil is the enemy; death is the enemy. Draw near to God.

What are your thoughts and feelings on this verse? Have you felt under attack spiritually? How does it comfort you to know other Christians struggle during this time too? What songs help you feel closer to God when under attack? What scriptures help you? Make a list of verses and songs to play when you feel particularly vulnerable.

---

[32] C.S. Lewis, *A Grief Observed* (New York: Harper Collins EBook, 2009), Location 133.

[33] Luke Terveen, *Hope for the Brokenhearted* (Colorado Springs, CO: Victor, 2006), 113.

DAY 28 REFLECTION

Look back over the verses and devotions. What speaks to you the most? As you read and meditate, record your thoughts. We looked at verses that speak of our true Home. I find focusing on Heaven, our true Home, very comforting. When I can take my mind and heart away from my pain and sorrow and try to focus on Heaven and the resurrection, I find comfort. As we look at John 11:25 we are reminded that we live even though we die. Our loved ones are more alive than ever! We read where Jesus says, "Blessed are those who have not seen and yet have believed." This is us. We can find comfort in these words.

We read where Jesus refers to the Kingdom in terms of a family, showing the continuity of life and relationships. I find it very comforting to focus on the continuity of life and relationships. If there were no continuity of life and relationships, our grief would take a different turn; after all, our relationships would truly be over. As it is, however, when we read the scriptures we see the continuity and know we are only temporarily separated. I find myself now sending sympathy cards that emphasize the temporary separation. We read one of my favorite verses that reminds us to set our sights on the realities of Heaven. And finally, we read about the spiritual warfare and are reminded to draw near to God.

I find great comfort in the verse that speaks of sitting at the feast of Abraham, Isaac and Jacob—the family. I find great comfort in focusing on Heaven. What brings you comfort? Record your thoughts and feelings for the week.

DAY 29

Since, then, you have been raised with Christ, set your hearts on things above, where Christ is, seated at the right hand of God. Set your minds on things above, not on earthly things. For you died, and your life is now hidden with Christ in God. (Colossians 3:1-3, NIV)

In his book *God's Story, Your Story*, Max Lucado creates a beautiful picture of our temporary home here and the true Home we look forward to. Max is describing his journey on one of his many travels and he had this thought:

The journey home is nice, but the journey is not the goal.... Suppose this announcement were heard: 'Ladies and gentlemen, this flight is your final destination. We will never land. Your home is this plane, so enjoy the journey.' Passengers would become mutineers. We'd take over the cockpit and seek a landing strip. We wouldn't settle for such an idea. The journey is not the destination. The vessel is not the goal. Those who are content with nothing more than joy in the journey are settling for too little satisfaction. Our hearts tell us there is more to this life than this life. We, like E.T., lift bent fingers to the sky. We may not know where to point, but we know not to call this airplane our home. In God's narrative, life on earth is but the beginning: the first letter of the first sentence in the first chapter of the great story God is writing with your life.... He is polishing you for your place in his kingdom. Your biggest moments lie ahead, on the other side of the grave.[34]

He goes on to add emphasis, "Scripture uses a starchy verb here. Zeteo (seek) is to 'covet earnestly, strive after, to inquire, desire, even require.' ....Head for home the way a pigeon wings to the nest or the prodigal strode to his papa. Obsess yourself with heaven!"[35]

I love his analogy of the plane. We do tend to think of this life as the destination, but it is not; it is the journey to our true Home. Our believing loved ones have departed from this temporary home and landed in our true Home, our true destination. We will join them, just as if they had taken a plane ahead of us on a trip.

When our youngest daughter moved to Hawaii, we flew to visit her many times. And as we stepped off the plane, she was always there smiling and full of love to greet us. We were all excited to be together again and embraced each other. Someday our loved ones will be there to greet us full of love as we step into our true destination. I am waiting on that day!

What are your thoughts and feelings on the verses and Lucado's words?

---

[34] Max Lucado, *God's Story, Your Story* (Grand Rapids, MI: Zondervan, 2011), 55.
[35] Ibid., 56.

DAY 30

But we are looking forward to the new heavens and new earth he has promised, a world filled with God's righteousness. And so, dear friends, while you are waiting for these things to happen, make every effort to be found living peaceful lives that are pure and blameless in his sight. (2 Peter 3:13-14, NLT)

The New Earth, a world filled with God's righteousness, will be eternal. Right now your loved one is with Christ in Heaven. But when Christ comes again and we are all part of the bodily resurrection, when we see that New Heaven and New Earth together with our loved one, we are truly Home.

Randy Alcorn writes, "God's redemptive plan climaxes not as the return of Christ, nor in the millennial kingdom, but on the New Earth."[36] Then we will have eternity with God. We will worship our Lord fully. I urge you to read *Heaven* by Randy Alcorn and *Heaven Revealed* by Paul Enns. These two men do a great job of explaining the intermediate Heaven, where our loved ones are now and the New Earth. Can you imagine a world filled with God's righteousness?

When my parents' dog of fifteen years died, Mom found herself completely alone in her house. After praying, she decided she needed another pet for company. We found a rescue unit that had rescued a small breed dog from a puppy mill. When we arrived at the rescue unit, there were many crates of dogs. And in the back were the two we had seen on the internet. The lady said, "Just pick either one." They looked alike since they had both come from the same breeder and most likely were sisters. Mom and I looked at each other; how do you pick? We knew we were not going to be able to pick just one, so she decided to take them both. As she was filling out the paperwork for adoption, I was putting on their new leashes to take them home. One of them was licking me all over my face so I could barely find her collar; the other was cowering in the back. As I put on their leashes, I found myself telling them: "You are going to your new home. Wait until you see what awaits you. You will be loved unconditionally and your new home is beautiful. And not only will you have someone that takes care of you and loves you, you will be together." And as I said that, I thought that my words sounded somewhat like the transition from Earth to Heaven. Even on our best days someone else is hurting. We live in a fallen world. All of our good times and beauty now are all glimpses of what is to come. Our loved one has left the fallen world and entered into a place filled with God's righteousness. We too will join our loved ones. And someday all believers will see the New Heaven and the New Earth. It is hard to grasp just how amazing Heaven will be. We are waiting on that day!

What are your thoughts on the verses and the story comparing our transition?

---

[36] Randy Alcorn, *Heaven* (Carol Stream, IL: Tyndale House, 2004), 87.

DAY 31

My eyes are dim with grief. I call to you, Lord, every day; I spread out my hands to you. (Psalm 88:9, NIV)

In discussing this Psalm, Dustin Shramek writes:

He called on God because he expected God to answer. But he didn't receive an answer. His hands remained empty day after day. This was when the pain was its deepest. Many of us can endure the worst kinds of suffering if God himself is filling our hands (and hearts) with comfort. But when we cry out for comfort and receive nothing, we are undone. Surely the Sovereign One who has ultimately brought about this suffering could at least comfort me in the midst of it, couldn't he? When this doesn't happen the suffering is magnified beyond our imaginings. [37]

There were times after Don went Home I would be in the floor on my prayer blanket just crying. I didn't know what to pray, and it didn't seem to matter because it didn't seem like God was listening anyway. I remember reading a comment once in a book on grief. Someone had concluded, "His eye is not on the sparrow." I knew that even though at times I did not feel God, I would not allow that thought to stay. I knew that the same God I had always trusted was there. I do not understand why He seems so far away when we need Him the most. But I know He is there.

I cannot overemphasize how having those scriptures memorized helps when you just say them over and over. And when nothing else helps, just say, "I trust you Jesus, even though I can't feel you right now." Or quote John 6:68: "To whom shall we go Lord? You have the words to eternal life." Shramek adds later that the Psalms many times end with a message of hope even though this Psalm may not. He points out the Psalm "Reminds us that we are not alone, God has not abandoned us even though it feels like it. Even though this one doesn't end with a message of hope, we know how many times the psalms do. The psalms remind us He is with us even though we don't feel Him."[38] Remember to hold to the hope in your darkest moments. Spread out your hands to God; He loves you and His eye is on you.

What are our thoughts and feelings on the verse and on Shramek's words? If there have been times you have not felt God, journal that experience.

---

[37] Dustin Shramek, "Waiting for the Morning During the Long Night of Weeping." John Piper and Justin Taylor (Ed). *Suffering and the Sovereignty of God*, (Wheaton, IL: Crossway, 2006), 183.

[38] Ibid., 54.

DAY 32

But our citizenship is in heaven. And we eagerly await a Savior from there, the Lord Jesus Christ. (Philippians 3:20, NIV)

We are citizens of Heaven. This world as we know it now, in its fallen state, is only temporary. Tony Evans writes, "Most People think we are in the land of the living on our way to the land of the dying. But actually we are in the land of the dying on our way to the land of the living."[39] We are not in our true Home, at least not the true Home as we will someday know it.

When Dr. Clara Reed was planning Dad's service she said, "We will have a celebration of Bro. Bob's Homegoing." She knew Dad was a citizen of Heaven. Dad went Home. Don went Home; your loved one went Home. We are citizens of Heaven. And the next part of the verse is more real to me than ever: "We eagerly await a Savior from there, the Lord Jesus Christ." Jesus is in Heaven with our loved one, but He is coming back to get us all. If we are not called Home through death, we will see Jesus coming back for us. We await Jesus' return, and even more eagerly now.

I have become obsessed with looking at the sky. My phone is filled with random pictures of the sky. Someday Jesus will come back on the clouds and we will all see. But for now, we hold to the promise that we are citizens of Heaven. If you travel out of the country, you may visit for a while, but your citizenship remains in your own country. There is a connection with our roots, with who we are, where we belong. When we received Christ as our Savior, we became citizens of Heaven. Randy Alcorn writes, "Note the verb in the statement: Our citizenship 'is,' not 'will be,' in Heaven. Although our citizenship in Heaven is present, our residence there is future."[40] Regardless of where we are now, we are just passing through. We know our true Home awaits us. Our loved ones are there now; they have claimed their citizenship. And someday we will reside there as well with our loved ones, with Our Savior. We are waiting on that day.

How does this verse speak to you? What are your thoughts on celebrating a Homegoing?

---

[39] Tony Evans, *Tony Evans Speaks Out On Heaven and Hell* (Chicago, IL: Moody, 2000), 7.

[40] Randy Alcorn, *Heaven* (Carol Stream, IL: Tyndale House, 2004), 252.

DAY 33

But those who die in the LORD will live;
their bodies will rise again!
Those who sleep in the earth
will rise up and sing for joy!
For your life-giving light will fall like dew
on your people in the place of the dead! (Isaiah 26:19, NLT)

"Those who die in the Lord will live." Even though we go immediately to Heaven to be with our Lord, for those who die in the Lord, there will be a day their bodies will rise again. Even in the Old Testament, God was reassuring His people of His plan. Some scholars say the above scripture is referring to Israel as a nation; others see it as referring to both the nation and the bodily resurrection. Isaiah is full of prophecy not just for that time period, but looking ahead to the Messiah and the New Earth.

It is reassuring to read prophecy in the Old Testament because the prophecies remind us of the eternal plan. Scripture shows us things that were prophesied and came true within Isaiah's lifetime; things that came true with Jesus' birth, death, and resurrection. Prophecies show us future events that have not yet occurred. As Randy Alcorn writes, "The hope of the ancient Israelites was not only for their distant offspring but also for themselves. They longed for God's rule on Earth, not just for a hundred years, or a thousand years, but forever."[41] Alcorn goes on to say, "God's people are not looking for deliverance from Earth, but deliverance on Earth. That's exactly what we will find after our bodily resurrection."[42]

We long for that time too. We long for a time when we will once again live on this Earth, a New Earth. We will be with our believing loved ones again on this Earth. We will sing for joy because we will be with Christ. We are waiting on that day!

What are your thoughts and feelings on this verse? What are your thoughts on Randy Alcorn's statement?

---

[41] Randy Alcorn, *Heaven* (Carol Stream, IL: Tyndale House, 2004), 144.
[42] Ibid., 144.

DAY 34

For this world is not our permanent home; we are looking forward to a home yet to come. (Hebrews 13:14, NLT)

For here we do not have an enduring city, but we are looking for the city that is to come. (Hebrews 13:14, NIV)

I love the way the New Living Translation translates this verse using the word "home." Paul Enns writes, "We are pilgrims looking for another world, a better world. Nothing else on this earth can provide that incomparable comfort, that ultimate resolution to our greatest dilemma – to anticipate a glorious, unending reunion and fellowship with loved ones, never, never to end."[43]

One day right after Don was called Home, as I was crying I heard myself say, "I just want to go Home." The words just came out of my mouth. I was in my home on Earth. A place I love. A place Don and I built when we were young, where we have raised our girls, where we have lived for over thirty-two years. But at that moment, Home was with Don, Home was with Our Lord, Home was our permanent Home. Mercy Me has a song that I listened to over and over called "Homesick":

> Help me Lord cause I don't understand your ways
> The reason why I wonder if I'll ever know
> But, even if you showed me, the hurt would be the same
> 'Cause I'm still here so far away from home[44]

These lyrics sum up how I feel so perfectly. We are looking forward to our Home yet to come. And someday we will be there. It is a Home yet to come, but we have the promise that it will be. We are waiting on that day!

How does this verse speak to you? How does Paul Enns' statement comfort you? What are your thoughts on the words to Mercy Me's song?

---

[43]   Paul Enns, *Heaven Revealed* (Chicago, IL: Moody, 2011), 16.
[44]   Mercy Me, "Homesick." *Itunes Original.* MercyMe, 2008.

DAY 35 REFLECTION

As you read over the last six days, what thoughts come to you? We looked again at Colossians 3:1-3. I love these verses. It is not hard to set your heart on Heaven, especially when part of your heart is there. These verses are amazing to me. I have always liked the analogy Max Lucado gives about life on an airplane. I reflect on that analogy a lot as I grieve, trying to wrap my brain around the journey and the destination at verses that speak of Heaven as our true Home and where our citizenship truly is.

We look at verses that talk of the New Heavens and New Earth. I found incalculable comfort in reading Randy Alcorn's book *Heaven* and Paul Enns' book *Heaven Revealed*. The focus on the New Heaven and the New Earth is amazing.

We read the heartfelt Psalm that says, "My eyes are dim with grief." We can relate. As you read these Psalms, remember to journal your own feelings of grief.

We read verses that remind us of our true Home. Our citizenship is in Heaven. Our loved ones have gone Home. As hard as it is for us, they are Home! And finally, in Isaiah we read our bodies will rise. We will have a bodily resurrection. We are citizens of Heaven now. We eagerly look forward to the New Earth. We are waiting on that day! I love the word Homegoing. Our loved ones have gone Home. As you go back over the last week, take time to reflect. Soak in those things you may have missed. Record thoughts and feelings you have on the last six days.

DAY 36

I press on to reach the end of the race and receive the heavenly prize for which God, through Christ Jesus, is calling us. (Philippians 3:14, NLT)

Our loved ones have finished the race set before them. God calls us to run our race and He is there when we finish. I wish Don's race had not been so short. I wish we could all finish together. But that is not a part of God's eternal plan.

Don was an avid cyclist. His stamina was incredible. It was nothing for him to ride in bicycle rallies for 100 miles. Our race here is in doing God's work. Our earthly life with its day to day struggles and triumphs is our race. What we do here matters. Don and Dad ran a good race here on Earth. They pressed on and finished the race set before them, and God welcomed them Home. Your loved one finished his race, and God welcomed him Home.

I keep wondering what Dad and Don are doing. How amazing it must be to see Jesus! How amazing it must have been to look up and be welcomed Home! In his book, *Hope for the Brokenhearted*, Dr. John Luke Terveen writes about the day his daughter went Home to be with the Lord. She was at track practice and jumping hurdles. He gave a beautiful picture when he said, "She jumped over the hurdle and straight into her Saviors arms."[45] Regardless of how your loved one went Home, she finished the race set before her. We must press on to finish ours as painful as that might be. It may seem more like putting one foot in front of the other right now and remembering to breathe or just doing the next thing you know you have to do. But continue to pray and look to Jesus pressing forward as we wait for that day we are called Home. God does call us forward. It is hard to even move some days, but God does call us forward. A race is not always easy and there are times when we falter, times we feel like we can't go on, times we feel we can't take another step. But remember we aren't "moving on" which sounds like we leave someone behind. We are moving forward, towards Heaven.

We used to go hiking a lot. There were times when we would hike some pretty steep mountains. Don always had more stamina than I did, so there were times he was waiting on me. I would be thinking I could not make it to the top. But with his encouragement I would, and the view was always beautiful. We can make it to the top because God is calling us forward and the prize is in Heaven. We will see Jesus, and we will have a glorious reunion with our loved ones. We are waiting on that day!

What are your thoughts on the verses and Dr. Terveen's beautiful description? Journal any experiences you have similar to climbing the mountain or a race.

---

[45] John Luke Terveen, *Hope for the Brokenhearted* (Colorado Springs, CO: Victor, 2006), 17.

DAY 37

Then I saw a new heaven and a new earth, for the first heaven and the first earth had passed away, and there was no longer any sea. I saw the Holy City, the New Jerusalem, coming down out of heaven from God, prepared as a bride beautifully dressed for her husband. And I heard a loud voice from the throne saying, "Look! God's dwelling place is now among the people, and he will dwell with them. They will be his people, and God himself will be with them and be their God. He will wipe every tear from their eyes. There will be no more death or mourning or crying or pain, for the old order of things has passed away." (Revelation 21:1-4, NIV)

God will dwell among His people! There will be no more death, or mourning, or crying, or pain. That is the result of His eternal plan. When we received Christ as our Savior, we became a part of this plan. And someday we will live on a New Earth. The Holy City will be a part of the New Earth. We long for a time that there will be no more death. The pain right now is overwhelming. But someday we will live again on this Earth. God will dwell among us. We will be reunited with our loved one and never again go through the pain of death.

When Dad was in the hospital, we would be encouraged by something the doctor said, then later discouraged; the up and down news was like a roller coaster. The night before Dad went to Heaven, Don and I went to the hospital. Dad was propped back in the bed and he said, "I feel tired but it is a good tired." He had walked down the hall a bit. We left encouraged. The next day Dad took a turn for the worse, and then he was gone. Perhaps you have gone through something similar with the ups and downs, the tears, and then the hope. But someday the tears are going to end. Someday there will be no more crying. God will wipe away the tears. We will not need to cry because there will be no more death, no more mourning, or crying, or pain. It is hard to imagine that day right now because pain consumes you. Tears flow and the sorrow is heavy and so deep. But the pain will all end because God's dwelling place will be among us.

Randy Alcorn writes about this verse, "God's redemptive plan climaxes not as the return of Christ, nor in the millennial kingdom, but on the New Earth. Only then will all wrongs be made right. Only then will there be no more death, crying, or pain."[46] We are waiting on that day!

What are your thoughts and feelings on these verses? What are your thoughts on Randy Alcorn's words about God's redemptive plan?

---

[46] Randy Alcorn, *Heaven* (Carol Stream, IL: Tyndale House, 2004), 56.

DAY 38

Rejoice with those who rejoice; mourn with those who mourn. (Romans 12:15, NIV)

This scripture helps us understand that mourning is expected and it is okay. This passage does not say, "Cheer up those who mourn." Well-meaning people sometimes say things that are not so helpful. You did not just have surgery that you must get over. Don't let anyone rush you. You may need to be assertive. If you have trouble saying how you feel, then write it. Let people know you are hurting, and though you know they mean well, you do not need to be pushed. Tell them what you need from them.

Grief is universal, but how we grieve is a very individual thing. Some people want to be around other people; some do not. You are unique. Allow yourself to grieve as you need to grieve. The worst thing you can do is stuff your feelings and avoid grief. You are not going to grieve wrong. After God called Don Home I did not want to leave my house for a good while. I felt closer to Don at home in his recliner. Yet I have had some clients and friends who did not want to be at home. New Year's Eve after Dad went Home, we stayed up as we always had. Our family custom was to play forty-two, eat, and talk. My sister, Don, and Mom wanted to play forty-two because Dad loved it so much. My sister, Teresa, felt closer to Dad playing forty-two because Dad loved it. I, on the other hand, could not bear to play the game without Dad. Neither of us was wrong; our preferences reflected the way we felt. Our two daughters threw themselves into making a picture slide show and frames with pictures of the family when both Dad and Don went Home.

We have to find that place where we can express our grief. Journaling helps you process those needs. But you also have to communicate your needs to others. If people try to "help" you, pull, or push you to do something when you are not ready, tell them. Most people are not sure what to do.

One of Don's closest friends is, Jeff; they rode bikes and hiked together. Jeff and his wife Karen and Don and I often spent time together. After Don went Home, they came over. Jeff with tears in his eyes said, "I don't know what to say, so I am not going to say anything." But his tears said everything. He loved Don and he and his wife were hurting with me. Two friends, Penny and Gloria, would come over and sit and cry with me. Their love and their presence were immeasurable. Our family is extremely close, so we would be able to sit and cry and talk about how much we missed Dad and then Don. Some families do not always draw closer and distance makes loss so much more difficult. If you are in a situation where people pull away or push, try communicating how you all can grieve differently but still need to respect these differences.

How does this verse help you? Have you noticed people grieving differently?

DAY 39

See, I will create new heavens and a new earth. The former things will not be remembered, nor will they come to mind. But be glad and rejoice forever in what I will create, for I will create Jerusalem to be a delight and its people a joy. (Isaiah 65:17-18, NIV)

As you read this verse in Isaiah, hold on to the thoughts of the New Heavens and the New Earth. Remember there is an eternal plan, and there has been from the beginning of time. Throughout the Old and New Testaments are the promises of God that point us to the eternal plan. This world here and now is not all there is. When you wonder why bad things happen, remember that this world, as it is now, is all temporary. All of us have a time to be called Home. Someday, at the appointed time, Jesus will come back. Someday God will create a New Heaven and a New Earth. We will be glad and rejoice forever. Randy Alcorn says it very well, "Once we understand that all we love about the old Earth will be ours on the New Earth—either in the same form or another—we won't regret leaving all the wonders of the world we've seen or not yet see. Why? Because we will yet be able to see them."[47]

Melody, our oldest daughter, said, "Mom, I can see Dad checking out all the places to show us!" I know if God is indeed allowing those gone before to "check it out," then Don will. All of our family trips were adventures because he loved to take the back roads where ever we went. No tour busses for us. We have gone down trails that ended up being dead ends, but most of the time we discovered beautiful scenes. But maybe we will have to wait until the New Earth to check out those things together. Either way, we know that we will be glad and rejoice in what God has created.

Notice that God says, "But be glad and rejoice in what I will create, for I will create Jerusalem to be a delight." God's plan is to create something so beautiful that we, His people, will delight and rejoice in it. If we can hold to the thought of God's eternal plan as we mourn, it helps in two ways. One, the plan has always been there; it is eternal. We think in terms of right now and this moment, but there is a big plan that goes far beyond this moment in time and history. And second, the eternal plan is something we will delight in. Because of God's eternal plan, you will be reunited with your loved one in a place so wonderful that it will be a delight. We will be with those we love, so we will be even more delighted. We are waiting on that day!

How does this verse speak to you? What are your thoughts on Alcorn's words?

---

[47]   Randy Alcorn, *Heaven* (Carol Stream, IL: Tyndale House, 2004), 43.

DAY 40

I know that my redeemer lives and that in the end he will stand on the earth.
And after my skin has been destroyed, yet in my flesh I will see God; I myself
will see him with my own eyes—I, and not another.
How my heart yearns within me! (Job 19:25-27, NIV)

These above verses in Job are some I quote the most. If you just take a moment
to soak in these verses, it is amazing. Scholars think Job is the oldest book in
the Bible. Philip Yancey writes, "Seen as a whole, Job is primarily about *faith* in
its starkest form."[48] Job sees a day that God will walk on this Earth and he also
knows a day that, although his skin is destroyed, he will still see God in the flesh.
"With my own eyes—I, and not another. How my heart yearns within me!" You
and I will stand before our Lord. And we will see Him ourselves. I don't know
about you, but my heart is certainly yearning to see God. Our loved one already
has. And someday so will we.

The pain is all consuming right now, but when you stop and quote this
verse and meditate on it, it can bring you comfort. You, yourself, will see God.
God loves you. We cannot lose sight of the fact God loves us. We will see Him
ourselves. Randy Alcorn writes, "The prospect of seeing God eclipsed all of
Job's heartaches."[49] We have to remember that God is in control. We will see
Him. Our heart will still hurt, but we know that there is an end to that pain
because we know we will see Him. We know that our loved one has entered His
presence now.

Another awesome thing to take from this verse is the reminder of the
continuity of our lives in Heaven. In his book *Heaven*, Randy Alcorn quotes this
verse and adds, "But through all the changes I will still be who I was and who
I am. There will be continuity from this life to the next and I can say with Job,
'in my flesh I will see God; I myself will see him with my own eyes—I, and not
another.'"[50] He also writes, "Being with God is the heart and soul of Heaven."[51]
Remind yourself of this verse when you feel like God is far away. Quote this verse
when nothing in your life makes sense. I found Job comforting and reassuring,
and full of hope and faith. I shall see God; how my heart yearns within me. I
am waiting on that day!

Meditate on these verses. How can these verses comfort you now? Try memorizing
this verse and saying it aloud.

---

[48] Philip, Yancey, *Disappointment With God* (Grand Rapids, MI: Zondervan, 1992),
181.
[49] Randy Alcorn, *Heaven* (Carol Stream, IL: Tyndale House, 2004), 466.
[50] Ibid., 114.
[51] Ibid., 171.

DAY 41

Brothers and sisters, we do not want you to be uninformed about those who sleep in death, so that you do not grieve like the rest of mankind, who have no hope. For we believe that Jesus died and rose again, and so we believe that God will bring with Jesus those who have fallen asleep in him. For the Lord himself will come down from heaven, with a loud command, with the voice of the archangel and with the trumpet call of God, and the dead in Christ will rise first. After that, we who are still alive and are left will be caught up together with them in the clouds to meet the Lord in the air. And so we will be with the Lord forever. Therefore encourage one another with these words. (1 Thessalonians 4:13, 16-18, NIV)

Read all of 1 Thessalonians 4:13-18. I love this passage and we will use it again. We read, "We will be caught up *together with them* in the clouds to meet the Lord in the air." And it ends with, "Encourage one another with these words." I love what Randy Alcorn says about this passage:

Our parting is not the end of our relationships, only an interruption. We have not 'lost' them, because we know where they are. They are experiencing the joy of Christ's presence in a place so wonderful that Christ called it Paradise. And one day, we're told, in a magnificent reunion, they and we 'will be with the Lord forever. Therefore encourage each other with these words.'[52]

Later Randy Alcorn adds these beautiful and comforting words:

The notion that relationships with family and friends will be lost in Heaven, though common, is unbiblical. It denies the clear doctrine of continuity between this life and the next and suggests that our earthly lives and relationships have no eternal consequence. It completely contradicts Paul's intense anticipation of being with the Thessalonians and his encouraging them to look forward to rejoining their loved ones in Heaven.[53]

Focus on the encouragement of knowing you will be with your loved one again. Also note Paul doesn't say, "Don't grieve." Paul expects his readers to grieve, but he reminds them they have hope unlike those who are not believers. The pain of not having your loved one here is intense and real. The sorrow is deep. But the hope is real too. We must hold to that hope, and when we hold to the hope of Christ, we grow our faith. We are waiting on that day!

What are your thoughts on these powerful verses and on Alcorn's words?

---

[52] Randy Alcorn, *Heaven* (Carol Stream, IL: Tyndale House, 2004), 73.
[53] Ibid., 351

DAY 42 REFLECTION

As you reflect over the last six days, what speaks to you the most? We looked at verses that remind us we are running a race and that speak of God's calling us. We read the beautiful words in Revelation that speak of God dwelling with us! How absolutely powerful are these verses?

The verse that talks about mourning is important because it reminds us it is okay—and even expected—to mourn, and to not allow anyone to hurry us through the process. It reminds you to speak up for yourself and to allow yourself to grieve. I have clients that come in feeling guilty because they don't know how they "should" be. You need to allow yourself to grieve in the way you need to.

I love the thought of the New Heaven and the New Earth; I am waiting on that day! We will be with our loved ones again and we will be a place of delight. We will live with God. These verses on the New Earth are beautiful words of comfort. I find it amazing that Job, the book that some scholars think is the oldest, speaks of a resurrection. I continue to quote these verses. It brings me comfort.

The verses in Thessalonians give us that beautiful picture of being caught up in the clouds with our loved ones, and meeting Jesus together to be with Him forever. How beautiful to imagine being caught up with Jesus in the sky! Pick one or more of these verses to memorize. Reflect and meditate on the verses and devotionals for the last six days. Record your thoughts and feelings.

DAY 43

For ever since the world was created, people have seen the earth and sky. Through everything God made, they can clearly see his invisible qualities—his eternal power and divine nature. So they have no excuse for not knowing God. (Romans 1:20, NLT)

One day I was driving to work crying and talking to God. I said, "Where are you God? Are you there? I don't feel you. I need to feel you. I don't want to doubt you." And as I turned the corner and looked at the sky, the sun was shining magnificently between the clouds. Rays were illuminating the morning. And I thought, "Yes, you are here. The sky shows your majesty, your handiwork." God's magnificence in creation points us to Heaven.

I mentioned before that I began taking photos of the sky, marveling at how beautiful it is, how none of the beauty of creation can be an accident. Don and I have always appreciated the beauty of the outdoors. We built a family cabin in the mountains near Broken Bow, Oklahoma, right outside Beavers Bend State Park. The cabin is full of windows to have a clear view of God's beautiful creation. One morning not long after Dad went Home, Don and I were at the cabin. "I will Rise" by Chris Tomlin was playing through our speakers and the sun was streaming in through the huge windows. I was so moved I filmed the sun coming through the windows with the song playing in the background. When we listen to that song, we would think about Dad. He had been in pain, but he would rise again through Christ.

After Don went Home, I shut down and didn't want to move. But as I sat on our patio where we had spent so many mornings and I took in God's beautiful works, I had a desire to see anything of nature that would help me focus on God's handiwork. Where do you see those invisible qualities? Look around you. Notice God's hand in all of the beauty of creation. Your tears can blind your view. The pain can numb your ability to see God's handiwork. I am not saying that I am continually able to focus beyond the pain, because I can't. I have to constantly remind myself to look around me at the beauty of God's creation. Now I remind you as well: look around you. Look at the butterflies gracefully flying around. Listen to the birds singing and flying. Look at the trees, the flowers, and the wildlife. Feel the sun on your skin; see the clouds through the storm, the sunset as it casts a glow. Nature shouts God's handiwork. God is here, He loves you, and He is in control. His handiwork points us to Heaven.

How does this verse speak to you? Where can you see God's hand at work in creation? Take a minute to write about how you feel and see God's beautiful creation all around you.

DAY 44

Therefore we do not lose heart. Though outwardly we are wasting away, yet inwardly we are being renewed day by day. For our light and momentary troubles are achieving for us an eternal glory that far outweighs them all. (2 Corinthians 4:16-17, NIV)

Paul's light and momentary troubles were not light. He had been beaten and imprisoned. He knew his death could be at any moment. But Paul saw his troubles as momentary. Why? Because compared to eternity, everything here is momentary. We have an eternal glory to look forward to, and all of this pain and sorrow will be outweighed by that eternal glory. I know your pain and sorrow doesn't seem light. Sorrow is heavy, very heavy. Pain is relentless. Each day you wake up the reality hits you that the loss of your loved one is not a nightmare—or at least not one you can wake up from.

Sometimes at night you may not be able to sleep. If you do fall asleep, you wake up to the realization that it is another day you have to face without your loved one, and the nightmare continues. It seems like nothing you are experiencing right now can be real. Yet each day is a painful reminder to you that what you are experiencing must be real. One of my grief-stricken friends once said, "It feels like I am stuck in a twilight zone." As for me, I keep thinking this is all so surreal, a horrid nightmare. Nothing about this nightmare seems light or momentary. But we are viewing things through the lens of Earth and what we see, which is all temporary. This time here on Earth is just the beginning.

Steven Saint writes, "Why is it we want every chapter to be good when God promises that only in the last chapter will he make all the other chapters make sense, and he doesn't promise we will see the last chapter here?"[54] Paul knew that the last chapter was not on this Earth. He knew that there was an eternal glory. Your loved one has entered into his eternal glory. As believers we can look forward to the day we too will enter God's eternal glory. Even though nothing right now seems light or momentary, all of this sorrow will seem light and momentary when we see Jesus. We are waiting on that day!

What are your thoughts and feelings on this verse? How do you feel about Steven Saint's words about the last chapter?

---

[54] Steven Saint, "Sovereignty, Suffering, and the Work of Missions." John Piper and Justin Taylor (Ed). *Suffering and the Sovereignty of God* (Wheaton, IL: Crossway 2006), 120.

DAY 45

But it has now been revealed through the appearing of our Savior, Christ Jesus, who has destroyed death and has brought life and immortality to light through the gospel. (2 Timothy 1:10, NIV)

In the *Bible and the Future*, Anthony Hoekema writes:

The conquest of death, therefore, is to be seen as an essential part of Christ's redemptive work. Christ not only redeems his people from sin; he also redeems them from the results of sin, and death is one of them. And so we read in II Timothy 1:10 that, 'Christ has abolished death and brought life and immortality to light.' It is a fitting culmination of Christ's redemptive work that in the new Jerusalem there will be no more death (Rev. 21:4)[55]

We know that someday there will be no more death, but until that time comes those of us left behind face the overwhelming pain of death. However, through the pain, we must hold on to the knowledge that for the believer this "death" is not the end. We have the promise of life and immortality through Christ. And so as we mourn, and we hurt, and miss the physical presence of our loved ones, we know that they are safe and we will one day be with them. They are in our Lord's presence. Because of Christ's death and resurrection, we have that promise of immortality. He has abolished death for the believer. Paul Enns says it well:

Death will never overtake the believer. Immortality (athanasian) means precisely what a person anticipates, 'that which is not subject to death.' Death is gone, banished forever. Believers take on immortality. Although this mortal, earthly body is laid to rest in the grave, the real person, the soul and spirit, continued on uninterrupted as the believer is transported into glory. There the believer continues in genuine, real life and *immortality*.[56]

We can look forward to the New Jerusalem we will see with our own eyes. We can look forward to seeing Jesus in His glory, and we can look forward to being with our loved ones again. We are waiting on that day!

What does the verse say to you? What are your thoughts on the two quotes? How do they help you now?

---

55 Anthony A. Hoekema, *The Bible and the Future* (Grand Rapids, MI: Eerdmans), 84.
56 Paul Enns, *Heaven Revealed* (Chicago, IL: Moody, 2011), 36.

DAY 46

I have fought the good fight, I have finished the race, I have kept the faith. Now there is in store for me the crown of righteousness, which the Lord, the righteous Judge, will award to me on that day—and not only to me, but also to all who have longed for his coming. (2 Timothy 4:7-8, NIV)

This passage is talking about the day we will receive our rewards as believers, and shows us how the things we do here matter for eternity. We have a race to run and the rewards come as a part of His divine plan. Your loved one has fought the fight and finished the race. Dad had COPD and then developed lung cancer. He kept an amazing attitude, and was witnessing the entire time he was in the hospital. His oncologist, a wonderful Christian man who prayed for his patients, was amazed at Dad's attitude. Dad knew that there was a crown of righteousness in store for him. He fought the fight and finished the race. Don and Dad lived each day to the glory of God. Each day we are here we are called to run the race.

You may have lost a child and feel they did not get a chance to run the race. They ran their race, as short as it may have been. Each life is important to God, and each life touches others. Whether that life was new or one hundred years old, the race was set. Someday the things we don't understand now will all make sense. I agree there are many things in this life that from an earthly perspective do not make sense. If you try to make sense of it, you will feel like you are going crazy. Even as a therapist who knows mental health issues, there are days that I think: I am going to lose my mind. I cannot handle this anymore. Each day is a conscious effort to just be.

But we continue with each step because we know what we do here matters for eternity. Someday we will see Jesus and everything will make sense. The burdens we carry, the pain; it will all make sense in light of eternity. But also notice the last line in the verse above: "also to all who long for his appearing." As we finish our own race and fight the fight, we can look—and should look— forward to Christ's appearing. Recognizing the brevity of life, we should be praying for all those we know who do not know the Lord as we look forward to that day Jesus will appear. When Jesus appears, then and only then will the sorrow in this world go away. We are waiting on that day.

What are our thoughts and feelings on this verse? Do you long for Jesus appearing? How does that bring you comfort?

DAY 47

All these people were still living by faith when they died. They did not receive the things promised; they only saw them and welcomed them from a distance, admitting that they were foreigners and strangers on earth. People who say such things show that they are looking for a country of their own. If they had been thinking of the country they had left, they would have had opportunity to return. Instead, they were longing for a better country—a heavenly one. Therefore God is not ashamed to be called their God, for he has prepared a city for them. (Hebrews 11:13-16, NIV)

It is easy to read the scriptures and think of the stories about Abraham as history. Even though we know that history is a vital part of who we are and an important part of our faith, we might miss the bigger picture. Abraham died before fully recognizing the full promises of God. Reading these verses highlight the eternal plan. All of history and current events are part of a plan that will be fully realized in Heaven.

We have to stay focused on the eternal plan, and for those of us hurting it is even more important. Why? Because focusing on the eternal plan and realizing our eternal destination allows us to hold on to the hope of being with our loved one again. Without an eternity with Christ, without a Sovereign God, death would certainly be devastating. Knowing that we are moving toward the eternal plan and looking forward to a heavenly country allows us to hold to eternal hope and assurance.

The pain is ever-present, and holding to the eternal plan may not lessen the pain of not having our loved one with us. But just like any pain, knowing the source of it will eventually be gone allows us to faithfully endure. We will no longer be separated from those we love. We are foreigners on this Earth. Now as we long for that heavenly country, we can know the heavenly country is a reality. The answer to all of our questions, the answer to sorrow, is a heavenly one. God has prepared a city for us. We are all moving in that direction. Our loved ones just went a little sooner. We are waiting on that day!

Meditate on this verse. How does seeing Abraham's story as something more than history help you right now?

DAY 48

You have made my life no longer than the width of my hand. My entire lifetime is just a moment to you; at best, each of us is but a breath." Interlude. (Psalm 39:5, NLT)

Even a life of one hundred years is nothing compared to eternity. You may feel as I do: the here and the now is lasting painfully slow. But we are told repeatedly through the scriptures that this world as we know it is not all there is. This life is short in comparison to eternity. When you think you can't go on, and I know that feeling well, you have to remind yourself: this life is just a breath. The thought of the brevity of life gives me such an urgency to share God's message with others. We do not have any promise of a next breath! We know that all too well. We are dealing with the intense pain of a loved one; someone that did not take another breath. And the time we had with them was all too short. Yet people tend to think we have all the time in the world.

Don and I had talked about a will just a couple of weeks before he went Home. We wanted to talk to a lawyer about some property, and thought we really should get a will since we were both self-employed. Were we in a hurry? No. We were both healthy, active, and felt young. So there was no big hurry. We were wrong. Did it cause some problems that we didn't have a will? Yes, I had to deal with things at a time I was in so much pain I could not breathe. Fortunately, we found a Christian lawyer who was very compassionate. But I couldn't keep from thinking that this was hard and painful, but it was something that I was able to do with family help. Then when we think of life, many people have time due to sickness to prepare, but many do not. Don went Home suddenly and without warning, yet he went straight into the arms of our Lord because he was prepared spiritually. He also knew all of his relationships were sound and full of love. He was always prepared because he walked with God and lived his faith. There are many things we put off, thinking we have plenty of time to take care of that later. Salvation is one of those things that cannot be taken care of later; one day it will all be too late. That makes it even more important to have urgency for others' salvation.

Another area people postpone working on is relationships. So knowing our life is brief, it is important to invest in those relationships with each other—and our relationship with God. When our loved ones go Home, we become so aware of what is important. Even though we are hurting, spending time in prayer for those who are lost is important. We know how brief life is. And there is an urgency to make sure others get the eternal perspective. The eternal perspective allows us to know that we will be with our loved ones before we know it. We are waiting on that day!

What are your thoughts on the verse and today's devotional?

DAY 49 REFLECTION

Reflect back over the last six days. We looked at Romans 1:20 that speaks of God's handiwork. We know that as we look at the sky and the beauty in nature that we see what God has created. All of His works point us toward Heaven. We see verses that remind us this time on Earth is momentary compared to eternity. The time to us grieving seems painfully slow, but someday we will see how short it is compared to the eternal glory. The NLT used the word interlude after the verse in Psalm 39. The word in other translations is Selah. It's meaning is unknown but many think it means a rest. Reminding us to rest in Him.

We read that Jesus has destroyed death and because of Him, we have eternal life. Death is not the end. We read verses that remind us to finish the race set before us. These verses remind us no matter how short our loved one's life was; he or she ran their race.

It helps to be reminded that Abraham didn't see the end result of his promises, but he trusted God. We know we too can trust God and look forward to the heavenly city. We read again of the brevity of life. Reminding ourselves of the brevity of life and the eternal plan is important. It forces us to remember this world as we know it is temporary and brief. We have an eternity to look forward to. Death will be destroyed. We just need to remember to focus on God's handiwork, His eternal plan, our own continuity of life, and relationships as we wait on that day. Which verses seemed to speak to you the most? Pick one or more verses to memorize. Reflect on the devotionals and record your thoughts and feelings.

DAY 50

Why, you do not even know what will happen tomorrow. What is your life? You are a mist that appears for a little while and then vanishes. (James 4:14, NIV)

James 4:14 is another scripture passage to remind us that life is short. This verse also reminds us that we need to be about the Father's business. Our perspective has to stay focused on the eternal.

We have no guarantee of the next day or even the next breath. This world as we know it is not all there is. There is an eternity to celebrate and worship our Lord with our loved ones. Staying focused on the shortness of life, for those of us who are anxiously awaiting our reunions, is a way to keep an eternal perspective. Beth Moore says, "This verse can have a profound effect on the way we view human existence if we're willing to adjust our lens.... This life goes fast. A vapor. A mist. Picture someone exhaling warm breath into the freezing cold. There it is. Then it's gone."[57] She goes on to say:

God is the one with the real plan.... God is the only one looking through every layer and at every implication. He looks upon a situation in context to what is, what was and what is to come. His deliberations don't just involve immediate impact. He sees our place and our positions amid carefully woven generations.[58]

We have to try to keep the thought of the eternal plan in focus. God has the real plan. What we see is one part of that plan. What we do here matters, and as we take the next step, we are one step closer to Heaven; one day closer to Heaven. Remember we are one moment closer to seeing Jesus, to fully understanding and to being reunited with our loved one. We are waiting on that day!

What are your thoughts and feelings about this verse? How has your thoughts changed on this since your loved one has gone Home? How can focusing on the brevity of life comfort you?

---

[57] Beth Moore, *James Mercy Triumphs* (Nashville, TN: Lifeway 2012), 151.
[58] Ibid., 153.

DAY 51

You will keep in perfect peace those whose minds are steadfast, because they trust in you. (Isaiah 26:3, NIV)

Isaiah 26:3 joined my most quoted list. One day this verse came up on my Bible verse app. As soon as I read it, I thought, "This describes Don." I have to remind myself to say, "I trust you, Jesus, even though I don't feel you. Help me be steadfast in my faith." Peace comes with trusting Jesus. Even though we feel completely overwhelmed, even though we don't understand, even though our world has fallen apart and we are broken and lost, God is in control. I will trust Him. Steven Curtis Chapman's song "I will Trust You" is about choosing to trust God in the face of overwhelming pain. I listen to it over and over. These powerful words show the relentless pain and sorrow of having a child go Home all too soon.

> I don't even wanna breathe right now
> All I wanna do is close my eyes
> But I don't wanna open them again
> Until I'm standing on the other side
>
> I will trust You, trust You
> Trust You, God, I will
> Even when I don't understand
> Even then I will say again
>
> You are my God, and I'll trust You
> And with every breath I take
> And for every day that breaks
> I will trust You
> I will trust You
> And when nothing is making sense
> Even then I will say again
> God, I trust You[59]

Listening to this amazing song helps you focus on God. Focus on God and choose to trust Him even when you don't understand. Quoting this verse and making the choice to trust God and telling Him that I trust Him helps me stay focused. We want the peace that comes with being steadfast because we trust in God. But when faced with sorrow and pain, trust can be hard; therefore, we must choose to trust Him. Pray for help to be steadfast. And then we can say, "I trust you God even in the darkest of nights when I don't feel you."

Write your thoughts on the verse and the powerful lyrics. Choose to trust.

---

[59]   Steven Curtis Chapman, "I Will Trust You." *Beauty Will Rise*. Sparrow, 2009.

DAY 52

None of us can hold back our spirit from departing. None of us has the power to prevent the day of our death. There is no escaping that obligation, that dark battle. And in the face of death, wickedness will certainly not rescue the wicked. (Ecclesiastes 8:8, NLT)

The day of our death is certain unless we are here when Jesus comes again. Some people are told they have an illness and began to prepare for that possibility; some are taken suddenly. We ask people to pray with us for healing and sometimes God heals. But sometimes the healing is realized in Heaven. Max Lucado writes, "We don't like to say good-bye to those we love. But if we believe what the Bible says about Heaven is true, and I believe it is, then the ultimate prayer, the ultimate answered prayer, is heaven."[60]

We can ask people to pray, and the Bible tells us to, but ultimately everyone Jesus healed died. One of our assistant ministers was battling with cancer. He came to see me when Don went Home, and we talked about his own battle. Less than a week later he was in the hospital. I went to see him; we prayed and talked about Heaven and Don and how the true healing was in Heaven. Two days later he was healed, because two days later he stepped into Heaven into the waiting arms of Jesus. We cannot stop that day. God is sovereign, and He is in control. What we can do is hold to our hope in Christ. Because of Christ, death is not the end for believers. We are promised an eternity with Christ. We look forward to that day. We ask Him to help us have an eternal perspective and to trust him despite the pain and sorrow. We are saved by Christ. Your believing loved one was saved, and now is safe in our Savior's presence. The ultimate healing is in Heaven. We will have a reunion in Heaven someday. And when we do there will be no more days of death. We are waiting on that day!

What are your thoughts and feelings on this verse? What are your thoughts on Max Lucado's words?

---

[60] Max Lucado, *For These Tough Times* (Nashville, TN: W Publishing, 2006), 75.

DAY 53

And if our hope in Christ is only for this life, we are more to be pitied than anyone in the world. (1 Corinthians 15:19, NLT)

At family gatherings we nearly always end up talking about how God has blessed our family. Holidays are spent together, and God is given the glory. Don and I would sit on our deck or patio and nearly all conversation would end up with how very blessed we were. One weekend before Dad went Home, we were all at our cabin in the woods. We sat out on the deck of the cabin discussing Heaven. Our talk turned to family and reunions in Heaven and the continuity of life. Dad said, "Ann, it is the nature of God." God ordained the family. He chose Abraham to be the father of a nation. Our family's hope has always been in Christ for this life and for eternity.

When we have a loss that shakes our world completely, especially if we are not feeling God, we may lose sight for a moment of what we have always believed. Our belief that we have always held to before this loss is still true; we can't let shock and sorrow cloud that fact. Our hope in Christ is not just for this world. Christians and non-Christians alike have both good and bad things happen to them. A lot of people talk about how lucky they are, and what a great life they have. But only Christians can say, "Our hope is not just in this life." We have hope in Christ in this life for sure, but it is for the next life too. Our eternal life with Christ is what we have that is different. Our reunion with our loved ones, our family, is a promise. We have the promise of a resurrection and a New Heaven and a New Earth.

Our hope is in Christ. Right now you need to remember what your hope in Christ means more than you ever have in this life. Your hope is in Christ, and it is not just for this life. We have an eternity to worship Christ. We have an eternity to celebrate with our family. We have an eternity to get to know other believers. I have wondered if Dad and Don are meeting relatives they had heard about but never met. Is Don meeting my grandparents, who he never met? Is he meeting his grandparents? Is Dad getting to spend time with his Dad? I think so. And I can't wait until I join that party. We are waiting on that day.

Meditate on this verse. How does it help you? What are your thoughts about the nature of God?

DAY 54

For the Word of the LORD holds true,
and we can trust everything he does. (Psalm 33:4, NLT)

The Word of the Lord holds true. When your world is torn apart, it is hard to hold to anything. Things do not feel right and nothing makes sense. You may find yourself crying all the time. You may find yourself feeling irritable, or feeling like no one understands. You might feel isolated or abandoned. There are times you may feel that you are losing your mind. Feelings seem to overwhelm you. The darkness of the nightmare seems never ending. The abyss of pain and sorrow seem never ending. But what we do know is the Word of the Lord holds true.

So when those feelings overwhelm you, when nothing makes sense, when the nightmare threatens to consume you, remember His Word. His Word tells us that our hope is in Christ. His Word tells us that we are promised eternity. His Word tells us that there will be no more death. His Word tells us He has prepared a place for us. His Word tells us we will be with our loved ones with Christ forever. Read the scripture passages in the Bible that seem to speak to you the most. Memorize the verses that remind you what His Word says. Satan will tell you that you are abandoned. Satan will tell you that if God loved you, He would not have taken your loved one. Satan will tell you to doubt. But Satan is the author of lies. The Word of the Lord holds true. We can trust everything the Lord does, because we know He is in control.

We know God has an eternal plan. We know that this world, as we know it, is not all there is, and that we have an eternity to live with Jesus. Look around you and see the Creator's handiwork. Remember His work in your own life. Read all the prophecy that has been fulfilled and has yet to be filled. God's Word holds true and we can trust everything He does.

How does this verse speak to you? What feelings threaten to overwhelm you? What verses can you hold to right now to remind yourself of God's Word?

DAY 55

For now we see only a reflection as in a mirror; then we shall see face to face.
Now I know in part; then I shall know fully, even as I am fully known. (1
Corinthians 13:12, NIV)

There is so much we don't see and we don't understand. Don would say he hoped
when he got to Heaven we could watch a replay of everything like the parting
of the Red Sea. Maybe he could watch Jesus' baptism or the Transfiguration.
He wanted to watch the walls of Jericho come down. I don't know if we will be
able to see these things in Heaven or if Don already has. But I know we will see
fully, and I can't wait.

I can't wait until the day that I don't wonder what God is telling me—that
I don't have to pray, "Is that you God" because I will know it is Him. We won't
have to wonder if this is from God. We will know fully. I think that will be
absolutely awesome. For now, though, we are in the valley of confusion and
sorrow. We wonder where God is, or if we have heard His voice. There are times
I have wondered if what I thought was from God or if it was just my own desires.
There will be a day that confusion is gone, because we will know fully. Steven
Curtis Chapman's song "Questions" voices some of these feelings:

> And where are you God
> Cuz I am finding life to be
> So much harder than I had planned

> Know that I am afraid
> To ask these questions
> But You know they are there

Chapman questions the pain and suffering and what happened in his own life,
but he finishes with the beautiful words:

> But isn't there a day of redemption coming
> Quickly Lord, come quickly
> Lord, come quickly[61]

We have to hold to this promise that someday we will see fully. But for now, we
trust Jesus. We pray even though we aren't sure we hear Him. We pray for others,
we quote scripture, and we listen to songs about Him. We spend time with Him.
We know someday we will see fully. We are waiting for that day!

What are your thoughts and feelings on the verse and the today's devotional?

---

[61]   Steven Curtis Chapman, "Questions." *Beauty Will Rise*. Sparrow, 2009.

DAY 56 REFLECTION

As you read back over the last six days, reflect on the verses and devotionals that spoke the most to you. We look at two verses that speak of the brevity of life, one in James and one in Ecclesiastes. We need the constant reminder that our life is but a mist; we have no control over the day we die. Our loved ones went Home because it was their time. We don't understand, but we hold to the promise of eternity. We will be reunited. We wait on that day!

Isaiah 26:3 is a beautiful verse that reminds me of Don. Truly Don was steadfast in his faith and in his life. As I quote this verse I feel peace. We become steadfast when we trust in God. We choose to trust. We also looked at not having the control we think we do. God is in control, not us. Choosing to trust in God, even when you do not feel Him and when you are completely overwhelmed, is a step of faith. God sees that faith and will help you as you make this journey.

Our hope is in Christ. We have an eternity to worship Him and be with our loved ones. I quote 1 Corinthians 15:19 every day. Pain can consume us, so we have to remind ourselves that our true Home is with Jesus. Our hope is not just in this life, even though it matters; our hope is in Jesus Christ and the eternal life. And lastly we read that we shall see Him face to face and know fully. What exciting words in 1 Corinthians! Record your thoughts and feeling as you reflect over the last week. What did you need to hear the most this week? How is God speaking to you?

DAY 57

But why should I fast when he is dead? Can I bring him back again? I will go to him one day, but he cannot return to me. (2 Samuel 12:23, NLT)

Some people interpret this verse to mean David will go to the grave with his son. However, a vast majority that I read interpret this as David's knowledge that he would actually go to his son in eternity. I have to agree with the authors that see this as referring to eternity. Paul Enns writes, "David understood, he would be reunited in Heaven with his son."[62] Randy Alcorn writes, "I personally think David, in his agony, was consoling himself with the belief that he would one day join his son in Heaven."[63] Why would David be so distraught while he prayed that his son would live, only then to be able to calmly say that he could go to him someday if he didn't think he would actually be with his son in person? It would seem like David had the knowledge that there was more than the grave. Of course, David wanted his child to live, just as we would want our loved one to live if given the choice. But our hope in Christ gives us the assurance of Heaven. Every day I listen to the beautiful and heartfelt words in the Mercy Me song "Homesick":

In Christ, there are no goodbyes
And in Christ, there is no end
So I'll hold onto Jesus with all that I have
To see you again
To see you again[64]

The desire to be with your loved one is intense. Perhaps you are reading this and you have lost a baby as David did. Jesus said, "Let the children come to me." Children are precious in His sight. Your precious baby is with our Savior and someday you will go to that baby. No matter how old the person is that we love, we long to go with him or her. Until the day we do, we must trust that Jesus has them and we must trust His promises. We are waiting on that day!

What are your thoughts and feelings on this verse? What are your thoughts on the quotes and the lyrics to the song?

---

[62] Paul Enns, *Heaven Revealed* (Chicago, IL: Moody, 2011), 160.

[63] Randy Alcorn, *Heaven* (Carol Stream, IL: Tyndale House, 2004), 355.

[64] Mercy Me, "Homesick." *Itunes Original*. MercyMe, 2008.

DAY 58

But thank God! He gives us victory over sin and death through our Lord Jesus Christ. (1 Corinthians 15:57, NLT)

As believers, we have victory of sin and death though our Lord Jesus Christ. It is because of this victory we know that our believing loved one is with Jesus now. And we will be reunited one day. As we mourn now, we know our loved one entered into Jesus' presence.

Max Lucado writes, "You and I might wonder why God took them home. But they don't. They understand. They are, at this very moment, at peace in the presence of God."[65] We may focus on not having our loved ones with us. But they are focusing on being with Jesus. We too have to focus on the fact we have victory through Jesus and we will someday be with our loved one praising God.

Keeping an eternal perspective does not stop your pain, but it does allow you to hold to the hope of the victory in Christ. Because we have this hope, this victory in Jesus, we will see Jesus. Because we have this victory we will be reunited with our loved ones. When the pain seems overwhelming today or the memories overtake you, thank God for the victory your loved one has. I know the pain and sorrow are harder sometimes than others. But I also know that it seems to help me when I say, "Thank You, Lord that I have such an amazing love that the intensity of the loss would be this deep." Thank God that because of the victory in Christ we will have eternity to praise and worship Him with our loved ones. We are waiting on that day.

How does focusing on the victory over sin and death through Jesus help you? How does thanking God for such a deep love help you cope with the pain? What other thoughts come to you as you read this verse?

---

[65]   Max Lucado, *For These Tough Times* (Nashville, TN: W Publishing, 2006), 75.

DAY 59

Who will separate us from the love of Christ? Will tribulation, or distress, or persecution, or famine, or nakedness, or peril, or sword? Just as it is written, "FOR YOUR SAKE WE ARE BEING PUT TO DEATH ALL DAY LONG; WE WERE CONSIDERED AS SHEEP TO BE SLAUGHTERED." But in all these things we overwhelmingly conquer through Him who loved us. For I am convinced that neither death, nor life, nor angels, nor principalities, nor things present, nor things to come, nor powers, nor height, nor depth, nor any other created thing, will be able to separate us from the love of God, which is in Christ Jesus our Lord. (Romans 8:35-39, NASB)

Nothing can separate us from God's love. We are secure in our faith and His love. Right now, the absence of your loved one feels like a nightmare that won't end; a nightmare you would love to wake up from and find you have your life back. It seems inconceivable that you are without the one you love. The feelings are so overwhelming and so intertwined. You may feel afraid, anxious, sorrowful, aching, angry, confused, and the list goes on. But in all the feelings, there has to be the knowledge that Jesus holds us.

Nothing can separate us from God's love. Nothing could separate your believing loved one from God's love. Paul listed it all and included death. Paul included every power that is, that was, or that will be; nothing can separate us from God's love. Hold on to that belief. Your loved one is safely in Christ's presence. Max Lucado writes, "While we are shaking heads in disbelief, they are lifting hands in worship. While we are mourning at a grave, they are marveling at heaven. While we are questioning God, they are praising God."[66] Paul knew that he faced death every day. And he also knew nothing would separate him from God's love. You may even feel abandoned right now. If you are not feeling God in your pain, it is easy to fall into the feeling that He doesn't care or you would feel Him. Nothing will separate us from God's love. Your loved one is praising God. Your loved one is surrounded by God's glory and His presence.

The hard part is being here without the person you love. But the promise is that nothing can separate us from God's love. So as hard as this temporary separation is we will hold on to Jesus, and someday we will be in His presence. We will be with our loved one praising God together. We are waiting on that day!

Meditate on this verse. What thoughts and feelings come to you as you meditate? How does knowing Paul literally faced death each day help you understand his words even more?

---

[66] Max Lucado, *Max on Life* (Nashville, TN: Nelson, 2010), location 3246.

DAY 60

Martha said to Jesus, "Lord, if only you had been here, my brother would not have died." (John 11:21, NLT)

In his book *He Still Moves Stones*, Max Lucado writes:

Her words are echoed in a thousand cemeteries. If you had been here, my brother would not have died,… The grave unearths our view of God. When we face death, our definition of God is challenged. Which, in turn, challenges our faith. Which leads me to ask a grave question. Why is it that we interpret the presence of death as the absence of God? Why do we think that if the body is not healed then God is not near? Is healing the only way God demonstrates his presence?… the same voice will speak again. There will be no more death. Jesus made sure of that.[67]

In His song "Questions", Steven Curtis Chapman asks, "Where were you God, I know you had to be right there." And in the same song he sings, "You know that I believe and Come quickly Lord come quickly."[68] Maybe you prayed for healing or maybe it all happened so quickly that you didn't have a chance to pray for healing. But in any situation, God is not absent. On the contrary, He was more real in that moment to our loved ones than ever before. Dad and Don and _____ are in His presence in a very real way. They have experienced His glory as never before. From the smallest child to the oldest saint, when God called them into His presence, they were safe in His arms. Our arms and hearts ache, but we hold to the knowledge our loved ones are in our Savior's arms experiencing His presence and the glories of Heaven.

Lazarus was raised but he ultimately died to this Earth. And ultimately, Mary, Martha, and Lazarus were together again with Jesus in a very real way; just as we will be with our loved ones in the presence of Jesus praising and worshiping Him. We know someday there will be no more death. Hallelujah! We are waiting on that day!

How does this verse speak to you? What are your thoughts and feelings on the statement by Max Lucado? Steven Curtis Chapman?

---

[67]   Max Lucado, *He Still Moves Stones* (Dallas, TX: Word, 1993), 187.
[68]   Steven Curtis Chapman, "Questions." *Beauty Will Rise*. Sparrow, 2009.

DAY 61

I make known the end from the beginning, from ancient times, what is still to come. I say, 'My purpose will stand, and I will do all that I please.' (Isaiah 46:10, NIV)

I read a number of books on God's sovereignty after Don went Home. Even though I do not understand why bad things happen, I have to remember and know God is sovereign. God has a purpose. From the beginning, God has made known the ending. Anthony Hoekema writes, "Because God is the Lord of history, history has meaning and direction. We may not always be able to discern God's purpose in history, but that there is such a purpose is a cardinal aspect of our faith. [69] God knows best. He is in control.

We can't always see God's purpose, especially when we are overcome with grief and our life feels out of control. But we have to trust God. We know the beginning and we know how it all ends. We have Genesis and Revelation and everything in between. God will bring it all together. His purpose stands from ancient times and what is still yet to come.

Joel Rosenberg is an author who rose to fame after his first fictional book. The reason he became famous is because his books seem prophetic. But because he is a Christian, he is quick to give God the glory. Most of his books are based on Ezekiel 38 and 39. He writes fiction based on those chapters, but because those chapters are prophecy they are being played out now in our time. Much like Joel Rosenberg had predicted through his fiction, real life happens. How did Rosenberg know to write those words? The words are in the Bible. Events prophesied are amazing to watch when they unfold.

Prophecy can help comfort you. Why? Because God has an eternal plan, and when you watch history unfold you can be comforted. This short span of life we all have is part of the plan. We have to hold to the knowledge that the best is yet to come. We will see how all history played out one day. One day we will see the glorious accumulation of God's plan. We will see Jesus. We will see the New Heaven and the New Earth. And we will have an eternity to worship our Lord with our loved one. As we wait on that day, we must remind ourselves that we will choose to trust our Lord. His purpose stands forever.

What thoughts and feelings come to you as you read this verse? How does focusing on God's sovereignty comfort you right now?

---

[69] Anthony A. Hoekema, *The Bible and the Future* (Grand Rapids, MI: Eerdmans), 28.

DAY 62

But you have come to Mount Zion, to the city of the living God, the heavenly Jerusalem. You have come to thousands upon thousands of angels in joyful assembly, to the church of the firstborn, whose names are written in heaven. You have come to God, the Judge of all, to the spirits of the righteous made perfect. (Hebrews 12:22-23, NIV)

Believer's names are written in Heaven. When we receive Christ our name is written in Heaven. In his book *Heaven*, Randy Alcorn points out in this verse that, "This is written in present tense."[70] We come to Mount Zion as believers. This means that we are already citizens. We are already invested in Heaven. And someday, we will be made perfect. We will come to the heavenly Jerusalem. Thousands of angels are singing in joyful assembly. Just think your loved one is experiencing awesome sights and sounds as you read this. It is hard to stay focused on what your loved one is experiencing when you hurt so badly. The sorrow is so heavy and so fatiguing. But there is hope for the future. That future takes us to the heavenly city. The future we have because our names are written in Heaven. Something else Alcorn points out about this verse is worth pondering.

This verse and others like it suggest that God created Earth in the image of Heaven, just as He created mankind in His image.... C.S. Lewis proposed that, 'The hills and valleys of Heaven will be to those you now experience not as a copy is to the original, nor as a substitute to the genuine article but as the flower to the root or the diamond to the coal.'[71]

We have a shadowy glimpse of what Heaven will be like; we have a promise of our names written in Heaven. Your loved one is there now, rejoicing with the angels. We have the promise of Heaven too. We are waiting on that day!

How does this verse speak to you? How does focusing on your loved one rejoicing with the angels help you?

---

[70]   Randy Alcorn, *Heaven* (Carol Stream, IL: Tyndale House, 2004), 192.
[71]   Ibid., 54.

DAY 63 REFLECTION

Read over the last six days and reflect on the verses and devotionals. We read David's words and find comfort that he knew he would go to his son. We will join our loved ones in Heaven. When I listen to the lyrics of "Homesick" by Mercy Me, the words resonate with me. We read verses that speak of God's glory and of death not being the end. We see verses that remind and promise us nothing will separate us from God's love. Nothing!

We also looked at verses that speak of God's sovereignty. I find comfort in focusing on God's sovereignty. I may not understand why, and will not understand why this side of eternity, but I don't have to because we have a sovereign God that is in control. David Powlison says about sovereignty:

Death, mourning, pain and tears will be no more (Rev.21:4). Life, joy, and love get last say. His sovereignty is going somewhere. People miss that when they make 'the sovereignty of God' sound as if it is implied fatalism, like Islamic *kismet*, like *que sera sera*, like being realistic, and resigned to life's hardship.[72]

We will join our loved ones in the city of the living God. Nothing will separate us from the love of our sovereign God. He will bring us to a Home He has prepared. A Home in which our loved ones are already present, waiting for us. We will join them someday! We are waiting on that day! Record your own thoughts and feelings on the verses and devotionals of the last six days. What day's devotionals seem to speak to you the most?

---

[72] David Powlison, "God's Grace in Your Suffering," John Piper and Justin Taylor (Ed). *Suffering and the Sovereignty of God* (Wheaton, IL: Crossway, 2006), 159.

DAY 64

Teach us to realize the brevity of life, so that we may grow in wisdom. (Psalm 90:12, NLT)

When we truly grasp the brevity of life, we can grow in wisdom. I think most people are caught up in this world to the extreme. However, when you have someone you love go Home, the brevity of life is clearly highlighted. If we know and truly accept that life is brief, then we focus more on eternity. We get caught up in things—in success and in everything life has to offer. We can make a choice to live now to the glory of God because everything we do matters in eternity. It is a huge mistake to not recognize the brevity of life. We have a false sense of security or control. Our security is in Christ, period. Anything else is not secure.

In the past several decades there have been numerous times when people have decided that the world was going to end. The media played it up, and of course, nothing happened. But I would always have a client or someone say, "Do you think it might be the end of the world?" But the bottom line is, regardless of when Christ comes again, life is still brief. None of us have a guarantee of a next breath. I remember reading about a runner on a beach being hit by an airplane. I can imagine this was a healthy young man who would have thought that he was relatively safe running on the beach. If anyone told him to watch out for airplanes, it would have sounded ludicrous. But the unthinkable happened. Recognizing the brevity of life grows wisdom because then we focus on eternity.

I don't know what loss you have had that brings you to this devotion, but I know that regardless of age, you wish the life of your loved one had been longer. If we compare the number of years to eternity, it is nothing. I found a Mother's Day card that Don had given me the Mother's Day before he went Home. In it he had written, "God has blessed me beyond measure with you." God did bless us beyond measure on this Earth in the brevity of life He gave us. So now I try to focus on the fact that if this life is so blessed, and Heaven is better, how amazing will Heaven be? How amazing will it be to be reunited with those we love and worship Christ together again? And in Heaven there is no brevity; Heaven is everlasting! We are waiting on that day!

What are your thoughts and feeling on this verse? What are your thoughts on my statement about Heaven is better and how amazing that must be? Why do you think the psalmist said, "so that we may grow in wisdom"?

DAY 65

You saw me before I was born. Every day of my life was recorded in your book. Every moment was laid out before a single day had passed. (Psalm 139:16, NLT)

Don't be afraid! I am the First and the Last. I am the living one. I died, but look—I am alive forever and ever! And I hold the keys of death and the grave. (Revelation 1:17-18, NLT)

Read Job 14:15 and Ecclesiastes 8:8a along with these verses. We tend to think if we eat right, take care of ourselves, make good choices, etc., we will be rewarded with a long and prosperous life. But we know all too well that there are no guarantees to a long life because of what we do or do not do. We also know we are not in control; God is.

God has our eternity in mind. He has our days planned before we are born. We will not go a second before God is ready, and we will not stay on this Earth a second longer than He wants. And although the pain is overwhelming for those of us left behind, the comfort comes in knowing God is sovereign. We may not understand why God has chosen to take our loved one when He did, but the important thing is: *He has our believing loved ones.* Our believing loved ones are safely with God, and they went at their appointed time. They lived the exact number of days God had determined for them. Nancy Guthrie makes an excellent point on this subject:

This means you can surrender all the if-onlys that taunt your thoughts.....This means that when you face the death of someone you love, you don't have to surrender that person to an unknown, uncaring nothingness. You can rest, knowing that the person you love who knows Jesus is safely in his care and under his loving control. Jesus holds the keys.[73]

In grief therapy we know that the "what ifs" or the "if only" thoughts are very normal. These thoughts can persist and deepen your grief. But as Nancy points out we must let those go. Instead, rest in the promise that your loved one is with Jesus. Jesus holds the keys to death. Jesus prepares a place for us. Jesus will take us to live with Him forever. Our loved ones have gone Home before us, but it is their true Home. As believers, we will join them at the appointed time. We will have an eternity to worship God with our loved ones. We will be reunited with them and we will live forever with our Lord.

Meditate on all the verses. If you are struggling with the what ifs, let them go.

---

[73] Nancy Guthrie, *Hearing Jesus Speak into Your Sorrow* (Carol Stream, IL: Tyndale House, 2009), 145.

DAY 66

I think it is right to refresh your memory as long as I live in the tent of this body, because I know that I will soon put it aside, as our Lord Jesus Christ has made clear to me. (2 Peter 1:13-14, NIV)

When I was a child growing up, we liked to go camping. Don and I continued that tradition with our girls. We would always look for just the right spot and then put up the tent. We have many wonderful memories of camping, but I was always ready to put the tent down and go home. After all, a tent is only a temporary shelter. I wanted my shower and my bed. We have many good experiences here on Earth in our temporary tent, but someday we will be in our true Home, our permanent Home.

Peter is purposefully describing that he is in a temporary dwelling because he knew that his time to depart this Earth was drawing near. He was using all of his remaining time to make sure others were living to the glory of God. In the verse right before this one, he is encouraging believers to stand fast, and that they would be richly welcomed into the eternal kingdom. The word he uses to put aside has the meaning of depart. Paul Enns points out the words have the same meaning used to describe Israel's departure from Egypt to their new home and he adds, "Peter used the same expression, 'departure,' to refer to 'laying aside of earthly dwelling'. Josephus also uses it for 'riding out… for setting off.' Where? To the believer's new home! It pictures a journey to the believer's home in heaven."[74]

Peter even knew how he was going to die. Jesus had told him before He ascended. Peter is basically saying, "I am about to leave this temporary body, so let me keep reminding you what is important." Peter was not afraid; he knew where his eternal and permanent destination was.

We know our bodies will age. We cannot do the things we once did. Our body, as it is now, is temporary. Our body wears out. But we lay this tent aside when we depart to be with Christ. Your loved one has left the temporary tent to be with Christ. Our loved ones just broke camp before we did. But we will join them someday. Someday we will all have a bodily resurrection and the bodies raised will not be temporary. We are waiting on that day!

What are our thoughts and feelings as you read this verse? What are your thoughts on Peter knowing he was about to depart, and yet still wanting to remind others of what is important? How does this verse speak of his assurances?

---

[74] Paul Enns, *Heaven Revealed* (Chicago, IL: Moody, 2011), 40.

DAY 67

Let us hold tightly without wavering to the hope we affirm, for God can be trusted to keep his promise. (Hebrews 10:23, NLT)

Let us hold unswervingly to the hope we profess, for he who promised is faithful. (Hebrews 10:23, NIV)

Hebrews 10:23 is a verse I quote consistently. Sometimes I say, "God, I hold unswervingly to the hope I profess because I know You are faithful. I choose to hold to the hope I profess." I think saying it in first person allows us to use the scriptures as affirmations.

I received Christ at a very young age. I have professed my love for Christ and my hope in Christ for most of my life. I cannot let that be swayed now. Now that I need to feel God and be assured of that hope more than ever, I cannot be swayed. Holding on can be very hard to do at times. But God is faithful. We must hold on to that faithfulness. Pain and sorrow rip you in half, and it is hard to not waver. You feel like there is nothing to even stand on because your world has been completely ripped apart. So the only thing you can hold on to is the hope of Christ. Our hope is in Christ. Our hope for eternal life is in Christ.

I would wake up in the night with the searing pain of knowing the loss was real; it was not a nightmare. Each time I would wake up, I would quote this verse. Each time the doubt would threaten to overcome me, I would quote this verse. I continue to quote this verse. Steven Curtis Chapman sings:

> You are faithful!
> You are faithful!
> When you give and when You take away,
> even then still Your name
> is faithful!
> You are faithful!
> And with everything inside of me,
> I am choosing to believe
> You are faithful.[75]

So for now, we hold unswervingly to the hope we affirm as we wait on that day, because we know God is faithful.

How does this verse speak to you? Write down those times you may feel you are wavering and ask God to help remind you of this verse. How do Steven Curtis Chapman's lyrics comfort you?

---

[75]   Steven Curtis Chapman, "You Are Faithful." *Beauty Will Rise.* Sparrow, 2009.

DAY 68

Then Christ will make his home in your hearts as you trust in him. Your roots will grow down into God's love and keep you strong. And may you have the power to understand, as all God's people should, how wide, how long, how high, and how deep his love is. (Ephesians 3:17-18, NLT)

Joseph Stowell looks at the early Christians and has these thoughts:

It is precisely because their hearts were focused on heaven—as Screwtape observes, 'rooted in eternity'—that the early church members effectively prompted a redemptive revolution so powerful that if formed and framed the entire western culture for centuries. Because they were keenly aware that heaven was their home Christians were willing to suffer, share and love without thought of return.[76]

Roots go deep and they are stabilizing. During times of grief, when nothing seems right anymore, when you don't understand life anymore, when nothing makes sense to you, cling to those roots. Cling to what you know to be true. God loves you. God loves the one you love. There is so much we may not understand right now. But someday in eternity we will understand more fully. For now, we have to cling to those roots and trust Him. Trust that God has everything under control. Trust there is an eternal plan. Trust your loved one is safely in Heaven in the presence of Jesus. In the song "Homesick," Mercy Me sings:

And I close my eyes and I see your face
If home's where my heart is then I'm out of place
Lord, won't you give me strength to make it through somehow
Won't you give me strength to make it through somehow
Won't you give me strength to make it through somehow

I've never been more homesick than now[77]

In God's love you will find the strength, not on your own power. I kept saying, "I can't do this." I can't. I really can't. It is only through God's strength that any of us can take the next steps until God calls us Home. Hold to the roots of your faith. He loves you.

What are your thoughts on the early Christians' focus on Heaven and eternity?

---

[76] Taken from *Eternity*,©2006 by Joseph M. Stowell, and used by permission of Discovery House Publishers, Grand Rapids, MI 49501. All rights reserved, 45.

[77] Mercy Me, "Homesick." *Itunes Original*. MercyMe, 2008.

DAY 69

Trust in the LORD with all your heart;
do not depend on your own understanding. (Proverbs 3:5, NLT)

There is no way in your own understanding that you will make sense of this loss. You absolutely will have to trust in the Lord and with all your heart. Jesus knows your heart is broken; He knows your heart. Do not try to make sense of this loss. Because only in light of eternity and His understanding will everything make sense.

I asked every day, "Why?" And every day I said I would stop asking why. Max Lucado writes, "For those who trust God, death is nothing more than a transition to heaven. Your child may not be in your arms, but your child is safely in his."[78] Trusting is hard when you are hurting so deeply and your arms ache to hold the one you love, or to be held by the one you love. This is precisely why trust is so important. We cannot depend on our own understanding under such painful circumstances. The sorrow and pain blind us to that understanding. Focus on all that God has done for you; focus on the eternal destination. Continue to say, "I trust you God even though I do not understand."

Philip Yancey writes,

The big picture, with the whole universe as a backdrop, includes much activity that we never see. When we stubbornly cling to God in a time of hardship, or when we simply pray more, more—much more—may be involved than we ever dream. It requires faith to believe that, and faith to trust that we are never abandoned, no matter how distant God seems.[79]

I trust you God, even though I don't understand, and I don't feel You right now. I know You are there, and I lean on You, not on myself. I choose to trust You.

Many of you may have memorized this verse as a child. How does it speak to you now at this time? What are your thoughts on the quotes?

---

[78] Max Lucado, *Fearless* (Nashville, TN: Nelson, 2009), 64.
[79] Phillip Yancey, *Disappointment With God* (Grand Rapids, MI: Zondervan, 1992), 265.

DAY 70 REFLECTION

As you read back over the last six days, what are your thoughts? We looked at verses that speak of the brevity of life. We read several verses that remind us that our days are determined and that Jesus holds the keys. Be sure you read all the verses. Space would not allow me to put all the verses on the page. But when you read them all you recognize God has this very moment in our loved ones' lives and in our lives. We looked at the "what if" and the "if only" thoughts that can overwhelm us. Yet the Bible shows us that we are not in control. If you are holding on to the "what ifs" and the "if only", pray that God gives you peace. The enemy will have you believe if you had only done something, things would be different. But Jesus holds the keys to death, not us.

We looked at Peter standing firm and unafraid, even though he faced death, because he knew this life was temporary. Peter looked forward to the permanent, seeing this life and body as temporary. His example of a tent is something we can all relate to. We long for a permanency, and that will come. We also looked at verses that remind us to hold unswervingly to the hope we profess. I have to remind myself the hope I have always professed is very real. I cannot waver now. I will hold to that hope. We also looked at the verse about not relying on our own understanding. We can't rely on our own understanding. Our understanding fails us and life does not make sense to us. The only way to handle grief is to not lean on our understanding, but to hold unswervingly to the hope we profess. We recognize we are all walking Home and we must hold unswervingly to the hope we profess. Choose one or more verses to memorize this week. Write your thoughts and feelings on what God seemed to be saying to you this past week.

DAY 71

God has now revealed to us his mysterious plan regarding Christ, a plan to fulfill his own good pleasure. And this is the plan: At the right time he will bring everything together under the authority of Christ—everything in heaven and on earth. (Ephesians 1:9-10, NLT)

"This is the plan. At the right time God will bring everything under the authority of Christ—everything in Heaven and on Earth." That is a pretty amazing statement. It doesn't get clearer than Paul's statement. There is an eternal plan. Our lives on this Earth, as we know it, are brief. Our focus needs to be on the eternal plan.

Read this amazing statement by Paul Enns:

In Egypt the Israelites celebrated the Passover Feast 1,400 years before the time of Christ's earthly life. At that event, on the fourteenth day of Nisan, the Israelites killed the Passover lamb at twilight (Ex 12:6) which, according to Josephus, was three in the afternoon. Jesus was the fulfillment of the Passover prophecy; the lamb slain on the fourteenth of Nisan foreshadowed the coming of Christ. When did Christ die? On the Passover, the fourteenth of Nisan, at 3:00 p.m., *precisely* the time the Father had ordained (John 19:14; Mark 15:33)[80]

When I read this passage I was amazed. How intricately detailed was the event of the perfect Passover Lamb, the Lamb of God! It is hard to wrap my brain around the fact that God planned all of that down to the very minute. God is fulfilling His perfect plan to the precise detail, and He will bring it all together. We have a part in God's eternal plan. Our loved one has a part in His eternal plan. Today all we can see and feel is our pain and sorrow. The absence of the one we love is overwhelmingly painful, and we wonder, "How can this be?" But at the right time it will all come together, and when it does we will understand. We will be with our loved one again. We will see Jesus, and He will bring it all together. There is a plan for you. Pray God will be glorified even in your suffering, and that He will teach you to have an eternal perspective as you wait on that day and fulfill His plan for you.

What are your thoughts and feelings on these verses? What are your thoughts on Paul Enns' details about the exact times? How can praying that God will be glorified in your suffering help you?

---

[80] Paul Enns, *Heaven Revealed* (Chicago, IL: Moody, 2011), 48.

DAY 72

Father, I want those you have given me to be with me where I am, and to see my glory, the glory you have given me because you loved me before the creation of the world. (John 17:24, NIV)

As I read this verse, I have to agree with Paul Enns:

This statement should cause us to 'stop and reflect.' *Jesus wants us to be with Him—in close fellowship!* Can we begin to comprehend the magnitude of that statement? That should, first of all, be a comfort to us when a loved one dies. They are immediately with Christ and in fellowship with Him. Moreover, they are precisely where Jesus wants them to be—with Him. One day that will be the privilege and joy of all of us who know Him—we will be in close fellowship with Him and with our loved ones. What a phenomenally wonderful future we have![81]

As believers, we have this promise: we will be with Jesus. We will see His glory. Jesus' prayer shows us there was a plan before the creation of the world. Jesus loves us so very much that He wants us with Him. Our loved ones are with Jesus; they are seeing His glory. We, as believers, will see Him too, and we will be reunited with our loved ones for eternity.

Since before the creation of time, the plan was for Jesus to come and save the world through His perfect sacrifice. Each life on this Earth, as we know it, is brief; life here is temporary. Jesus goes beyond this short time on Earth, though; He desires us to be with Him forever. And we will be. Your loved one already is. The pain of not having our loved ones here, the emptiness that you feel at their absence is still very, very real. The promise that our loved ones are with Jesus now in His glory, and that someday we will be too is also very, very real. We can't see Heaven with our eyes now; we have to hold on by faith. Remind yourself that your loved one is where Jesus wants him or her to be, and someday you will be too. We are waiting for that day! Come, Lord Jesus! Come!

Meditate on these words. How does this verse speak to you? What are your thoughts and feelings on Paul Enns' words?

---

[81] Paul Enns, *Heaven Revealed* (Chicago, IL: Moody, 2011), 178.

DAY 73

For to me, to live is Christ and to die is gain. (Philippians 1:21, NASB)

A friend of mine had this verse tattooed on her ankle. When she thought about the time she would be reunited with her thirteen-year-old son, she would find comfort in this verse. Citing Philippians 1:21 and 2 Corinthians 5:8, Anthony Hoekema says, "What we enjoy now is just the beginning. We shall enter into the full riches of eternal life only after we pass the portal of death... Death for the Christian is therefore not the end but a glorious new beginning."[82] It is very hard to think of our loved ones in a glorious new beginning without us, but we will be with them again. If we can wrap our brains around the thought, it helps to try to picture them with Jesus. Try to understand that as much as we hurt and are filled with sorrow, they have gained glory in Christ. Our loved ones are there ahead of us. But we will be in Heaven too. They are in glory. Surrounded by glory, our loved ones truly know God's presence. It would be amazing if for only one minute we could see past the pain to their life in Christ now. I know it is hard to see past the pain and to picture that glorious scene. Your pain is so real, so searing, and so deep. But we must continue to remind ourselves of where our loved ones are now.

Regardless of how the end here came, now our loved ones have gained. You may have lost a loved one in a violent way, or maybe you watched them suffer. Watching someone suffer, or knowing someone we love had something horrific happen to them, can be excruciating. We must hold to the truth that no matter how he or she left, your loved one is now better than ever. Your loved one has passed through the portal, and now he is in glorious surroundings. Our loved ones will be in Heaven waiting on us when we get there, and we will be reunited with them. We will have an eternity to be with them praising and worshiping God. We are waiting on that day!

How does this verse speak to you? What are your thoughts on Anthony Hoekema's words? What are your thoughts on our loved ones will be there waiting on us?

---

[82] Anthony A. Hoekema, *The Bible and the Future* (Grand Rapids, MI: Eerdmans), 85.

DAY 74

For the perishable must clothe itself with the imperishable and the mortal with immortality. When the perishable has been clothed with the imperishable, and the mortal with immortality, then the saying that is written will come true: "Death has been swallowed up in victory." (1 Corinthians 15:53-54, NIV)

Paul Enns writes, "Our physical body, now subject to sin, decay, and death, will be indestructible in heaven and no longer subject to control by sin."[83] Randy Alcorn writes, "Continuity is evident in passages that discuss resurrection, including 1 Corinthians 15:53... It is this (the perishable and mortal) which puts on that (the imperishable and immortal). Likewise, it is we the very same people who walk this Earth, who will walk the New Earth."[84] So much time is given in the scriptures to looking forward to that day that we are resurrected. The resurrection is the hope and encouragement of the New Testament.

Nearly every book I read, when quoting this scripture, emphasized the continuity in the resurrection. Those of us who have had loved ones go before us want to know that death doesn't end relationships. If you have had a child go Home, you want to know that child will still be your child. You want to hold that child in your arms again. All of us want that loved one to be waiting on us, to hear his voice again, to see his smile again. Anthony Hoekema writes, "There must be continuity, for otherwise there would be little point in speaking about a resurrection at all. The calling into existence of a completely new set of people totally different from the present inhabitants of the earth would not be a resurrection."[85]

Our dear friend Dillon wrote a beautiful poem about Don and me. I have shared it in the back of this book. He also wrote in the first few days these words that I hold dear to me, "It is the clear separation between the temporary things of earth and the real things of eternity. Your pain comes from a loss of a love that is built in eternity, and only one of that incredibly rare nature could lead to this. You had amazing years while it was shared on earth, and you will have magnificence in eternity celebrating it together." We all have that desire for that continuity of life and relationships. We need to know that there will be a day that we will have an imperishable and immortal body. Until that day the saints wait in Heaven. We wait for Jesus to call us Home or come back for us, but it will happen. And when Jesus does, death will be swallowed up in victory.

What are your thoughts and feelings on the passage and the quotes?

---

[83]   Paul Enns, *Heaven Revealed* (Chicago, IL: Moody, 2011), 78.

[84]   Randy Alcorn, *Heaven* (Carol Stream, IL: Tyndale House, 2004), 115.

[85]   Anthony A. Hoekema, *The Bible and the Future* (Grand Rapids, MI: Eerdmans), 251.

DAY 75

No longer will there be any curse. The throne of God and of the Lamb will be in the city, and his servants will serve him. (Revelation 22:3, NIV)

Randy Alcorn writes: "'No longer will there be any curse.' If the Bible said nothing else about life in the eternal Heaven, the New Earth, these words would tell us a vast amount."[86] We live in a fallen world under a curse. Bad things happen every day. All anyone has to do is look at the news. All around us is chaos. Death is a part of that fallen world. But we know that there will be a day when the curse is lifted. We will not live in a fallen world; the pain will be gone. As Philip Yancey writes:

In its 'plot' the Bible ends up very much where it began. The broken relationship between God and human beings has healed over at last, and the curse of Genesis 3 is lifted. Borrowing images from Eden, Revelation pictures a river and a tree of life. But this time a great city replaced the garden setting—a city filled with worshipers of God. No death or sadness will ever darken that scene.[87]

When Christ comes again, and the New Heaven and the New Earth are established, we will live in a perfect world. The curse is no more. It is an awesome thought to try to imagine what we long for now. We are in pain because of the curse. We can't see fully now, we have to hold to our faith when everything seems out of control to us. Our world has been torn apart, our heart broken. But there will be a day when this all changes. There will be a day there will no longer be a curse. Imagine that day, a day that death and sadness will be no more. A day that the broken relationship between God and humans is healed and we can be in His presence.

Imagine that garden scene, the city where the throne of God is dwelling. On the day the curse is lifted we will serve Him in Heaven. The curse is lifted and we see Jesus. Right now our believing loved ones are not in this fallen world. They are safe in the arms of our Savior. And someday we will all be in Heaven, and someday we will live again on this Earth. We are waiting on that day!

What are your thoughts and feelings on this verse? What are your thoughts and feelings on the quotes?

---

[86] Randy Alcorn, *Heaven* (Carol Stream, IL: Tyndale House, 2004), 105.

[87] Philip Yancey, *Grace Notes* (Grand Rapids, MI: Zondervan, 2009), 141.

DAY 76

For the Word of God is alive and active. Sharper than any double-edged sword, it penetrates even to dividing soul and spirit, joints and marrow; it judges the thoughts and attitudes of the heart. (Hebrews 4:12, NIV)

I cannot emphasize enough how powerful quoting scripture is. There are nights I cannot go to sleep. There are nights I wake up crying out. There are days that feel like I am totally encompassed in pain and darkness. I have learned to quote the many verses that help me. I repeat them over and over and feel the anxiety lessen. Very early on when I didn't feel God at all, wondered if He was even there, and doubt would creep in, I would quote John 6:68: "To whom shall I go Lord?" I would quote 1 Cor. 15:19 when I became focused on this life to remind myself our hope in Christ is not just in this life. Heb. 10:23 helps to remind me to hold unswervingly to the hope I profess. Col. 3:1-3 reminds me to fix our minds and hearts on Heaven. Job 19:25-27 helps me to focus on my Redeemer lives and I shall see Him in my flesh. When I was full of questions and anxiety, I would quote Isaiah 26:3 to remember that God keeps us in peace whose mind is on Him. John 11:25 reminds me Jesus is the resurrection and the life. I would quote scripture to remind myself that our citizenship is Heaven, to remind myself that there is an eternal plan, that God is sovereign, and that this world is not our Home. And the list goes on and on.

The Bible tells us the Word of God is alive and active. You can quote His Word anytime; let it fill you as you repeat it over and over. If I can't sleep, I alternate between praying and quoting scripture. During the day, when everywhere I look I see our life together and Don's absence screams at me, I quote 2 Cor. 4:18 to remind myself to focus on what is unseen, not on what is seen. God is always with us, but at times He may feel distant. Chris Tiegreen suggests, "The Spirit of God is always with us and in us, but sometimes we can sense His practical Presence only in the Word He inspired."[88]

I started quoting these verses immediately, mainly because they were a lifeline to me. But as I read this scripture it became more real to me. It wasn't just that I needed to remind myself what God said, although I did; it wasn't just to hold to those promises because if I didn't I would sink into an abyss of complete despair and hopelessness, although that was true too; it was because the word of God is alive and active. The claiming of those words brings strength and comfort within me through Jesus. That is why His Word is so important.

Meditate on this powerful verse. If you have not been memorizing and quoting Scripture, start now. Journal verses that comfort you.

---

[88] Chris Tiegreen, *The One Year Experiencing God's Presence Devotional* (Carol Stream, IL: Tyndale House, 2011), December 1.

DAY 77 REFLECTION

As you reflect over the last six days, what stands out to you? We read verses in Ephesians that are a clear statement of the eternal plan. When I read Paul Enns' statement of the precise detail I am amazed. We read the magnificent verse that tells us Jesus wants us to be with Him. This verse can bring us comfort—Jesus wants our loved ones and us with Him!

We read verses that remind us death will be swallowed up; it has been defeated so we can now say, as Paul did, "To die is gain." We read verses that remind us the Earth is now under the curse, but one day the curse will be gone. All of these verses are powerful.

Reminding ourselves that Jesus wants us with Him, should cause us to stop and reflect on how Jesus wants our loved one with Him. Jesus' Words are very powerful. Randy Alcorn reminds us that reading the curse is lifted is powerful in itself. How true are those Words to you? And, finally, we read Hebrews 4:12, a verse that tells us why memorizing Scripture can bring us comfort. If you have not been memorizing Scripture, start now. If that seems daunting to you, start small. Write some passages on index cards and carry with you to read aloud. Reflect over the last six days and record your thoughts and feelings. What this past week seemed to resonate most with you?

DAY 78

He says, "Be still, and know that I am God;
I will be exalted among the nations,
I will be exalted in the earth." (Psalm 46:10, NIV)

I have always loved to read. After Don went Home, I re-read *Heaven* by Randy
Alcorn. I had read it the first time after Dad went Home. I followed *Heaven* with
reading more and more books. I guess I thought I was going to find the answer
in all the books. I read books on Heaven, grief, the sovereignty of God, hearing
God, strengthening your faith, prophecy, etc. In eight months I had read over
80 books. That was in addition to the Bible and devotionals. I had two friends
within a few days apart say to me, "Ann, stop. Just be still." And they were right.
I was so busy reading to calm myself that I was not being still. I was frantically
searching for God, but not being still to hear Him.

Being still can be hard. The books were of value, some more than others.
And I think God did speak to me through many of the books. I have referred
to many of the books through this devotional because they are so valuable. But
I was so frantic that I could not be without a book to read. I needed to be still.
I needed to rest in Him. And then I slowly started to read again. I know some
people can't read because they can't focus and they might be about being "busy"
with something else. Whatever you might find to busy yourself with, make sure
you have time to be still and just know that He is God.

Pain and sorrow can make everything an effort. Physically and emotionally,
you become exhausted. Grief and sorrow make you very weary. It takes all your
strength to just do what you have to do. And many things get left undone. Being
still is important for that very reason; you are weary. You not only need to rest to
hear from God, you need to rest physically and emotionally. Rest is something
that does not come easily in grief. Check in with yourself, see if there is a need
for you to be still, and just know that He is God.

What does the verse say to you? Are you struggling to be still? Spend time today
making a conscious effort to be still. Record your thoughts.

DAY 79

Wait for the Lord;
be strong and take heart
and wait for the Lord. (Psalm 27:14, NIV)

Waiting on God can be hard. Being strong when you are broken is hard. You cannot handle grief in your own strength. The psalmist tells us to take heart and wait for the Lord. One translation says not to despair. It is hard not to despair or feel weak when we feel such pain and sorrow. When we don't feel God, we may be scared and confused, but God is with us even when we can't feel Him. When we don't feel Him, we truly have to wait on Him.

Priscilla Shirer writes, "We must believe He is working on our behalf even when He chooses not to say a single word. In His silence, He speaks volumes to us. He commands us to wait on Him and focus our attention on His Holiness."[89] Write in your journal and process those feelings. Listen to music that helps you focus on God's holiness. In the song "Broken Hallelujah" Mandisa sings:

> When all that I can sing
> Is a broken hallelujah
> When my only offering
> Is shattered praise
> Still a song of adoration
> Will rise up from these ruins
> I will worship You and give You thanks
> Even when my only praise
> Is a broken hallelujah[90]

Shattered praise may be all you can muster right now. But worship Jesus, wait on Him, and focus on His holiness. Know that while you wait on that day—that glorious day that we see Jesus in all His glory and are reunited with our loved one—we trust that God is in control. Right now, what God wants is us to wait on Him.

What are your thoughts and feelings on this verse? What are your thoughts and feelings on Priscilla Shirer's words? What are your thoughts on Mandisa's lyrics in "Broken Hallelujah"?

---

[89]   Priscilla Shirer, *Discerning the Voice of God* (Chicago IL: Moody, 2007), 149.
[90]   Mandisa, "Broken Hallelujah." *Freedom*. Sparrow, 2009.

DAY 80

My flesh and my heart may fail, But God is the strength of my heart and my portion forever. (Psalm 73:26, NASB)

Someone you love's flesh and heart has failed. But God was the strength of their heart and their portion forever. He is the strength of your heart and your portion forever. Our bodies will wear out. Our bodies fail us. God does not. And forever is what we are concentrating on. We long for that day that we know our heart and flesh will not fail. I know there are times even now that I wonder how a heart that hurts as much as mine can continue to beat. There are times that the pain and sorrow hit you like a ton of bricks, and it sucks the life out of you. Greg Laurie says this so well:

But sometimes the reality that my son is gone pierces my heart like a sword, and I say, 'Oh God. I can't believe this! I can't handle this pain!' But then I will preach to myself and I will say, 'Now Greg, listen to me. Your son is alive in the presence of the Lord, and you are going to see him again before you know it in heaven.' And I will remind myself of the promises of God.[91]

I know the feeling all too well of the reality piercing my heart like a sword. And I too have cried, "I can't believe this is real. I can't handle this anymore, not a second more." But then like Greg, I have to remind myself that Don and Dad are in the presence of the Lord. I will join them, and we will be together worshiping God forever. God is our strength. We know this body fails, but God does not. He is our stability. God has eternity planned. We are just waiting on that day. And while we do we have to remind ourselves constantly of the promises of God.

What are your thoughts and feelings on this verse? What are your thoughts and feelings on Greg Laurie's statement?

---

[91]   Greg Laurie, *Hope for Hurting Hearts* (Dana Point, CA: Kerygma, 2008), 25.

DAY 81

He who dwells in the shelter of the Most High Will abide in the shadow of the Almighty. I will say to the LORD, "My refuge and my fortress, My God, in whom I trust! (Psalm 91:1-2, NASB)

In times of sorrow, our refuge and our fortress must be in God. He is faithful. There are days I feel like I can't go another day. The sorrow is so heavy. Every day is hard and painful, and then you have those special days that are even more painful. The holidays, birthdays, anniversaries, any day that was special to you and your loved one becomes a day of painful memories. Memories you would not trade for anything, and memories you are so thankful to have. But the reminder that you no longer have that person with you is overwhelming. The empty spot at the table, in the bed and in the family room shout the absence of someone you love. The only refuge in this time is God.

Read Psalm 91:1-2 with the verse in 2 Cor. 1:3 that tells us that God is the God of all comfort. God is the Father of compassion, and the God of all comfort. He is our refuge and our fortress, my God, in whom I trust. Charles Stanley writes, "When you are down, the Holy Spirit knows exactly how to encourage you. When you are grieving, the Holy Spirit knows the balance between shedding tears of grief and gently wiping them from your cheeks. He is at work to comfort you through every trial and adversity."[92] There is great comfort in seeing our Savior's eternal characteristics. Steven Curtis Chapman's lyrics are much like the words of the psalmist:

> I will trust You, trust You
> Trust You, God, I will
> Even when I don't understand
> Even then I will say again[93]

As Dr. Luke Terveen writes, "No matter how alone we may feel, the Lord has not abandoned us but always remains there for us, powerful to help and to save."[94] Find ways now to dwell in God. Make sure you have quiet time to pray, read His Word, and journal. Do not try to deny your feelings and run away from God in your pain. Dwell in the shelter of the Most High; abide in the shadow of the Almighty. He is your refuge. I will trust you God.

How are you dwelling in God? Journal your thoughts and feelings.

---

[92] Charles Stanley, *Enter His Gates* (Nashville, TN: Nelson, 1998), 69.

[93] Steven Curtis Chapman, "I Will Trust You." *Beauty Will Rise*. Sparrow, 2009.

[94] John Luke Terveen, *Hope for the Brokenhearted* (Colorado Springs, CO: Victor, 2006), 69.

DAY 82

At this, Job got up and tore his robe and shaved his head. Then he fell to the ground in worship. (Job 1:20, NIV)

Job had just found out all of his beloved children had been killed. We are told that he would offer sacrifices on behalf of his children on the chance that they may have sinned. He hears the devastating news of the tragedy, and he tears his robe and shaves his head. In anguish, he falls to the ground. But even in his anguish he worshiped God.

I knew that no matter what, I was going to hold on to Jesus, even when I didn't feel Him. I continue to have to, because without Him there is no hope. Job must have felt the same way. But notice something else: he visibly showed his grief. He didn't put on a face to act like all was okay. People may try to push you to be "ok." Nancy Guthrie says it well: "Sometimes it seems like the people around us think that because we know the one we love is in heaven, we shouldn't be sad. But they don't understand how far away heaven feels, and how long the future seems as we see before us the years we have to spend on this earth before we see the one we love again."[95] She also points out: "Job tore his robe and shaved his head. He hurt. And he was not ashamed to show how deeply he hurt.... Your tears do not reflect a lack of faith."[96]

I think sometimes people think that if their faith is strong enough that they should not show their emotions. Our faith consoles us, but we still hurt without the ones we love now. You are the one who goes to bed without your loved one beside you. You are the one whose arms ache to hold your loved one. You are the one who looks around and sees his absence everywhere. You are the one who longs to hear her voice, see his smile, and feel the touch of your loved one. And when you don't, it hurts inconsolably. The only thing that will bring you comfort is holding on to Jesus. We do not know how long it will be before we see our loved ones again, and it still hurts beyond belief. But in our pain we also know that there will be a reunion. So we worship as Job did. Nancy Guthrie makes an excellent point to ponder: "Surely our worship in the midst of pain and sorrow is particularly precious to God— because it costs us so much. Worship is not made easier, but it becomes all the more meaningful when offered from a heart that is hurting."[97]

Reflect on today's verse and quotes. Have well meaning people tried to rush? Have your tried to be "strong" and denied your grief?

---

[95] Nancy Guthrie, *Holding On to Hope: A Pathway Through Suffering to the Heart of God* (Wheaton, IL: Tyndale,2002), Location 128.

[96] Ibid., Location 141.

[97] Ibid., Location 172.

DAY 83

Praise be to the God and Father of our Lord Jesus Christ! In his great mercy he has given us a new birth into a living hope through the resurrection of Jesus Christ from the dead, and into an inheritance that can never perish, spoil or fade. This inheritance is kept in heaven for you. (1 Peter 1:3-4, NIV)

Our inheritance is kept in Heaven for us. Our inheritance will NEVER perish, spoil, or fade. Peter wants us to focus on what we have in Heaven. We can focus on Heaven because of the hope that we have through the resurrection of Christ. Our hope is in Christ.

In *A Grace Disguised*, Jerry Sittser writes, "But life here is not the end. Reality is more than we think it to be. There is another and greater reality that envelops this earthly one. Earth is not outside heaven, as the philosopher Peter Kreeft wrote; 'it is heaven's workshop, heaven's womb.'"[98] This life is just a warm up. Peter tells us we have our inheritance kept in Heaven for us, in our true Home. Your loved one is in Heaven now. Your inheritance is still waiting on you.

It is a comforting thought when we think of what is waiting for us in Heaven. We will be with God in a place designed for us to dwell with God. We have an inheritance waiting; we have our loved ones waiting. We have an eternity to explore and learn. It is only with an eternal perspective that we can hold to all of the wonderful things we have waiting on us in Heaven. Randy Alcorn writes, "God has made himself closely identified with Heaven. It is His place…. Jesus wants us to anticipate Heaven to enjoy the magnificence of it."[99]

We have a living hope. How amazing does that sound? Our hope is alive. This is the hope that we hold to; that we profess. This is the inheritance that we look forward to. And being reunited with our loved one is a part of that hope. We are waiting on that day!

How do these verses speak to you? How does thinking about an inheritance in Heaven comfort you?

---

[98] Jerry Sittser, *A Grace Disguised: Expanded Edition* (Grand Rapids, MI: Zondervan, 2004), 193.

[99] Randy Alcorn, *Heaven* (Carol Stream, IL: Tyndale House, 2004), 202.

DAY 84 REFLECTION

Reflect over the devotionals and verses for the last six days. We looked at verses that remind us to be still and to wait on God, who is our strength and our shelter. I have heard people say they can't concentrate and they are afraid to think. They might say all that they can do is watch TV, play electronic games, distract themselves with people, or….. But if we are not careful all of these things, while not necessarily bad, are ways we can be "busy" and not be still. As you reflect over your time, be honest with yourself. Are you being still and waiting on God?

We read verses in the Psalms. Verses that remind us God is our strength and portion. And verses that remind us He is our refuge and fortress. When we are broken and our strength fails, these words in the Psalms are powerful. God is our refuge. We will trust Him and we will be still before Him.

We saw how Job outwardly and visibly mourned, but still worshiped God. We hear how Nancy Guthrie reminds us our tears do not reflect a lack of faith. It is okay to outwardly mourn; it is not a sign of weak faith. Even though we know our loved ones are with Jesus, we still miss them. We don't know how long it will be before we are with our loved ones, and we miss them very much. Our grief and sorrow are very real and powerful, and it is okay to show that grief and emotion. But in our grief and sorrow we hold to the everlasting hope. We also read that our inheritance is stored up for us in Heaven. We know that even though we hurt now, we will be with our loved ones again. We will be with Jesus, and so we hold to Him now.

I want to remind you again, if you read a quote from an author that resonates with you, find and read his or her book. There are many powerful books of others that can help you in your time of grief. Record your thoughts and feelings as you reflect over the readings in the last six days.

DAY 85

As the new heavens and the new earth that I make will endure before me,"
declares the Lord, "so will your name and descendants endure. From one New
Moon to another and from one Sabbath to another, all mankind will come and
bow down before me," says the Lord. (Isaiah 66:22-23, NIV)

The above verses in Isaiah can comfort us for more than one reason. The eternal
plan is evident in all prophecies. I think that is why it is so important now to
remind ourselves of those prophecies. The New Heaven and the New Earth are
talked about throughout the Old Testament and the New Testament. There is
great comfort in thinking about the New Heaven and the New Earth because
that is where God will dwell among us. The New Earth is where the curse will
be lifted, and there is no more death. We will once again be with our loved ones
without death and pain. Looking forward to that time brings us hope.

I am also struck by the words, "Your name and your descendants endure."
He is talking about the nation of Israel and the covenant with Israel. When
we receive Jesus as our Savior, we are adopted into the family of God, and we
are included in this new covenant. But in looking at the nation of Israel, it was
started through Abraham. God chose one man to build a nation, a people set
apart, His chosen people. This one man and his descendants are Israel. It strikes
me how much family and descendants play into God's eternal plan. These verses
underscore the importance of family to God. We are a part of God's family, but
He also made us a part of a family here. Since there is continuity in Heaven,
then those descendants and family lines will stay important. When I read these
words, I find comfort.

Most of you reading this are probably grieving a family member. A spouse, a
child, a parent, a sibling, grandparent, grandchild, aunts, uncles, nieces, nephews,
or cousins have gone on before you. Perhaps you are grieving the loss of a dear
friend who feels as close as family. God has used friendship throughout the Bible
like Jonathan and David, and Jesus had many dear friends that He seemed closer
to. Take comfort in those family and friendship relationships being reunited.
Randy Alcorn writes, "Deep and joyful human relationships will be among
God's greatest gifts in Heaven—relationships that by God's grace will never
end."[100]

What are your thoughts and feelings on these verses? What are your thoughts
and feelings on Alcorn's statement?

---

[100] Randy Alcorn, *Heaven* (Carol Stream, IL: Tyndale House, 2004), 57.

DAY 86

But Stephen, full of the Holy Spirit, gazed steadily into heaven and saw the glory of God, and he saw Jesus standing in the place of honor at God's right hand. And he told them, "Look, I see the heavens opened and the Son of Man standing in the place of honor at God's right hand!" As they stoned him, Stephen prayed, "Lord Jesus, receive my spirit." (Acts 7:55-56,59, NLT)

I wish desperately to see the Heavens open up right now and I am sure you do too. We can take comfort in what Stephen saw. Paul Enns uses the verse as one of several to show the nearness of Heaven:

Stephen was looking into heaven! 'The Heavens opened,' indicating that heaven was not distant but nearby, in another realm. The language was strong and clear as Stephen describes what he sees. He saw the blaze of the *Shekinah* glory of God. He saw Jesus standing at the right hand of God—which was unique since Jesus had previously taken His seat at the right hand of the Father, His work being completed (Luke 22:69; Eph. 1:20; Col. 3:1). Why was Jesus standing? He was welcoming Stephen into Heaven![101]

Nearly every book I read that quoted this verse emphasized that Jesus was standing to welcome Stephen. Paul Enns also writes:

This is a strong reminder of what awaits every believer departing this old earth. The believer immediately transitions into heaven and is welcomed home by Jesus Himself. The Lord opened the portals of heaven, allowing Stephen to see into the realm of heaven, which would be a strong comfort and encouragement to every believer.[102]

No matter what the circumstance of our believing loved ones' departure, Jesus welcomed them Home. Stephen's was a violent and painful death. He was the first recorded death of a believer after Jesus' resurrection. James' death followed shortly after. We may dwell on how our loved ones went Home, especially if they suffered. I don't begin to understand why some suffer or have violent deaths. To have to deal with violence happening to someone you love would be overwhelming. But as we read about Stephen, we see that even in the midst of a horrific stoning, Stephen looked and up and saw Jesus; that view of Jesus eclipsed whatever pain he felt that moment on Earth. Stephen saw Jesus, and in that moment he forgave the people murdering him and said, "Lord Jesus, receive my spirit." Jesus has received the spirit of your believing loved one. We hurt, but we rejoice that those we love are with Jesus. They are Home.

Meditate on these verses and quotes. What are your thoughts and feelings?

---

[101] Paul Enns, *Heaven Revealed* (Chicago, IL: Moody, 2011), 53.
[102] Ibid., 53.

DAY 87

God has now revealed to us his mysterious plan regarding Christ, a plan to fulfill his own good pleasure. And this is the plan: At the right time he will bring everything together under the authority of Christ—everything in heaven and on earth. (Ephesians 1:9-10, NLT)

It is hard to understand why bad things happen. It is hard to understand the pain and suffering in the world. You may be asking why someone you love is no longer with you. It is hard not to ask why. Why didn't we have longer with those we love? But even if we knew why our loved one was taken, the hurt would be the same. The lyrics to Mercy Me's song are so very true:

> Help me Lord cause I don't understand your ways
> The reason why I wonder if I'll ever know
> But, even if you showed me, the hurt would be the same
> Cause I'm still here so far away from home[103]

This verse in Ephesians helps redirect me to the eternal perspective. The prophets of the Old Testament prophesied about the Christ, but even they did not fully understand. Philip Yancey talks about dual prophecies (prophecies that had meaning for the immediate future and also for the end times), and how they can be confusing. He also states that it helps us understand that God's timing and our timing are not the same. In fact, understanding timing can help us understand the eternal perspective. Yancey makes an excellent point:

I believe this prophetic device, admittedly confusing, offers a glimpse into how God views history. As 'Seers,' the prophets have insight into God's perspective, and for a God who lives outside the constraints of time, sequence is a minor issue. The Lamb, says the apostle Peter, 'was chosen before the creation of the world, but was revealed in the last times for your sake' (1 Peter 1:20). Paul added that God also chose his followers 'before the creation of the world' (Ephesians 1:4). Similarly, our hope of eternal life was promised 'before the beginning of time' (Titus 1:2). Long before Einstein's theory of the relativity of time and space, the New Testament writers established some truths as, quite literally, timeless.[104]

God is timeless. This life is not all there is, and we will have an eternity to understand. God has everything in this life and the next under control and at the right time God will bring it all together. We have to trust Him.

What are your thoughts and feelings on the verses and quotes?

---

103   Mercy Me, "Homesick." *Itunes Original.* MercyMe, 2008.
104   Philip Yancey, *Grace Notes* (Grand Rapids, MI: Zondervan, 2009), 391.

DAY 88

This hope we have as an anchor of the soul, a hope both sure and steadfast and one which enters within the veil. (Hebrews 6:19, NASB)

The author of Hebrews is confirming our hope is in Christ. He uses two descriptors: an anchor and a veil. An anchor holds the ship steady until it is ready for departure. Our hope in Christ is an anchor for our soul. We are anchored to Christ, and have His promise as a guarantee of eternal life.

The veil has to do with the sanctuary. In the following chapters of Hebrews the author talks about Christ being the High Priest that sits in the inner sanctuary of the true tabernacle, Heaven. In the Old Testament the veil separated the people from the Holy of Holies. The veil was ripped in half from top to bottom when Jesus was crucified. We no longer have the separation. We have direct access to our God. So the imagery is of us having direct access to Jesus, and of us being anchored to Jesus. Jesus is steadfast and sure. He will keep us safe and guaranteed until our departure to Him in Heaven.

Grief knocks everything steady out from under you. The waves of the storm threaten to topple you. All you can do is hold to Christ. He is the anchor of the soul. Our hope is always in Him. Our believing loved ones' departure from this Earth brought them to Jesus and to the hope we profess. In the midst of the storm, when you do not feel Jesus, He has you anchored. There are times you may seem steadier than others. There are times that you feel God and emotions seem smoother, and the next moment you feel lost and alone. Life is tumultuous, and grief the worst pain that can be imagined. The feelings that accost you threaten to overtake you. Casting Crowns sings, "Praise you in the Storm" and the word ring true.

> I stumbled in the wind
> You heard my cry to you
> And you raised me up again
> My strength is almost gone
> How can I carry on
> If I can't find You
>
> But as the thunder rolls
> I barely hear You whisper through the rain
> "I'm with you"[105]

We have an anchor; it is our hope in Christ. Even in this storm Jesus holds us.

What are your thoughts and feelings on the verses and the lyrics?

---

[105] Casting Crowns, "Praise You in This Storm." *LifeSong*. Reunion Records, 2005.

DAY 89

For Christ must reign until he humbles all his enemies beneath his feet. And the last enemy to be destroyed is death. (1 Corinthians 15:25-26, NLT)

Randy Alcorn writes, "Death is painful and it's an enemy. But for those who know Jesus, death is the *final* pain and the *last* enemy."[106] All of us readily agree death is an enemy. You may feel anger. Anger is a normal part of grief. For some it is more pronounced than for others. Some people are angry with someone, some are angry at God, some are just angry. I think we would all agree that we are angry with death. Death is the enemy. Death is real for now, but as painful as it is for us, it is not the end for our loved one. Our believing loved ones have been ushered into Christ's presence. Someday death itself will be destroyed; there will be no more death. Paul Enns writes:

Christ is destined to reign as king and as doing so He has authority over every realm and enemy, over Satan and his domain, and over every aspect of nature including death....Through His death and resurrection, Christ has indeed conquered death. The scripture says death will be abolished, meaning He will bring death to an end. It will be no more.[107]

Randy Alcorn writes:

Christ's mission is both to redeem what was lost in the Fall and to destroy all competitors to God's dominion, authority and power. When everything is put under his feet, when God rules all and mankind rules the earth as kings under Christ, the King of kings, at last it will be as God intends. The period of rebellion will be over forever, and the universe, and all who serve Christ, will participate in the Master's joy![108]

The eternal plan has been from the beginning to do away with death; it will be destroyed. But for now death is the enemy, and it is overwhelmingly painful for us. Hold to the knowledge that for our believing loved one's death is the last enemy. Our loved ones are safely with our Lord, and we will be too someday. Someday we will see Jesus, and once again we will worship Jesus with our loved ones. We are waiting for that day.

What are your thoughts and feelings on these verses? Write about any feeling of anger you might be experiencing. How can viewing death as the enemy help?

---

[106] Randy Alcorn, *Heaven* (Carol Stream, IL: Tyndale House, 2004), 467.
[107] Paul Enns, *Heaven Revealed* (Chicago, IL: Moody, 2011), 44.
[108] Randy Alcorn, *Heaven* (Carol Stream, IL: Tyndale House, 2004), 93.

DAY 90

I pray that the eyes of your heart may be enlightened in order that you might know the hope to which he has called you, the riches of his glorious inheritance in the saints and his incomparably great power for us who believe. (Ephesians 1:18, NIV)

I pray, as Paul does, that the eyes of your heart be enlightened. Read this verse in Ephesians carefully. Paul knew how hard it is to grasp the hope, the riches, the inheritance, and the great power that was ours in Christ. There is such a huge spiritual warfare going on that right now all your eyes see are the tears. But we can pray as Paul did that the eyes of our heart be enlightened to know the hope of Jesus Christ and His glorious inheritance. I know how hard it is to hold to all the unseen riches and eternal perspective when all you see are tears. I listen to the song "See" by Steven Curtis Chapman every night. The song sounds as if God has opened the eyes of Chapman's heart to write this:

Right now
All I can see are clouds of sorrow

But from the other side of all this pain
Is that you I hear
And calling out to me?

Saying "See, it's everything you said that it would be
And even better than you would believe.
And I'm counting down the days until you're here with me
And finally you'll see"[109]

Someday we will see Heaven and all the inheritance with our own eyes. For now we have to pray for God to open the eyes of our heart and to help us see and hear those glorious riches He has for us. Pray that we are not so overwhelmed with the pain that we miss those things He may be telling or showing us.

As you meditate on this verse, how does it speak to you?

---

[109] Steven Curtis Chapman, "See." *Beauty Will Rise.* Sparrow, 2008.

DAY 91 REFLECTION

As you read back over the last six days, what speaks to you the most? We read verses in Isaiah that speak of the New Heaven and the New Earth. And we see in this verse in Isaiah that, "Your name and descendants endure." As we grieve family or close friends we can find comfort in these words. We certainly can find comfort as we look forward to the day the New Earth is established.

We also see the nearness of Heaven as we read about Stephen seeing Heaven open up, and Jesus standing to meet him. We can try to envision Jesus meeting our own loved ones. Realizing how horrific a stoning would be for Stephen and yet he sees Jesus and all is made right. We can find comfort in this story as we think of our own loved one's departure.

We read about the eternal plan and having an eternal perspective. And we see that hope is an anchor for our soul. When the doubts, the storms, and the grief overwhelm us, we have an anchor—it is our hope in Jesus Christ. If you are artistic you might trying drawing an anchor and focusing on how powerful our Anchor is.

As we read the last enemy to be defeated is death, we look forward to that day. Then we read the prayer that God opens the eyes of our heart. I pray that now for all of us, that God opens the eyes of our heart. I pray that we can truly feel His love and know His eternal plan since the beginning of the ages. And that we truly hold to the hope as an anchor for our soul. As you reflect over the last week, record your thoughts and feelings. How is God speaking to you?

DAY 92

Dear friends, now we are children of God, and what we will be has not yet been made known. But we know that when he appears, we shall be like him, for we shall see him as he is. (1 John 3:2, NIV)

There are things in this life we don't know, things we don't understand now. But John tells us one day we shall be like Jesus and we shall see Him as He is. I cannot wait for that day. Randy Alcorn writes, "The apostle John was Christ's dearest friend on earth and he 'fell at Jesus feet as though dead' (Revelation 1:17). We will see Christ in his glory. The most exhilarating experiences on Earth, such as white water rafting, sky diving or extreme sports will seem tamed compared to thrill of seeing Jesus."[110]

I listen to Mercy Me's song "I Can Only Imagine" often. We played the song at Dad's and Don's service. We want to imagine, we try to imagine, but nothing will compare to seeing Jesus as He is. Just think: our loved ones are experiencing Jesus' glorious presence right now. When I am overcome with pain and crying, I try to refocus by imagining what Don and Dad are experiencing. Even though I want my life back, would I really want to take them away from the magnificence they are experiencing? It is hard to imagine as much as I try. But someday I won't have to imagine; someday I too will see Jesus as He is. We will see Jesus' radiance. We will be in His glorious presence forever and truly know Him.

When we do see Jesus, we will become like Him. Paul Enns writes, "Moreover, we will be transformed spiritually as well; our mind, heart, and will then shall reflect only spiritual vitality. In that realm, 'we shall see Him'."[111] When we see Jesus and become more like Him, what we don't understand now will make sense. The sorrow will be no more. We have an eternity to spend with Jesus. We are waiting on that day!

What are your thoughts and feelings on this verse? How does thinking about seeing Jesus and being like Him bring you comfort?

---

[110] Randy Alcorn, *Heaven* (Carol Stream, IL: Tyndale House, 2004), 180.
[111] Paul Enns, *Heaven Revealed* (Chicago, IL: Moody, 2011), 174.

DAY 93

For he was looking forward to the city with foundations, whose architect and builder is God. (Hebrews 11:10, NIV)

Don was a well-known and respected home builder in our community. His faith and steadfastness was known among the community. He would tell people, "I build the house; you make it a home." He put time, effort, and caring into all of his houses. After Dad went Home to be with the Lord, Don and I were reading *Heaven* by Randy Alcorn. We read the part where Alcorn discusses work on the New Earth, and pointed out that the first person Scripture described as filled with the Spirit was a craftsman. Alcorn quoted Exodus 31:1-6, where it tells us that God filled Bezalel with the Spirit and chose him to engage in all kinds of craftsmanship.[112] I told Don that he would have something to do in Heaven since he is builder. People are not going to need a counselor anymore, but building will apparently continue.

Don built a house for one of our church members. She wrote me a card after he went Home to be with the Lord. And she wrote, "Our home is strong and full of love just like the man who built it." I wept as I read it because it was so thoughtful and so true. Just think: if a mere mortal can build a strong and loving home, what can we expect from God as the architect and builder of Heaven? Heaven will be strong and full of love just like its builder.

I have tried to imagine Don checking out everything after he got to Heaven. He is such a perfectionist in building; I can almost see him being overwhelmed with the beauty of what he sees. I can't help but wonder if he and Dad checked those things out together. We have something to look forward to, a heavenly city whose foundations are designed and built by God. Can you imagine how much care and design God has put in our eternal place? This is all a part of the eternal plan. Spend a moment contemplating the city of which God is the architect and builder. Try to imagine what Heaven might be like for your loved one and for us when we join our loved ones some day. We are waiting on that day!

How does this verse speak to you? How does thinking about God putting so much detail in the foundations of the Heavenly city comfort you?

---

[112] Randy Alcorn, *Heaven* (Carol Stream, IL: Tyndale House, 2004), 443.

DAY 94

The LORD God planted a garden toward the east, in Eden; and there He placed the man whom He had formed. Out of the ground the LORD God caused to grow every tree that is pleasing to the sight and good for food; the tree of life also in the midst of the garden, and the tree of the knowledge of good and evil. Now a river flowed out of Eden to water the garden; and from there it divided and became four rivers. (Genesis 2:8-10, NASB)

Randy Alcorn writes:

The word *paradise* comes from the Persian word *pairidaeza,* meaning 'a walled park' or 'enclosed garden.' In the Septuagint, the Greek translation of the Old Testament, the Greek word for paradise is used to describe the Garden of Eden. Later, because of the Jewish belief that God would restore Eden, paradise became the word to describe the eternal state of righteousness, and to a lesser extent, the present Heaven.... Eden was not destroyed. What was destroyed was mankind's ability to live in Eden. There's no indication that Eden was stripped of its physicality and transformed into a 'spiritual entity.' It appears to have remained just as it was, a physical paradise removed to a realm we can't gain access to—most likely the present Heaven because we know for certain that's where the tree of life now is (Revelation 2:7).[113]

One of the things Don and I loved to do was landscape every spring. We spent several weekends going from nursery to nursery, carefully picking out plants and then planting around our deck, our patio, and our front porch. We loved the time together planning, planting, and seeing the results of our efforts. As the first spring approached after Don went Home, I could not bear to work in the yard without him. But then our friend Penny invited me over. As she and I sat on her back porch talking, I gazed over her yard. She and her husband Greg had landscaped their yard beautifully, and as we talked about Heaven the thought came to me: this is similar to what Heaven will be like. The beauty of the different flowers, the falling water from the fountain, and the vegetable and fruit trees all reminded me of what Eden might be like. Notice this verse says "pleasing to the sight." God wants His people to enjoy the beauty He has created. I decided to plant all the flowers like Don and I would plant. Don had built a dry stream the year before he went Home, and the perennials he had planted started blooming. I bought and planted our favorite plants. But as I did I felt close to Don, and close to God. And as I sat outside and listened to my music, I thought of Heaven and the beauty Don and Dad are experiencing now.

What can you do to help visualize the natural beauty of Heaven, of Eden-like qualities? Meditate on this verse as you take in the beauty around you.

---

[113] Randy Alcorn, *Heaven* (Carol Stream, IL: Tyndale House, 2004), 55-56.

DAY 95

And they were calling to one another: "Holy, holy, holy is the Lord Almighty; the whole earth is full of his glory." (Isaiah 6:3, NIV)

Isaiah is describing the view of Heaven that God revealed to him. When Isaiah sees the splendor and holiness of God, he cries out, "Woe to me!" Isaiah was immediately aware of his sinfulness and his unworthiness, but God allowed him to see this scene, and a seraph flew to him and touched his mouth with coal. The whole earth is full of God's glory. And in that glory we recognize His holiness. After Dad went to Heaven I saw this note he had written in his sermon notes. The note said, "All the material in the universe is as if it were a message in code from God." I ponder those words. God's glory is everywhere.

On days that I feel so completely isolated from God, I try to remember to look around at the sky, the plants, and the surroundings. The whole Earth is full of God's glory. When we focus on God's glory we can't help but sing of His holiness. In Heaven they sing, "Holy, holy, holy is the Lord Almighty." When we sing of God's holiness, it allows us to focus on His holiness. Sometimes I sing along with Steven Curtis Chapman's "Our God is in Control."

> And we'll sing holy, holy, holy is our God
> And we will finally really understand what it means
> So we'll sing holy, holy, holy is our God
> While we're waiting for that day
>
> We're waiting for that day
> We'll keep on waiting for that day
> And we will rise
> Our God is in control
>
> (Holy, holy, holy)
> (Holy, holy, holy)
>
> Our God is in control[114]

We serve a holy, loving, faithful, and sovereign God. He is above all things and His glory fills the Earth. His holiness and sovereignty assure us that He is in control. Our loved ones are with Him singing of His holiness in His presence. What an awesome thought to think of our loved ones praising God with the angels. We will join them someday. We are waiting on that day!

Meditate on the verses and the lyrics. Sing about and focus on God's holiness.

---

[114] Steven Curtis Chapman, "Our God Is In Control." *Beauty Will Rise*. Sparrow, 2008.

DAY 96

You guide me with your counsel, and afterward you will take me into glory. (Psalm 73:24, NIV)

God takes us into glory. Your believing loved one is in glory with Christ. Even though being here without our loved ones is incredibly painful, we are still on this Earth for God's purpose. He will guide us, and when He is ready He will take us into glory. When we become so enamored with this world and all it has to offer, our focus is taken off of God and His plan. But all along He has a plan to guide us and bring us Home. Paul Enns quotes the psalmist and writes,

God directs our lives, all the details, event after event, year after year, and then precisely at the right time, He takes us Home. God determines the number of days we spend on earth. They are different for each of us. Some live longer lives, some shorter. Then at the end of our days, He receives us home, into the brilliance of His heavenly home.[115]

The loss of a loved one is hard on those of us left behind. We miss everything about those we love. We live by faith not by sight, but with the pain of grief, we can lose focus. It can be hard to stay focused on eternity when we want to have our life the way it was. As we read this verse in the Psalms, we focus on God's guiding us and knowing that He will take us Home to glory too. When Jesus takes us Home, we will see the glorious wonders of Heaven, we will see Jesus in all His glory, and we will be with those we love.

For now, ask God to guide you with His counsel. Continue to pray that you will feel His presence, and that you will have the assurance and hope that only He can give. Pray that you can glorify Him even in your pain. Know that God is guiding you now, even though you may not feel Him. God has a plan that you are a part of, and although that plan included the loved one who has gone before you, there is more for you to do before He calls you Home. I know that I am ready and hoping that Jesus comes soon, or calls me Home soon. But I also know it is not my decision to make. He will call me to glory when He is ready, just like He did Dad and Don, and like He did your loved one. God is sovereign; He has a plan. Trust Him now.

As you meditate on this verse, how does it speak to you?

---

[115] Paul Enns, *Heaven Revealed* (Chicago, IL: Moody, 2011), 48.

DAY 97

But I am hard-pressed from both directions, having the desire to depart and be with Christ, for that is very much better. (Philippians 1:23, NASB)

Early Christians were ever ready to go Home and be with the Lord. The first believers had seen the resurrected Jesus. Those who did not see Him personally saw His power through His disciples. When someone you love more than life itself goes before you, you have a whole new view of Heaven and of life. Perhaps your view of Heaven and life has become much more like the early Christians; the desire to go to Heaven is stronger. We know our loved one is with Christ. I relate so well to how Dr. John Luke Terveen felt when his daughter went Home:

I found myself overwhelmed with the desire to depart and join her in Jesus' presence in heaven. I was not disillusioned, nor was I suicidal but, I simply felt the same yearning for death Paul had – seeing it as 'gain' in so many ways. I could almost taste Heaven's reality at that moment. Yet I knew that my life or death was not my decision to make whatever my desire might be.[116]

It is also worth pointing out Paul's emphasis on how much better Heaven will be. He tells us that to depart and be with Christ in Heaven is much better. I love the way Paul Enns states this in his book *Heaven Revealed*:

This is earth; our future lies in heaven. Heaven is always better than earth – in every dimension. There is no realm in which earth is better. In no way will we ever be poorer in heaven than on earth. Everything will be better in heaven. That is an underlying principle that we must continually bear in mind. Do you have a good relationship with your spouse? It will be better in heaven. Are you surrounded by a lot of love on earth? We will experience more love in heaven.[117]

It is hard to imagine that something so wonderful here on Earth could be better by far, but it will be. We are waiting on that day!

As you meditate on this verse, how does it speak to you? What are your thoughts on the quotes?

---

[116] John Luke Terveen, *Hope for the Brokenhearted* (Colorado Springs, CO: Victor, 2006), 179.

[117] Paul Enns, *Heaven Revealed* (Chicago, IL: Moody, 2011), 158.

DAY 98 REFLECTION

Read back over the last six days, meditating on each verse as you do. We read verses that remind us that we will be like Jesus and someday we will see Him as He is. Isn't that an amazing thought? We read verses that tell us God is the architect and builder of the city we will call Home. The Creator has created a city for us to live with Him for eternity. Since Don was a builder, I find particular interest in these verses. Our friend Hong's words mean so very much to me. I know how much goes into planning and building. God is the ultimate builder. We see the Garden of Eden as a glimpse of Heaven, and try to imagine how Paradise might be as Eden is described in Genesis. As you read these verses, try to think of the magnificence of what our loved ones are experiencing.

We are told Isaiah glimpsed into Heaven and focused on the Holiness of God. I quoted one beautiful song on the holiness of God, but there are so very many. Perhaps you have your favorite song on the holiness of God. If not, search through old hymns and new songs. The more we focus on the holiness of God, the more we understand Him and His sovereignty.

We are reminded that God will guide us while on Earth and then bring us into His glory. He has already brought our loved ones into His glory. We are reminded that Heaven is better by far. Our loved ones have been taken into God's glory where they see Jesus as He is. They see the beauty and awesomeness of Heaven, which we can only try to imagine. We know that we will be with our loved ones someday. We know for now He will guide us as we wait on that day He will call us to His glory. We are waiting on that day! Record your thoughts and feelings as you reflect on the verses and devotionals of this past week. What resonates with you the most?

DAY 99

Yet what we suffer now is nothing compared to the glory he will reveal to us later. (Romans 8:18, NLT)

If you are reading this devotional because someone you love has gone Home, then you are most likely suffering with the deep sorrow and pain that comes with grief. Even with the knowledge of where our loved ones are, the absence of our loved one is still very painful, and we suffer. But Paul tells us this is nothing compared to the glory that will be revealed to us later.

Some of you may have watched your loved one suffer. Your loved one is no longer suffering. The person you love has entered into Heaven, and at the very moment they did the suffering was gone and your loved one's view was of Christ and His amazing love. I wish we could have just a peek of what was going on in Heaven, just a glimpse of the glorious moment to see Jesus. But unfortunately, we don't get that glimpse now. Someday, however, Heaven will be revealed to us, just as it was to our loved ones.

For now, no matter how much it hurts, remember the pain is nothing compared to the glory He will reveal to us later; this is the eternal perspective. Randy Alcorn says of this verse: "Paul offers us a perspective on how to view the hardships of life in a fallen world."[118] When we can grasp an eternal perspective, we can view our present suffering through a different lens. Suffering is a part of a fallen world. But as believers, God has something wonderful prepared for us. We know it will be awesome. He will reveal His glory to us as He has our loved ones. We are waiting on that day!

What are your thoughts and feelings on this verse? Does this verse help you view suffering through a different lens? What are your thoughts on your loved one seeing God's glory revealed?

---

[118] Randy Alcorn, *Heaven* (Carol Stream, IL: Tyndale House, 2004), 226.

DAY 100

The creation looks forward to the day when it will join God's children in glorious freedom from death and decay. For we know that all creation has been groaning as in the pains of childbirth right up to the present time. (Romans 8:21-22, NLT)

Someday all of creation will be restored. All of creation looks forward to that day of restoration. I know I do. Because of the curse, we live in a fallen world. There is death and decay. Someday there will be freedom from death and decay. Randy Alcorn states, "Christ will turn back the curse and restore to humanity all that we lost in Eden, and he will give us much more besides."[119]

As I write this, part of the United States is dealing with a drought and another part is dealing with wildfires. Yet another area is bracing for a tropical storm that will bring possible flooding and destruction. When will it all end? It will end when the Earth is restored, and we are living on the New Earth. All of creation will be at is best without death. That includes us. Our loved ones have already entered into a place of beauty and grandeur with no more death and decay. And when God restores the Earth all of creation will share in that glorious freedom. This speaks not just of our hope in the freedom from death but also in the glorious plan that includes all of creation.

Don and I visited California, and we drove through a redwood forest. We were captivated by the magnificent redwood trees. We took pictures trying to capture how small we were in comparison. But no picture does the scenery justice. The summer before that, we visited the beautiful Blue Ridge Parkway in the Smoky Mountains. We would pull over and take in the beautiful water flowing down the mountainsides, with waterfalls around the next corner. We would stop and eat, and put our feet in the cool waters. I could go on and on about the beauty of creation. But just think: as beautiful as this world is, it will be restored to an even more beautiful world and it will be perfect. There will be no death. We can all groan for that day when we, as God's children—and all of creation—will be freed from the death and decay of this fallen world. I am waiting on that day!

What are your thoughts and feeling on these verses? What are some beautiful areas of nature that you have visited in the past? How does thinking about beautiful scenes in nature in light of creation being restored comfort you?

---

[119] Randy Alcorn, *Heaven* (Carol Stream, IL: Tyndale House, 2004), 187.

DAY 101

And we believers also groan, even though we have the Holy Spirit within us as a foretaste of future glory, for we long for our bodies to be released from sin and suffering. We, too, wait with eager hope for the day when God will give us our full rights as his adopted children, including the new bodies he has promised us. (Romans 8:23, NLT)

In yesterday's devotion, we talked about all of creation groaning for the New Earth. As believers we look forward to that day when we are released from sin and suffering. Randy Alcorn writes, "That's the final resurrection, when death will be swallowed up and sin will be reversed, never again to touch us. This is what we should long for and live for. Resurrection will mean many things—including *no more sin*."[120] Paul Enns writes:

This is *the* day. There is a day coming when all of the suffering, all of the maladies of this life are destroyed, when we, in our glorified bodies will live in Heaven, on the new earth, eternally fulfilling God's ordained purpose for us. We too yearn and wait for that day. And we will live in fellowship with God and with our redeemed loved ones in a perfect environment, in a heaven of indescribable beauty and perfect environment.[121]

Our loved ones have been released from the sin and suffering and are eagerly awaiting the day when we can all be a part of the bodily resurrection, and the day we live on the New Earth. We are still among the sin and suffering, but someday we will not be. Just think of the view that our loved ones now have. They get to wait in the presence of Jesus, surrounded by His glory. We are waiting for the day God calls us Home as well, whether it is through death or whether we are here when He comes again. But either way, we have been given a promise. God is faithful. We will see Him face to face, and we will be reunited with our loved ones. Someday there will be no more suffering or sin. I cannot wait for the day that sin is not present; when we do not battle our sin nature, nor have spiritual warfare, because we are in the presence of Jesus. Come, Lord Jesus. Come.

What are thoughts and feelings on this verse? What are your thoughts on the quotes?

---

[120] Randy Alcorn, *Heaven* (Carol Stream, IL: Tyndale House, 2004), 316.
[121] Paul Enns, *Heaven Revealed* (Chicago, IL: Moody, 2011), 15.

DAY 102

For our struggle is not against flesh and blood, but against the rulers, against the powers, against the world forces of this darkness, against the spiritual forces of wickedness in the heavenly places. (Ephesians 6:12, NASB)

I know I have mentioned several times that you are at your most vulnerable when you are grieving. I want to emphasize the enormity of the spiritual warfare that surrounds you right now. There were so many times I was on my face crying, "I cannot do this anymore. Please, God." There are still times I feel that I can't do this anymore. You may feel isolated and alone, even with people around you that love you. You may not feel God even when you are crying out, and when that occurs you may doubt God. But there is so much going on we do not see. This verse in Ephesians is a graphic picture of the unseen world. As Philip Yancey points out:

Very often disappointment with God begins in Job-like circumstances. Why me? Why does He seem so distant? He goes on to say that as readers of Job we see behind the curtain to a contest being waged in the invisible world. But in our own trials we will not have such insight. When tragedy strikes we will live in a shadow, unaware of what is transpiring in an unseen world.[122]

You may feel engulfed by darkness, and that can be a breeding ground for anxiety and doubt. But we know that God is sovereign. He loves you. God has an eternal plan. Draw closer to God by staying in His Word, listening to music, quoting scripture, praying, and journaling. It is important that you remember even though you have questions and you may not feel God, He is with you.

Our redeemed loved ones are no longer a part of the spiritual warfare; they are safely with our Father. But those of us left behind have it much harder. We are still a part of that fallen world, and we still struggle, but we are not alone. We know who wins the war. Jesus will be triumphant. He has already defeated the devil. Remind yourself of His sovereignty. Remind yourself that your redeemed loved one is now at rest from the spiritual warfare. Someday we will see Jesus and be with Him, and we will be with our loved ones. For now, keep reminding yourself of what you know is true. God is faithful.

Reflect on this verse. How does it comfort you to know that our redeemed loved one no longer has to worry about spiritual warfare? Write those things down that help you the most when you feel the darkest.

---

[122]   Phillip Yancey, *Disappointment With God* (Grand Rapids, MI: Zondervan, 1992), 193.

DAY 103

Your eternal Word, O LORD,
stands firm in heaven. Your faithfulness extends to every generation,
as enduring as the earth you created. Your regulations remain true to this day,
for everything serves your plans. (Psalm 119:89-91, NLT)

The above verses remind us that God's eternal plan will happen. He is in control. His faithfulness extends to us, just like it did to Abraham and all the generations of believers that have come since. His Word is eternal. Mark Hitchcock writes, "Bible prophecy reveals to us there is an end. It reveals to us there is a purpose and a goal—for this world, for creation, for humanity, and for everyday life."[123]

When we are grieving, our world has been ripped apart. We feel very unstable, lost, and broken. Reminding ourselves that God is still in control is important. I know this loss and time of your life is not what you would have chosen. We may question if God is in control. But what we have to remember is that this stay on Earth is temporary. God is eternal. His Word is eternal. Everything serves God's eternal plan. You may be thinking: "How can this tragedy serve His plan?" I don't know. I do know, though, that I have to believe God is sovereign, and regardless of how I feel, He is still in control. I see one part of life, my little part right here in this time frame, and it hurts unbearably. But this life is so brief compared to eternity. I do not see the whole picture, only God does. From the beginning God has had a plan, and all things are working toward that eternal plan. And someday, we will understand.

John Piper writes, "The evil and suffering in this world are greater than an of us can comprehend. But evil and suffering are not ultimate. God is. Satan, the great lover of evil and suffering, is not sovereign. God is."[124] So for now we have to quote scriptures and remind ourselves that our God is faithful. His faithfulness extends to every generation. His Word stands firm in Heaven. Heaven is where our redeemed loved ones are right now. Heaven is where we will be, and when we are we will sing with the psalmist, "Holy, Holy, Holy." We will understand this glorious plan and how it unfolded. We are waiting on that day!

Meditate on these verses. How do the verses speak to you? How does focusing on God's sovereignty and His eternal plan bring you comfort now?

---

[123] Mark Hitchcock, *The End* (Carol Stream, IL: Tyndale, 2012), 9.

[124] John Piper, "The Sovereignty of God in Suffering," John Piper and Justin Taylor (Ed). *Suffering and the Sovereignty of God*, (Wheaton, IL: 2006), 129.

DAY 104

He replied, "You are talking like a foolish woman. Shall we accept good from God, and not trouble?" (Job 2:10, NIV)

I included this verse because I needed to remind myself that God has blessed me beyond measure. Not that I needed to remind myself because I had never forgotten, but because I knew in the pain I had to remind myself He was the same God that has always blessed me. With all my heart, I am eternally grateful for everything God has done in my life. I cannot start claiming that things are unfair. This world is not about me.

I have received so many blessings from God. Yes, I am broken that He has taken two of those wonderful blessings. But how can I accept all the good and then cry, "Foul"? No, I cannot cry "foul" now. I tried to. I thought: How unfair. But each time, I had to remind myself God had been more than fair to me. He has blessed me beyond measure. He is faithful. I had a wonderful dad. My parents raised my siblings and me in an incredibly loving home and taught us about God's love from the time we were born. And we remain very close today. I met Don when I was fourteen and we have had the most amazing relationship ever. God gave us two wonderful daughters. I am blessed and I am grateful. I wish that God had allowed Dad and Don more time with us on this Earth. I miss them both unbelievably. My pain and sorrow are ever-present. But I can't accept all the wonderful blessings, and then decide God isn't good. God is good. If this world were all there was it would be very sorrowful indeed. But we know this world is not all there is. We know that we will indeed be with our loved ones again. We know that the same wonderful and good Father who has blessed us here has a wonderful eternity planned for us.

As Paul Enns says so beautifully, "Should we think that God would give us a wonderful, loving relationship with family and friends for forty or fifty years, only to be terminated, never to be enjoyed again? Impossible!"[125] We can accept this trouble and this pain because we know this life here is not all there is. We know God is good. We know this time on Earth is all temporary. We look forward to the day when we will see Jesus and this trouble is no more. We are waiting on that day!

What are your thoughts and feelings on this verse? Have you struggled with the same feelings? What are your thoughts on Paul Enns' statement?

---

[125]   Paul Enns, *Heaven Revealed* (Chicago, IL: Moody, 2011), 159.

DAY 105 REFLECTION

Read over the last six days. Meditate and reflect on how God may have opened your eyes. We read verses that give us a perspective on how to view life's hardships. We know we are suffering now but we also know there is a day coming that God will reveal His glory. Our suffering will pale in comparison. We hold to the beautiful thought of God's glory revealed. We read that all of creation, including us, groans for the future glory and restoration of all things. Perhaps you have taken trips where you were surrounded by amazing sights of this Earth. Try to imagine how the beauty we see now will look restored on the New Earth.

We read again of the spiritual warfare. Our struggle is not against flesh and blood but against the spiritual forces of wickedness. This is a sobering thought and we hold to Our Redeemer. But we can rejoice that our loved ones are no longer in this fallen world as we look forward to the day we are all with Jesus.

We read that God's Word is eternal, and His eternal plan stands firm. God's eternal plan is the most amazing thing to read. We are such a small part of His plan, but we are a part of the plan. He has an eternal plan, and because His Word stands eternal, we know we will all be with Him. We know that God has everything under control even when we don't understand. We are also reminded that when we don't understand right now, we can't lose sight of how faithful God has been in our lives. We may not understand now, but because we remember God's faithfulness in the past, we know He has all things in His control. We now groan for that future glory. We know all creation groans for restoration. We also know that trouble and suffering will all seem light and momentary when we see Him as He is. We are waiting on that day! Record your thoughts and feelings as you reflect over this past week's devotionals. What verses seem to speak to you the most?

DAY 106

But you must remain faithful to the things you have been taught. You know they are true, for you know you can trust those who taught you. You have been taught the Holy Scriptures from childhood, and they have given you the wisdom to receive the salvation that comes by trusting in Christ Jesus. (2 Timothy 3:14-15, NLT)

When I read this verse in 2 Timothy it hit home very deeply. As we have talked about earlier, we know that when God seems far away it easy to start doubting. I have said so many times, "Where are you God?" When God seems far away, if we do not hold fast to what we know to be true, doubts can creep in. I think that is why this verse seems so powerful to me. We must remain faithful to what we have been taught. We know what we have been taught and believed our whole lives is true. When we made the decision to receive the salvation of Jesus Christ there were no doubts.

Remain faithful to what you have been taught, what you have always known to be true. During this time of spiritual warfare, holding to what you know is important. Reflect on your life and remember when you received Christ. Remember those who taught you, whether it was your family, friends, or someone that just took the time to show you the scriptures and lead you to Christ. You trusted those who taught you, and you trusted Christ. His Word has not changed. Death is not the end. Your loss is devastating right now. Life is overwhelmingly painful. But this world is not all there is. When you received Christ, you received salvation. You were saved from Hell and received the promise of Heaven. Your hope in Christ is rooted in eternity.

Yes, life is painful right now, and it will continue to be painful. Memories flood your mind. You can't go anywhere that you don't have memories and they are bittersweet. You are thankful you have the memories and the times that created those memories, but you long to have your life back. C S Lewis wrote, "So many roads lead to thoughts of H." (H was in reference to his wife.)[126] We cannot escape the pain of grief. But we cannot escape the faithfulness of God either. Remind yourself you know His Word is true. We can trust those who taught us; we can trust our God. Remain faithful to Him.

Meditate on these verses. How do the verses speak to you? Write those times in your life when you felt the strongest in Christ, and knew the truthfulness of what you have been taught. How can remembering help you now?

---

[126]   C. S. Lewis, *A Grief Observed* (New York: Harper Collins EBook, 2009), Location 52.

DAY 107

Simon Peter asked him, "Lord, where are you going?"
Jesus replied, "Where I am going, you cannot follow now, but you will follow later." (John 13:36, NIV)

"You will follow later." Following Jesus to Heaven is a beautiful thought. Jesus was preparing His disciples for His death. John 13:1 tells us, "Jesus knew that the time had come for him to leave this world and go to the Father." In verse 33 He tells them, "I am with you a little while longer." He goes on to tell them that where He is going they cannot come. Of course, Peter wanted to go with Jesus. But Jesus lets Peter know that he cannot follow now, but he will come later. Peter insists that he wanted to follow Jesus now and that he would lay down his life for Him. Jesus tells Peter that he will indeed deny Him three times. But in between all of the confusion of the day, Jesus gently tells Peter, "You will follow later." I think those words can have meaning for us right now in our grief. Our believing loved ones have entered into Heaven. We will follow.

Your loved one is in the presence of Jesus. And you will follow. Dr. John Luke Terveen writes, "No passion grips the soul of one who grieves the loved one more than a desire to be together again."[127] In the book *We Shall See God*, Randy Alcorn writes, "Augustine said, 'We have not lost our dear ones who have departed from this life, but have merely sent them ahead of us, so we also shall depart and shall come to that life where they will be more than ever dear to us, and where we shall love them without fear of parting.'"[128]

Jesus knew His disciples would grieve. Jesus wanted Peter to remember that someday Peter would be able to follow. You hold to the thought of following your loved one to Heaven. Jesus has prepared a place for us. Jesus has our believing loved ones in Heaven with Him. And when it is time, we will follow. I find great comfort in the beautiful thought that we will follow. I am waiting on that day!

What are your thoughts and feelings on this verse? Have you been gripped with the desire to be with your loved one again? Does it bring you comfort to know you will follow?

---

[127] John Luke Terveen, *Hope for the Brokenhearted* (Colorado Springs, CO: Victor, 2006), 146.

[128] Augustine, as cited by Randy Alcorn in *We Shall See God* (Carol Stream, IL: Tyndale House, 2011), 95.

DAY 108

Nevertheless do not rejoice in this, that the spirits are subject to you, but rejoice that your names are recorded in heaven. (Luke 10:20, NASB)

When we receive salvation through Jesus, our names are recorded in Heaven. Jesus had sent the seventy out on a mission, and they returned excited. They had a good mission and told Jesus: "Even the demons are subject to us in your name." Jesus confirmed their experience, and told them He saw Satan fall from Heaven. Jesus told them He has given them authority over the enemy. And the mission was triumphant. But then He told His disciples that the real joy was that their names are recorded in Heaven.

Jesus knew that the disciples were excited now and rightfully so, but He also knew they would be in for suffering on this Earth very soon. Jesus' followers had a long road ahead of them; He wanted them to stay focused on the real joy, and that was that their names written in Heaven. No matter what happens in this life on Earth, we have the joy of Heaven. Amazing, isn't it? The real excitement is in Heaven. When your loved one received Christ, his or her name was written in Heaven. And when God called _____ Home he or she went straight to Heaven to be with our Lord. We have the same promise. Randy Alcorn writes:

Anticipating Heaven doesn't eliminate pain, but it lessens it and puts it in perspective. Meditating on Heaven is a great pain reliever; it reminds us that suffering and death are temporary conditions. Our existence will not end in suffering and death—they are but a gateway to our eternal life of unending joy.[129]

This is one of my favorite quotes of Randy Alcorn's. Meditate on Heaven. You will, in God's timing, be in Heaven with Him and with your loved ones! We are waiting on that day!

What are your thoughts and feelings on this verse? What are your thoughts and feelings on Alcorn's quote?

---

[129]   Randy Alcorn, *Heaven* (Carol Stream, IL: Tyndale House, 2004), 460.

DAY 109

In Jerusalem, the LORD of Heaven's Armies will spread a wonderful feast for all the people of the world. It will be a delicious banquet with clear, well-aged wine and choice meat. There he will remove the cloud of gloom, the shadow of death that hangs over the earth. He will swallow up death forever! The Sovereign LORD will wipe away all tears. He will remove forever all insults and mockery against his land and people. The LORD has spoken! (Isaiah 25:6-8, NLT)

These verses in Isaiah give us a beautiful view of the New Earth. We will feast with our family and other believers. God will remove the cloud of gloom, and the shadow of death that is now hanging over the Earth. He will swallow up death forever! The pain and sorrow that we feel now will be gone. These verses are an amazing look into the future. When we received Christ as our Savior we are included in this future. Feasts and banquets create images of fun and togetherness. And we are even told that the food will be delicious. But to think that there will be no bad thing to mar the amazing time together is even better.

When we get together as a family there is nearly always a meal planned. Meal times create times for bonding, laughing, talking, reminiscing, and just loving each other. Just think: someday, once again, we will be eating and drinking with our loved one. Family meals without Dad and Don are so hard now. Their place at the table is noticeably and painfully empty. There are so many wonderful memories, and for each one I am thankful. But the pain of not having them here with us now is overwhelming. When we eat those favorite foods without them, it is painful. But someday, someday, we will eat with those we love again. And then there will be no fear of anything happening. Because death will be gone! We will truly enjoy each other; and best of all, we will be in God's presence.

Paul Enns writes, "We will be so fulfilled in fellowship and celebration with family and friends and the Lord Jesus that there is no earthly experience to compare. The present fellowship we enjoy is only a foretaste of the joy in Christ's kingdom."[130] The pain now is real, and not having our loved ones with us now is so very hard. But there is comfort in knowing that we have the hope and assurance of Heaven, and that as Christians we will be reunited with our loved ones. We have this beautiful scene in Isaiah to look forward to! We are waiting on that day!

Reflect on these verses. Have you thought about eating and drinking in Heaven with your loved one someday?

---

[130] Paul Enns, *Heaven Revealed* (Chicago, IL: Moody, 2011), 70.

DAY 110

Therefore my heart is glad and my tongue rejoices; my body also will rest secure, because you will not abandon me to the realm of the dead,
nor will you let your faithful one see decay. You make known to me the path of life; you will fill me with joy in your presence, with eternal pleasures at your right hand. (Psalm 16:9-11, NIV)

We will not be abandoned to the realm of the dead. As redeemed people we have a path to Heaven. And as King David wrote, we will be filled with joy in God's presence and we will have eternal pleasures in His presence. Randy Alcorn writes:

When there's fulfillment, when there's beauty, when we see God as he truly is—an endless reservoir of fascination—boredom becomes impossible.... Freedom from sin will mean freedom to be what God intended, freedom to find far greater joy in everything. In Heaven we'll be *filled* with joy and eternal pleasures.[131]

Our loved ones are in God's presence already and they are filled with joy in His presence. I know it is hard to focus on what our loved one is seeing because we can't see if for ourselves. But we know God's presence is magnificent and there will be eternal pleasures!

I want to rejoice that Dad and Don are experiencing incalculable joy. And I do rejoice for them, but the pain in not having them here threatens my focus. So I have to stay focused on Jesus and Heaven. Because right now, Don, Dad, and _____ are focusing on Jesus and the awesomeness of His presence. The few times that Don and I would be apart, we would always want to describe what we were seeing to the other one. We wanted to share with each other whatever experience we had. Not being able to share this with Don and wondering everyday what he is doing is painful. But I have to hold to the promise that I will know someday. I will experience that joy and eternal pleasure along with Don and Dad. So for now, I keep praying that God teaches me to have an eternally perspective; that I can rejoice that Don and Dad are seeing Jesus and filled with joy in His presence. I have to hold to the promise that I will join them someday, and we will have eternal pleasures with Jesus. I am waiting on that day!

Have you tried to imagine your loved one filled with joy in Christ's presence? Have you thought about what eternal pleasures may be in Heaven?

---

[131] Randy Alcorn, *Heaven* (Carol Stream, IL: Tyndale House, 2004), 410.

DAY 111

He has made everything appropriate in its time. He has also set eternity in their heart, yet so that man will not find out the work which God has done from the beginning even to the end. (Ecclesiastes 3:11, NASB)

God has set eternity in our hearts. We all have an awareness of something bigger than us; that there is more. Unfortunately, that search for fulfillment can lead to things other than God. But when we recognize that yearning for more is about eternity, we can ask Him to teach us how to have that eternal perspective. When a loved one goes Home, the reality of eternity is never more important. This is the time to hold to that reality, to study what the Bible tells us about Heaven and eternity. Joseph Stowell writes:

Life is most disappointing, most despairing, when it is lived as though this world is all we have. Questions have few answers, and crisis become all consuming. Thankfully, this is not the only world. Christ connects us to the eternal world to come and provides for us an eternally redeemed world within. This present world makes sense only when we live here in light of these other worlds.[132]

There are many things we cannot understand, especially if we view life through one lens: the here and now. I think our default is to look at life through the here and now, but we seem to always know there is more. That feeling is eternity set in our hearts. So we must focus through the lens of eternity.

Notice also in this verse there is, once again, reference to God's eternal plan. God has a plan from the beginning and He has made everything appropriate in its time. God's eternal plan is seen through an eternal lens. We pray that God teaches us how to view things in light of eternity. He has set eternity in our hearts. We just have to hold to what God has set in our hearts: eternity.

What are signs to you that God has placed eternity in our hearts? What are your thoughts on the statement viewing life through in light of eternity?

---

[132] Taken from *Eternity*, © *2006* by Joseph M. Stowell, and used by permission of Discovery House Publishers, Grand Rapids, MI. All rights reserved, 11.

DAY 112 REFLECTION

Reading over the last six days, what speaks to you now? We read verses that speak of us remaining faithful to what we have been taught. I think it is important to remember what we have been taught; what we know to be true. We may lose sight of what we know to be true as we grieve, but it is more important than ever to remind ourselves of what we have been taught. Reflect back on your salvation. We read the verses where Jesus is preparing His disciples for His death. He knew they would grieve deeply, and He knew they would want to be with Him. Jesus promises they will follow. We will follow. He knows how much we miss our loved ones. He knows that we will follow, and we will be with our loved ones, and we will all be with Jesus. What a day that will be!

We also read that our names are written in Heaven, and that is cause to rejoice. We are reminded to meditate on Heaven. Our names are written in Heaven, and Jesus reminds us that our name written in Heaven is what is important. We are given a beautiful picture of the New Earth; of family eating together and rejoicing. God will wipe away every tear, and we will all be together worshiping Him forever. Have you thought of eating and drinking in Heaven with your loved one again? How amazing is that thought! We are waiting on that day! We are reminded there are eternal treasures in Heaven. Our loved ones are in the presence of God and filled with joy. It is hard to see past our pain, but when we think on their joy, it can be comforting.

Finally we are told God has put eternity in our hearts, and we are reminded of the eternal plan. Can you think of ways that you know that eternity has been placed in your heart? Record your thoughts and feelings as you reflect on the devotionals of this past week. What does God seem to be saying to you now?

DAY 113

Go out and stand before me on the mountain," the LORD told him. And as Elijah stood there, the LORD passed by, and a mighty windstorm hit the mountain. It was such a terrible blast that the rocks were torn loose, but the LORD was not in the wind. After the wind there was an earthquake, but the LORD was not in the earthquake. And after the earthquake there was a fire, but the LORD was not in the fire. And after the fire there was the sound of a gentle whisper. When Elijah heard it, he wrapped his face in his cloak and went out and stood at the entrance of the cave. And a voice said, "What are you doing here, Elijah?" (1 Kings 19:11-13, NLT)

I have always liked these verses, but lately I am reminded once again of the significance. I want the voice of God to be audible and say, "Ann," to shake the mountain and to cause rocks to fall but I don't get that. I am trying to hear the whisper. I think I am guilty of looking for the huge and missing the small. I pray that God lets me hear a whisper, and that I will know it is His whisper. I am reminded of the times that I felt confident that I had sensed God's prompting me to do something.

But when Don went Home, I felt no prompting. I second-guessed everything. What if it is just a coincidence? I had more than one person tell me I was over-thinking everything. I think maybe we become desperate to hear God, and that very desperation blocks us from hearing Him. Michelle looked lovingly at me one day and said, "Mom, I think you would explain away the burning bush right now." Maybe she is right. So how do you stop that? Keep praying. I noticed that there were times I would feel what can best be described as a swelling from within. Almost like a small, uneventful wave washing in on the beach, filling the sand where there had been no water. But then it would recede, leaving the sand dry again. This ebb and flow seemed to go on. I would think I heard something maybe felt something, and then it would ebb away. I just held on to Jesus by praying, continuing to write in my journal, and listening to the music. It seemed like slowly, very slowly, the flow in would stay longer. There are times I feel like maybe this is God prompting me, and I try to hold on to that thought. There have been several times I felt more strongly that God was showing me something, and I wrote those thoughts down. There are still times God seems distant. There are times I think, "Is that you, God?" But I have to hold to the thought that maybe those times are my whisper. I still want the mighty wind, and I will continue to pray for the mighty wind. But I am thankful for the whisper.

Write the times you feel like maybe you are hearing from God. Are they loud and clear or are they whispers you strain to hear?

DAY 114

O LORD, how long will you forget me? Forever?
How long will you look the other way? How long must I struggle with anguish in my soul, with sorrow in my heart every day?… But I trust in your unfailing love. I will rejoice because you have rescued me. (Psalm 13:1-2,5, NLT)

In *A Grief Observed*, C.S. Lewis writes that when a friend died he had the assurance of his continued life; even his enhanced life. He says upon the death of his wife, "I have begged to be given even one hundredth part of the same assurance about H. There is no answer."[133] The intensity of the sorrow makes you feel like God has forgotten you. The psalmist says it beautifully, "How long must I struggle with the anguish in my soul, with sorrow in my heart every day?" You know this struggle and perhaps you feel as C.S. Lewis did, craving the assurance that can only come from God. And yet God seems so silent.

Notice, however, the psalmist's line after pouring out his heart to God, "But I trust in your unfailing love." I know that I must trust in His unfailing love, even though I am not feeling it. I have memorized and quoted scriptures throughout my life, but never so much as now. You need to remind yourself through God's Word that God's love is unfailing. God is faithful to keep His promises. We just have to trust God and keep our hearts and minds on the eternity of His promises and His love. God's eternal plan will prevail. There is pain and sorrow in the fallen world. But since the beginning of time, we have His Word that there is more than this life. God is timeless. God's love is true and faithful. We have the hope of eternity, and we have God's unfailing love. Remember the times past that you have felt His love and blessings, and know He is still close even though you don't feel Him. Comfort Manyame's song "Watching Over You" gives a beautiful picture of God's love,

I'm watching over you,
Even though it seems I am so far away
I'm watching over you,
I'm as close to you as the next breath that you take
I'm watching over you,
I've been wiping every tear drop from your face
I'm watching over you, In your darkest night my light will shine the way[134]

Does God feel far away? Reflect on the verses and the lyrics. Remember times past when you have felt God. Journal your thoughts and feelings.

---

[133] C. S. Lewis, *A Grief Observed*, (New York: Harper Collins EBook, 2009), Location 216.
[134] Comfort Manyame, "Watching Over You." *Draw Me Near.* Comfort Manyame, 2010.

DAY 115

"Men of Galilee," they said, "why do you stand here looking into the sky? This same Jesus, who has been taken from you into heaven, will come back in the same way you have seen him go into heaven." (Acts 1:11, NIV)

Can you imagine how the disciples must have felt? They had gone through the sorrow and grief of watching Jesus die on the cross, and their own lives threatened. They would have been devastated, sorrowful, and afraid. Then, when Jesus came back just like He said He would, the joy they must have felt! Reading about Jesus' interaction with His disciples is important. Randy Alcorn tells us if we study Christ's interactions after His resurrection with the ones He appears to you will notice something:

You will see how similar they are to his interactions with these same people before he died. The fact that Jesus picked up his relationship where they'd left off is a foretaste of our own lives after we are resurrected. We will experience continuity between our current lives and our resurrected lives, with the same memories and relational histories.[135]

Jesus spends time with them in His resurrected body teaching them about the kingdom. Before He ascends, Jesus tells them to wait on the Holy Spirit, and they will be His witnesses. Keeping in mind all the disciples had been through, now they watch as Jesus ascends to Heaven right before their eyes. I can imagine that they were in awe of what they had just seen, and probably wanted to shout, "No, wait! Take us too!"

Angels appear and say, "Why do you stand there looking up? The same Jesus who has been taken from you to Heaven will come back the same way you have seen Him go into Heaven." In His resurrected body, in all His glory, Jesus will come back for us. Jesus is coming back! Joel Rosenberg calls Israel the epicenter. The Gospel spread from Israel and Israel is where Jesus will come back. All eyes are on Israel as I write this. Israel is truly the epicenter.

Jesus rules from Heaven and He will return for us. His interactions with His disciples show the continuity of eternity. Jesus left clear instructions; the angels, through His Word, tell us how He is coming back. Everything is clearly planned and orchestrated. God will someday restore the Heavens and the Earth. We will see all the accumulation of history and God's eternal plan. Our believing loved ones have been taken from us into Heaven, but we will be with them again. We are waiting on that day!

How do you feel about the statement that Christ's interaction after His resurrection was similar to those before He died? Does this comfort your?

---

[135] Randy Alcorn, *Heaven* (Carol Stream, IL: Tyndale House, 2004), 118.

DAY 116

Godly men buried Stephen and mourned deeply for him. (Acts 8:2, NIV)

Stephen was violently stoned for his faith and he was faithful to the end. Witnesses had watched him cry out as He saw Heaven open, and Stephen saw Jesus standing to greet him. They had heard him forgive his killers and pray for Jesus to take him Home. The godly men who buried Stephen may have even eventually died for their faith. We do not know who they were, but we know all of the disciples but one most likely died violently for their belief that Jesus was the Messiah. And yet with such a strong faith that they were also ready to die themselves, these godly men mourned deeply for Stephen. Why? Because they loved him, and because even though they had the hope of Heaven and the resurrection, Stephen was not with them physically. They missed him very much.

Mourning deeply is not a sign of little faith; it is a normal reaction to loss. And even though we haven't truly "lost" that person, because we know as Christians our loved one is in Heaven, we have lost our loved one physically with us for the time being, and that is very, very hard. People are uncomfortable with others' pain and may try to rush you through your grief. You need to clearly communicate your own needs, and not allow anyone to rush you through grief. Grief is personal. It helps to read books by other Christians who have gone through losses. I have referred to several throughout this book. There are number of books written on grief, but I found it best to thumb through the books first. Not all the books written on grief are helpful. I found some very odd books as well as some very helpful ones. I encourage you to allow yourself to grieve in the way that you need to, but don't deny the grief or try to avoid the pain. Sorrow is a normal reaction to loss and even when we know where our loved ones are, we still miss them. As for me, I agree with Greg Laurie, who says that what helps him is, "Thinking about heaven. The more I think about heaven the better things are."[136] I am waiting on that day!

Do you feel like people are rushing you through grief? If so, what do you need to tell them? Do you need to seek out more reading on grief for Christians?

---

[136] Greg Laurie, *Hope for Hurting Hearts* (Dana Point, CA: Kerygma, 2008), 93.

DAY 117

The company of the prophets at Bethel came out to Elisha and asked, "Do you know that the Lord is going to take your master from you today?" "Yes I know," Elisha replied, "so be quiet." (2 Kings 2:3, NIV)

Prophets twice came to Elisha to ask him if he knows Elijah is being taken that day. Twice Elisha basically replies, "Yes, I don't want to talk about it or think about it, so leave me alone." Three times Elijah tells Elisha that he needs to go on, and three times Elisha tells Elijah he isn't leaving him. I have read 2 Kings a number of times, but I don't think I understood how hard Elijah's departure was on Elisha until I was grieving. He loved Elijah; Elijah had been his mentor and he was with him daily. He didn't want to think about being without him.

When Dad was in the hospital the last time, he kept telling me about business matters to take care of when he was gone. I said, "But Dad, you will be able to do that when you get out." I really didn't want to think about Dad not getting out of the hospital. Even knowing that he had cancer, and knowing he would be called Home, I didn't want to think about him not being here with us. I didn't even have the chance with Don. One minute my perfectly healthy husband was working out and we are packing to go out of town, and the next I was lost in an abyss of sorrow. A couple of times Don and I would talk about how hard it would be to be without each other, and usually we finished the conversation by deciding we would just go together. Of course, we have no control over when we go Home, but we could not think about not being together. No one wants to think about being without those they love. The thought of being without our loved ones is so painful that we choose not to think about it, except when the loss happens you go to that painful place whether you want to or not.

Elisha was a strong man of God. The Bible records nearly twice as many miracles for Elisha than Elijah and both were great prophets of God. Even though Elijah didn't die, he still wasn't here with Elisha. I have well-meaning people ask if it is getting any better. No, grief doesn't get better; you don't get accustomed to being without someone you love and who is such an important part of your life. No one wants to think about being without their loved ones before loss happens, and no one wants to live without them after it happens. But for whatever reason, we are here. I would love to have seen the angels take Don and Dad Home like Elisha got to see Elijah's departure, but I didn't. I know, though, where Dad and Don are. Your grief is very real and no matter how strong your faith is, it is hard to be without those you love. But we know God has our believing loved ones now. We will have an eternity to be with our loved ones and worship our Savior. We are waiting on that day!

Reflect on this scripture passage. Can you identify with Elisha?

DAY 118

From one man he made all the nations, that they should inhabit the whole earth; and he marked out their appointed times in history and the boundaries of their lands. (Acts 17:26, NIV)

This verse in Acts is a clear statement on the eternal plan and sovereignty of God. "From one man He made all nations." He ordained when in history each one of us would live and where we would live. And He determined when we would come Home. Randy Alcorn points out,

Since God determined the time and exact places you would live, it's no accident which neighborhood you grew up in, who lived next door, who went to school with you, who was part of your church, youth group, who was there to help you and pray for you. Our relationships were appointed by God, and there is every reason to believe they will continue in Heaven.[137]

It is a beautiful thought that our relationships are appointed by God. When you read this verse, it clearly shows God's hand in the details.

Someone you love very much has gone Home to be with the Lord, but that person was not in your life by accident. God placed your loved one in your life. He cares about relationships; Christianity is a relationship with God. God is the one that made relationships important. He is the one who created you to love. The pain you feel now is born out of the intense love you had for the one you mourn. We don't understand why our loved one was taken now. Some people have a much longer life than others, and it is hard for us to understand.

If we focus on God's sovereignty and His eternal plan, we know that He has orchestrated our lives. God set the time you would be born, the relationships you have, the places you live, and the time you go Home. We can focus on trusting Him now. We can trust that the same God who gave us such a wonderful relationship will see it through to eternity. We are waiting on that day!

What are your thoughts and feelings on this verse? Does God appointing when and where you are in history help you see, as Randy Alcorn said, that even our relationships are appointed by God and that they will continue in Heaven?

---

[137] Randy Alcorn, *Heaven* (Carol Stream, IL: Tyndale House, 2004), 357.

DAY 119 REFLECTION

Reflect back over the last week. Was there a particular devotional that spoke to you? We read verses that show God often speaks in a gentle whisper; Elijah had to be waiting and listening. As you read these verses I hope you took time to listen. I hope you took time to meditate on what you may actually being hearing. We read how the psalmist struggled with anguish in his soul and with sorrow in his heart. That is a vivid description of our own pain. But the psalmist ends with He will trust in God's unfailing love. The lyrics from "Watching Over You" speak to my heart.

We also see a powerful verse that show the disciples watching as Jesus is taken to Heaven, and hearing the promise that He would return to this Earth. As I read back over the last week to summarize, I noticed these words in Acts: "who has been taken from you into heaven." Even though I know it isn't about me, I still feel at times like Don and Dad have been taken from me to Heaven. They are taken from us here physically, but only temporarily. This verse reminds me that even though they are in Heaven, because Jesus lives and will come back, our loved ones live. We will be reunited someday with our loved ones. We are waiting on that day!

We saw how godly men grieved deeply as they buried Stephen, lost in their own pain yet knowing he was with Jesus. We saw how Elisha, a godly prophet that God used mightily, didn't want to even talk about the loss of his friend and mentor. He knew Elijah was going to be taken up, and could not bear the loss of someone he loved. Even though he had strong faith and was used mightily, he grieved deeply. I think both of those verses show us that strong faith still misses and mourns our loved ones. We mourn deeply now, but we also know that this life here is not the end. We read verses that remind us of God's eternal plan and His sovereignty. We read how God has determined when we live in history and our relationships throughout life. How awesome is that thought? When I think of how God planned our lives, I am amazed. Our relationships are appointed by God. This verse in Acts is amazing and brings me great comfort. Can you imagine Heaven, knowing He appointed our relationships here? We are waiting on that day! Record your thoughts and feelings for the week. What devotionals resonate with you the most?

DAY 120

For we don't live for ourselves or die for ourselves. If we live, it's to honor the Lord. And if we die, it's to honor the Lord. So whether we live or die, we belong to the Lord. (Romans 14:7-8, NLT)

Romans 14:7-8 makes me think of my dad. We had rushed him to the hospital late one night to learn his lung had collapsed. He had tubes in his side, and was connected to all sorts of machines. Dad had never even been in the hospital for all of his seventy-eight years until the last few months of his life. Dad elected to have a surgery that many thought he would not live through. But he knew he did not want to live connected to tubes either. And even though Dad was the one in the hospital and the one in pain, he was the one talking about Jesus to everyone that came in. When Dad told us he wanted to go ahead with the surgery, he quoted these verses. He knew his life was in the Lord's hands. If God wanted Dad to live, then he would, and God would be glorified. But if God wanted Dad to come Home, Dad said that was great too, because whether he lived or died, he belonged to the Lord. And I knew that was true, but it was very hard to think of Dad not being there with us.

Right now, you are feeling how hard it is to be without your loved one. Sorrow is an abyss of pain. Being without those we love is very painful and sorrowful. But when we can focus on the fact that none of us as Christians live for ourselves or die for ourselves, we can focus more on eternity. If we are living, it is to honor God. When God calls us Home it is to honor Him as well. Because either way, as redeemed people we belong to God. I have to remind myself Dad and Don belonged to God all along, whether they lived or whether He called them Home, they are His. When we want to say, "Why did you take him away from me?" we have to remember our loved one belongs to God, and we belong to God.

I pray God helps me to honor Him while I am waiting on Him to bring me Home. Because whether I live or die, I belong to God. We will all be together again in God's perfect plan, because we do belong to Him. I am waiting on that day!

How does this verse speak to you? What are ways you can honor God even in your grief?

DAY 121

In the same way, the Spirit helps us in our weakness. We do not know what we ought to pray for, but the Spirit himself intercedes for us through wordless groans. And he who searches our hearts knows the mind of the Spirit, because the Spirit intercedes for God's people in accordance with the will of God. (Romans 8:26-27, NIV)

In his book *Prayer: Does it Make a Difference?* Philip Yancey says, "Though we feel ignorant in our prayers, the Spirit does not. Though we feel exhausted and confused, the Spirit does not. Though we feel lacking in faith, the Spirit does not. God is not so far off that we need to raise our voices to be heard. We need only groan."[138] There have been so many times that I just fell on my face and cried, not knowing what to say, and not knowing how to say it. I know I hurt. I just want everything the way it is "supposed" to be. I want my life back. But I know that I am not going to wake up from this horrid nightmare this side of Heaven. When I "wake up" it will be in Heaven, and life will all make sense in light of eternity. But in the meantime praying can be hard.

We are told the Holy Spirit intercedes with groans. In our crying out we have to trust He is listening, that we have an intercessor, and that God feels our pain. God sees the whole picture where we cannot. Grief is so exhausting and painful. We become so weary. There are times we just have to groan. And in those times the Holy Spirit is interceding for us. It is a beautiful thing to grasp that the Holy Spirit intercedes when we have no words, He loves us that much. Although it is hard to grasp when we are hurting, we know that we are loved and though we may not have the words, the Holy Spirit does. We have the Holy Spirit, our Comforter, interceding for us. We just have to bring ourselves into His presence and cry out. We don't have to pray the perfect prayer; we don't even know what to say. We just have to bring ourselves to our Father. The Holy Spirit will intercede.

What are your thoughts on these verses? If you have cried out not knowing what to say, how can you find comfort in knowing the Holy Spirit intercedes?

---

[138] Philip Yancey, *Prayer: Does It Make a Difference?* (Grand Rapids, MI: Zondervan, 2006), 112.

DAY 122

There he was transfigured before them. His face shone like the sun, and his clothes became as white as the light. Just then there appeared before them Moses and Elijah, talking with Jesus. (Matthew 17:2-3, NIV)

Both Paul Enns and Randy Alcorn refer to the verses on the Transfiguration, among others, to confirm that we are not disembodied beings while we are in Heaven. When someone we love goes Home before us, it opens so many questions. Between the sorrow of not having them with us and the questions about what are they doing, and what it is like for them, it can become completely overwhelming. But the more we know about Heaven, the more comforting it is. We don't want to be misguided and we certainly don't want to look beyond what the Bible tells us, but when we can find glimpses in the Bible, it is there for us to know. The apostles knew Moses and Elijah and they obviously had never met them. But they knew who they were immediately. Paul Enns writes:

But what happens at death, before the resurrection? Recall that at the transfiguration of Christ, Moses and Elijah appeared to Peter, James and John (Matt. 17:3). The three disciples recognized Moses and Elijah. Clearly those two had physical bodies through which they were identifiable. They are identified as 'men' (Luke 9:30), hardly the designation of a spirit.[139]

Randy Alcorn writes:

Because they'd already gone to Heaven (Moses having died and Elijah having been taken from Earth in a whirlwind), if souls in the present Heaven are disembodied, God would have had to create temporary bodies for them when they came from Heaven to be with Jesus on the mountain. If so, they would have gone from being disembodied to embodied, and after the Transfiguration become disembodied again to await the final resurrection.[140]

These glimpses in the Bible can bring us comfort. I find comfort in Don and Dad looking like looking like themselves, but reflecting the glory of God. I can only begin to imagine how glorious it is for them to be in Jesus' presence. Your loved one is still the same person in Heaven that they were here—only glorified. They are in the presence of the radiance of Christ, and they reflect His glory. What a glorious thought!

Reflect on these verses and quotes. What are your thoughts and feelings?

---

[139] Paul Enns, *Heaven Revealed* (Chicago, IL: Moody, 2011), 74.
[140] Randy Alcorn, *Heaven* (Carol Stream, IL: Tyndale House, 2004), 60.

DAY 123

Praise be to the God and Father of our Lord Jesus Christ, the Father of compassion and the God of all comfort, who comforts us in all our troubles, so that we can comfort those in any trouble with the comfort we ourselves receive from God. (2 Corinthians 1:3-4, NIV)

A good friend of ours wrote a song called "We Know He Cares." Jeff was the principal when I was a counselor at a small school. Jeff wrote this song in honor of a former student of ours, a beautiful young woman who had battled breast cancer, but at the young age of thirty-two went Home. Jeff wrote these words knowing he had a rare disorder that would most likely be fatal. The words to the song Jeff wrote lament how unfair life seems at times, but the chorus says it all, "We know He cares, He gave His Son."[141]

God is the Father of compassion and the God of all comfort. We do know God cares because He gave His Son. He loves us. The other thing to take from this verse is that God, in comforting you, will then use you to comfort others. The songs I have recommended were all written out of pain. God has used the artist's pain to comfort millions of others. The books on grief that meant the most to me were those written by someone in grief. Other books that spoke to me were written by those who were grieving. Paul Enns book on Heaven, written after his wife went Home suddenly, resonated with me. He understood. This quote in Randy Alcorn's book *Eternal Perspectives* sent me on a search:

If I knew that never again would I recognize that beloved one with whom I spent more than thirty-nine years here on earth, my anticipation of heaven would much abate, to say that we shall be with Christ and that that will be enough, is to claim that there we shall be without our social instincts and affections which mean so much to us here.... Life beyond cannot mean impoverishment, but the enhancement and enrichment of life as we have known it here at its best.[142]

After reading this quote I had to search for W. Graham Scroggie's book since it was out of print. He wrote it in 1930 after his beloved wife went Home. Scroggie understood. God is the God of compassion, He knows how you feel, and He loves you. He will comfort you by His presence, by others that He has comforted, and He will use you to comfort others.

Reflect on this verse. What are your thoughts on today's devotional?

---

[141] Jeff Sweet, "We Know He Cares." *The Gospel Through Music.* Jeff Sweet, 2012.

[142] William Scroggie, as cited by Randy Alcorn in *Eternal Perspectives, A Collection of Quotations on Heaven, the New Earth, and Life After Death* (Carol Stream, IL: Tyndale House, 2012), 367

DAY 124

Because we know that the one who raised the Lord Jesus from the dead will also raise us with Jesus and present us with you to himself. (2 Corinthians 4:14, NIV)

In verse 12 of this chapter in 2 Corinthians, Paul tells his readers that he and his companions are facing death. But he also tells them he will continue to preach because he knows that Jesus' death and resurrection will result in eternal life for him, his companions, and for those believers reading. He continues to tell the Corinthians that because Jesus was raised from the dead, so will we who believe. We have the assurance of the bodily resurrection and eternal life. We can take comfort in knowing our loved ones are with Him now, and that someday we will all be raised together.

Paul goes on to tell them he continues to preach because of his faith. And then Paul tells his readers that God will unite them and bring them together to Himself. Paul's statement is a clear statement of continuity. As Paul Enns writes:

Scripture is clear; there is a continuity of the earthly personality and body with the personality and body that we will have in the resurrection on the new earth. That has many implications. We will continue the relationship with the people we loved on this earth. The fellowship will be enormous—but we won't be limited by time constraints![143]

Paul was so sure of what he believed, even knowing he could die at any time. But he also knew that what he believed in resulted in the ones he loved and cared for also having eternal life. Paul knew that someday they would be together presented to God. And so will we be presented with our loved ones. We are waiting on that day!

What are your thoughts and feelings on this verse? What are your thoughts on the statement by Paul Enns? How does recognizing the continuity of who we are in eternity bring you comfort?

---

[143] Paul Enns, *Heaven Revealed* (Chicago, IL: Moody, 2011), 138.

DAY 125

A faith and knowledge resting on the hope of eternal life, which God, who does not lie, promised before the beginning of time, and which now at his appointed season he has brought to light through the preaching entrusted to me by the command of God our Savior. (Titus 1:2-3, NIV)

Our faith is resting on the hope of eternal life. This hope is not wishful thinking, but assurance. These verses give a clear statement of God's eternal plan promised before the beginning of time, and at His appointed season He brings this purpose to light. These two verses are packed with eternal truths. God's Word is truth. We have His promise.

The prophets would have loved to have seen the Messiah. The prophets had prophesied thousands of years in the past, and people had looked for the Messiah, but in God's appointed time Jesus the Messiah came. Jesus brings life to all those that receive Him. Through faith we know we have the hope of eternal life. We know God's plan is eternal. We know where our believing loved ones are. And we know we will someday join them. We also know that there will be a New Heaven and a New Earth. At the appointed time God's plan will all come about. Just like at the appointed time our loved one went Home. You have to now hold by faith to the hope of eternal life. We know it is true. Dr. John Luke Terveen writes:

Hope for now and for the future is wrapped up in relationship with Jesus, whose resurrection carries the assurance of new life for all who, by faith, invite Christ to dwell in their hearts. That is where our hope ultimately resides—Jesus. The loss of a loved one can hurt so badly that we just want to shut our eyes and get away from it all.[144]

Jesus has the answers; He is our hope. Immerse yourself in His Word and His promises. Dr. Terveen writes about the two men on the road to Emmaus and how they did not recognize Jesus at first, but He opened their eyes.

Hope is alive because Jesus is alive. Jesus comes and— sometimes even unrecognized by us—opens our eyes again to his life-giving power. He does this by opening our minds anew to his Word. How easy to forget God's Word in the throes of grief and loss. But that would be the greatest tragedy.[145]

What are your thoughts and feelings on these verses? Have you shut your eyes to God's Word? If so, how can Dr. Terveen's words help you?

---

[144] John Luke Terveen, *Hope for the Brokenhearted* (Colorado Springs, CO: Victor, 2006), 134.

[145] Ibid., 134.

DAY 126 REFLECTION

Looking back over the last week, what stands out to you the most? We read verses reminding us as believers that whether we live or die, we belong to the Lord. What an amazing promise that is. Each time I read Romans 14:7-8 I think of Dad saying those very words, and knowing it to be true. We read verses that remind us the Holy Spirit intercedes for us. If you are like me, that is powerful because so often the pain is so overwhelming I don't know what to pray. I only know to call His name. It is a wonderful thought to know the Holy Spirit intercedes for us.

We read about the Transfiguration and we recognize how powerful these verses are. The Transfiguration is a clear statement of continuity of life and people, and with that would be relationships. The comfort that comes from just reading about the Transfiguration is amazing. To know Don and Dad are right now Don and Dad reflecting the glory of Jesus, and to know they will be waiting on us to join them, is an awesome thing to hold on to. Can you feel that with _____? We also see verses that remind us of how we receive comfort and how we can comfort others. We read of others who shared their pain to comfort us.

We see more verses that emphasize God's eternal plan, and that He had that plan since before the beginning of time. I take comfort in all these verses. As you reflect, record those verses and devotionals that bring you the most comfort.

DAY 127

I must go on boasting. Although there is nothing to be gained, I will go on to visions and revelations from the Lord. I know a man in Christ who fourteen years ago was caught up to the third heaven. Whether it was in the body or out of the body I do not know—God knows. And I know that this man—whether in the body or apart from the body I do not know, but God knows—was caught up to paradise and heard inexpressible things, things that no one is permitted to tell. I will boast about a man like that, but I will not boast about myself, except about my weaknesses. Even if I should choose to boast, I would not be a fool, because I would be speaking the truth. But I refrain, so no one will think more of me than is warranted by what I do or say, or because of these surpassingly great revelations. (2 Corinthians 12:1-7a, NIV)

Paul had a glimpse of Paradise. These verses tell us Heaven is closer than we may think. The awesome and amazing scene that Paul saw was inexpressible for him. I like the way Paul Enns says this:

Paul was given a glimpse of heaven's glory, to sustain him in the time of suffering, reminding him of the magnificent glory that awaited him.... This is a reminder to us that amid the suffering and trials of life, a heavenly perspective is necessary. Only those who keep their eyes fixed on the glory to come will endure the trials and sufferings in the present.[146]

Although later John sees Heaven and was told to write about it, Paul was not to write what he had seen at this time. But we know that because of this great revelation he willingly went into situations knowing he would die. Many times he shows us how this vision impacted him. Among other verses, these come to mind: Phil. 1:21—"to die is gain"; Phil. 1:23—"Heaven is far better"; and Col. 3:1-4, in which he told us to keep our minds and hearts focused on Heaven. These are just a few verses, but Paul wrote many to show that he was looking forward to Heaven. Paul's vision sustained him and motivated him. We may not get this glimpse as Paul did, or as we would desire to. But we do have the scriptures that tell us much about Heaven. The more you read on Heaven, the more you can recognize how important it is to stay focused on it and the eternal plan. In *We Shall See God*, Randy Alcorn says, "Life on Earth matters, not because it's the only life we have, but precisely because it isn't—it's the beginning of a life that will continue without end on a renewed Earth. Understanding Heaven doesn't just tell us what to do, but why."[147]

How does understanding how and why Paul focused on Heaven comfort you?

---

[146] Paul Enns, *Heaven Revealed* (Chicago, IL: Moody, 2011), 19.
[147] Randy Alcorn, *We Shall See God* (Carol Stream, IL: Tyndale House, 2011), 86.

DAY 128

And God raised us up with Christ and seated us with him in the heavenly realms in Christ Jesus, in order that in the coming ages He might show the incomparable riches of his grace expressed in his kindness to us in Christ Jesus. (Ephesians 2:6-7, NIV)

All scriptures that pertain to Heaven catch my attention and focus. Anthony Hoekema put a different thought on these verses that really caught my eye. He writes, "In the believer's Christian experience, therefore, there is real continuity between this age and the next."[148] We know from other places in the scripture there is continuity as I have cited throughout the devotionals. But if we take all the verses that talk about our citizenship already being in Heaven, it speaks of clear continuity in even more places in the Bible.

We are told that God will show us the incomparable riches of His grace expressed in His kindness to us in Christ Jesus. Many of the authors I read think the coming age is referencing eternity. Some see the coming age as the millennial kingdom. Whether the coming age references eternity or the millennial kingdom the good news is that when we receive Christ we are seated spiritually with Him in the heavenly realm. Someday that will be a physical reality. Right now our loved ones are truly in the heavenly realm. They have made that next step and are able to see so much of the incomparable riches of His grace. As J. Sidlow Baxter writes, "Whatever different quality of life may be ours hereafter, this much is sure for the Christian: heaven will perfect and perpetuate all that earth has made sacredly dear."[149]

We have so much to look forward to in the coming ages. Our loved ones have entered the heavenly realm now. We will join them. All of us who receive Christ are raised up at salvation to be seated with Him in the heavenly realms, and in the coming ages we will know even more of the incomparable riches of His grace. Eternity with Christ will be perfect. We are waiting on that day!

What are your thoughts and feelings on these verses? What are your thoughts on Anthony Hoekema's statement? What are your thoughts on J. Sidlow Baxter's statement?

---

[148] Anthony A. Hoekema, *The Bible and the Future* (Grand Rapids, MI: Eerdmans, 1979), 39.

[149] J. Sidlow Baxter, *The Other Side of Death* (Grand Rapids, MI: Kregel, 1987), 63.

DAY 129

You love him even though you have never seen him. Though you do not see him now, you trust him; and you rejoice with a glorious, inexpressible joy. The reward for trusting him will be the salvation of your souls. (1 Peter 1:8-9, NLT)

Peter was with Jesus at the beginning of His ministry, and he saw the resurrected Christ. But he recognized the people he was writing to and even more through the ages, including us, that would love Jesus even though we have not seen Him. Peter is encouraging them and us. In the verses before this one Peter is encouraging his readers because he knows they are suffering. He is reminding them that their reward for trusting God is salvation, and so is ours. Our loved ones trusted Him and they passed from this life to Heaven as a result of that trust. Now, we have to trust Jesus. Perhaps this is the hardest time that it has ever been for you to trust Him. As I quoted C.S. Lewis earlier, "You never know how much you really believe anything until its truth or falsehood becomes a matter of life and death to you."[150]

Just as Peter's readers are suffering, you are suffering. It is so easy to doubt right now, but it is ever important to stay focused on Jesus and trusting Him. Peter is encouraging all of us who believe by faith to trust even though we do not physically see Jesus. As Steven Curtis Chapman sings in "I Will Trust You":

> I don't even wanna be right now
> I don't wanna think another thought
> And I don't wanna feel this pain I feel
> And right now, pain is all I've got
>
> It feels like it's all I've got, but I know it's not
> No, I know You're all I've got
> And I will trust You, I'll trust You
> Trust You, God, I will
> Even when I don't understand, even then I will say again
> You are my God, and I will trust You[151]

Just like Stephen Curtis Chapman, I have to say it again and again. "I will trust You, You are my God." When we suffer, it is more important than ever to trust. Listen to your songs, quote scripture and trust Him.

How does this verse speak to you? How do Peter's words of encouragement to those who had not seen Jesus (which would include all of us) relate to you now?

---

150 C. S. Lewis, *A Grief Observed* (New York: Harper Collins EBook, 2009), Location 327.
151 Steven Curtis Chapman, "I Will Trust You." *Beauty Will Rise.* Sparrow, 2008.

DAY 130

He will take our weak mortal bodies and change them into glorious bodies like his own, using the same power with which he will bring everything under his control. (Philippians 3:21, NLT)

As long as we live in a fallen world our mortal bodies are weak. People get sick. Accidents happen. Evil is in the world. But Paul is reminding us that one day Jesus will take our weak mortal bodies and change them into glorious bodies like His own. Paul goes on to tell us that Jesus will bring everything under His control. No longer will we live in a fallen world, and no longer will our bodies wear out. Whatever our loved ones look like right now, and there seem to be different interpretations of what that might mean, they are still the person we love, only perfected. Someday, when the plan is brought to climax and there is a bodily resurrection, our bodies will be like Jesus' glorified body. We have so much to look forward to.

When Jesus brings everything under His control, we will have glorified bodies. We will walk, talk, and eat with our loved ones again. We will worship God with our loved ones again. The first Easter without Don was painful because he was always by my side. Our friend Barbara texted me the week after Easter. She said, "My thoughts were on the difficulty of the day for you... one side rejoicing his seat by our Savior and yet sad that the seat next to you was empty...eternity cannot get here soon enough to escape the reality of your heartbreak, but it is coming." She summed up my feelings so beautifully. The day is coming. We will be reunited with our loved ones, and we will worship our Savior. We are waiting on that day!

How does this verse speak to you? How does the thought of glorified bodies like Jesus' comfort you?

DAY 131

They serve in a system of worship that is only a copy, a shadow of the real one in heaven. For when Moses was getting ready to build the Tabernacle, God gave him this warning: "Be sure that you make everything according to the pattern I have shown you here on the mountain." (Hebrews 8:5, NLT)

The author of Hebrews stresses that the system of worship is a copy of the real one in Heaven. So is all of Earth a copy of Heaven? Here are Randy Alcorn's thoughts on this question:

The book of Hebrews seems to say that we should see Earth as a *derivative* realm and Heaven as the *source* realm. If we do we'll abandon the assumption that something existing in one realm cannot exist in the other. In fact, we'll consider it likely that what exists in one realm exists in at least some form of the other. We should stop thinking of Heaven and Earth as opposites and instead view them as overlapping circles that share certain commonalities.[152]

Randy Alcorn goes on to suggest that it does stand to reason that if God created man in His image, He created Earth in Heaven's image. In his book *Eternal Perspectives*, Randy Alcorn quotes C.S. Lewis: "The hills and valleys of Heaven will be to those you now experience not as a copy is to an original, nor as a substitute is to the genuine article, but as the flower to the root, or the diamond to the coal."[153]

I agree with Randy Alcorn's thoughts. The book of Hebrews does seem to say that Earth is a derivative realm and Heaven the source realm. If we keep this thought in mind we can perhaps try to imagine a shadow of what our loved one is seeing. This summer has been hot and dry but I have diligently tried to keep the flowers we planted the year before. The purple perennial flowers that have come back are plentiful this year. Every time I go out to water them, I wonder what the flowers look like in Heaven. What do we see that our loved ones are seeing more intently? We don't have the answer to that question, nor will we know for sure until we are in Heaven with them. But we can know that our loved ones are with God, and it has to be glorious. We are waiting on that day!

What are your thoughts and feelings on this verse? What are your thoughts on the quotes?

---

[152] Randy Alcorn, *Heaven* (Carol Stream, IL: Tyndale House, 2004), 53.

[153] C. S. Lewis as cited by Randy Alcorn in *Eternal Perspectives, A Collection of Quotation on Heaven, The New Earth and Life After Death* (Carol Stream, IL: Tyndale House, 2012), 383.

DAY 132

For Christ did not enter into a holy place made with human hands, which was only a copy of the true one in heaven. He entered into heaven itself to appear now before God on our behalf. (Hebrews 9:24, NLT)

Christ entered Heaven to appear before God on our behalf. The verses before Hebrews 9:24 are showing how the earthly tabernacles required priest and sacrifices. But with Christ's death and resurrection He has purified us by His blood, so there is no need for daily sacrifices in the temple. Christ died once for all of us, and His blood cleanses us. Jesus is the reason that our loved ones, who received Him, are now in Heaven. Our loved ones are in their true Home, the true holy place not made with human hands. All the places here on Earth are only a copy of the true Home in Heaven. Randy Alcorn says, "The earthly sanctuary was a copy of our true one in Heaven. In fact, the New Jerusalem that will be brought down to the New Earth is currently the intermediate or present Heaven (Hebrews 12:22)"[154] He goes on to give a compelling reason to believe that if it is physical on the New Earth then it is most likely physical now in Heaven. He suggests our thinking is often backward. He states, "We tend to start with Earth and reason up toward Heaven, when instead we should start with Heaven and reason down toward Earth."[155]

We must try to wrap our brain around the magnificence of where our loved ones are; the magnificence of what Christ did for us that allows us to enter into His presence and His glory. Pain and sorrow can rob us of our eternal focus. I am convinced that pain and sorrow are so overwhelming that they consume all of our senses. The only way to begin to try to focus is to recognize how all-consuming pain and sorrow can be and to willfully and thoughtfully focus on God's Word to remind us what is true while we are waiting on that day!

How does this verse speak to you? What are your thoughts on, "We should start with Heaven and reason down toward Earth"?

---

[154] Randy Alcorn, *Heaven* (Carol Stream, IL: Tyndale House, 2004), 54.
[155] Ibid., 154.

DAY 133 REFLECTION

Reading back over last week, what speaks to you the most? We read verses that show us Paul's visit to Heaven. Paul's visit was so powerful and so amazing that it sustained him throughout his life. His awe inspiring experience of Heaven continues to encourage us as we read Paul's writings. These verses also remind us of the nearness of Heaven. We know that Christ is seated at the right hand of God and when we receive Him as Savior, we are seated with Him in the heavenly realms.

We read verses that emphasize the continuity of life in the coming ages. Peter reminds us that the reward for trusting Jesus, even though we didn't see Him, is our salvation. The verses that tell us the promise of glorified bodies reminds us to keep an eternal perspective. We read verses that show us this Earth is a copy—a shadow—of Heaven. When we see the beauty around us in a fallen world, it reminds us what amazing sights our loved ones must be seeing now in a perfected place. If this world is only a copy and a shadow, what intense colors and beauty they must be experiencing. And finally, we saw that Jesus appears before God on our behalf. Powerful verses this week focus us on Heaven. Record your thoughts and feelings as you look back over the week of devotionals. What seems to speak to you the most?

DAY 134

While we wait for the blessed hope—the appearing of the glory of our great God and Savior, Jesus Christ. (Titus 2:13 NIV)

After his fourteen-year-old daughter was called Home to be with Our Lord, Dr. John Terveen wrote a wonderful book called *Hope for the Brokenhearted.* His comments on this verse are appropriate for all of us hurting right now. He shared that since he has been a Christian he has always looked forward to Jesus' return, whether he understood it fully or not. But then he goes on to say after his daughter went Home how he felt:

Jesus' return became much more than just good doctrine. It meant life, love, and hope for me. I discovered within myself a deep and passionate yearning for Jesus' appearing as never before. Now I love the very thought of 'blessed hope' (Titus 2:13) of Jesus' soon return, for I know that at His return, the pain of separation from Jesus himself and believing loved ones will end. We will all be together and embrace one another again.[156]

I so agree with Dr. Terveen because I too have a deep and passionate longing for Jesus' return. I am drawn to those books and conversations that talk of Jesus' return. I am waiting; waiting on this blessed hope. Waiting on our Lord Jesus to come back, waiting on His appearance. I am waiting on that day I see Jesus in His glory, and I am waiting on that day I am reunited with Don and with Dad. As Christians we know that we have that hope. When you have someone that you love so much go Home before you, that waiting takes on a whole new meaning; that hope takes on a new meaning. It is a blessed hope and as believers we have that hope. As Dr. Terveen also points out, "Probably the oldest Christian prayer preserved in the New Testament is the Aramaic word, 'Maranatha' (1 Corinthians 16:22), a cry that means 'Our Lord Come!'" [157] And so I say, "Maranatha." We are waiting...

Meditate on this verse. Have you too found new meaning in the "blessed hope?" What are your thoughts on Dr. Terveen's statements?

---

[156] John Luke Terveen, *Hope for the Brokenhearted* (Colorado Springs, CO: Victor, 2006), 196.

[157] Ibid., 196.

DAY 135

In my vision at night I looked, and there before me was one like a son of man, coming with the clouds of heaven. He approached the Ancient of Days and was led into his presence. He was given authority, glory and sovereign power; all nations and peoples of every language worshiped him. His dominion is an everlasting dominion that will not pass away, and his kingdom is one that will never be destroyed. (Daniel 7:13-14 NIV)

Daniel is an amazing book. The prophecies in Daniel can be established in history. And yet we know there is more to come. Many scholars see these verses as a reference to the millennium, and many see them as referring to the eternal kingdom. But Paul Enns makes this point, "This is a strong statement that Christ's kingdom is eternal. These words cannot be restricted to the millennial rule of Jesus; Christ's kingdom is longer and greater than one thousand years. It is what God prepared from the beginning in Eden. It is eternal kingdom. It is forever."[158] I like the way Paul Enns describes the eternal kingdom. So either way you look at the verse, it means forever. Forever is beautiful.

When the New Heavens and the New Earth are established, Christ will rule and we, as believers, will be a part of that kingdom. You look around now and so much of what you see is a part of you and your loved one. And the pain of not having our loved ones here to experience life is overwhelming. Their absence is everywhere. But with an eternal perspective we know that we will be with our loved ones again, and this time there will be no separation, no death. We will live in Christ's everlasting kingdom. We will experience life as never before. Christ was given authority, glory, and sovereign power. His dominion is everlasting. As believers, we are a part of that kingdom. Your believing loved one is waiting on you, waiting on that moment in time when Christ comes again and His everlasting kingdom is established on Earth. Your kingdom come, Lord. We are waiting on that day!

What are your thoughts and feelings on these verses? How does recognizing that Daniel's prophecies have been proven through history and knowing there is more to come speak to you now? How does thinking of the New Earth comfort you?

---

[158] Paul Enns, *Heaven Revealed* (Chicago, IL: Moody, 2011), 61.

DAY 136

He who is the faithful witness to all these things says, "Yes, I am coming soon!" Amen! Come, Lord Jesus! (Revelation 22:20, NLT)

I poured myself into reading when Don went Home. Besides the many books on Heaven I read, I also found books on prophecy to be comforting. I never really understood prophecy, and usually was not drawn to books written on the end times. But now, everything has changed. There is comfort in knowing that even though I don't feel God, He is in control. When you look at prophecy, the eternal plan is so much more evident. Many of the prophecies on Christ in the Old Testament were fulfilled with His first coming; we can watch events now unfolding that were prophesied thousands of years ago. And we know many are yet to be fulfilled. When doubts hit me, I remind myself of those things, those tangible events. Prophecy helps me keep an eternal perspective.

During one of the times that I was crying out to God for something more tangible, something I knew that was from Him, I got an unexpected text from our pastor. Chet texted me and asked if he could share a quote with me. His text was this:

Yes, Jesus said, 'I am coming soon.' Paul reminds us to comfort one another with these words, and that Jesus IS coming soon. How many of us comfort ourselves with these words, much less one another? For Jesus said, 'Behold, I am coming soon, to repay every one for what he has done.' Yes, come Lord Jesus. Are you ready to comfort one another with these words.... Jesus said, 'I am coming soon.'?"[159]

Chet had no idea I was finding comfort in prophecy and Jesus' return, so when I got that text I was touched and thought, "Okay, God. Maybe You had him send that to me." And as I started to respond how much I appreciated it, I got the next text from him. Chet told me that quote was from a book he was reading, but the clincher for me was the quote was actually from a book my dad had written. Dad had written a short book called *Bro. Bob Blasts* that was a collection of his sermons in the early 70's—over forty years ago. There were only a small number published by a local publishing company and all proceeds went to the church. Our pastor had the book because my sister had given him a copy a while back, long before Don's departure. So for me, at that moment in time, something from my dad at the moment I needed it was so comforting. That moment brought together God's timing, family, and comfort. Come, Lord Jesus, come. We are waiting on that day!

How does this verse speak to you? What are your thoughts on my experience?

---

[159] Bobby Bryan, *Bro. Bob Blasts* (Paris, TX: Dewitt, 1972), 27.

DAY 137

Why, Lord, do you reject me and hide your face from me? (Psalm 88:14, NIV)

The psalmist is obviously hurting. I don't know what was going on his life, but his deep pain and feeling of isolation is evident. We may feel like God is hiding His face, but we know He isn't. God is not rejecting us. Dustin Shramek reminds us:

No amount of good theology is able to take the pain out of suffering. Too often we allow ourselves to believe that a robust view of God's sovereignty in all things means that when suffering comes it won't hurt. God's sovereignty doesn't take away the pain and evil that confronts us in our lives; it works them for our good. [160]

I think that sometimes I get the pain confused with not feeling God, as if pain signals God's absence. But if I stop and think about the truth, I know that if I had a major operation I would feel pain. The pain from the trauma to my body would still be there, and it would not mean God was not with me. This pain you and I feel now is even more real because we know the true healing of this pain will only happen in Heaven. Only in Heaven when we see Jesus fully will the pain stop. Then we will see Jesus and be in His glorious presence, and we will see our loved ones. Then no longer will we be separated from those we love. No longer will we wonder where God is because we will be in His presence. We will not feel like He has rejected us or hidden His face from us because we will be in His glory. Evil is gone, pain is gone, death is gone. We will be surrounded by the glory of God.

But for now, for this painful time, what is there to do? How do we hold to that fact that we know God is with us even if we don't always feel Him? We write what we know to be true, we say it out loud, and we listen to songs that say it. We pray. Sometimes I would get an email or a text or a card from family or friends to let me know I was not alone. I knew I always had people praying for me and for us as a family. If you do not have a church home, family, or friends praying for you, call a local church ask to be put on their prayer list. Allow the body of Christ to pray for you and to minister to you. God has not rejected you; He loves you.

Meditate on this verse. Can you identify with the psalmist? What are your thoughts on Dustin Shramek's statement? Do you feel as I do that you may get the pain confused with God being absent?

---

[160] Dustin Shramek, "Waiting for the Morning During the Long Night of Weeping." John Piper and Justin Taylor (Ed). *Suffering and the Sovereignty of God*, (Wheaton, IL: Crossway 2006), 175.

DAY 138

God is our refuge and strength, A very present help in trouble. Therefore we will not fear, though the earth should change And though the mountains slip into the heart of the sea; Though its waters roar and foam, Though the mountains quake at its swelling pride. Selah. (Psalm 46:1-3, NASB)

As I was reading this verse it struck me that grief feels like these verses describe. The Earth or your world does change. It feels like mountains fall into the sea and the waters roar and the Earth quakes. All that seems stable isn't, when you are grieving. Your world is literally shaken to the foundations. But the one thing that does remain is God. He is our refuge and strength. Even though there are times we do not feel Him in our grief, in those times even more than ever we must cling to Him. God is our refuge. A refuge is a place of shelter. God will hold us when we can't feel the Earth below us and when everything feels like chaos, God has us.

I have snippets of the night that Don went Home burned in memory. There are things I can't remember; there are other things I can't forget. I do remember at the hospital crying, "I can't do this, I can't do this." People said, "Yes, you can." But you can't. I can't. I can only in God's strength—and I have to hold to Him every second to even make it through that second. You may be looking at your situation and thinking, "I can't do this." And you are right: you can't on your own. But God is our refuge and our strength. It is in His strength that you will have to depend. God is a very present help but you may not feel Him there; you just have to trust that He is.

When I was a child and we went on vacations we would always stay at a hotel with a pool. It was a really big deal to have the pool. I was always scared of the water, but my dad would stand in the pool and coax me to jump; he would be there to catch me. And I would jump because I knew my daddy was there to hold me up when I went under. I trusted him. Even when the water temporarily blurred my vision, I knew Dad wouldn't leave me. God is our Father, our ever-present help. There are many, many times through this sorrow that I do not feel God with me, but I know He is. I know that with all the shaking of my world and everything seemingly falling apart that God is in control. He will not leave me. I have to trust in His promises, and trust that God is my refuge and my strength. I may lose sight of His refuge with all the chaos, but He is still here with me. I trust God even though I don't feel Him at times. He is in control.

What are your thoughts and feelings on this verse? Can you identify with the feelings of the world falling apart? Thinking of God as your refuge and strength, how do you hold to Him?

DAY 139

Truly, truly, I say to you, that you will weep and lament, but the world will rejoice; you will grieve, but your grief will be turned into joy. (John 16:2, NASB)

Jesus knew His disciples would weep and grieve. He knew how much they would miss Him. Jesus tried to prepare His disciples, but He knew their (and our) hearts. In his book *If God is Good*, Randy Alcorn quotes Nancy Guthrie:

'I think we expected our faith to make this hurt less, but it doesn't. Our faith gives us an incredible amount of strength and encouragement while we had Hope, and we are comforted with the knowledge that she is in heaven. Our faith keeps us from being swallowed by despair. But I don't think it makes our loss hurt any less.' Randy adds after the quote, When I interviewed David and Nancy Guthrie, they said God stood with them *in* their pain, but God did not *remove* their pain. Those separated in death from their loved ones don't *want* the pain to go away entirely because if it did, it would minimize the importance of their relationship. Nancy Guthrie says, 'It is only natural that people around me often ask searchingly, 'How are you.' And for much of the first year after Hope's death, my answer was, 'I'm deeply and profoundly sad.'[161]

As you continue reading Alcorn's interview with the Guthries you see that she felt blessed to have people want to share her sorrow but was sad when others wanted to "fix her." People do tend to want to fix the grief but they can't, and sometimes we have to gently remind them of that. The important thing is for you to remember that it is okay for you to grieve. Jesus knew we would weep and lament. Your faith does not take away the pain; I think that is something maybe we all think before the loss. We rely on our faith to help us, but we aren't prepared for the depth of the pain that comes with the loss of a loved one. Sorrow is like an abyss and it is overwhelming and heavy.

We cry and we grieve deeply, and Jesus knew we would, but the important part is the last line of this verse, "our grief will turn to joy." When we see Jesus and we are reunited with our loved ones, our grief will turn to joy. But don't rush it now. Hold on to your faith; it is what will hold you in your pain. It is what gives you the hope of Christ to know that someday when you see Jesus, the pain will go away; and not only will it go away, it will turn to joy. We will be with our Savior, we will be reunited with those we love, and we will have an eternity to rejoice with them. We are waiting on that day!

Reflect on the verse and the comments of Nancy Guthrie. I can identify with what Nancy Guthrie is saying. Can you?

---

[161] Randy Alcorn, *If God Is Good Faith in the Midst of Suffering and Evil* (Colorado Springs, CO: Multnomah Books, 2009), 365.

DAY 140 REFLECTION

Reflect back over the last six days. What stands out to you? We read verses that remind us of our blessed hope. We read how Dr. Terveen and others talk about losing a loved one. Suddenly that blessed hope becomes even more real as we wait on that day. Can you identify with Dr. Terveen's thoughts? We read another verse in Revelation telling us Jesus is coming soon and how holding to those prophecies bring us hope. Jesus tells us to comfort each other with those words; He is coming soon! We are waiting on that day! What were your thoughts on my experience? I can tell you that day, I cried as I realized what God was giving me in comfort.

We read Daniel and the amazing prophecies fulfilled, with some yet to be fulfilled. Daniel helps us see the eternal plan and the sovereignty of God. We will read more from Daniel. We read several verses that remind us that our faith and beliefs do not protect us from pain. Even though we have hope, we still grieve and hurt. We mourn. We may not feel God's presence and we cry out to Him, but we also remember He is our refuge and our strength. Jesus Himself tells us we will weep and lament; we will grieve. But then He promises us our grief will turn to joy because He is coming back. We can all hold to that promise that our grief will turn to joy; that Jesus is coming back soon. Someday this nightmare will end; someday our mourning will turn to joy. We will see Jesus; we will be reunited with our loved ones. We will have an eternity to worship Him with our loved ones. We are waiting on that day! Record your thoughts and feelings as you reflect over the last six days of devotionals. What resonates the most with you?

DAY 141

I myself will see him with my own eyes—I, and not another. How my heart yearns within me! (Job 19:27, NIV)

One thing that has become evident as I read books by others who are grieving is how the loss of our loved ones snaps our attention to Heaven in a way that becomes more pronounced than ever. Of all the books I read, the ones that meant the most to me were the ones that echoed what I felt. And what I noticed is how much Heaven and an eternal perspective is a central theme in all of them. One of the books I discovered as I was nearing the end of these devotionals was Nancy Guthrie's *Holding onto Hope*. She wrote the book after losing a child, and knowing as she wrote that another child would be going to Heaven soon. Her words are profound. And like me, she found comfort in Job. She writes:

When you lose someone you love, heaven becomes much more of a reality, much more than a theological concept or theatrical cliché. In the midst of his suffering, Job's deepest desire is not just for the suffering to end but for eternity in the presence of God to begin. I have come to the place where I believe a yearning for heaven is one of the purposes and one of the privileges of suffering and of losing someone you love. I never had the yearning before, but I do now. You see, a piece of me is there. And all too soon, I will have two children waiting for me there. I now see in a much fuller way that this life is just a shadow of our real life—of eternal life in the presence of God.[162]

She goes on to say, "Do you find yourself yearning for heaven in the midst of your sorrow or difficulty? Perhaps that is a part of the purpose in your pain—a new perspective, a proper perspective, about life on this earth and the life after."[163] Her thoughts are worth pondering.

This verse in Job is powerful. When we read Job, we may get lost in all the dialogue, but we must remember that Job lost all of his children. He certainly had his eye toward eternity. Job says his heart yearns within him. My heart yearns within me to see Jesus. I know Don and Dad are with Our Redeemer now, and every day I wonder what they are doing. But I know Dad and Don are better by far just as your loved one is. God is in control, and I know I will see Jesus myself. I know I will be reunited with Don and with Dad. We will have an eternity to worship Jesus with our loved ones. How my heart yearns within me. I am waiting on that day!

What are your thoughts on the verse and the quote by Nancy Guthrie?

---

[162] Nancy Guthrie, *Holding On to Hope: A Pathway Through Suffering to the Heart of God* (Wheaton, IL: Tyndale, 2002), Location 419.

[163] Ibid., 438.

DAY 142

The time came when the beggar died and the angels carried him to Abraham's side. The rich man also died and was buried. In Hades, where he was in torment, he looked up and saw Abraham far away, with Lazarus by his side. (Luke 16:22-23, NIV)

I love the thought of the angel carrying our loved ones to Heaven. I love the thought of an angel carrying me to Heaven. In a number of the books I read on Heaven, these verses in Luke were included for obvious reasons. There is a lot we can learn about Heaven in this passage. For one, many people do not think this was a parable but an actual event. Why? Randy Alcorn explains it best:

Did you know that this is the only parable Jesus told in which he gave a specific name to someone in the story? Naming Lazarus suggests that Jesus was speaking of a real man who had that name.... Perhaps Jesus intended for us to picture people in the afterlife as real humans with thoughts and capacities (and perhaps even forms), and with the same identity, memories and awareness from their lives on earth.[164]

I had never thought about the fact that it might not be a parable. But after reading Alcorn and others, I have to agree it is most likely not a parable, but indeed a true story. However, whether this is a parable or not, there is still a lot we can learn from this passage; it was important enough for Jesus to tell us about. In the book *Heaven*, Alcorn talks a lot about what we can learn from this passage in its entirety. But the people in this passage, as Alcorn points out, have a clear identity, memories of their family, and of their actions on Earth. Even the man in Hades is presented as caring about his family on Earth. How much more would those in Heaven be caring? There is so much to take from these verses. And continuity is one of them. Continuity of our identity, our memories, our thoughts, our family, and our life as we knew it is clearly shown here in these verses. I hold to all these truths we find in these verses. I find the message so reassuring. Your loved one is your loved one. He is safe in Heaven. The very thing that make them the people we love is still there and will still be when we join our loved ones in Heaven. And we will still be us. The reunion will be awesome. We are waiting on that day!

What are your thoughts and feelings on these verses? What are your thoughts on this being an actual event not a parable?

---

[164]   Randy Alcorn, *Heaven* (Carol Stream, IL: Tyndale House, 2004), 63.

DAY 143

Now the one who has fashioned us for this very purpose is God, who has given us the Spirit as a deposit, guaranteeing what is to come. (2 Corinthians 5:5, NIV)

To know we have a deposit that guarantees us Heaven is amazing. The Holy Spirit is our guarantee. In *Disappointment with God*, Philip Yancey writes, "The Spirit will not remove all disappointment with God. The very titles given to the Spirit—Intercessor, Helper, Counselor, Comforter—imply there will be problems. A deposit guaranteeing what is to come."[165] What is to come? He goes on to say, "The Spirit reminds us that such disappointment is temporary, a prelude to an eternal life with God.... But the Spirit whispers of a new reality, a fantasy that is actually true, one into which we wake for eternity."[166]

Remember there is an eternal plan and God has a purpose. We have the Holy Spirit as a deposit guaranteeing us of this eternal plan. It helped me as I read *Disappointment with God* to be reminded to look at all of life through the eternal lens. The very titles the Holy Spirit is given does imply there will be problems here in this life. But we have the hope and that guarantee of what is to come.

As the pain envelopes you, hold on to that guarantee, that promise of eternity. The purpose of God that we see unfolding in history and in events now is crucial to hold to. As believers we will take part in God's eternal purpose and the New Heaven and New Earth. If we lose sight of the eternal perspective, we cannot handle the pain. But knowing we have that guarantee and knowing it will be glorious gives us the peace that comes from God. He has an eternal plan. We have to look through our eternal lens to see the guarantee of what it to come. We are waiting on that day!

How does this verse speak to you? What are your thoughts on the fact that the titles of the Holy Spirit remind us there will be problems here? How does the thought of knowing that you have a guarantee comfort you?

---

[165] Phillip Yancey, *Disappointment with God* (Grand Rapids, MI: Zondervan, 1992), 67.

[166] Ibid., 167.

DAY 144

Who then is the one who condemns? No one. Christ Jesus who died—more than that, who was raised to life—is at the right hand of God and is also interceding for us. (Romans 8:34, NIV)

It is a beautiful picture to think of Christ interceding for us. I tried to imagine Jesus interceding as I was praying. I admit sometimes picturing Jesus interceding can be hard to imagine. When you are blinded by pain it is hard to imagine anything but your own pain. But we know there is spiritual warfare going on all around us. We know that we are loved and that Jesus sees our pain, knows our very thoughts, and knows our heart; so we know He is interceding for us. To know He intercedes for us is something to hold on to. Because of His death and resurrection we are not condemned but are promised life eternal.

Philip Yancey says, "I fall back on the promise that Jesus prays for me—as he did for Peter—not that I would never face testing, nor even fail, but that in the end I would allow God to use the testing and failure to mold me into someone more useful for the kingdom, someone more like Jesus."[167]

Perhaps even as Christ is interceding for us, so are our loved ones. I tried to imagine Jesus interceding for me, and that perhaps even Don and Dad interceding for our family. It is hard to be here without our loved ones with us. Yet somehow we must be where we can continue to glorify God and further His kingdom. Knowing that Christ is interceding for us can help strengthen us. We can find comfort in these words. We are loved, and Christ is at the right hand of God interceding for us. Jesus loves us and He is ever interceding, and someday He will bring us Home. We are waiting on that day!

What are your thoughts and feelings on this verse? How does imagining Christ interceding for you comfort you? What are your thoughts of your loved one interceding for you?

---

[167] Philip Yancey, *Prayer: Does It Make a Difference?* (Grand Rapids, MI: Zondervan, 2006), 88.

DAY 145

For as in Adam all die, so in Christ all will be made alive. But each in turn: Christ, the firstfruits; then, when he comes, those who belong to him. Then the end will come, when he hands over the kingdom to God the Father after he has destroyed all dominion, authority and power. For he must reign until he has put all his enemies under his feet. (1 Corinthians 15:22-25, NIV)

Adam brought sin into the world, and with sin came death. But Christ brought life, eternal life. Jesus is the firstfruit. And because of Jesus, we who receive Him as our Savior will also receive everlasting life. We belong to Jesus; because we belong to Him and because He has dominion we are promised eternal life. In the book *Heaven*, Randy Alcorn writes:

Christ's mission is both to redeem what was lost in the Fall and to destroy all competitors to God's dominion, authority and power. When everything is put under his feet, when God rules all and mankind rules the earth as kings under Christ, the King of kings, at last all will be as God intends. The period of rebellion will be over forever, and the universe, and all who serve Christ, will participate in the Master's joy![168]

As we focus on the eternal plan we hold to the fact that death will be destroyed. This was the plan from the beginning. Christ will put all His enemies under His feet. Satan will be no more; death will be no more. We will all live with Christ on the New Earth. And since we know there is continuity, we know that I will still be me, you will still be you, Don is Don, my dad is my dad, Bob. And your loved one is still _____. And since we know this, we know we will live together in continuity in a world that is no longer under the curse. We will see Jesus, and know Him fully. We are waiting on that day!

As you meditate on these verses, how do they speak to you? What are your thoughts on the continuity of who we are? How does that bring you comfort?

---

[168] Randy Alcorn, *Heaven* (Carol Stream, IL: Tyndale House, 2004), 93.

DAY 146

As the deer pants for streams of water, so my soul pants for you, my God.
My soul thirsts for God, for the living God.
When can I go and meet with God? (Psalm 42:1-2, NIV)

Reading back through the Psalms, this verse spoke to me. When God seems silent, you do pant for Him and you do thirst for Him. You do want to go and meet with God. This verse was so on target for how I was longing to hear from Him. I quote this passage often, but the question seems to still be, "When can I go and meet with God?" Set aside time to spend with God away from the distraction of TV or anything else that you may be allowing to distract you. Find a time that you can set aside to read the Bible and pray. Meditate on the verses you read. If you don't know where to start, start with the Psalms. The Psalms are full of times when David and other psalmists cried out to God in their darkness.

When we are truly thirsty for water, nothing satisfies but water, and we actively pursue finding that drink. There are times now when you are thirsty for God but can't find Him. Making that time to spend focused on Him, even if you do not feel Him, is important. If you do not know what to pray, pray the Lord's Prayer, pray for others, pray a psalm, or just pray His name. Don't give up, just like you would not give up looking for the water. When can I go and meet with God? We can set that time aside now to meet with Him, but we know that someday we will truly go and meet with Him.

We know that our believing loved ones have truly met with God. Until the day that you and I can go meet with God in Heaven, we must truly thirst for Him here. When we do, we must make sure we have set that time aside to pray and to listen. Ask God to let you hear Him and then look and listen.

What does this verse say to you? Have you set aside times to spend in His presence? What are you doing to hear Him?

DAY 147 REFLECTION

As you read over the last week, what speaks to you? We read verses that speak of Job, a father, yearning for Heaven. What were your thoughts on Nancy Guthrie's statements? I thought her words on our yearning being a part of the purpose of our pain to be very interesting. Our loss does give us a new perspective—the proper perspective as Nancy says. Our loss snaps our attention to Heaven and we yearn for that day.

We read verses that show a clear consciousness in eternity, one that speaks of continuity, of care and concern for family. I find the thoughts by Randy Alcorn, and shared by several other authors that suggest that Luke 16:22-23 is not a parable very interesting. The verses in Luke are a clear statement of continuity of life and relationships. If someone in Hades has care and concerns for his family, then how much more will that be true for our loved ones in Heaven? I find great comfort in these verses.

We read the Holy Spirit is given as a guarantee of what is to come and the eternal plan. We also read that Christ is the firstfruit, and He interceding for us, which speaks of the eternal plan and His eternal love for His children. And we see David yearning and thirsting to meet with God, which encourages us to set aside time to spend with God so we can hear Him. These are all powerful verses. Which ones bring you the most comfort? As you reflect back over the week, record your thoughts and feelings.

DAY 148

The Lord appeared to us in the past, saying: "I have loved you with an everlasting love; I have drawn you with unfailing kindness." (Jeremiah 31:3, NIV)

Jeremiah is prophesying to the Israelites about to go into captivity; they will be in captivity for seventy years. But God is assuring the faithful remnant that He loves them with an everlasting love. God loves you with an everlasting love. Our focus must always be on the eternal perspective. All of humanity is marching in the direction of eternity. But what you can't lose sight of is that God does love you. God loves the one He called Home.

You are hurting and perhaps feel far away from God right now. You may wonder how He loves you if you are hurting this much. But if we look at God from a timeless perspective we know this dot in time is just a small part of eternity. The best is yet to come. He loves us. He loves you. He loves those He has called Home. Remind yourself of God's love. Ask God to let you feel His love. But don't lose sight of the fact that He loves you with an *everlasting* love. God's love will not end. Think of the words to Comfort Manyame song, "Watching over you":

> I'm watching over you,
> Even though it seems I am so far away
> I'm watching over you,
> I'm as close to you as the next breath that you take
> I'm watching over you,
> I've been wiping every tear drop from your face
> I'm watching over you, In your darkest night my light will shine the way
> I love you, and I will never let you go[169]

God loves you with an everlasting love. He draws us with unfailing kindness. He will never let us go.

What are your thoughts and feelings on this verse? How does focusing on God's love help you right now? What are your thoughts to the words from "Watching Over You"?

---

[169] Comfort Manyame, "Watching Over You." *Draw Me Near.* Comfort Manyame, 2010.

DAY 149

Trust in him at all times, you people; pour out your hearts to him, for God is our refuge. (Psalm 62:8, NIV)

It is okay to pour out your heart to God. He hears you. Just remember to keep trusting Him as you do. I continue to pour my heart out to God every day. I can't help but do that. There are times when I say things I might not want to say in front of anyone else, but I know I can say them to God. He knows my heart anyway. But that is okay, because God wants us to pour our hearts out to Him. Quoting this verse, Greg Laurie writes:

In the same way, even in our worst pain, we should cry out to God. Sometimes you and I don't do that. Sometimes we allow trouble and trauma and hardship to cause us to be angry with God, so that we withdraw from Him and don't want to talk to Him. No, my friend, that's why you need Him more than ever! Cry out to Him with your doubts. Cry out to Him with your pain. He will patiently and lovingly hear you. He might set your crooked thinking straight as you seek Him, but He wants you to pour out your pain. He loves you. [170]

Notice the first part of this verse: "Trust in Him at all times." We will have hard times. It is much easier to trust in the easy times. But when it comes to something like what you are facing right now, a hard time doesn't even seem to sum it up. It is devastating. However, it is more important than ever to trust God. He has an eternal plan. This life is just a miniscule part of God's eternal plan. The real action is in Heaven. However, this life does matter. What we do here while we are alive goes into eternity, but the time here is short in comparison to eternity. God knows how hard this loss will be in our limited perspective though, and He is okay with us crying out to Him. He is our refuge. We just have to trust Him no matter what we feel at the time. We need Him more than ever, and He wants us to pour our hearts out to Him; He is our refuge.

What are your thoughts and feelings on this verse? What are your thoughts and feelings on Greg Laurie's statement?

---

[170] Greg Laurie, *Hope for Hurting Hearts* (Dana Point, CA: Kerygma, 2008), 26.

DAY 150

You keep track of all my sorrows. You have collected all my tears in your bottle. You have recorded each one in your book. (Psalm 56:8, NLT)

This Psalm is very comforting. Mark Talbot writes,

But God, David knows, has kept count of his nightly tossings; he has numbered his futile wanderings; he has kept track of all of David's sorrow. He has put David's tears in a bottle and written all of his anguish in his book. And David knows that the God who cares for him that much will not abandon him. 'This I know,' he declares, 'that God is for me.'[171]

It is easy to wonder if God really cares how much you are hurting, especially if you do not feel Him. But He does and He keeps track of our tears. God loves us so much that He gave us His son. This sorrow and this pain is not the end of the story. Mark goes on to say:

Moreover, we will not always, right now, have these answers for ourselves. But in glory the answers will be clear, when we see Jesus face to face. Then we will see that God has indeed done all that he pleased and has done it all perfectly, both for his glory and our good, for the light of Jesus' countenance—in that light of life'—we will see that through our sufferings our loving Father has been conforming us to the likeness of his Son.[172]

So go ahead and cry, recognize your sorrow is a natural part of your love. But also recognize that God loves you. As Comfort Manyame sings:

I'm watching over you, I've been wiping every tear drop from your face[173]

And as Steven Curtis Chapman sings:

He'll wipe every tear from our eyes
And make everything new, Just like He promised Wait and see[174]

Our tears may continue to flow but God continues to love us.

What are your thoughts on this verse? On God's storing your tears?

---

[171] Mark R. Talbot, "All the Good that is Ours in Christ," John Piper and Justin Taylor (Ed). *Suffering and the Sovereignty of God*, (Wheaton, IL: Crossway, 2006), 76.
[172] Ibid., 77.
[173] Comfort Manyame, "Watching Over You." *Draw Me Near.* Comfort Manyame, 2010.
[174] Steven Curtis Chapman, "See." *Beauty Will Rise.* Sparrow, 2008.

DAY 151

And He said to him, "Truly I say to you, today you shall be with Me in Paradise." (Luke 23:43, NASB)

In his book *One Minute After You Die*, Erwin Lutzer writes:

What can we expect one minute after we die? While relatives sorrow on earth, you will find yourself in new surrounding which just now are beyond our imagination. Most probably, you will have seen angels who have been assigned the responsibility of escorting you to your destination, just as the angels who carried Lazarus into Abraham's bosom.[175]

Paul Enns writes,

But in moments the pain and misery [of the thief] would transition to unspeakable glory and joy. Not some time in the future but this very day... only moments away... he would breathe celestial air. As Oswald Sanders has said, 'The moment we take the last breath on earth, we take our first breath in heaven.'[176]

Although we are in sorrow here, our believing loved ones are not. The more I try to focus on the joy Dad and Don were experiencing, the more I can try to shift from my own pain. We see darkness and overwhelming pain. Our loved ones see glorious surroundings, they see Jesus face to face, and they see Paradise. We too will see glorious surroundings, we too will see Jesus face to face, and we too will see Paradise. And we will be reunited with our loved ones. As Mercy Me sings in "Homesick":

> In Christ, there are no goodbyes
> And in Christ, there is no end
> So I'll hold onto Jesus with all that I have
> To see you again
> To see you again[177]

Today your loved one is with Jesus in Paradise. When Jesus is ready, we will be in Paradise. We are waiting on that day!

What are your thoughts and feelings on the verse and quotes?

---

[175] Erwin Lutzer, *One Minute After You Die* (Chicago, IL: Moody, 1997), 63.

[176] Paul Enns, He*aven Revealed* (Chicago, IL: Moody, 2011), 41- 42

[177] Comfort Manyame, "Watching Over You." *Draw Me Near*. Comfort Manyame, 2010.

DAY 152

Furthermore, because we are united with Christ, we have received an inheritance from God, for he chose us in advance, and he makes everything work out according to his plan. (Ephesians 1:11, NLT)

Because we are united with Christ, we have received an inheritance from God. That inheritance includes Heaven and eternity. God makes all of history work out according to His plan. Anthony Hoekama's thoughts on this verse:

God is in control of history. This does not mean that he manipulates men as if they were puppets; man's freedom to make his own decisions and his responsibility for the decisions are at all times maintained. But it does mean that God overrules even the evil deeds of men so as to make them serve his purpose.[178]

There are many bad things that happen in this world, and it is hard to understand why. But this world as we know it is not all there is. God will work everything out to His final plan. This part of history that we see is a small part of history. It is a huge part of history to you; it is your life. But in His plan, everything comes together in eternity. We shall know Jesus fully, and understand so much more. Then, and only then, will all of this we do not understand now make sense. We know we will understand, because we have an inheritance from God. Because of this inheritance we have security in knowing that no matter what happens here, God is in control. In this huge plan that has been unfolding since the beginning of time, we can only see a small part. But the eternal plan is so much bigger than any of us can imagine. If we focus just on this dot of time, it becomes crushing. But we recognize that when we were united to Christ, we became a part of something so much bigger. We now have an inheritance that is a part of God's plan, and everything will work out according to His plan; we hold to that promise.

Do we understand it all? No, but we do know we can trust God. When all else fails, we hold to that trust and to that promise. Our believing loved ones have taken a part of their inheritance. They have seen Jesus face to face; they are in Heaven surrounded by His glory. Our loved ones see so much more than we do now. We just have to hold to these promises until the day we are called to see our inheritance. We are waiting on that day.

What are your thoughts and feelings on this verse? Does focusing on an eternal plan and our inheritance comfort you? Why or why not?

---

[178] Anthony A. Hoekema, *The Bible and the Future* (Grand Rapids, MI: Eerdmans, 1979), 27.

DAY 153

Now may our Lord Jesus Christ himself and God our Father, who loved us and by his grace gave us eternal comfort and a wonderful hope, comfort you and strengthen you in every good thing you do and say. (2 Thessalonians 2:16-17, NLT)

We have eternal comfort and hope through the grace of God. Our comfort and hope comes from and will last forever; it is eternal. It is because we have eternal hope that we can even have comfort. Without the knowledge of eternity, what hope would there be? People can say our loved ones live on in our memories. Well, it is great to have memories. I am so blessed to have the wonderful memories that I do. Memories are comforting, but the true comfort lies in eternity. The true comfort is not that you have those wonderful memories or that your loved one's legacy lives on, which is great, but the true comfort lies in our eternal comfort and hope. The true comfort comes in knowing we will be reunited with them; they are more alive than ever.

As Paul Tripp writes, "Suffering temporarily steals our comfort and pleasure. But forever guarantees that all of this is temporary. Eternity tells every child of God that the bulk of our existence will be lived in a place of eternal peace, rest, and joy. Life in the hereafter, with all of its perfect beauty, will be eternal."[179] We do take comfort in our memories, but when we know that our loved ones are with our Savior we can truly have comfort. We take comfort in knowing that our loved ones are in Heaven, and knowing where they are can strengthen us now. We know we will be reunited with our loved ones and that we have eternity to worship God together. Allow God to comfort you now with those thoughts, and allow that to strengthen you to make it through the day, knowing that you will step into eternity yourself when He calls you Home. We are waiting on that day!

How does this verse speak to you? What are your thoughts on Paul Tripp's statement?

---

[179] Paul Tripp, *Forever Why You Can't Live Without It* (Grand Rapids, MI: Zondervan, 2011), Location 1736.

DAY 154 REFLECTION

Reading back over the last week, what do you find the most comforting? We read verses that show us God loves us with an everlasting love. When we reflect on God's everlasting love and unfailing kindness, we can truly feel comforted. There may be times we do not feel His love. But when we reflect on our lives and relationships with those we love, we *know* we are loved. We *know* God's kindness is unfailing. We read verses that tell us God wants us to tell Him how we feel, to pour out our hearts to Him, and that He is our refuge. God loves us so much that He knows each tear we shed. These verses all together show us God's love, His eternal love.

We read verses that show us we go immediately to be with Jesus as we draw our last breath. These same verses reassure us where our believing loved ones are; they are with Jesus in Paradise. We read verses that tell us God gives us eternal comfort; that we have eternal comfort and an inheritance. It is amazing to see all the verses that talk about eternity. God is eternal. He loves us, He comforts us, and He knows our tears. He has an eternal plan which is crucial for us to hold to. God is eternal, and His love and comfort are eternal. All of these verses help us focus on an eternal perspective. All of these verses remind us this short span of time we are on Earth, is not all there is. We have an eternity with our loving God. We will have an eternity with our loved ones praising God and His unfailing love and kindness. We are waiting on that day! As you reflect on the last week, record your thoughts and feelings. What seems to speak to you the most?

DAY 155

But I trust in you, Lord; I say, "You are my God." My times are in your hands;
(Psalm 31:14-15a, NIV)

David was running from enemies and yet affirming that no matter what, God
is his God and he will trust Him. Steven Curtis Chapman sings:

> You are my God, and I'll trust You
> And with every breath I take
> And for every day that breaks
> I will trust You
> I will trust You
> And when nothing is making sense
> Even then I will say again[180]

There are days that all you will be able to say is, "You are my God and I trust
you." In the darkness when nothing makes sense, remember your life is in His
hands. He is your God, and despite feelings of fear and doubt, you must trust
Him. Sing it, say it, write it. Your believing loved one's life was in God's hands,
and He took him Home. There is a day we will all go Home.

None of us wants to think about death happening when we are enjoying
life here, and it is precisely because we get so caught up in this life that we forget
this time here is temporary. The translation used in today's Bible verse says, "My
times are in your hands." Our times can mean our life, our future… everything
about us. The bottom line is that God is in control and we have to trust Him.
Jerry Sittser writes:

My despondent mood casts a shadow over everything, even over my faith. On
those occasions I find it hard to believe anything at all. But then I gain perspective.
I remind myself that suffering is not unique to us. It is the destiny of humanity. If
this world were the only one there is, then suffering has the final say and all of us
are a sorry lot, but generations of faithful Christians have gone before and will come
after, and they have believed or will believe what I believe in the depths of my soul.
Jesus is the center of it all. He defeated sin and death through his crucifixion and
resurrection.[181]

We do have to gain perspective, an eternal perspective. Like David, even though
we are despondent, we know that God is our God. Trust Him.

How do the verses and quotes speak to you today?

---

[180] Steven Curtis Chapman, "I Will Trust You." *Beauty Will Rise*. Sparrow, 2008.
[181] Jerry Sittser, *A Grace Disguised: Expanded Edition* (Grand Rapids, MI: Zondervan, 2004), 169.

DAY 156

I have told you all this so that you may have peace in me. Here on earth you will have many trials and sorrows. But take heart, because I have overcome the world. (John 16:33, NLT)

Jesus told us we would have trials and sorrows. We were never promised we would not have sorrows. This fallen world guarantees trials and sorrows. But the good news is Christ has overcome the world, and He tells us because of that we have peace in Him. Peace—true peace—can only come from Jesus. Anything else is fleeting. In *Disappointment with God*, Philip Yancey writes:

Jesus offered no immunity, no way *out* of the unfairness, but rather a way *through* to the other side. Just as Good Friday demolished the instinctive belief that this life is supposed to be fair, Easter Sunday followed with its startling clue to the riddle of the universe. Out of the darkness a bright light shone.... We need more than a miracle. We need a new heaven and a new earth, and until we have those, unfairness will not disappear.[182]

No matter what happens in this fallen world, Jesus has overcome it. Because He has overcome the world we have the promise of peace that comes from Him. He has our believing loved ones with Him right now. Someday we will be with Him as well. Someday we will all be together on the New Heaven and the New Earth. Our focus is on the eternal perspective. Jesus prepared His disciples for the trials and sorrows they would face. Take heart even in your pain and sorrow now. I know how overwhelming the pain can be. I am amazed at how heavy sorrow is, and yet along with the heaviness comes a cavern of emptiness. It seems like something empty should not be so heavy. But sorrow is like that and it is relentless. Jesus knew that we would have sorrow, and He prepares us with the best answer possible. He has overcome the world!

What does this verse say to you? How would you describe sorrow? How does knowing that Jesus prepared His own disciples for their sorrow allow you to see there is an answer?

---

[182] Phillip Yancey, *Disappointment with God* (Grand Rapids, MI: Zondervan, 1992), 207.

DAY 157

Jesus responded, "Didn't I tell you that you would see God's glory if you believe?" (John 11:40, NLT)

This verse in John is in response to Martha's concern that if Jesus rolled the stone back on her brother's grave, there would be a terrible smell. Can you imagine what she must have been feeling? The pain and the sorrow of her brother's death, and now Jesus was saying to roll back the stone. Dare she get her hopes up? Logic says, "It has been four days; this could be a disaster." But Jesus' response is, "Didn't I tell you that you would see God's glory if you believe?" Dr. Terveen writes:

John ties everything back to Jesus' focus on *God's glory* announced at the beginning of the story. To see the glory of God means to see the greater things God was doing in the life of Jesus. Lazarus's death and raising points ahead to Jesus' death and resurrection, the 'glory of God' through which God will bring life to everyone who believed in Jesus. We dare not miss the point. Jesus possesses in himself the sovereign authority and power to give life. 'See me and believe in me.' Jesus is saying and you are seeing the 'glory of God.' You, too, can inherit life forevermore through trusting in me. I am the resurrection and life.[183]

You are reading this because someone you love very much has entered Heaven. And the reason our loved ones can enter Heaven is because they trusted in Christ as their Lord and Savior. Jesus tells us if we believe we will see God's glory. Our loved ones are in God's glory now. We have to hold to what we believe. Dr. Terveen goes on to say,

I also believe that the sign of Lazarus and his loved one's reunion points to Jesus performing a far greater reuniting of those who have believed in him. He will bring us back together again, to live with one another in heaven. Is it any wonder we who believe long to go to heaven? It is our blessed hope.[184]

Let Dr. Terveen's beautiful words of blessed hope sink in. We will be all brought together again with our loved ones to live with one another in Heaven. How amazing is that statement? We are waiting on that day!

How does this verse speak to you? What are your thoughts and feelings on Dr. Terveen's statements?

---

[183] John Luke Terveen, *Hope for the Brokenhearted* (Colorado Springs, CO: Victor, 2006), 107.

[184] Ibid., 107.

DAY 158

The LORD will protect you from all evil; He will keep your soul. The LORD will guard your going out and your coming in From this time forth and forever. (Psalm 121:7-8, NASB)

We read verses like this and think, "Well, then why am I hurting? God did not protect my loved one." If this life were all there is, that would well be true. But notice what He is protecting us from is "all evil." And notice He will keep our soul from this time forth and forever. Clearly the psalmist did not expect to live forever, so what does this mean? I think we have to look at the eternal perspective. God protects believers from the evil one. We live in a fallen world with constant spiritual warfare. But God is sovereign and no matter what the devil may throw at us, God will protect us from evil. He keeps our soul. He guards our going out and coming in from this time forth and forevermore. He guarded our loved ones straight into His glory. He has their soul. He has our soul and will guard it straight into His glory.

During this time of pain God will guard you from the evil one. We know this is a time of spiritual warfare. The first part of this chapter states, "I will lift up my eyes to the mountains; from where does my help come? My help comes from the LORD who made heaven and earth." In "Praise You in the Storm," Casting Crowns sing:

> I raise my hands and praise the God who gives
> And takes away
> I lift my eyes unto the hills
> Where does my help come from?
> My help comes from the Lord
> The Maker of Heaven and Earth[185]

Lift your eyes to the maker of Heaven and Earth. He sees your pain; He knows what you are going through. He is guarding you and protecting you from evil. He will keep your soul from now into eternity, just like He has our loved ones. Our loved ones are safe, truly safe, because they are with Jesus, just as we will be when Jesus calls us Home. We are waiting on that day!

How does this verse speak to you? What is the hardest part for you in keeping your eyes on Him?

---

[185] Casting Crowns, "Praise You in This Storm." *LifeSong.* Reunion Records, 2005.

DAY 159

Keep me as the apple of your eye; hide me in the shadow of your wings. (Psalm 17:8, NIV)

Apple of your eye "refers to the pupil, a delicate part of the eye that is essential for vision and that therefore must be protected at all costs."[186] God referred to Israel as the apple of His eye. David prayed that God would keep him as the apple of His eye. Don read this and began to pray that we would always put God first and be the apple of each other's eye. He would say that with God as our center focus and each other second, our relationship would always stay God-centered and therefore be strong. And our marriage stayed strong. We are one in every way: spiritually, physically, and emotionally. As I was reading this the memories of this special part of our relationship filled my heart.

We can take comfort in knowing that God does protect us. He loves us as the apple of His eye. The words "shadow of your wings" is a metaphor for protection. We know God loves us and protects us. No matter how much we hurt now, we are protected for eternity. God will keep us as the apple of His eye and under the shadow of His wings until He calls us Home. We may suffer here, but nothing will happen that is beyond His reach.

A few days after God called Don Home, my friend Vi recommended a song called "Draw Me Near." I started looking for the song she suggested. I "stumbled" on an album by the same name, "Draw Me Near," by Comfort Manyame that had a song "Watching Over You." I listened even though it was not the song she meant for me. As I listened, my tears flowed. The words were beautiful even before I got to the part that included the words, "apple of my eye." Since those were Don's and my words to each other, I felt as if God were comforting me with this song. It wasn't by accident I found this song:

> Even though it seems I am so far away
> I'm watching over you,
> I'm as close to you as the next breath that you take
> I'm watching over you,
> I've been wiping every tear drop from your face
> I'm watching over you, In your darkest night my light will shine the way
> I love you, and I will never let you go
> I'll carry you, and every burden that you bear
> You are the apple of my eye[187]

Allow the power of the Psalm and the song to wash over you. God loves you.

---

[186] NIV Study Bible, Kenneth Barker Ed. (Grand Rapids, MI: Zondervan, 1985), 283.
[187] Comfort Manyame, "Watching Over You." *Draw Me Near.* Comfort Manyame, 2010.

DAY 160

I give them eternal life, and they shall never perish; no one will snatch them out of my hand. My Father, who has given them to me, is greater than all; no one can snatch them out of my Father's hand. (John 10:28-29, NIV)

When we receive Christ as our Savior we are given eternal life. We will not perish; no one can snatch us away. God is greater than any force around us, including death. We have this promise. We have this assurance of His care. As we keep an eternal perspective, we can find comfort. Many people point to this verse to show the security of the believer. If your loved one received Christ as his Savior, he is secure in His hands. We live in a fallen world, and many times bad things happen that we cannot understand or explain. But if you hold to our promise of eternal life, then you can know that despite what happens here, despite the influence of a fallen world, God holds us securely. God's grace covers those who are His children.

Hold to thoughts of Heaven and eternity and know that we have security as believers. Our security lies in Christ. Nothing this world or the devil throws at us can stop the love of Jesus. Jesus' Words of eternal life are powerful. Your believing loved one entered in eternity. There are a number of devotionals in this book that talk about trusting God and that God is faithful. What do we trust Him about? This verse is one of the very things that remind us what it means to trust Him. We trust that Jesus has us securely with Him and nothing can separate us. Jesus has been telling His listeners that He is the shepherd and those who receive Him are His sheep. When we receive Christ as our Savior this is our promise. We trust that Jesus has us in His hands. We trust that we have eternal life. We trust our children are with Him. We trust that our loved ones are with Him. We trust that we are so secure that no one can snatch us from our Father's hands because He is greater than all. Our loved ones are safe in His arms. They have crossed into the Heavenly realm. God is greater than all. Trust Him.

What are your thoughts and feelings on this verse? How does the security of the Father's hand comfort you?

DAY 161 REFLECTION

Looking back at the last week, what seems to speak to you? We read verses that remind us our life is in God's hands. We must trust Him to hold us. We read Jesus' own words that we will have trials and sorrows, but we also read His own words that tell us He has overcome the world. It is a powerful thought to remind ourselves, Jesus has overcome the world. Jesus tells us that if we believe we will see God's glory. We also read Luke Terveen's words that the story of Lazarus is a far greater statement. We will all be brought together again with our loved ones in Heaven. We are waiting on that day!

We read verses that remind us the Lord protects us from evil and brings us to Him forever. As we read these words in Psalm 121 we might wonder if that includes us. We may not feel protected right now. However, we know that He does guard us. He protects us straight to Him.

We read that we are the apple of His eye which means He loves and protects us. I truly believe that God directed me to the song "Watching Over You." He knew what I needed at that moment and He was reassuring me of His love and of Don's. My editor suggested I change the words, "We are one in every way" to we were one. But I choose to leave it at we are. I believe Don and I are still one. I cried as I listened to this song the very first day. I have listened to "Watching Over You" every day since Don went Home. God's loving kindness in giving me this song is powerful to me. This verse in the Psalms tells us that we are loved. God loves us. We are the apple of His eye. He is watching over you now.

And lastly we read that we are secure in Jesus. Nothing can snatch us out of His hand. These verses in John give us comfort and security. All these verses remind us of God's eternal purpose and plans. We will see His glory. We will be with Him forever. He has an eternal plan. Our loved ones have entered into His glory; we will join them. We are waiting on that day. Focusing on the words of the last week, record your thoughts and feelings. What do you feel like God is laying on your heart this week?

DAY 162

But the plans of the Lord stand firm forever,
the purposes of his heart through all generations. (Psalm 33:11, NIV)

Once again we see the plans of the Lord will stand firm forever. His purpose is through all the generations. When we focus on His eternal plan, we are able to feel the firmness, the stability, the security. Asher Intrater writes:

I believe the Bible to be true and trustworthy. As such, it must be internally consistent from Genesis through to Revelation. Genesis starts with the creation of heaven and earth; Revelation ends with the creation of the new heavens and the new earth. What God intended in the beginning is brought to completion in the end.[188]

Intrater quotes a Shabbat Hymn from the 16th century in which the Rabbis say, "What is final in deed is first in thought."[189]

From the beginning of time God's plan was conceived and throughout the Bible we see how that plan unfolded. As believers, we are a part of that plan, but our part is a small part of the whole plan. We have to be able to look beyond this part that we are in, and trust that all of this is working toward that eternal plan. Someday we will see how this unfolds. In his book *Disappointment with God*, Philip Yancey likens life to a play in which we see what unfolds in front of us, but we can't see what is happening behind the stage. We can only see our part, and sometimes we are not even sure what that is. But that is where reading God's Word and trusting Him comes in. His Word assures us of a plan, and we can see how that plan is unfolding throughout history and how it continues to unfold. Trusting Him when your world has fallen apart is hard, because what you see is devastation, lost dreams, and emptiness. But what you don't see is eternal, and it is planned. We will participate with our loved ones in that eternal, unseen world. For now, we hold to the promise that the purposes of His heart stand firm forever.

How does this verse speak to you? What are your thoughts on the statement by Asher Intrater?

---

[188] Asher Intrater, *Who Ate Lunch With Abraham?* (Peoria, AZ: Intermedia, 2011), IV. Website: www.reviveisrael.org.
[189] Ibid., IV

DAY 163

And God raised us up with Christ and seated us with him in the heavenly realms in Christ Jesus, in order that in the coming ages he might show the incomparable riches of his grace, expressed in his kindness to us in Christ Jesus. (Ephesians 2:6-7, NIV)

Randy Alcorn writes, "As Christians, we're linked to Heaven in ways too deep to comprehend. Somehow, according to Ephesians 2:6, we're already seated with Christ in Heaven. So we can't be satisfied with less."[190] This is not the only verse that says we are already raised with Christ. In Colossians 3:4, Paul writes that our life is hidden in Christ as he exhorts us to think on Heaven. Anthony Hoekema points to this verse among several to point out that, "In the believer's experience, therefore, there is real continuity between this age and the next."[191]

Death is the portal that we must pass through before Heaven, but we are already guaranteed that spot because once we receive Christ as our Savior we have a place in Heaven. Most authors I read refer to the coming ages as eternity with Christ. The coming age will be on the New Earth. During the ages to come He will show us, or reveal to us even more of the incomparable riches of His grace. There is so much we cannot see or understand right now on this Earth. Even focusing on Heaven and eternity, the pain and sorrow continues unrelentingly; but with that pain is the assurance of the coming ages. We have the assurance that Heaven is our true Home. The assurances of eternal life can comfort us in our pain, because we know our loved ones are already there in Christ's presence, already seeing so much more than we can imagine. We also know that we will be with them again, and we can all experience the revelation of His incomparable riches. We will have an eternity to learn more and more about the incomparable riches of God. If you ponder the words "incomparable riches," that phrase tells you that God has provided riches for us that have no comparison. And we know it is expressed in Christ Jesus. So we know that heavenly realms are awesome. We can't begin to imagine what our loved ones are experiencing, even though we would like to. We have a taste of wonderful times here with our loved ones, so we know that Heaven will be even more awesome. We are waiting on that day!

How do these verses speak to you? What are your thoughts on the quotes?

---

[190] Randy Alcorn, *Heaven* (Carol Stream, IL: Tyndale House, 2004), 458.
[191] Anthony A. Hoekema, *The Bible and the Future* (Grand Rapids, MI: Eerdmans, 1979), 39.

DAY 164

For I am the Lord your God
who takes hold of your right hand
and says to you, Do not fear;
I will help you. (Isaiah 41:13, NIV)

When I was a little girl I had an active imagination, and I walked and talked in my sleep. One night I vividly remember waking up in the night and not being able to find the door. I was pounding on the wall yelling for help. My dad calmly came into my room and turned on the light, and said, "Ann, I am here." I was standing on my bed at the opposite wall to the door. I felt dumb, but relieved. Grief and sorrow have a way of trapping you in the dark. David Powlison writes:

God seems invisible, silent, far away. Pain and loss cry out loud and long. Faith seems inarticulate. Sorrow and confusion broadcast on all channels. It is hard to remember anything else, hard to put into words what is actually happening, hard to feel any force from who Jesus Christ is.... Pain and threat are completely engrossing. You're caught in a swirl of apprehension, anguish, regret, confusion, bitterness, emptiness and uncertainty.[192]

We know in our best of times that God loves us and tells us not to fear. There have been so many times that I have not felt God and wondered where He was. It has taken me a long time to realize I was pounding in the dark and God was always there. It just takes a long time to hear, "I am here." And sometimes even after you start to feel Him, you lose that feeling just as quickly, because once again the darkness descends on you. But God is the Lord your God; He tells us to not fear—that He will help us. Focus on all the things that allow you to remember His love, and though you may not feel Him or see Him, you still know in your heart He is there holding your hand even in the darkness. You may be like me: pounding on the wall of darkness; but we just have to stop to listen and know that He is with us after all.

How does this verse speak to you? Think and write of a time that you were scared and your own fear kept you from seeing or hearing what you needed.

---

[192] David Powlison, "God's Grace in Your Suffering," John Piper and Justin Taylor (Ed). *Suffering and the Sovereignty of God* (Wheaton, IL: Crossway, 2006), 149.

DAY 165

When Christ, who is your life, appears, then you also will appear with him in glory. (Colossians 3:4, NIV)

When Christ comes again it will be in full glory and as a conqueror. The saints will appear with Him in glory. Wherever Christ is, there is glory in His presence. Certainly the appearance of Christ coming again will be awesome, just as the appearance of Christ is awesome when He calls us Home to Heaven. When I am missing Don at my side and crying, I try to remind myself that Don is in the glory of Jesus right now. No matter how much it hurts here and no matter how much I miss them, Dad and Don are experiencing a glorious presence that we cannot even imagine. I try to focus on how they must look even now. Because Dad and Don have stood in Jesus' presence they must reflect His glory. I wonder what they are doing. I try to think about how it must be for them.

However we read this passage—whether it is the rapture or Christ coming to overthrow Satan and establish His kingdom, to be with Christ is to see His glory. Spurgeon wrote, "The complete personhood of every believer shall be perfected in the glory of Christ."[193] In Heaven we retain who we are, but we are perfected because we are with Christ.

There are a wealth of scriptures that point us to Heaven and eternity. Yet most of the time we move along, not giving Heaven and eternity much thought until someone we love is in Heaven. Now the reality of the brevity of life hits like a ton of bricks, but we have the scriptures to refocus us on eternity. Take heart in all the verses you read that point you to the eternal perspective. Continue to pray for that eternal perspective. Focus on Christ and His glory, where your loved one now is. Continue to focus on what we are all called to focus on: Christ, who is our life. We are waiting on that day!

What are your thoughts and feelings on this verse? Write your thoughts on what appearing with Him in glory might mean to you and your loved ones.

---

[193] Charles Spurgeon, as cited by Randy Alcorn in *We Shall See God* (Carol Stream, IL: Tyndale House, 2011), 201.

DAY 166

His intent was that now, through the church, the manifold wisdom of God should be made known to the rulers and authorities in the heavenly realms, according to his eternal purpose that he accomplished in Christ Jesus our Lord. (Ephesians 3:10-11, NIV)

In the verses right before this passage, Paul talks about God's secret plan or mystery. The mystery was hidden in the past but now revealed. That secret or mystery is God's redemption of the world, Jew and Gentiles through Jesus Christ. Arnold Fruchtenbaum writes, "The mystery which was previously unrevealed was the fact that Jewish and Gentile believers will make up one new entity, the Body of the Messiah, the Church."[194]

Before the beginning of time, God has had His eternal plan and purpose. All of history has moved toward this and is continuing to move. Even the spirit world knows God has an eternal purpose. The same God who plans every detail and has this eternal purpose has us in His plan. Think of all the prophets in the Old Testament who prophesied about the Messiah coming, but weren't quite sure how it would unfold. As we grow closer to the time of Jesus' return, we can see even more clearly how all His purposes are playing out. Take comfort in His sovereignty and His eternal plan. The same God who has us in His plan has _____ safely in His presence.

Remind yourself that we are such a small part of history and yet we, as believers, are included in this eternal plan. We, as believers, are a part of the Church. We have an eternity to learn how this has all unfolded and someday all that we don't understand will all make sense. When we look at the grand scale of eternity and God's eternal plan we can find assurance of His sovereignty and our eternal security with Christ. We will worship again with our loved ones. We are waiting on that day!

How do these verses speak to you? Write your thoughts on the mystery that has been revealed and how you can find assurance in the eternal purpose.

---

[194] Arnold G. Fruchtenbaum, *The Footsteps of the Messiah* (Tustin, CA: Ariel, 2003), 673.

DAY 167

Because God's children are human beings—made of flesh and blood—the Son also became flesh and blood. For only as a human being could he die, and only by dying could he break the power of the devil, who had the power of death. Only in this way could he set free all who have lived their lives as slaves to the fear of dying. (Hebrews 2:14-15, NLT)

This passage in Hebrews is amazing. I really like what Paul Enns has to say about these verses:

What a phenomenal truth! The writer of Hebrews encourages us to not fear death because Jesus Christ destroyed the power of death as if it no longer existed. Those who were enslaved to the fear of death have been set free.... That refers to us! Followers of Jesus set free from the fear of death.[195]

Jesus came in the flesh. The Moody Handbook of Theology states:

Through His death and resurrection Christ has destroyed the power of death. Through the incarnation Jesus took on humanity, died an atoning death for the sins of the world and thereby conquered the adversary who held the power of death.[196]

We no longer need to fear death. Death is ugly and it hurts those of us left behind. But it has no power over the believers. _____ went straight to the presence of our Lord. We do not need to fear death because it is not the end for the believer. Of course we pray for healing because we do not want to be separated from those we love, even for a little bit. Every morning I wake up and the realization hits me again and again that this was not a nightmare I can wake up from on this Earth. The empty place beside me screams at me every morning and night. Everything around me screams the absence of Dad and Don. But this I know, Don and Dad are better than okay. They are with Jesus. Someday I will join them. I am waiting on that day. In the meantime, I pray that I glorify Jesus. He paid the ultimate price so that we do not have to fear death anymore. Even if we die the most horrifying death here, we are still met by Jesus. He has conquered the power of death, and we have the promise of eternal life with Him. We are waiting on that day!

How do these verses speak to you? Write your thoughts on "Jesus Christ destroyed the power of death as if it no longer existed."

---

195 Paul Enns, *Heaven Revealed* (Chicago, IL: Moody, 2011), 34.
196 Paul Enns, *The Moody Handbook of Theology Revised and Expanded* (Chicago, IL: Moody, 2008), 384.

DAY 168 REFLECTION

Read over the last week, what brings you the most comfort? We read that God's eternal plan and purpose of His heart stands firm forever! We read the words, "through all generations." God has an eternal plan and has since before the beginning of time. When we stay focused on this measure of time we can lose sight of that eternal truth. We read a quote from Asher Intrater. He will be quoted more throughout the devotional. I discovered him mid way through writing this book. Asher Intrater is a Messianic Jew and his books and writings are very insightful. His website is www.reviveisrael.org.

We read verses that remind us we are already seated with Christ in Heaven which underscores the continuity of our lives. We read verses that comfort us with the knowledge that God holds our hands. He loves and cares for us even though there are times we may not feel Him. Christ will appear in glory and we will appear with Him in His glory. Our loved ones are already in His glory. These verses speak of the eternal perspective and plan and that the entire heavenly realm knows this plan will come to pass. We read verses that assure us we do not need to fear death. Jesus became flesh and by His death and resurrection, He broke the power of death. He has destroyed death as if it no longer existed. I have quoted Randy Alcorn frequently. His website is www.epm.org. EPM stands for Eternal Perspective Ministries. I encourage you to visit both of the websites and explore the books and writings of both Randy Alcorn and Asher Intrater.

As you reflect back over the week of devotionals, record your thoughts and feelings. What seems to resonate with you the most?

DAY 169

Therefore, since we have so great a cloud of witnesses surrounding us, let us also lay aside every encumbrance and the sin which so easily entangles us, and let us run with endurance the race that is set before us. (Hebrews 12:1, NASB)

Certainly the author of Hebrews has just been talking about the saints in the past who have persevered with faith. But several authors that I read seem to think that the cloud of witnesses can also include our believing loved ones who have gone before us. Randy Alcorn writes:

The imagery seems to suggest that those saints, the spiritual athletes of old, are now watching us and cheering you on from the great stadium of Heaven... The unfolding drama of redemption, awaiting Christ's return, is currently happening on Earth. Earth is center court, center stage, awaiting the consummation of Christ's return and the establishment of his Kingdom. This is a compelling reason to believe that the current inhabitants of Heaven would be able to observe what's happening on Earth.[197]

J. Sidlow Baxter writes, "I think that to be really fair to the passage we must believe that those invisible spectators are said to be watching us *now*. If then, *they* observe us are our departed Christian loved ones debarred from doing so? Is not a reasonable presumption that they too see us, watch us, and know what is happening to us?"[198]

Although not referencing this verse, Joni Erikson's statement relates very well to it. She writes:

Could it be that our loved ones in glory are able to love us now? Pray for us now? Love does not die; it cannot die because it cannot fail. Love is a part of a departed saint's being, not his body, but his person. I'm convinced that Billie now loves her husband Cliff with a purer, holier and more intense love than ever known on earth. And even if she is able to observe the mistakes, blunders, and tears of her loved ones on earth, she has the benefit of an end-of-time view, she is able to see the bigger, better picture.[199]

Maybe the cloud of witnesses does include our loved ones. There is compelling reason to think our loved ones are aware and perhaps praying. Regardless, we must run the race before us until He calls us Home.

What are your thoughts and feelings on the verse and the quotes?

---

[197] Randy Alcorn, *Heaven* (Carol Stream, IL: Tyndale House, 2004), 70.

[198] J. Sidlow Baxter, *The Other Side of Death* (Grand Rapids, MI: Kregel, 1987), 57.

[199] Joni Eareckson Tada, *Heaven: Your Real Home* (Grand Rapids, MI: Zondervan, 1995), 202.

DAY 170

Then the King will say to those on His right, Come, you who are blessed of My Father, inherit the kingdom prepared for you from the foundation of the world. (Matthew 25:34, NASB)

This is an amazing statement: "prepared for you from the foundation of the world." What a clear statement of the eternal plan. This is what Jesus will say as He ushers in the New Heaven and the New Earth for eternity. It is amazing to think this was all planned from the foundation of the world. Randy Alcorn writes:

God hasn't changed His mind; he hasn't fallen back on Plan B or abandoned what he originally intended for us at the creation of the world. When Christ says, 'take your inheritance, the kingdom prepared for you since the creation of the world,' it's as if he's saying, 'This is what I wanted for you all along. This is what I went to the cross and defeated death to give you. Take it, rule it, exercise dominion, enjoy it; and in doing so, share my happiness.[200]

Paul Enns writes:

We hear the word "inherit," and we think of something special that we receive— that someone has passed on to us. But our inheritance through Christ will surpass anything that this has to offer. We are beneficiaries of the glorious kingdom of Christ – living on a perfect earth, enjoying, luxuriating in a perfect world, devoid of all sin. All the prophecies of Christ's glorious kingdom will culminate on the new earth, to be enjoyed by God's people.[201]

Don and Dad are in Heaven, just as _____is in Heaven right now in the presence of Christ. Those we love are still looking forward to the New Earth someday which they and we will enjoy together as a part of our inheritance planned since the foundation of the world. We have all of eternity to explore that New Earth. The reunion of loved ones and the ability to worship together unhindered by sin will be absolutely amazing. When the darkness and pain seem to overtake you, it is okay to cry and mourn because we miss them. But as we look for comfort, look toward this glorious inheritance that is ours. We are waiting on that day!

How does this verse speak to you? Write your thoughts on the quotes.

---

[200] Randy Alcorn, *Heaven* (Carol Stream, IL: Tyndale House, 2004), 102.
[201] Paul Enns, *Heaven Revealed* (Chicago, IL: Moody, 2011), 63.

DAY 171

Remember the things I have done in the past. For I alone am God!
I am God, and there is none like me. Only I can tell you the future before it
even happens. Everything I plan will come to pass, for I do whatever I wish.
(Isaiah 46:9-10, NLT)

God is sovereign. He knows what will happen before it happens. We have to
remember that no matter how bad life looks, no matter how much we hurt and
don't understand, God is sovereign. I don't know your circumstances. I know
that if you are reading this book, you are hurting because someone you love has
gone Home. Maybe your loss involved someone suffering, or maybe it was a
violent death. We cannot understand all that happens here. But we have to hold
to the fact that God is sovereign. There is pain and suffering all around us. John
Piper writes, "The evil and suffering in this world are greater than any of us can
comprehend. But evil and suffering are not ultimate. God is. Satan, the great
lover of evil and suffering, is not sovereign, God is."[202]

Paul Enns writes:

The entire focus of our concern is this life—here and now. But this is incorrect
thinking. The span of our threescore and ten on this earth is but a slight sliver of time
when eternity is considered.... our life does not consist only of our earthly existence.
We are eternal, and the drama of our earthly events must be evaluated alongside a
heavenly perspective. Only then will we come to terms with the difficulties of this
life.[203]

We go to be with Jesus immediately. So the pain and suffering are no more for
those who have gone before us. There will be a reunion someday. There will be a
New Earth and we will live eternally with Jesus and never again will there be death
or suffering. I suspect that then, as we look back, whatever we have gone through
will not look nearly as large as it does now. Now the pain is consuming. I have
talked to many people that have lost husbands, children, loved ones ten or more
years ago. All are looking forward to that day to be with their loved ones again.
They are still full of sorrow. But even after all these years of pain and sorrow, when
we see our loved ones again it will seem short compared to an eternity with them
worshiping Jesus. When we see Jesus, all will be understood. God is in control.

What are your thoughts and feelings on the verses and quotes?

---

[202] John Piper, "The Sovereignty of God in Suffering," John Piper and Justin Taylor
(Ed). *Suffering and the Sovereignty of God*, (Wheaton, IL: Crossway, 2006), 29.

[203] Paul Enns, *Everything Happens For A Reason* (Chicago, IL: Moody, 2012), 175.

DAY 172

The righteous person may have many troubles, but the Lord delivers him from them all. (Psalm 34:19, NIV)

I think so often we read verses in the Bible and take them to mean that right now things will be wonderful. Many times we do have wonderfully blessed times on this Earth, but we also have many troubles here. We hear speakers quote verses all the time that would lead us to believe that all we need to do is pray for wealth and prosperity, and if we are faithful, God will deliver. I had a client whose child had multiple disabilities. The leaders in her church told her the child would be healed if her faith was strong enough. Don't get me wrong, I do believe God heals. I have seen Him heal. But I also believe that there are times God chooses not to heal. I believe His eternal plan is one that we cannot always understand or give reason to from this earthly perspective. I also believe God causes some to prosper financially to glorify His work. However, prosperity is not measured in worldly wealth. God has a plan and we are a part of that plan, but it does not mean this life is just for our happiness. God does, however, give us many blessings that result in happiness here on this Earth. We know that Heaven is even better. But here and now in this world as we know it we will have troubles.

Dustin Shramekin, in "Waiting for the Morning During the Long Night of Weeping," writes: "Let us not so quickly go from the affliction to the deliverance and thus minimize the pain in between. God's promise of deliverance does not mean that he will immediately deliver us. For some deliverance only comes with death."[204] Ponder those words for just a moment: "For some deliverance only comes from death." We must get away from thinking that everything will end well here. This world as we know it is all temporary. We are here to fulfill His kingdom. For some of us the time we have here is longer than others. But all believers have a purpose to fulfill, and then they are called Home. The righteous may have many troubles as this verse clearly states. We are not immune from trouble here at all. We know unless we are here until Jesus comes again, we will all face death. But God keeps us safe and delivers us to Himself. And being with Jesus is the best place of all to be.

What are your thoughts and feelings on this verse? What are your thoughts on the statement: "For some deliverance only comes with death"?

---

[204] Dustin Shramek, "Waiting for the Morning During the Long Night of Weeping." John Piper and Justin Taylor (Ed). *Suffering and the Sovereignty of God* (Wheaton, IL: Crossway, 2006), 179.

DAY 173

Let us then approach God's throne of grace with confidence, so that we may receive mercy and find grace to help us in our time of need. (Hebrews 4:16, NIV)

If ever there was a time of need in our life, now is certainly that time. When someone you love departs from this Earth it is your darkest hour. Often you do not feel God. The pain consumes you. The ache within is relentless. When Dad was taken Home I felt this void and heaviness. I longed to hear him say, "I love you too, baby." Don and I both grieved Dad's going Home. Dad was like a dad to Don. Don was there to hold me even though he too grieved. When Don was taken so abruptly I was shattered into a million pieces. Nothing made sense anymore.

I have an internal magnet that seems to be constantly searching for my other half. If ever I needed to find mercy and grace, it is now. The writer of Hebrews tells us to approach God's throne with confidence. Although you may not feel confident right now, give all those thoughts to God. He loves you. You may have to approach God even though you are not confident feeling and even though you do not feel Him. Just let God know you trust that He is with you in spite of your pain. The verses prior to this one are the ones that remind us that Jesus is our high priest, One that is capable of sympathizing with us. Jesus had been tempted in every way, yet was without sin. So when we go to Jesus, we have confidence that He understands and loves us and He will listen. Dustin Shramek writes:

When we read the story of Christ's passion, we often gloss over the astounding statement. The Son of God who is the Father's beloved and delight was forsaken. He was abandoned and left all alone. Being forsaken by his friends was one thing, but being forsaken by his Father was quite another. The depth of this pain is greater than we can know. There has been no greater pain in all of history. In the midst of our pain we may feel alone and believe that no one has hurt as badly as we hurt. But it isn't true. Jesus Christ has felt such pain; indeed, he has felt pain that would have destroyed us. He is able to sympathize.[205]

In this very hour of need, you can approach God's throne even in the all-consuming pain, and you can know He truly knows and loves you. He will give you grace and mercy in your time of need.

Reflect on the verse and quote. What are your thoughts?

---

[205] Dustin Shramek, "Waiting for the Morning During the Long Night of Weeping." John Piper and Justin Taylor (Ed). *Suffering and the Sovereignty of God* (Wheaton, IL: Crossway, 2006), 187.

DAY 174

Dear friends, do not be surprised at the painful trial you are suffering, as though something strange were happening to you. But rejoice that you participate in the sufferings of Christ, so that you may be overjoyed when his glory is revealed. (1 Peter 4:12-13, NIV)

Tuesday night before Don went Home, I found an app for my iPhone that I "stumbled" across; it is John 3:16 Promises. I liked it because the verse would pop up on my phone at a specified time. The first time I got a verse it was on Wednesday and it was on marriage. The Thursday after Don went Home this verse, 1 Peter 4:12-13, was the one that popped up. For the next week every verse was either on grief or assurances of some kind.

I clung to this verse in 1 Peter at that moment I saw it. I was so blinded by pain, I could not breathe, I could not think, I could not walk. I was in a nightmare I was sure I would wake up from; I had to. This pain could not be real. A friend, whose young thirteen-year-old son died suddenly and violently, clung to this verse as well. Dustin Shramek, commenting on this verse, writes:

Indescribable pain and grief is normal, even for Christians. Our fears, anger, doubts, and everything else we feel in our pain don't make God nervous or uncomfortable with us. God still loves us, and he is still for us. When we are in the pit of despair we must look around and see that only God can bring us out. There is no other hope. And what's more is God is committed to bringing us out. He alone is holy and therefore He alone can help us.[206]

Peter warned his readers that there will be painful trials. Months later, I was talking to our friend about this verse and even wondered if I had taken it out of context. After all, I was not being persecuted for being a Christian like the people Peter was most likely writing to. Our friend, who is dealing with a terminal illness, said, "I think anything that has the potential to make us doubt and have to cling to our faith can be seen as a trial or persecution." This is perhaps the most difficult trial of your life. Hold to the promise that there will be a day when His glory is revealed and on that day we will be overjoyed. Peter knew he would be crucified. He knew ahead of time how he would die, yet he can say these Words with conviction. Our loved ones have seen Christ in His glory and are overjoyed. We are waiting on that day!

Reflect on the verses. What are your thoughts on the present suffering?

---

[206] Dustin Shramek, "Waiting for the Morning During the Long Night of Weeping." John Piper and Justin Taylor (Ed). *Suffering and the Sovereignty of God* (Wheaton, IL: Crossway, 2006), 189.

DAY 175 REFLECTION

Looking back over the last week, what brought you comfort? We read verses that remind us we have a cloud of witnesses watching, and we contemplate our loved ones perhaps occasionally seeing us. What are your thoughts on our loved ones occasionally seeing us and perhaps interceding? Does that thought bring you comfort?

We read verses that remind us we have an inheritance that has been planned from the foundation of the world. Verses that are a clear statement on an eternal plan and inheritance remind us of the continuity of our lives. We read verses that remind us God is sovereign. God Himself tells us that He can tell us what will happen before it happens. He also tells us that if He plans it, then it will most certainly happen. The sovereignty of God is so important to hold to because when nothing else makes sense we have to know we have a God who is in control and has had a plan from the beginning of the world.

We also read verses that tell us we are going to suffer and have trials and troubles, one in the Old Testament and one in the New Testament. But we are also told He will deliver us even if that means in death. Death delivers us to God. We are told that when Jesus is revealed in all His glory, we will be overjoyed; that is the day the pain stops. We read that we can approach God's throne of grace with confidence and receive His mercy and grace because Jesus has paid the price. Jesus knows our suffering because He Himself has suffered. Record your thoughts and feelings on the devotions of the past week. What seemed to speak to you the most in the past week?

DAY 176

He will wipe every tear from their eyes. There will be no more death or mourning or crying or pain, for the old order of things has passed away. (Revelation 21:4, NIV)

Dustin Shramek writes:

And as we wait for the coming dawn, the return of the Son of God, we can know that we are not alone. Jesus himself endured the long night of weeping, and God promises to carry us even when we don't feel his arms around us. While we are on earth, there often will be deliverance from many of our sufferings—there will be many mornings that will dawn and bring with them joy. But the ultimate morning comes when Jesus returns. That is when true shouts of joy will come and when all tears will be wiped away.[207]

The sorrow will always be with you. A huge part of your life is gone, and it has changed you. Our task is to glorify Him now and further His kingdom. You can glorify God and further His kingdom even in your sorrow.

We know that there will be a day when God will wipe away all of our tears and with that day comes the promise of no more death, mourning, crying or pain. What a glorious thought.

God has an eternal plan and all of this suffering will be no more. Allow this to bring you closer to God, not push you away from Him. We have a promise: there will be no more death, mourning, crying, or pain; all of these will be gone for good. But for now Dustin Shramek reminds us:

The morning will dawn and God will remove every tear (Rev.21:4), but God is not just concerned about the morning, the new day when you can shout for joy. He is with us even in the night when there is nothing but the weeping, when the tears are so thick that we can't see. When we are in the deepest pit and the darkness weighs on our souls and God feels so absent that we wonder if He is even real...[208]

God is with you through your sorrow and He promises a new day. Hold to that promise and allow Him to see you through this night of weeping, a night that seems to last forever. But know that morning will come. We are waiting on that day!

Reflect on the verse and the quotes. What are your thoughts?

---

[207] Dustin Shramek, "Waiting for the Morning During the Long Night of Weeping." John Piper and Justin Taylor (Ed). *Suffering and the Sovereignty of God* (Wheaton, IL: Crossway, 2006), 190.
[208] Ibid., 184-185.

DAY 177

He (Jesus) must remain in Heaven until the time comes for God to restore everything, as he promised long ago through his holy prophets. (Acts 3:21, NIV)

Peter was calling his listeners to repentance and assuring them that the holy prophets had prophesied that God would restore all things as His eternal plan. Peter reminds his listeners, which includes us, that Jesus had accomplished part of the plan and was waiting until the day He would finish the plan; then, all things would be restored. When all things are restored then we will live for eternity on the New Earth with Christ. Asher Intrater writes:

Ultimately, God will restore all things. There is nothing that will not be restored. This includes everything planned at creation; everything prophesied to Israel; everything promised to the church. It includes all things in heaven and earth (Eph. 1:10). God's commitment to restore all things is a source of great hope and encouragement to us all.[209]

I agree with Asher Intater's words, "God's commitment to restore all things is a source of great hope and encouragement to us all." When the darkness of grief consumes you, the feeling that your world is destroyed and will never again be okay is overwhelming. If this life was all there is, then that would indeed be the truth. However, because we know that one day God will indeed restore all things, we have hope and that hope is awesome. This Earth will be restored, our bodies will be restored, and our relationships will be restored.

Randy Alcorn's book *Eternal Perspectives* is an extensive collection of quotes and scriptures on Heaven, New Earth, and life after death. One of the quotes by J. Paterson-Smyth in the *Gospel of the Hereafter* was, "Did God implant that divine love in her only to disappoint it? God forbid! A thousand times, no. In that world the mother shall meet her child, and the lonely widow shall meet her husband, and they shall learn fully the love of God in the rapturous meeting with Christ's benediction resting."[210] Hold to the comfort that _____ is in Heaven with Jesus. When we are called Home we will be in Jesus' glorious presence, our true and ultimate longing. With that promise also comes the promise of the total restoration of all things. We are waiting on that day!

How do today's verse and quotes speak to you?

---

[209] Asher Intrater, *Who Ate Lunch With Abraham?* (Peoria, AZ: Intermedia, 2011), 163, www.reviveisrael.org.

[210] J. Paterson-Smyth as cited by Randy Alcorn in *Eternal Perspectives, A Collection of Quotations on Heaven, The New Earth, and Life After Death,* (Carol Stream, IL: Tyndale House, 2012), 211

DAY 178

In the time of those kings, the God of heaven will set up a kingdom that will never be destroyed, nor will it be left to another people. It will crush all those kingdoms and bring them to an end, but it will itself endure forever. (Daniel 2:44, NIV)

Daniel is an amazing book, full of prophecy, full of eternal truths. Paul Enns writes about this verse:

Heaven is described as a kingdom numerous times in Scripture; it is the eternal kingdom Christ will inaugurate at His second coming. The phrases, 'never be destroyed... endure forever,' are reminders that the kingdom exceeds the thousand years of the millennium. The kingdom is eternal. It is heaven's rule on earth.[211]

When you study the prophecies and see how things have unfolded just as they were prophesied, you are reminded that God is in control and that He has an eternal plan. As we focus on keeping an eternal perspective, it is crucial to keep in mind these amazing prophecies. Having an eternal perspective means understanding that there is an eternal kingdom we all look forward to. This Earth will be restored and God's kingdom will endure on the New Earth. Kingdoms and nations have come and gone. God has appointed each nation and called them according to His eternal purpose. But His kingdom, the ultimate kingdom, will endure forever. As believers we are a part of that kingdom and will live forever with Him.

Grief threatens your very stability. It knocks the world completely out from under you, and when that happens it so hard to hold on to anything. But knowing that we, as believers, are a part of the kingdom that endures forever is rock solid. Erwin Lutzer writes, "But it is reasonable to assume that there is continuity between the earthy kingdom and the eternal heavenly kingdom."[212] There is continuity in the kingdoms, in His people, and in our relationships. His kingdom will endure forever. We are waiting on that day!

As you reflect on the verse and the quotes, how do they speak to you?

---

[211] Paul Enns, *Heaven Revealed* (Chicago, IL: Moody, 2011), 27.
[212] Erwin Lutzer, *One Minute After You Die* (Chicago, IL: Moody, 1997), 90.

DAY 179

But in the account of the burning bush, even Moses showed that the dead rise, for he calls the Lord 'the God of Abraham, and the God of Isaac, and the God of Jacob.' He is not the God of the dead, but of the living, for to him all are alive. (Luke 20:37-38, NIV)

Randy Alcorn took many of Charles Spurgeon's sermons and created a book entitled *"We Shall See God."* In one of the sermons on these verses Charles Spurgeon writes:

A living God is the God of living men; and Abraham, Isaac, and Jacob are still alive.… It is clear that they live *personally*. It is not said, 'I am the God of the whole body of the saints in one mass.' But, 'I am the God of Abraham, Isaac, and Jacob.' God will make his people to live individually. My mother, my father, my child—each will personally exist.… As Abraham is not lost to Isaac nor to Jacob nor to God nor to himself, so are our beloved ones by no means lost to us. We are by no means deprived of our dear ones by their death. They are; they are themselves; and they are ours still.[213]

Afterword Randy Alcorn writes, "A name denotes a distinct identity. As Spurgeon insists, the fact that people in Heaven can be called by their earthly names demonstrates that they remain the same people—without the bad parts—forever."[214] Jesus was speaking to the Sadducees who did not believe in a resurrection and were trying to trick Jesus. Jesus knew exactly what to say, and in these few sentences, said volumes.

One of the things I struggle with the most is how our relationships will be in Heaven. I know I am not alone. Many of the books I read were written by those struggling as well. Jesus is the One we worship, and He is the main focus of Heaven. He also is the one who gave us the loving relationships that we are now grieving. And while nothing stops the overwhelming pain of not having our loved ones with us, holding onto the continuity of whom we are and our relationships give us the hope and assurance we so desperately need.

Some use Jesus' next words in this passage about marriage to promote the idea that relationships in Heaven are not the same, especially marriage. I confess I struggled with this the most. But several authors I greatly respect specifically note Jesus' words are in context of procreation. We will have no more need to procreate as couples, but relationships, according to Jesus' other words, continue. Do not allow Satan to rob you of this truth.

Reflect on the verses and quotes. How important is continuity to you?

---

[213] Charles Spurgeon, as cited by Randy Alcorn in *We Shall See God*, (Carol Stream, IL: Tyndale House, 2011), 33-36.

[214] Randy Alcorn, *We Shall See God* (Carol Stream, IL: Tyndale House, 2011), 37.

DAY 180

For God saved us and called us to live a holy life. He did this, not because we deserved it, but because that was his plan from before the beginning of time—to show us his grace through Christ Jesus. (2 Timothy 1:9, NLT)

Here is another verse that tells us of the eternal plan from the beginning of time; it is all part of the eternal perspective. Before we were born, God had in place the plan of salvation through Jesus Christ. Before man ever sinned, the plan of redemption was in place. In God's timing Jesus Christ came and showed us grace. We are saved through no effort of our own. Christ died in our place for the atonement of our sins, and His resurrection assures us as believers that we go straight into His presence. Because of His grace we are promised an eternity in Heaven.

When we think of Heaven we think of all the blessings of being in His presence and the New Heaven and the New Earth. Our loved one is right now in Heaven and a part of this blessing. God is sovereign and His plan stands eternally.

One thing that is hard to understand is why certain things happen. If God is sovereign, He could have stopped this death. He could have prevented the cancer, the accident, the heart attack, the attack, the death. God could have and He did not. But if we look at everything through the eternal perspective, we remember we will all die unless we are here when Christ comes again. This life is not all about our happiness here on Earth. All of history, all of our lives, marches toward the eternal plan of eternity. There has been a plan since before the beginning of time. This Earth is not here just for our pleasure. Yes, God does grant us pleasure here, but there is also much pain and heartache as you well know. Only in eternity will there be true happiness. God has saved us and called us to live a holy life. We are given this promise of eternity through the grace of God, because we choose to believe and receive Him as our Savior. When we make that decision we are given eternal life, a life that was planned before the beginning of time. Hold now to that thought of eternity. My loved ones and your loved ones have been called Home. But death is not the end. We have the promise of an eternal life through Jesus Christ. It was His plan before the beginning of time.

How does this verse speak to you? Can you see God's plan is not just for now, but for eternity? How does knowing God called you comfort you now?

DAY 181

For God was pleased to have all his fullness dwell in him, and through him to reconcile to himself all things, whether things on earth or things in heaven, by making peace through his blood, shed on the cross. (Colossians 1:19-20, NIV)

God will reconcile all things whether on Earth or Heaven to Him. As Anthony Hoekema writes, "Being a citizen of the kingdom, therefore, means that we should see all of life and all of reality in the light of the goal of the redemption of the cosmos.... This implies a Christian philosophy of history; all of history must be seen as the working out of God's eternal purpose."[215]

Randy Alcorn writes:

The breadth and depth of Christ's redemptive work will escape us as long as we think is it limited to humanity. In Colossians1:16-20, notice that God highlights his plan for the church, but then he goes beyond it, emphasizing 'all things, 'everything,' 'things on earth,' and 'things in Heaven.' God was pleased to reconcile to himself all things, on Earth and in Heaven. The Greek words for 'all things,' ta pana, are extremely broad in their scope... The power of Christ's resurrection is enough not only to remake us, but to remake every inch of the universe. [216]

God reconciles all things to Him through Christ's blood shed on the cross. As a part of God's eternal plan all of Heaven and Earth are subject to Him, and we will live forever with Him on the New Heavens and the New Earth. This plan of redemption has been planned from the beginning of time. We hold to that knowledge as we focus on an eternal perspective. All things are under God's rule, whether on Heaven or Earth. So what does that mean for us now? Our believing loved ones have passed through to the presence of God. We must continue here until He calls us Home, knowing that what we do matters for eternity. But also knowing that each day we seek God we are seeking His guidance. Each day is one day closer to Heaven and being with Jesus. We are waiting on that day!

What are your thoughts and feelings on this verse? What are your thoughts on the quotes? What are your thoughts and feelings about each day being one day closer to Heaven?

---

[215] Anthony A. Hoekema, *The Bible and the Future* (Grand Rapids, MI: Eerdmans, 1979), 54.
[216] Randy Alcorn, *Heaven* (Carol Stream, IL: Tyndale House, 2004), 126.

DAY 182 REFLECTION

Read back over the past week. What speaks to you the most right now? We read the beautiful words that bring us comfort and hope, that God will wipe away every tear and there will be no more death, mourning, crying, or pain. I quote Revelation 21:4 often. We are waiting on that day. We do cry and mourn now and we do suffer, but there will be a day we will not. We will be overcome with joy; we will see Jesus in all His glory. God will wipe away our tears and there will be no more death, mourning or pain! We are waiting on that day!

We read verses that remind us that God promises to restore all things, which gives us hope. The restoration of all things shows us He has an eternal plan and He is sovereign. Looking forward to that restoration of all things, including relationships, is something that can and does bring me hope. We read God's promises to set up an eternal kingdom. God's promises and prophecies bring me great comfort. An eternal kingdom means forever.

We read a verse in which Jesus tells us that God is the God of the living, and He calls Abraham, Isaac, and Jacob by their earthly names. The fact He does call them by name reminds us we are individuals loved by God, and is a clear statement of continuity of our individual lives. I find strong comfort in holding to that continuity of our lives and relationships. If you are grieving a spouse, perhaps you too have struggled with the verses on marriage. What are your thoughts on how many authors see this as referring to procreation, and not suggesting that relationships end?

When we read of the plan from the beginning of time, we are reminded to keep the eternal perspective because God's plan is eternal. We are told God will reconcile all things to Him, all things on Earth and in Heaven. As you read back over the last week record your thoughts and feelings. What brings you the most comfort this week?

DAY 183

Look to the LORD and his strength; seek his face always. (1 Chronicles 16:11, NIV)

Maybe you are seeking the Lord's face and you can't seem to find Him. Maybe you are not seeking Him because you are angry. The fact you are reading this devotional tells me you are seeking something. I think the hard part is seeking God and not feeling Him. Charles Stanley writes:

Adversity can wreak havoc in this life. But you can advance it as you face it with the long-term view of eternity. You can rest in the certain truth that your faithfulness and perseverance will be rewarded in eternity. The outcome of suffering, when entrusted to God's sovereign, kind hand, is always merciful. The sufferings of this life, Paul said, cannot compare to the 'glory that is to be revealed to us." (Rom 8:18) The light of God's countenance is upon you in your affliction. But one day you will see Him face-to-face, and that encounter will put all things into place. Sorrow and crying will flee away for all eternity.[217]

Continue to seek His face even when you feel He is far away. When God called Don Home and with the suddenness and shock, I did not feel God at all; He felt so far away. Then slowly God did not seem so far away. I continue to pray, read the Bible, books, journal, and listen to Christian music. I knew despite what I feel or do not feel I must look to the Lord and His strength. God is with me despite how I feel. He always has been and always will be. You, too, have to continue to seek His face; there is no way you can do this in your own strength. Set aside time in the day to seek Him. Going to Sunday School and church was very hard for me because Don and I did it together. So it took me awhile to go back to church, but I also spent many hours seeking God at home. Many people find comfort in going back to church immediately.

The important thing is in seeking God and how He leads you. But hearing and reading the Word of God reminds you that God is your strength. Do not isolate yourself or busy yourself to the point you are not seeking God. God sees your suffering. One day you will see God's face, and all of this pain and sorrow will be over. Seek His face and know beyond a doubt that He is with you.

What are your thoughts on this verse? What are your thoughts on the quote by Charles Stanley?

---

[217] Charles Stanley, *Enter His Gates* (Nashville, TN: Nelson, 1998), 94.

DAY 184

The LORD is good; his love is eternal
and his faithfulness lasts forever. (Psalm 100:5, GNT)

God loves us. You may not feel loved. Sorrow isolates you even though you are surrounded by people who do love you. Sorrow can make you feel isolated from God. But God's love is eternal and His faithfulness lasts forever. Nothing can separate you from God's love or His faithfulness; it is His character. He is immutable. Songs throughout the ages sing of God's faithfulness. This morning in church we sang an old hymn, "Great is His Faithfulness." As I read and sang the words, I reminded myself I have sung this song all of my life and always believed the words. I cannot doubt His faithfulness now even though I am broken and hurting. God is still faithful. C.S. Lewis writes, "We have to be continually reminded of what we believe. Neither this belief nor any other will automatically remain alive in the mind. It must be fed."[218] As Mandisa sings:

> Yet I trust in this moment
> You're with me somehow
> And You've always been faithful
> So Lord even now
> When all that I can sing
> Is a broken hallelujah
> When my only offering
> Is shattered praise
> Still a song of adoration
> Will rise up from these ruins
> I will worship You and give You thanks[219]

As Steven Curtis Chapman sings:

> You are faithful!
> You are faithful!
> When you give and when You take away,
> even then still Your name
> is faithful![220]

As countless songs through the ages remind us, God's faithfulness and love lasts forever. We have an eternity to praise God's goodness, and we will do that with our loved ones. We are waiting on that day.

How can you remind yourself of God's faithfulness and love?

---

[218] C. S. Lewis, *Mere Christianity*, (New York, NY: HarperCollins, 1952, 1980), 141.

[219] Mandisa, "Broken Hallelujah." *Freedom*. Sparrow, 2009.

[220] Steven Curtis Chapman, "Faithful." *Beauty Will Rise*. Sparrow, 2008.

DAY 185

For we know that if the earthly tent we live in is destroyed, we have a building from God, an eternal house in heaven, not built by human hands. Meanwhile we groan, longing to be clothed instead with our heavenly dwelling. (2 Corinthians 5:1-2, NIV)

Paul Enns writes, "The tent is a reminder that we are on a pilgrimage, like visiting a foreign country. A tent is temporary. After a brief sojourn on earth, we pull up stakes and trade in our tent for a heavenly home. We aren't made to live in a tent forever; we are made for a mansion."[221] As I mentioned previously, we did a lot of camping growing up and in turn Don and I took our girls camping. There is something about being in the woods and enjoying nature. There is always an adventure. But tents wear out, they leak, they sway in the wind. They are fun, but I was always ready to get back home. When you are camping you know the dwelling is not permanent. You wouldn't want the tent to be permanent.

These bodies we now have wear out, age, and can be destroyed. We know that our bodies are not permanent, even though we may act like they are at times. People spend all kinds of money on plastic surgery and ways to stay young. But the truth is our bodies are not meant to be permanent. But we have a building from God, an eternal house in Heaven, not built by human hands. God has fashioned us an eternal body that will not wear out. Paul states, "We groan, longing to be clothed with our heavenly dwelling." Paul longed to be with Christ in Heaven, to cast aside this earthly tent and take on his heavenly body. We can relate to that longing. Our loved ones have left their earthly tent behind to be in God's glorious presence. They are no longer groaning in this temporary shelter; they are in our true Home. These bodies, this world as it is now, is all temporary; none of this was meant to be our permanent home. Some of our tents do wear out; some do not even have the chance to wear out before they put on their heavenly dwelling. The younger the person, the more we may wonder why he or she didn't get the chance to "wear out." I don't know why. I know we don't control how long our tent will last, but as believers in Christ we do have the promise of a new permanent dwelling in Heaven, whenever that might be. Our loved ones have claimed their new dwelling now. We are waiting for that day we claim ours.

How does this verse speak to you? How can viewing this earthly body as a tent make a difference?

---

[221] Paul Enns, *Heaven Revealed* (Chicago, IL: Moody, 2011), 38.

DAY 186

We are confident, I say, and would prefer to be away from the body and at home with the Lord. So we make it our goal to please him, whether we are at home in the body or away from it. (2 Corinthians 5:8-9, NIV)

These verses are a clear statement on going to be with the Lord immediately. Paul was so sure that he would be with Jesus immediately that he preferred to go right then. But either way he wanted to please God. My continued prayer is, "Lord, let me glorify you while I am here; but I hope You are coming soon." I don't understand why I am left behind. I always thought Don and I would go together; after all, a lot of our ministry was together. We were strong together. I still wish we had gone together. And I look forward every day to the day God calls me Home.

I know, too, that I must make it my goal to please God whether I am here or at Home with Him, which makes it even more important to seek Him continually in order to be in His will. Every day I think I cannot do this one more day. I cannot handle this pain, this sorrow, the absence of my soul mate one more day. Yet here I am one more day. So each day, to get through the day, I must completely seek Him and be in His strength because I have none on my own. Paul Enns writes:

'To be at home' means 'to be among his own people.' Heaven is our true home. And believers have continuity with their earthly life, both in knowledge and physical form. They are recognizable and physically identifiable. These wonderful words should remove any fear, any question, and any doubt concerning the destiny of believers at death. We have a strong assurance of our future.[222]

Randy Alcorn writes, "The place changes but the person remains the same. The same person who became absent from his or her body becomes present with the Lord."[223] Our loved ones are present with the Lord and that is glorious for them. They are at Home with our Savior. We must continue to make it our goal to please Him now, to be a part of that eternal plan, and to glorify Him while we wait on that day that we too enter His presence and our true Home. We are waiting on that day!

What are your thoughts and feelings on this verse? What are your thoughts on the quotes? How are you glorifying God?

---

[222] Paul Enns, *Heaven Revealed* (Chicago, IL: Moody, 2011), 23.
[223] Randy Alcorn, *Heaven* (Carol Stream, IL: Tyndale House, 2004), 283.

DAY 187

Yet Jerusalem says, "The LORD has deserted us; the Lord has forgotten us." "Never! Can a mother forget her nursing child? Can she feel no love for the child she has borne? But even if that were possible, I would not forget you! See, I have written your name on the palms of my hands. Always in my mind is a picture of Jerusalem's walls in ruins. (Isaiah 49:14-16, NLT)

Perhaps some of you are reading this and you have a child that has gone Home. You know the impossibility of a mother feeling no love for her child. God is reaffirming that impossibility and then says, "But even if it were possible, I would never forget you. I have written your name on the palms of my hands." There are times when I felt God had deserted me. I could not feel Him. I would continue to say, "Where are you God?" The sorrow is so dark and overwhelming that it obscures our vision. Yet I know that there is nothing that would ever make me forget or love my children less. If I, in my weakness, know that, how much more can our loving heavenly Father hold on to us? We may feel God has deserted us but He has not. Hold on to what you know is true. Recall all God has done in the past. You know God loves you, you know that He will not desert you. Our names are written on the palms of His hands. Interestingly, some versions such as the NASB do not have the words "your name." That verse is translated, "Behold I have inscribed you on the palms of My hands." That is an amazing thought. Either way, God has us in His hand. Isaiah is comforting the people of Israel with God's love. And although this is written to the nation of Israel, Christianity is rooted in Judaism. We are grafted in as believers. God has us on the palm of His hand as well. He has not deserted us. One day we will all be a part of the New Jerusalem.

It is more important than ever that you draw close to God. Continue to pray even if it doesn't feel like God is near. Continue to read the Bible and listen to music that draws you closer to Him and allows you to rest in Him. Know that feeling this loss and His absence is normal in grief. But the feelings of God's absence will not last. God's love for you stands. He has not deserted you. He will not.

What are your thoughts and feelings on this verse? What are your thoughts about your name being written on His hands?

DAY 188

About three in the afternoon Jesus cried out in a loud voice, "Eli, Eli, lema sabachthani?" (which means "My God, my God, why have you forsaken me?"). (Matthew 27:46, NIV)

When the pain seems to overtake you, remember that Jesus knows your pain. Jesus felt abandoned as we read in this verse. When you want to cry out, "Why have you forsaken me?" know that Jesus understands. And know that He has not forsaken you. In "The Long Night of Weeping," Dustin Shramek writes:

When we read the story of Christ's passion, we often gloss over the astounding statement. The Son of God who is the Father's beloved and delight was forsaken. He was abandoned and left all alone. Being forsaken by his friends was one thing, but being forsaken by his Father was quite another. The depth of this pain is greater than we can know. There has been no greater pain in all of history. In the midst of our pain we may feel alone and believe that no one has hurt as badly as we hurt. But it isn't true. Jesus Christ has felt such pain; indeed, he has felt pain that would have destroyed us. He is able to sympathize.[224]

Dustin goes on to say:

He was abandoned but He did not forget one very important thing—the fact that God is holy. How does regarding God as holy help us in the midst of our suffering? What help is this when we are trapped in the pit and the darkness threatens to suffocate us? It helps us in two ways, First, in the midst of our pain, God's holiness is a life preserver that we can cling to in order to keep us from falling into the abyss. Second, it is because God is holy that he himself will keep us from falling into the abyss.[225]

Jesus took on all that pain and sorrow for us. He now intercedes for us. His sacrifice makes it possible for us, as believers, to have eternal life. _____ is with Him now. Jesus knows your pain and intercedes for you now. Jesus is holy, He loves you, and He has our loved one in His hands now.

How does this verse speak to you? What are your thoughts on Dustin Shramek's words?

---

[224] Dustin Shramek, "Waiting for the Morning During the Long Night of Weeping." John Piper and Justin Taylor (Ed). *Suffering and the Sovereignty of God* (Wheaton, IL: Crossway, 2006), 186.
[225] Ibid., 187.

DAY 189 REFLECTION

Reflect back over the last week of devotions. What speaks to you the most? We are reminded to seek God always. Even in this time of feeling alone and perhaps not feeling God, we know to continually seek Him. It is in seeking God that we begin to feel Him. We read verses that remind us that God is good, that He loves us with an eternal love, and that His faithfulness is forever. "Forever" and "eternal" are words that remind us of the eternal perspective. It is not about this limited time on Earth; it is about eternity. It has always been about eternity. God is good, He is faithful and He loves us with an eternal love.

We read verses that remind us our earthly tents are temporary and are made to be temporary, but we have an eternal home built not by human hands but by God. Our new bodies will be eternal and we groan for that heavenly dwelling. We read that Paul prefers to be away from this body and at Home with the Lord; words we can probably all relate to. But we also read where Paul says he makes it his goal to please God—whether in this body or away from it. So we are reminded that while we are waiting on that day we must make it our goal to please God and pray that we glorify Him. But while we wait and while we pray, we glorify God here. We also know that our believing loved ones are safe in the glorious presence of Jesus.

We are reminded that God will not desert us; that He cannot forget us because our names are written in the palm of His hand. God has us written on His hand! We read the agonizing words of Jesus as He cries out in a loud voice, "My God, My God why have you forsaken me?" We need to pause and remind ourselves that in the midst of our own pain Jesus felt completely alone and in anguish in that moment, so He knows our pain. He chose to go to the cross and feel that pain so that we have the assurance of eternal life. Our loved ones are with Him now because He chose that anguishing death for us. It is a staggering thought that brings us to our knees. These are all powerful words. Record your thoughts and feelings as you read over the last week of devotions.

What is God laying on your heart?

DAY 190

So do not fear, for I am with you; do not be dismayed, for I am your God. I will strengthen you and help you; I will uphold you with my righteous right hand. (Isaiah 41:10, NIV)

Fear and dismay are two emotions you are most likely feeling. God knows your heart. He knows that you are in a situation that will create those feelings but He is with you. Despite your circumstances He is still your God. He will strengthen you and uphold you. Chris Tiegreen writes, "God promises victory to those who endure, so He gives us enough strength—usually just enough so that faith is still required—to keep us going."[226] As Casting Crowns sings:

> And I'll praise You in this storm
> And I will lift my hands
> For You are who You are
> No matter where I am
> And every tear I've cried
> You hold in Your hand
> You never left my side
> And though my heart is torn
> I will praise You in this storm[227]

As I listen to this song, I am struck by these words, "That you are who you are no matter where I am." God is still our God; no matter where we are or what we are going through, He is still God. He will strengthen us and hold us with His righteousness and holiness. Trust in His faithfulness and though your heart is torn, continue to praise Him in the storm knowing He has never left your side even in the midst of your fear and dismay. Hold to the knowledge that God is in control. Your believing loved one is with Jesus now, and Jesus is holding you through the storm. Trust Him, cry out to Him, and praise Him.

How does this verse speak to you? What feelings other than dismay and fear are you feeling? Can you trust God to strengthen you through them?

---

[226] Chris Tiegreen, *The One Year Experiencing God's Presence Devotional* (Carol Stream, IL: Tyndale, 2011), July 10.

[227] Casting Crowns, "Praise You in This Storm." *LifeSong.* Reunion Records, 2005.

DAY 191

Whoever has ears, let them hear what the Spirit says to the churches. To the one who is victorious, I will give the right to eat from the tree of life, which is in the paradise of God. (Revelation 2:7, NIV)

Anthony Hoekema tells us that the word Paradise is used in the New Testament three times: in this verse; in Luke 23: 42-43, where Jesus tells the thief on the cross he will be with Him that day in Paradise; and in 2 Corinthians 12:4, where Paul writes about being caught up in Paradise. In reference to Revelation 2:7, Hoekema writes, "We read about the tree of life which is in the Paradise of God—here again Paradise refers to the final state rather than the intermediate state." He goes on to show that we can conclude that we are immediately with Christ.[228] Randy Alcorn writes:

Eden was not destroyed. What was destroyed was mankind's ability to live in Eden. There's no indication that Eden was stripped of its physicality and transformed into a 'spiritual' entity. It appears to have remained just as it was, a physical paradise removed to a realm we can't gain access to –most likely the present Heaven, because we know for certain that's where the tree of life now is.[229]

It is an amazing thought to think of Dad and Don actually seeing the tree of life! How awesome that will be for them. And just as the tree of life is now in the present Heaven, when the New Earth is restored it will be a constant beauty for us to behold—and we will eat from the tree of life! We know from other verses it will constantly yield fruit in the New Earth. Take comfort in knowing that right now _____ is in Paradise in our Lord's presence. Our loved ones see the majestic wonders of God's glory and the place He has prepared. Can you see the eternal plan? The tree of life was in the Garden of Eden before the fall, and it is now in Paradise waiting on the New Jerusalem to come. God knew all along the plan for the tree of life. As a part of that eternal plan we will eat from the tree of life! Soon, very soon I hope, we will be in Paradise with our loved ones and other believers. All of history marches to the day when everything will be restored, and those who are victorious will eat from the tree of life that is preserved right now in Paradise. Hold to the eternal perspective. We are waiting on that day!

Meditate on this verse and the quotes. What speaks to you the most?

---

228   Anthony A. Hoekema, *The Bible and the Future* (Grand Rapids, MI: Eerdmans, 1979), 103.

229   Randy Alcorn, *Heaven* (Carol Stream, IL: Tyndale House, 2004), 56.

DAY 192

Jesus answered, "My kingdom is not of this world. If My kingdom were of this world, then My servants would be fighting so that I would not be handed over to the Jews; but as it is, My kingdom is not of this realm." Therefore Pilate said to Him, "So You are a king?" Jesus answered, "You say correctly that I am a king. For this I have been born, and for this I have come into the world, to testify to the truth. Everyone who is of the truth hears My voice." (John 18:36-37, NASB)

I think these verses in John are very powerful; they embody the eternal perspective and the eternal plan. Jesus could have stopped His crucifixion in an instant. He is the King of kings. But He had been born and come into the world for this very thing, to die for our sins and to set His eternal Kingdom. There was a song when I was growing up that had these words:

> He could have called ten thousand angels
> to destroy the world and set Him free.
> He could have called ten thousand angels
> but He died alone for you and me.[230]

Jesus had a clear plan and even though He knew the intense pain and abandonment He would feel, He chose to continue this plan. Jesus knew a whole different realm, a whole different kingdom. Jesus has a kingdom that will out-live all kingdoms. Philip Yancey writes, "But according to the Bible, human history is far more than the rising and falling of people and nations; it is a staging ground for the battle of the universe."[231]

Randy Alcorn writes, "He meant that his Kingdom isn't of the Earth as it is now, under the Curse. Although Christ's Kingdom isn't from the Earth, it extends to the Earth, and one day it will fully include the Earth and be centered on it."[232] Asher Intrater writes, "God has a design from the beginning of time. What happens at the beginning of the Bible is a foundation for what will happen at the end of the Bible."[233] Jesus is the truth. I pray that I hear Jesus' voice daily and that I can keep an eternal perspective while I wait on that day.

As you reflect on these verses and quotes, how do they speak to you?

---

[230] Ray Overholt, 1958.
[231] Phillip Yancey, *Disappointment With God* (Grand Rapids, MI: Zondervan, 1992), 189.
[232] Randy Alcorn, *Heaven* (Carol Stream, IL: Tyndale House, 2004), 207.
[233] Asher Intrater, *Who Ate Lunch With Abraham?* (Peoria, AZ: Intermedia, 2011), 169.

DAY 193

Your sun will never set; your moon will not go down.
For the LORD will be your everlasting light.
Your days of mourning will come to an end. (Isaiah 60:20, NLT)

Most authors I read see Isaiah 60 as a dual prophecy for Isaiah's time and for the New Jerusalem. We know these verses depict the New Jerusalem since God will be our everlasting light and our days of mourning will come to an end. When we mourn, we feel like each day is a nightmare; one that we know will be not be over until we open our eyes in Heaven. On that day when we open our eyes in Heaven, the mourning will stop because we are with our Lord. The Lord will be the everlasting light. Just think: His glory is so majestic and powerful that sun and moon will no longer be used for light. That thought is hard to fathom, isn't it? And even now our loved ones are experiencing His glorious light.

Death is hard on those of us left behind. The ones who are with God are experiencing fully the life everlasting. We weep and mourn and hurt, but this sorrow will end the day we see Jesus face to face. In describing Heaven as a place of blessedness and not a condition, William Scroggie wrote, "It is true that God is omnipresent, but surely we can say that it is with Him, though in a higher sense, as it was with the sun, which," says Van Oosterzee, in his *Christian Dogmatics*, 'shines everywhere, yet especially displays its full splendour in the firmament'."[234]

I thought about William Scroggie's words when I read this verse. We can see the sun now, but we can't look directly at it without it affecting our eyes. We know the sun is millions of miles away, yet we still feel and see its splendor here on Earth. It is probably one of the best ways in our limited comprehension to explain God's omnipresence; He is in Heaven but He is everywhere. In the New Jerusalem, we will no longer need the sun and moon for light because God will be the everlasting light. Our loved ones are seeing those things we read about and try to understand. They are experiencing His glorious light and fully understand. Someday we will experience those blessings with our loved ones. Then the mourning will stop, the nightmare will end, and our true Home will be realized. We are waiting on that day!

As you meditate on the verse and the quote, how do they speak to you?

---

[234] William Scroggie, *What About Heaven?* (London: Pickering & Inglis, 1954), 56.

DAY 194

Instead of the thornbush will grow the juniper, and instead of briers the myrtle will grow. This will be for the Lord's renown, for an everlasting sign, that will endure forever. (Isaiah 55:13, NIV)

Don and I planted our third crepe myrtle tree in September before God called Don Home November 2. Don loved crepe myrtle trees; really he just loved trees and flowers of all kinds. The year Don went Home the crepe myrtles seemed to abound. And each time I saw one of the trees I thought of him and this verse. I am not sure if the myrtle trees mentioned in the Bible is the same as a crepe myrtle, or is even a tree in the same family, but since they both have the name "myrtle," my mind naturally goes to that picture. Once again, we see a picture of the restoration of the land. Instead of the thorn bush and briers, beautiful trees like the juniper and the myrtle will grow. Nature will be restored to Eden-like conditions. God created this amazingly beautiful world we live in. Can you imagine what Heaven will be like and what the Earth restored will be like? I received an email recently with photos of nature around the world, all breathtaking. The last line on the email is, "Can you imagine what God has in store for us in Heaven if He did this on earth?" I thought that was a profound statement.

When we built a cabin in the woods, we had to clear the land. We bought the land in winter, and when spring came we realized it was full of poison ivy, thorns, and briars. Our whole family worked to clear the land, and underneath all of the weeds, briars, and poison ivy was a beautiful piece of land. The pine trees grew majestically; the dogwoods and other trees gave color in the spring. In the New Jerusalem there will be no thorn bushes or briars to clear. We will see the grandeur of His creation in perfection. Even now, what Don, Dad and your loved ones are experiencing is so much more than what our eyes can see here. When we look at nature now and take in the beauty that we see, we know it is just a shadow of what is to come, but we can have a faint glimpse of what our loved ones are seeing. And to know that best of all the ones we love are with the Creator makes the thoughts even more awe-inspiring.

Yes, we still have the sorrow and the pain now, because our loved ones are not with us. But we do hold to the fact that our separation is temporary and someday we will be in that same place as our loved ones. We will see the Creator, we will see the beauty of Eden, and we will see the restored Earth. And we will see our loved ones again. We are waiting on that day!

What are our thoughts and feelings on this verse? What specific scenes in nature help you think of the restored Eden?

DAY 195

And without faith it is impossible to please God, because anyone who comes to him must believe that he exists and that he rewards those who earnestly seek him. (Hebrews 11:6, NIV)

When we first got married, Don and I had a poster that had a picture of a kitten holding on to a tree branch, spread-eagle, back legs dangling. The caption read, "Faith isn't faith until it is all you are holding on to." We kept the poster to remind us during the hard times that if we say we rely on our faith, we have to mean it, not just in the plentiful and smooth times, but in the rough and hard times. We weathered through those hard times together and our faith grew. A loss of a loved one can feel like a shaky branch, and that you are alone hanging by the very end of your fingertips. You may wonder where God is. When those feelings hit, we have to remember that God does exist. You know that is true; you know He is the same God you have always believed in and relied on. When your faith is shaking and you do not feel God at all, it is easy to doubt, but hold on to Him with every fiber of your being. Earnestly seek God. The words *earnestly seek* mean to "search out, to seek after.… the seeker finds, or at least exhaust his powers of seeking."[235]

It is easy to feel completely abandoned and give up, but remember that it is more important than ever that you not give up. Cry out and earnestly seek God through prayer, reading His Word, and listening. Philip Yancey says that he thinks part of the difficulty comes from the "elastic way we use the word (faith)"[236] Yancey goes on to talk about childlike faith, and though it is important, there is another type of faith. He goes on to explain:

But Job, along with the saints of Hebrews 11, points to a different faith, the kind that I have circled around in this book on disappointment with God. Childlike trust may not survive when the miracle does not come, when the urgent prayer gets no answer, when a dense gray mist obscures any sign of God's concern. Such times call for something more, and I will use the musty word 'fidelity' for that hang-on-at-any-cost faith.[237]

Hang on at all cost right now. Our reward will come in eternity, when we see Jesus face to face. Believe and hold to your faith even if you feel you are barely holding on; still hold on while you are waiting on that day.

Reflect on your faith. Are you holding on at all cost?

---

[235] Rogers & Rogers, *The Linguistic and Exegetical Key to the Greek New Testament* (Grand Rapids, MI: Zondervan, 1998), 542.
[236] Phillip Yancey, *Disappointment with God* (Grand Rapids, MI: Zondervan, 1992), 230.
[237] Ibid., 230.

DAY 196 REFLECTION

As you reflect over last week, what stands out to you the most? We read that God holds us in His right hand. We may feel fear and dismay, but He will strengthen us and hold us. The song by Casting Crowns reminds us we may feel in a storm, but God never leaves our side. We read in Revelation that the tree of life that we read about in Genesis is in Paradise now. We contemplate that our loved ones see the Tree of Life right now in Paradise. I love how these verses point us to the eternal plan. The Tree of Life was in the Garden of Eden and is now in Paradise. God pays attention to every detail. He leaves us a map.

We read Jesus' own Words that tell us His kingdom is not in this realm. Our King is Jesus and His kingdom is eternal. There is a day coming when we will all see this New Kingdom in all its glory. What an awesome thought. We are waiting on that day! Reading those words encourage us to keep an eternal perspective.

We read several verses that talk about the New Earth. The land will be restored. The Lord is our everlasting light. We read the beautiful words, "There will be no more mourning." God knows our hearts; He knows how hard mourning is. Of all the beauty we can now see, when the land is restored it will all be magnified and the Lord will be our light... and it will be forever! We see how this fallen world has thorns and briars but someday the Earth is restored to the beauty God has planned. What specific nature scenes help you think of Eden?

Then we read about faith. Without faith it is impossible to please God. We read Philip Yancey's words that we need a "hang-on-at-all-costs faith." There is a whole dimension we cannot see. That thought brings me great comfort. Our loved ones right now see more clearly than they ever have, and more clearly than you and I can. But someday we will too. We are waiting on that day! Record your thoughts and feelings as you read back over the week. What day's devotional resonate with you the most?

DAY 197

For we live by faith, not by sight. (2 Corinthians 5:7, NIV)

We live by faith, not by sight. What this verse tells us is there is much we can't see, so we have to trust that what we don't see is very real. I really like how Asher Intrater describes the unseen:

The creation is divided into two halves, or two dimensions. One is visible and the other is not visible (Col 1:15-16). The part we cannot see is spiritual. The part we can see is physical. Yet, the invisible spiritual part is as real and corporeal as the physical part. The fact that we cannot see it does not mean that it is not there. Both operate according to laws, physical and spiritual. The invisible part was created first and the visible part was created from and out of the invisible part" (Heb. 11:3).[238]

When your world crashes, holding on to faith becomes even harder, but it is all the more important that you hold to your faith. We may stumble blindly at times in the dark, but we must hold to the knowledge that God is in control. No matter how out-of-control things feel, God is still in control. Sometimes it is harder to live by faith during times of grief because the person we love, the person we are used to seeing and being with is not here with us. We cannot touch our loved ones, see them, hear them, or be with them. Not having them with us knocks us down, and we want something real and tangible. The absence of what we want to see can lead to doubt. Quote this verse often; remind yourself that you live by faith, not by sight.

    Just because you cannot see _____ does not mean that he or she is not as real, even more real, than she has ever been. God is who you have always thought He was; He is in control. We will see the unseen someday. We just cannot see it right now. Right now, we have to hold on to the faith we profess, and remember that we must live by that faith not by sight. Someday you will see Jesus face to face. You will see the very real spiritual world. Right now Dad and Don and your loved one are all seeing more clearly than ever. Our loved ones are seeing that spiritual realm that they believed by faith. We have to wait until that day that we too will see. For now we remind ourselves that we live by faith and look forward to the day we will see. We are waiting on that day!

What are your thoughts and feelings on this verse? What are your thoughts on Asher Intrater's words?

---

[238] Asher Intrater, *Who Ate Lunch With Abraham?* (Peoria, AZ: Intermedia, 2011), 88.

DAY 198

Now Christ has gone to heaven. He is seated in the place of honor next to God, and all the angels and authorities and powers accept his authority. (1 Peter 3:22, NLT)

Jesus Christ ascended to Heaven after His resurrection. Now Jesus sits at the right hand of God. Colossians 3:1 tells us to fix our hearts and minds where Christ is seated at the right hand of God in Heaven. Heaven is our true Home, and Christ has prepared a place for us there. All angels and authorities and powers accept His authority. We have nothing to fear because Christ has conquered death and He is victorious. There will be a day when the final battle is won with Satan, but even now Christ has won the victory. All powers—not some, but all—are subject to His authority. Because Jesus is ruling from Heaven, we go straight to be with Him. All powers are subject to Him.

When you are overcome with the absence of _____, remember that _____ is now in Heaven. Our redeemed loved ones crossed into Jesus' presence immediately. Jesus has prepared a place for the youngest of His children to the oldest, and everyone in between. Keeping our focus on Christ in Heaven is important. As Charles Stanley writes:

Think about the comfortable feeling you have as you open your front door. That's but a hint of what we'll feel some day on arriving at the place our Father has lovingly and personally prepared for us in heaven. We will finally—and permanently—be 'at home' in a way that defies description.[239]

It is hard to not focus on the absence of our loved ones. We want to hold them, hear them, and see them. And that sorrow and pain is very real. But our loved ones are taken care of; it is us who feel the pain. One day Jesus will call us Home too. That glorious day we will see Jesus face to face. We will feel that love and see His glory, and we will be reunited with our loved ones. Come quickly, Lord! We are waiting on that day.

What are your thoughts and feelings on this verse? What are your thoughts on Charles Stanley's statement? How does holding to Christ's authority over all powers help you?

---

[239] Charles Stanley, *In Touch* Devotional, August 30, 2012.

DAY 199

Martha said to Jesus, "Lord, if only you had been here, my brother would not have died." (John 11:21, NLT)

Greg Laurie writes about Lazarus' death and resurrection and Mary and Martha's response. He writes, "To paraphrase it, *Where were you anyway, Jesus?*" He goes on to say, "I want you to notice something very important here. Jesus did not reprove Martha for what she said. Why do I bring this up? Because you need to know it is not wrong to tell God exactly how you feel."[240]

There are so many emotions that are flooding your mind and heart, which is another reason to journal. Journaling helps you sort through those feelings. It is very important in grief to express how you feel. Jesus did not chastise Martha. He loved Martha, Mary, and Lazarus. Jesus had eaten in their home and spent time with them. Clearly, Jesus had a close relationship with this family. Martha and Mary both told Jesus the same thing. They had banked on Jesus being there in time to heal their brother. They had faith He would and could heal their brother. Jesus saw their grief and wept with them, and never once did Jesus tell them they should not feel a certain way. We have a close relationship with Him too. Tell Jesus how you feel and ask to feel His presence and His love.

But also notice another of His responses to Mary and Martha, He wept with them. Then Jesus told them, "He who believes in me will live even though they die." We have a promise that we will live even though we die. I have heard others say that Jesus wept not just in grief but also because He knew that Heaven was a far better place for Lazarus to be. I think both of those thoughts are valid. Jesus felt their pain and their loss right at that moment, but He also knew Lazarus was far better off in Heaven. Jesus knew, too, that God would be glorified in Lazarus being raised, and that Lazarus would return to Heaven. So Jesus knew what was going to happen before He ever went to Mary and Martha; that is why He tarried to get back. Jesus knew how important this event was to show the glory of God; it was all part of the eternal plan.

Martha and Mary didn't know the plan; they just knew they hurt. They knew that the brother they loved and that Jesus loved was not with them. They had the hope of the resurrection in the last days, but they were not ready to say good-bye right then. We can certainly identify with how these women felt. Jesus also understood how Mary and Martha felt. But Jesus also knew the beauty of what awaited those who would live with Him for eternity. Tell Jesus how you feel, but hold to the promise of eternal life, where your loved one is now and where we will be when we join the ones we love. We are waiting on that day!

Reflect on today's devotion. Journal and pray your feelings.

---

[240] Greg Laurie, *Hope for Hurting Hearts* (Dana Point, CA: Kerygma, 2008), 24

DAY 200

The heavens proclaim the glory of God.
The skies display his craftsmanship. (Psalm 19:1, NLT)

Any time weather permitted, Don and I would sit outside in the evening and talk. Most of the time our talk would turn to how thankful we were, and how God had blessed us. There is something about sitting outside under the stars. We always loved a full moon. When you sit under the stars and a full moon it is hard to not think of God's glory. We built a cabin with windows to the ceiling to see the awesomeness of His creation. The camera on my phone is full of pictures of the sky. Cloud formations, the sunset, the sunrise, the sun's rays shining through the clouds all shout of God's majesty. When you don't feel God, step outside and look at the sky. None of the beauty and majesty of what you see could be here by accident. When the enemy shouts doubts in your ear and when you are not hearing God, look around. God shouts His handiwork from all of creation. God the Creator displays His craftsmanship in the skies.

Lisa Stilwell created and compiled the book *The Heavens Proclaim His Glory*. The book is full of powerful photos of space and beyond. In her book she has compiled pictures from the lens of the Hubble Telescope and quotes from various authors about the sky. I chose a few of those quotes: Abraham Lincoln: "I can see how it might be possible for a man to look down upon the earth and be an atheist but I cannot conceive how he could look into the heavens and say there is no God." Max Lucado: "By showing us the Heavens, Jesus is showing us His Father's workshop," and Kirk Cameron: "When I come to die, I want someone there with me who is stronger than death. I want to walk through the door of eternity with the Creator of the Universe, Life Incarnate, God who became man, died for me, defeated the grave, and calls me His friend. You can have all this world, just give me Jesus."[241]

We see God's glory as we look at the sky, and still there is much in the universe we cannot see with our own eyes. The same God that put all of the heavens in place has our loved ones safe in the place He has prepared. And God will bring us all to Him. We are waiting on that day!

What are your thoughts and feelings on this verse? On the quotes from the book? Take time to gaze at the sky today and tonight, meditate on the handiwork, write your thoughts and feelings.

---

[241] Abraham Lincoln as cited by Lisa Stiwell, *The Heavens Proclaim His Glory* (Nashville, TN: Nelson, 2010), 15. Max Lucado and Kirk Cameron as cited by Lisa Stiwell, *The Heavens Proclaim His Glory*, (Nashville, TN: Nelson, 2010), 151.

DAY 201

His purpose was for the nations to seek after God and perhaps feel their way toward him and find him—though he is not far from any one of us. For in Him we live and move and exist. (Acts 17:27-28a, NLT)

These verses follow the verse that we looked at earlier that tells us God has set the times and places for every person to live. Now we are told God's purpose was that we would seek after Him and find Him even though He is not far from any of us. When we are grieving, it may feel as if we are feeling our way in the dark. But God is all around us even if we don't feel Him. Chris Tiegreen writes:

In our quest for a deeper sense of God's presence, we need to remember much of what we seek is already all around us. We live and move and exist in God. He is present in every atom of creation, and if we are observant we can see not only His past handiwork as Creator but His current activity as Lord, Guide, Shield, Provider, Comforter, and Healer. Even when He seems far away, He never is. Whether we sense His presence or not, He is near.[242]

Hold to the knowledge that God has set His plan into motion since the beginning of time. God set times and seasons, and even when and where you would live. God has placed people in your life and all that time He has a plan for you and for the entire world. God's plan is eternal and in eternity we will realize the full extent of His plan. There is so much right now that may not make sense. When your arms ache to hold the one you love, to hear the voice of the one you love, to see the special smile, hear your loved one laugh, the pain and the ache is very real. But God knows His eternal plan. God wants us to seek Him, He knows we live and move and exist only through Him. God may have taken our loved ones Home as a part of His plan, but He has not left us. God holds them safely. He will call us Home, and we will be reunited. The hard part is being left here without the ones we love, so we must seek Him.

The NET translates "feel their way" as "grope around." That is what I feel like sometimes—that I am groping around to find God. But just like at night, if I grope around I am often right on what I am looking for. Be still and pray. Seek God's Word; seek His presence. Pray that you will see God in every way that you can, and that you will feel Him. Then be open to receive. It may not come as quickly as you like; but in diligently seeking Him, you will begin to feel that assurance.

What are your thoughts and feelings on this verse? How have you been seeking Him? When do you think you feel His assurance the most?

---

[242] Chris Tiegreen, *The One Year Experiencing God's Presence Devotional* (Carol Stream, IL: Tyndale, 2011), June 20.

DAY 202

Then Elisha prayed, "O LORD, open his eyes and let him see!" The LORD opened the young man's eyes, and when he looked up, he saw that the hillside around Elisha was filled with horses and chariots of fire. (2 Kings 6:17, NLT)

When we read verses like these that highlight the closeness of Heaven and the unseen realm, there is so much we can bring from these verses. The following quotes all find gems in these verses: Paul Enns writes:

When the Lord pulled back the curtain, a powerful army was nearby! Where had this army come from? Heaven!... Heaven is near us yet in a different sphere is implied... the servant saw into the new realm... While it is true that Elisha saw in another dimension, it is probably better to state that Elisha saw with both his physical eyes and spiritual eyes. It was not a vision.[243]

Randy Alcorn says:

It could be argued these horses and chariots (with angelic warriors) exist beside us in our universe, but we are normally blind to them. Or they may be in a universe beside ours that opens up into ours so that angelic beings—and horses, apparently—can move between universes.[244]

Asher Intrater writes:

That we do not see the unseen part of creation does not mean that it cannot be seen. It is unseen to us but it is not "un-seeable." Under normal circumstances we ought to be able to see both dimensions. Before Adam and Eve sinned, they were able to see both. At the time they sinned, their sight became restricted. It was as if a barrier was placed between the seen and the unseen realm in order to prevent us from seeing the spiritual part.[245]

We are told throughout Scripture there is more to this world than we see. However close Heaven may be, we know it is the dwelling place of God. Jesus sits at His right hand, and Jesus has a place prepared for us. Our loved ones are already there. We will see this wonderfully awe inspiring place with our own eyes. We will be reunited with loved ones, and our eyes opened. I wish we could glimpse Heaven now, but we have to trust Jesus while we wait on that day.

As you reflect on the verses and quotes, how do they speak to you?

---

[243] Paul Enns, *Heaven Revealed* (Chicago, IL: Moody, 2011), 50.

[244] Randy Alcorn, *Heaven* (Carol Stream, IL: Tyndale House, 2004), 49.

[245] Asher Intrater, *Who Ate Lunch With Abraham?* (Peoria, AZ: Intermedia, 2011), 88.

DAY 203 REFLECTION

Look back over the last week and reflect on the devotionals. We read that we live by faith, not sight. This verse in 2 Corinthians is short but profound. We do not live by sight, we live by faith. I really like how Asher Intrater talks about the unseen. We know how much we want to see our loved ones. We are visual creatures. But this is where we must remind ourselves, we live by faith. Someday we will see but for now we hold to Jesus in faith.

We read where Christ is in Heaven ruling and every power accepts His authority. He has the authority over all, not just some things but all things. The victory has been won. We know Heaven is our destination. The verses also remind us God is in control.

We read how Martha tells Jesus, "If only you had been here." She echoes what we all wonder, "Why didn't you stop this, Jesus?" I never tire of the story of Jesus with Mary, Martha, and Lazarus; we will read it several more times. The story of Jesus raising Lazarus from the dead and His compassion for the family is rich, it is timeless, and it reveals so much. I find great comfort in reading this story over and over. Jesus loves this family just like He loves your family and mine. He cares when we hurt, and someday He will make all things right. We are waiting on that day!

We read that the Heavens proclaim God's glory; the skies His craftsmanship. We are reminded to stop and look at the magnificence of God's work, especially when He seems far away. Truly take time this week to look at the sky. Notice the heavens do proclaim the glory of God. Meditate on His Word as you look at His craftsmanship. We read that God wants us to seek Him. We may feel like we are in the dark groping around and alone, but God is not far away and we are encouraged to seek Him.

We read the exciting account of God opening Elisha's servant's eyes to see the heavenly realms. It reminds us of the nearness of Heaven and the unseen realm. We know our loved ones are in the unseen realm. We would all love that glimpse of Heaven, but for now we trust and believe Heaven is amazing and our loved ones are there, and we will be reunited with them. We are waiting on that day! As you reflect back over the week, record your thoughts and feelings.

What do you feel like God is laying on your heart this week?

DAY 204

"For I know the plans I have for you," declares the Lord, "plans to prosper you and not to harm you, plans to give you hope and a future." (Jeremiah 29:11, NIV)

I will confess that as I read this verse, I had difficulty with it. I felt harmed already so that just didn't seem to fit. My future without Don didn't seem right; all of our dreams included both of us in them. Perhaps you are feeling the same way. Maybe your child went Home and with that child all your future dreams and hopes; maybe, like me, you lost a spouse you had plans of a future with, and the list could go on and on. Whoever it was, you feel harmed. So what does this verse mean? After all, people put this verse on cards, so if you are already feeling harmed, how does it make sense?

As I read Jeremiah, I realized this was in a letter to exiles. They had been exiled from Jerusalem. They were taken captive to a foreign country, and God tells them they are going to be in exile for 70 years. This likely means that some of those people never returned to Israel. Some of them lost loved ones along the way. And all of them eventually died. Jeremiah was put in prison and lowered into a muddy cistern to be left alone to die. So what about all of those bad things? Perhaps this means again that we must have an eternal perspective. We have already seen where many of the prophecies in the Old Testament have a dual prophecy. Part of the prophecy is for the time period it was written, and part of it for the coming of the Messianic Kingdom.

We know that some of the Israelites came out of exile and rebuilt the temple. But we know also that in 70 AD the Israelites were scattered again. We know that the Jewish people got their land back in 1948. We know that one day in the New Heaven and the New Earth, there will be a New Jerusalem. So God is always working His eternal plan for His people.

We know that God uses this time on Earth to make us more Christlike for His eternal kingdom. So perhaps this verse in Jeremiah is really about an eternal focus. God's plan for us is not just for this life; in fact, much of the plan to prosper us and give us a future and a hope are really pointing toward eternity. We have read so much on the New Heavens and the New Earth. We know all history marches toward God's redemption of His creation. We know then we will have no more death, mourning, pain or crying. God has a plan, and although there are many times He does keep us from physical and emotional harm, there are many times we are harmed in some way. But if we keep an eternal perspective, we know that the true healing, the true future, the true plan is eternal. We are waiting on that day!

Have you struggled with this verse? Reflect on the loss of future dreams. How does reading this verse in light of eternity change things for you?

DAY 205

As you look forward to the day of God and speed its coming. That day will bring about the destruction of the heavens by fire, and the elements will melt in the heat. (2 Peter 3:12, NIV)

"As you look forward to the day of God" is a promising statement. As I have mentioned before, prophecy became the second most read subject of mine, second to Heaven. Why? For one thing, when the doubts would hit, it was very comforting to remind myself that despite what I feel—or don't feel—I know the Bible is full of prophecies that have come true and prophecies that are being fulfilled before our eyes.

When we were teenagers in the seventies, Don and I would talk about the prophecies and specifically a verse that said the whole world would watch. I can remember Don and I discussing how that would happen. I also vividly remember during Desert Storm how CNN exploded on the scene and literally the whole world watched as the war unfolded. And of course now we have FOX and various other news channels that we can watch in real time. I can watch something live from my iPhone. Watching as the world watches is just one example of how we are watching prophecy unfold. There are so many things foretold that we didn't understand, how it could happen. Now we know.

And second, prophecy is important because I look forward even more to the day when Jesus returns. I know that day I will see Jesus, the mourning will turn to joy because we will be with Him. And on that day I will be reunited with Don and with Dad. You will be once again with _____.

In *Heaven Revealed*, Paul Enns writes on this verse in 2 Peter: "Peter was describing the renovation of the New Earth."[246] "This is the sphere where sin took place; it is renovated in anticipation of eternity."[247] This verse clearly tells us to look forward to that day. Randy Alcorn writes, "If we understand what a 'new heaven and new earth' means, we will look forward to it. (And if we're not looking forward to it, we must not yet understand it)"[248] I was looking forward to the day of Jesus' return before but even more so now. I am waiting on that day...

What are your thoughts and feelings on this verse? Read the headlines for this week. Which of those things that you read point to prophecies fulfilled, and how does that affect you?

---

[246] Paul Enns, *Heaven Revealed* (Chicago, IL: Moody, 2011), 95.

[247] Paul Enns, *The Moody Handbook of Theology Revised and Expanded* (Chicago, IL: Moody, 2008), 131.

[248] Randy Alcorn, *Heaven* (Carol Stream, IL: Tyndale House, 2004), 470

DAY 206

But because Jesus lives forever, he has a permanent priesthood. Therefore he is able to save completely those who come to God through him, because he always lives to intercede for them. (Hebrews 7:24-25, NIV)

How powerful are these words in Hebrews to you? Jesus intercedes for us. This chapter outlines how Jesus became the high priest for us. His death and resurrection paid the price for our sins instead of the sacrifice of bulls. By the blood of Jesus we are cleansed once and for all and because of His sacrifice, He saves us completely. Jesus understands our pain, and He intercedes for us. Philip Yancey writes:

As Jesus once prayed for Peter, now He prays for us… In fact the New Testament's only glimpse of what Jesus is doing right now depicts Him at the right hand of God 'interceding for us.' In three years of active ministry, Jesus changed the moral landscape of the planet. For nearly 2000 years since, He has been using another tactic: prayer.[249]

When you do not feel God and He seems far away, remember prayer still makes a difference. Remember that Jesus is interceding for you. Remember that Jesus hears you calling out to Him, so don't give up calling out to Jesus and holding to Him. We have been saved completely. Our loved ones are safely at Home. We have the hard part, but we are not alone. Jesus is praying for us too. Do not allow the enemy to keep you from praying, to shut God out. Keep talking to God, knowing that Jesus is also interceding. Pray for others, pray that you would feel Jesus, pray for understanding; but above all, pray.

We have the promise of eternal life. Our redeemed loved ones are in Jesus' presence even now. Perhaps our loved ones are praying for us too. We know we have a cloud of witnesses; we know the martyrs in Revelation know what is going on here on Earth; we know the rich man in Hades knew, and wanted to get word to his family. There is so much in the unseen world we don't see or know, but what we do know is Jesus saves us completely and He intercedes for us. That is a beautiful promise. We can tell Jesus that we will trust Him even though we may not understand or even though we don't feel Him. We can say, "I know you are interceding for me. I know you have _____ safe with you in our true Home. I trust you, Jesus."

How do these verses speak to you? How does picturing Jesus interceding for you affect you?

---

[249] Philip Yancey, *Prayer: Does It Make a Difference?* (Grand Rapids, MI: Zondervan, 2006), 88.

DAY 207

But let me reveal to you a wonderful secret. We will not all die, but we will all be transformed! It will happen in a moment, in the blink of an eye, when the last trumpet is blown. For when the trumpet sounds, those who have died will be raised to live forever. And we who are living will also be transformed. (1 Corinthians 15:51-52, NLT)

These verses in 1 Corinthians describe the bodily resurrection. Even though our loved ones are now with Christ in Heaven, there will be a day when Christ returns and takes all believers still alive. On the day Jesus returns, not only will the bodies of those still alive be transformed in a blink of an eye, those who have already gone to Heaven will have a bodily resurrection. All of our bodies—whether here or raised from the grave—will be transformed and perfected. I go to the cemetery and think if Jesus returned right now I could join Don and Dad immediately, and we would all have transformed bodies. But we do not know when the time of Jesus' return will come; we do know, though, that the day of Jesus' return will indeed come.

Paul Enns writes, "Changed means 'changed into something far better and vastly superior to the former'—yet there remains the identity and continuity with the old. We remain the same persons, yet we are renovated into perfection in every respect."[250] I wish we could not be talking about death right now. I wish we had gone Home together. But for whatever reason, God has left us here and our loved ones have gone Home. Our task is to seek God, to glorify Him, and to serve Him until the day He calls us Home or that He comes back for us. Jesus understands our pain, and He intercedes for us. We have to continue to pray for God to show us how to live for now with the promise of eternity, knowing that we will be reunited with our loved ones. Pray that we glorify Him and serve Him. We will see Jesus, and we want our actions to be pleasing to Him. We want to know that despite our pain, we seek and serve Him. We will see Jesus, and we will live with Him forever. We will be reunited with our loved ones and have an eternity to spend with them. We are waiting on that day!

As you meditate on this verse and the thoughts of today's devotion, how do they speak to you?

---

[250] Paul Enns, *Heaven Revealed* (Chicago, IL: Moody, 2011), 228.

DAY 208

This man (Jesus) was handed over to you by God's deliberate plan and foreknowledge; and you, with the help of wicked men, put him to death by nailing him to the cross. But God raised him from the dead, freeing him from the agony of death, because it was impossible for death to keep its hold on him. (Acts 2:23-24, NIV)

As horrible as the events were leading to Jesus being taken by the angry men and standing before the rigged trial, it was all part of God's eternal plan. God's deliberate plan was for Christ to die on the cross and to be resurrected. It was impossible for death to keep its hold on Jesus. And because of His death and resurrection, we are free from the penalty of death. Instead, we live even though we die; death has no power over the believer. _____ is with our Lord. These Scriptures reinforce the eternal plan. God used wicked people to bring about His sovereign will. That did not excuse them from their actions; Peter is very clear that they were at fault. But God used even bad things for His will.

I don't know the circumstances of how your loved one went Home. I know just six weeks before Don went Home, our cousin, Keith, a godly man, a fire chief, and a strong family man, was brutally murdered. I have worked with people who have had loved ones die violently. I have watched people suffer with cancer and other terminal illnesses. I pray daily for those Christians in other countries who are being persecuted and dying for their beliefs. I don't pretend to understand why. I know we live in a fallen world. I know God is sovereign. I know that death has no hold on us as believers. God's eternal plan comes to fruition with the New Heaven and New Earth. All that happens here and now is but a brief moment in comparison to eternity. We are all on a journey Home and we serve Him now and do what He calls us to do until He calls us Home.

When we get to Heaven there will be understanding far beyond what we can understand now. We have to trust Jesus despite the circumstances. Jesus has overcome death. Death is a portal to Heaven. We have to take that journey unless we are here when Jesus returns, but either way the destiny of believers is Heaven. Our true home is Heaven with our Savior. How we die will not seem as important once we are in Heaven with our Savior. It is important to hold to God's faithfulness, His eternal plan, and His promises. We will see God; we will be with Him, and with our loved ones. We will have an eternity to praise and worship Jesus. We are waiting on that day!

What are your thoughts and feelings on these verses? What is the most difficult thing about the way your loved one went Home? How can recognizing God's sovereignty and eternal plan help you?

DAY 209

Grace and peace to you from God our Father and the Lord Jesus Christ, who gave himself for our sins to rescue us from the present evil age, according to the will of our God and Father. (Galatians 1:4, NIV)

Randy Alcorn writes:

The world as it was and the world as it will be, is exceedingly good. The world as it is now, inhabited by humanity as we are now, is twisted. But this is a temporary condition, with an eternal remedy; Christ redemptive work. Not all worlds and all ages are evil, but only this world in this present age. When Jesus calls Satan 'the prince of this world' (John 14:30; 16:11) and Paul calls Satan 'the god of this age' (2 Corinthians 4:4), it's a relative and temporary designation. God is still God over the universe, still sovereign over Earth and over Satan. But the devil is the usurper who has tried to steal Earth's throne from man, God's delegated king of the Earth. In his time, God will take back the throne, as the God-man Jesus Christ, at last restoring and raising Earth.[251]

This present age means the days prior to the return of Jesus. The world was evil in Paul's day and it has continued. As we get closer to Jesus' return, the world seems to grow in wickedness. All you have to do is read the headlines to recognize how evil this present age is. We live in a fallen world. But the good news is Christ has rescued us from this evil age. Yes, we are in this fallen world, but we have the promise of eternal life. We have the promise of the new age that will be ushered in when Christ returns and the Earth is restored. As Randy states, this is all temporary and the eternal remedy is through Christ's redemptive work. We will live on the restored Earth where Christ reigns. The words "according to the will of our God and Father" speak again of the eternal plan and the eternal perspective. Our loved ones are now in His presence. If God calls us Home, we wait in Heaven in His presence out of this evil age; if He returns, He takes us with Him. This world in its fallen state is all temporary. Hold to the eternal perspective. We have been rescued; our loved ones are rescued. We are waiting on that day...

What are your thoughts and feelings on this verse? What are your thoughts on the statement by Randy Alcorn?

---

[251] Randy Alcorn, *Heaven* (Carol Stream, IL: Tyndale House, 2004), 228.

DAY 210 REFLECTION

As you look back over last week, what speaks to you? We read God's plan not to harm us but to prosper us. Perhaps we read it skeptically at first, but then we are reminded of the audience and that we are looking at God's eternal purpose. We must keep the eternal perspective. As you read this verse in Jeremiah and others like it, read those verses before and after. Have you struggled with verses like these? When we read the chapters and verses before and after, and notice the entire message, often we see the eternal focus.

We are told to look forward to the day of the Lord. The prophecy shows us God will refine and restore this Earth. We all look forward to that day of Jesus' return even more than we did before. I encouraged you to read the headlines. Truly just in the last few years everything seems to be speeding up exponentially. So much that is happening we can see as having been prophesied. There is comfort in prophecy. There is comfort in looking forward to Jesus' return. Come Jesus come!

We read Jesus intercedes for us. How powerful is the thought of Jesus interceding for us? We read about our bodily resurrection and we will live forever together. We can find comfort in the word *forever*. We see several verses that remind us of the eternal plan and purpose of God.

Jesus rescues us from this evil age. We live in an evil age but God is sovereign and He is eternal, this fallen world is temporary. We wait on that plan to come to fruition, we know it will. He has rescued us. We read that God's deliberate plan was for Jesus to die the horrible death on the cross for our salvation, a thought so amazing it is hard to comprehend. Because of Jesus' death, we have salvation and victory over death. We have an eternity with Jesus because of His sacrifice. We are so thankful for His grace and redemption. As you read back over the last week, record your thoughts and feelings. What day's devotional speaks to you the most?

DAY 211

Lord, you alone are my portion and my cup; you make my lot secure.
The boundary lines have fallen for me in pleasant places; surely I have a delightful
inheritance. I will praise the Lord, who counsels me;
even at night my heart instructs me. (Psalm 16:5-7, NIV)

As the initial searing pain and shock begins to stabilize, I try to focus on
how God has blessed me. When all seems lost, and darkness and brokenness
threatens to overtake you, remember that God's hand has been on you. When
I look at my life, I know that He has blessed me in so many ways far more than
I deserve. I hurt now, but I know that God is in control. I have to trust in Him
and in my inheritance as a believer. God is sovereign. He has established those
boundary lines and my lot in life. I would not trade a moment of my life God
has so generously given me. I know God will keep me secure and bring me into
His presence just like He did Don, and just like He did Dad, and just like He did
your loved one. I will praise His name.

As you pray, recall the many things He has blessed you with throughout your
life. Focus on God and His holiness. Listen to songs that allow you to focus on
His holiness and His goodness. Recall the times of blessing with your loved one.
Look forward to the times of blessings to come in eternity.

As you lay down at night, pray for God's counsel even in your sleep. Ask the
Holy Spirit to speak to you and let you feel Him. Chris Tiegreen writes, "Ask Him
every night before you go to sleep to fill you with His will—to 'program' your
mind with divine downloads that set your course from within. Then be sensitive
to the ways He leads. You can let your heart instruct you because He instructs
your heart."[252] I wish I could tell you that I always have an immediate answer,
but I do not. Many times I go to bed and wake up not feeling any differently.
But slowly, as you seek Him, you will feel more of His presence within. It is hard
at times to say the boundary lines have fallen in pleasant places when you feel
anything but pleasant. But we know that God has blessed us. We do not like
where we are right now, but we also know He loves us and that He will bring
everything together. We have the inheritance of eternal life. Depending on God
right now is what you must do. He alone is your portion and cup. Praise Him for
what He has done and for what He will do in eternity.

How do these verses speak to you? Tonight as you pray for Him to instruct your
heart and then listen to what He may say. Journal now the blessings you know
God has given you.

---

[252] Chris Tiegreen, *The One Year Experiencing God's Presence Devotional* (Carol Stream,
IL: Tyndale, 2011), May 17.

DAY 212

Give thanks to him who made the heavens so skillfully. His faithful love endures forever. Give thanks to him who placed the earth among the waters.
His faithful love endures forever. Give thanks to him who made the heavenly lights— His faithful love endures forever. The sun to rule the day,
His faithful love endures forever. And the moon and stars to rule the night.
(Psalm 136:5-9, NLT)

The same God that made the heavens so skillfully, who created the Earth and waters, made the heavenly lights, set the sun in place for day, and moon and stars at night, is the same God who loves you faithfully and endures forever. He is the same God who called your loved one Home. He is the same God who has a place for His children for eternity, and He is the same God who has established an eternal plan. This entire Psalm is composed of verses that exhort us to give thanks, and the response is, "His faithful love endures forever." The *NIV Study Bible* refers to this as a "liturgy of praise to the Lord as Creator and as Israel's Redeemer."[253] The Lord is our Creator and our Redeemer. He sent His only son to die for our sins, to redeem us, and to give us eternal life.

As you read this psalm, perhaps you can add your own verses. Give thanks to God for giving me such a wonderful husband and dad, His faithful love endures forever. Give thanks to God for our amazing life and love, His faithful love endures forever. The Thanksgiving one year after Don went Home and three years after Dad went Home, my eighteen-year-old nephew, Carson, posted this beautiful post on facebook:

Sometimes the things that we are most thankful for aren't even a part of this world anymore. I am thankful for my family that is physically here with me today. I am also thankful for the impact that my granddad and uncle left on me when they went to their permanent home. I know you aren't here anymore, but I know that we will meet up again one day.

Thanks to God; His faithful love endures forever. You fill in your own blank. Go back to your life and think not only of the loved ones you have, but the times in your life when God has blessed you. Focus on His faithful love that endures forever, His eternal plan, and give thanks that we have His faithful love. God is faithful and we can trust Him.

Read the whole chapter of Psalm 136 and write your own verses. Meditate on what you read and write. How can focusing on His faithful love enduring forever and His acts of love toward you comfort you now?

---

[253] *NIV Study Bible*, Kenneth Barker Ed. (Grand Rapids, MI: Zondervan, 1985), 930.

DAY 213

He will swallow up death forever. The Sovereign LORD will wipe away the tears from all faces; he will remove the disgrace of his people from all the earth. The LORD has spoken. (Isaiah 25:8, NIV)

God is sovereign and His plan through the ages culminates in the New Heaven and the New Earth where death will be swallowed up forever, and where God will wipe away every tear. Isaiah, speaking the Word of God foretells the destruction of death. And he ends it with, "The LORD has spoken." Randy Alcorn writes:

Jesus came not only to save spirits from damnation. That would have been, at most, a partial victory. No, he came to save his whole creation from death. That means our bodies too, not just our spirits. It means the Earth, not just humanity. And it means the universe, not just the Earth. Christ's victory over the Curse will not be partial. Death will not just limp away wounded. It will be annihilated, utterly destroyed.[254]

Throughout the Bible, God's sovereignty and His eternal plan is emphasized over and over. The New Heaven and the New Earth and eternal life is emphasized over and over. We just have to let those eternal truths soak in. We have to hold to the promises we read. We have to trust God and believe.

Right now the tears continue to flow and the thought of the sovereign Lord wiping them away seems far away. Our pain is all-consuming. We wake up and our loved one is not with us. We go through the day and our loved one is not with us. Other people go on as if there is nothing wrong, and we want to shout, "How can you do that? Can't you see that everything is not okay?" Grief's pain is only slightly visible to others, but you know how deep and intense the pain is inside of you. People say time heals; it does not. Over time, God helps you feel His comfort and peace, but the loss and pain is always there. What we can hold to is that someday that pain will be gone because God will swallow up death forever, and He will wipe away our tears. Healing will come in Heaven. For now we trust that God is faithful. We trust our loved ones are safely in His presence. We trust in God's sovereignty. And we look forward to that day.

How does this verse speak to you? What are your thoughts and feelings on the statement by Randy Alcorn?

---

[254] Randy Alcorn, *Heaven* (Carol Stream, IL: Tyndale House, 2004), 107.

DAY 214

No longer will there be a curse upon anything. For the throne of God and of the Lamb will be there, and his servants will worship him. And they will see his face, and his name will be written on their foreheads." (Revelation 22:3-4, NLT)

These verses in Revelation are beautiful and bring comfort and hope to all that grieve. Randy Alcorn writes:

God will lift the Curse, not only morally (in terms of sin) and psychologically (in terms of sorrow), but also physically (in terms of thorns in the ground). The curse is real, but it is temporary. Jesus is the cure for the curse. He came to set derailed human history back on its tracks. Earth won't be put out of its misery; it will be infused with greater life than it has ever known, at last becoming all that God meant for it to be.[255]

The throne of God and of Jesus is in Heaven even now, and when all is restored and the New Heaven and the New Earth are established we will see Him and His name will be on our foreheads. This is such an intimate portrayal of the relationship with God. We will serve God and worship Him. Even now our loved ones are with Him. Alcorn writes, "Not only will we see His face and live, but we will likely wonder if we ever lived before we saw his face! To see God will be our greatest joy, the joy by which all others will be measured."[256]

The awe in being before God's throne is indescribable now. It is an amazing thought that God's name will be on us. We are God's, and He claims us. Even now as you read this, our redeemed loved ones are in His presence. When I feel like I cannot go on, I try to focus on how wonderful Heaven is for Don and Dad and how amazing it is for them to actually be in Heaven. God has it all under control, and I see only a small portion. I see and feel my pain, I see our family's pain but God sees the whole picture. God sees the eternal plan. Our loved ones are okay; they are in the throne room of God. As believers, we will be too, in God's timing. We wait for the day there will be no more curse upon anything. We await the day that Jesus calls us all Home and restores all of creation to what He has planned. We are waiting for the day we will once again be with our loved ones, praising God before His throne. We are waiting on that day!

Meditate on these verses. Thinking of where your loved one is, and thinking of what is to come, write your thoughts and feelings.

---

[255] Randy Alcorn, *Heaven* (Carol Stream, IL: Tyndale House, 2004), 108.
[256] Ibid., 172.

DAY 215

Now over the heads of the living beings there was something like an expanse, like the awesome gleam of crystal, spread out over their heads. Now above the expanse that was over their heads there was something resembling a throne, like lapis lazuli in appearance; and on that which resembled a throne, high up, was a figure with the appearance of a man. (Ezekiel 1:22,26, NASB)

Read and ponder the words to these verses carefully, allowing the words to sink in your heart. Can you visualize what Ezekiel saw? Asher Intrater writes:

The book of Genesis states that God created the world with a firmament between heaven and earth. Until this time no one had ever seen it. The root of the word firmament means a surface someone can stand on. According to Ezekiel's description, there is a spiritual surface, relatively transparent, that stretches over our heads, like the ceiling of a lower apartment that becomes the flooring of the upper apartment. It is obviously made of a material or energy substance that we do not have on this earth.[257]

There are so many Scriptures about the seen and the unseen. We go about our daily lives unaware of the unseen. However, when someone we love is a part of that unseen world, it becomes much more real. We wonder what he is doing. How close is she? Ultimately we have to trust that God has everything under control. Our loved ones are with Jesus so that tells us enough. But still there is part of us that longs to know more.

We may have read over this verse in Ezekiel before and found it confusing. But as we start to meditate on it and read Asher Intrater's insightful words, pictures can come more clearly. Perhaps the division between Heaven and Earth is not so far away. The grandeur of just this one description is mind-boggling. Ezekiel had a glimpse into something, and as a result he had a dynamic message and closeness with God that is amazing.

Don had such an appreciation of the beauty of nature. When we would go into the mountains, he would be driving and exclaiming over the awesome scenery, and we would be peering over the side of the mountain reminding him to watch the road. I can only imagine how he reacted to seeing something like Ezekiel describes. I can imagine his and Dad's responses. We mourn, but they are in awe. Our loved ones know so much more fully. I have wondered if our loved ones even know when our arrival date might be; are they looking as forward to our arrival as we are? We trust that the unseen is there even though we can't see it. We know God is faithful and true. We look forward to that day!

Meditate on these verses. What pictures come to mind? What are your thoughts on these verses and Asher Intrater's descriptions?

---

[257] Asher Intrater, *Who Ate Lunch With Abraham?* (Peoria, AZ: Intermedia, 2011), 90.

DAY 216

Jesus said to her, "Your brother will rise again." Martha answered, "I know that he will rise again in the resurrection at the last day." Jesus said to her, "I am the resurrection and the life; he who believes in Me will live even if they die." (John 11:23-25, NIV)

In his book *Hope for Hurting Hearts*, Greg Laurie makes an excellent point on these verses. He writes:

Jesus was saying to His grieving friend, 'Martha, listen to me. 'Death is not the end! You are acting as though it is over with. It's not over with.' I think at this point He was talking about something greater and more profound than even the resurrection of Lazarus, which He would accomplish within that very hour. After all, raising Lazarus from the dead—exciting and joyful as that may have been—was only a temporary proposition! Lazarus would just have to die again in a few years.... So I don't think the essential message of the Lord's statement is, 'I'm going to raise your brother up from the dead.' I think the bigger message was this: 'Death is not the end. This is temporary. One day I will get rid of death altogether, and whoever believes in me will live forever.'[258]

There is a lot of attention and rightfully so, about Lazarus being raised from the dead. Jesus' raising Lazarus from the dead was a powerful message then and now. But Lazarus did eventually die again. I agree with Greg Laurie that there was a bigger message. Death is not the end. Jesus knew one day He was getting rid of death forever, and we would live forever. Until He establishes the abolishment of death completely we have a physical death now, but we do not die spiritually. Our loved ones have entered Heaven to be with Jesus now, but they live; and we will join them. Someday Jesus will do away with death altogether.

Notice also here that Jesus doesn't say, "Your brother will rise again, but you won't be brother and sister in Heaven." He says, "Your brother." Jesus knows that family ties are important to her now and will be in eternity. He knew her heart and her grief. Jesus had eaten with this family and knew their strong family ties. He loved them and they loved Him. In Jesus' consoling her He assured her of her brother's life, and that he would live even though he died. Your child, your parent, your spouse, your grandparent, sibling and your grandchild are still your loved ones. And as believers we will live forever with Christ. It is a beautiful promise straight from Jesus. We are waiting on that day!

As you meditate on these verses, how do they speak to you? What are your thoughts on the statements by Greg Laurie?

---

[258] Greg Laurie, *Hope for Hurting Hearts* (Dana Point, CA: Kerygma, 2008), 30.

DAY 217 REFLECTION

Read over the last week. What brings you the most comfort? We read God is our portion. God has set the boundary lines of our life. I am always amazed as I think back over what God has done. Our family moved to Detroit, Texas, when I was fourteen. Of all the places God could have moved my Dad and Mom He chose a little town in East Texas with a population of about 600 wonderful people. And in that very town I met the love of my life. How amazing was that boundary line?

We read to give thanks and that God's faithful love endures forever. Try filling in your own blanks and remind yourself of His unfailing love. Truly when we focus on His unfailing love, we can feel His love. We read the awesome words, "He will swallow up death forever." He will restore the whole of creation. He will remove the disgrace of His people. Then we read He will remove the curse. The throne of God is in Heaven. His name is written on our foreheads; we will see Him face to face. We ponder the thought of our loved ones seeing Him face to face. They are by the throne of God. It is so awesome that it is hard to grasp. We will be restored and reunited. We are waiting on that day!

We read the awesome picture of Heaven in Ezekiel and we are reminded of the nearness of Heaven; the majesty of Heaven. Meditating on those words brings me comfort. If you have not visited Asher Intrater's website, www. reviveisrael.org I encourage you to do so. You can receive Revive Israel updates via email.

We read again about Martha. And we read Greg Laurie's thoughts that Jesus was saying, "Death is not the end." The beautiful promise from Jesus that we will live. Jesus loved this family. He knew that Martha longed to be reunited with her brother, just as we long to be reunited with our loved ones. Jesus says we will. Hold and savor those words. Reflect back over the week and record your thoughts and feelings. What is God laying on your heart this week?

DAY 218

So we fix our eyes not on what is seen, but on what is unseen, since what is seen is temporary, but what is unseen is eternal. (2 Corinthians 4:18, NIV)

Paul tells us to fix our eyes on what is unseen. That is difficult to do. We are very physical creatures and our eyes are used to seeing our physical location. But Paul is telling us there is an unseen world that is eternal. All that we see is temporary. I love Asher Intrater's words on the unseen realm:

When Adam and Eve sinned in the Garden of Eden, the Bible says that they all of a sudden 'saw' their nakedness. The fact that they saw their nakedness was not an increase in vision but a decrease of vision. At that moment they saw carnal things, but loss of sight of spiritual things. This was not a small myopic loss of vision; this was an enormous fall into spiritual blindness. At that moment they stopped seeing an entire dimension of reality.[259]

The barrier is more internal than it is external. The barrier is a limitation in human eyes. It is not so much a limitation on our physical eyes as it is a limitation on our spiritual eyes, the eyes of our heart (Eph. 1:16). The veil in the Temple matched a spiritual veil on our hearts. When anyone turns to Yeshua in faith, that veil begins to be removed (2 Cor. 3:16). Until one is born again, he cannot see the spiritual world (kingdom of God). However, with the new birth comes a potential to see the things of the spirit. (John 3:3).[260]

(Asher Intrater is a Messianic Jew; Yeshua is Jesus' name in Hebrew which is what He would have been called when He walked on the Earth. Jesus is the English version of the Greek word for Yeshua). We are comfortable with the tangible—what we can see, and the physical—what we can touch. The physical reality of our loved one is one of the things we miss so much now. We can't see, touch, or hear our loved one, so his absence is painful and sorrowful. But if we could only see with our spiritual eyes we would see so much more. Of course, there is a reason we can't: God in His sovereignty has made the heavenly realm unseen. But I do pray that God will open the eyes of my heart, and that He lets me see and hear Him with my spiritual eyes and ears. Focusing on Heaven and knowing that there is an unseen world, a spiritual world, brings me comfort. Don, Dad and _____ are in Heaven. They can see what we long to see. Our loved ones have the ability to see the "unseen," the entire dimension that we cannot see, but someday we will too. We are waiting on that day!

Meditate on the amazing verse and quotes; how do they speak to you?

---

[259] Asher Intrater, *Who Ate Lunch With Abraham?* (Peoria, AZ: Intermedia, 2011), 99.
[260] Ibid., 80.

DAY 219

Brothers and sisters, we do not want you to be uninformed about those who sleep in death, so that you do not grieve like the rest of mankind, who have no hope. For the Lord himself will come down from heaven, with a loud command, with the voice of the archangel and with the trumpet call of God, and the dead in Christ will rise first. After that, we who are still alive and are left will be caught up together with them in the clouds to meet the Lord in the air. And so we will be with the Lord forever. Therefore encourage one another with these words. (1 Thessalonians 4:13, 16,-18, NIV) Read all of vs.13-18

Apparently Paul was answering some concerns about loved ones that had died before Jesus' return. Paul is assuring his friends that those who have "fallen asleep" will come back with Jesus when He returns. Paul tells his friends that their loved ones' bodies will be raised first and those who are still alive will be changed and *will be caught up together* with them in the clouds (emphasis mine). They were going to be together again with their loved ones. The point was that Paul wanted to assure his friends they didn't have to grieve like those that had no hope. They had hope because they trusted in Jesus. They were going to be with their loved ones again with Jesus; it doesn't get any better than that.

Any time our family is together, conversation will go to something about our faith. Of course, now that Dad and Don are in Heaven we talk about Heaven even more. But we have always talked about God's goodness and faithfulness. We worshiped God together. Just think: there will be a day we will worship God in an even more exciting way because the object of our worship will be right there, visible in all His glory. Thinking about the resurrection and being with Jesus is amazing to contemplate.

These verses reassure us of relationships. Paul knew his readers were grieving because someone they loved had gone before them. Paul's words reassure us all. As Randy Alcorn writes, "Throughout the ages, Christians have anticipated eternal reunion with their loved ones."[261] In *One Minute After You Die*, Erwin Lutzer writes:

Of course, dear widow, your husband who is in heaven continues to love you as he did on earth. Today he loves you with a fonder, sweeter, purer love. It is a love purified by God. Your child loves you; so do your mother and father. There is no more a break in love than there is in continuity of thought. Death breaks ties on earth but renews them in heaven.[262]

Meditate on this verse. What are your thoughts on the two quotes?

---

[261] Randy Alcorn, *Heaven* (Carol Stream, IL: Tyndale House, 2004), 95.

[262] Erwin Lutzer, *One Minute After You Die* (Chicago, IL: Moody, 1997), 66.

DAY 220

Abraham breathed his last and died in a ripe old age, an old man and satisfied with life; and he was gathered to his people. (Genesis 25:8, NASB)

We can read over this verse in Genesis and not grasp the full meaning of what it says. "He was gathered to his people." The following quotes are deep insights on the words. First, the words of Paul Enns:

Scripture is also clear that there will be recognizable reunion with family members immediately at death. When Abraham died, "he was gathered to his people" (Gen 25:8; 25:17; 35:29; 49:29,33). The picture is further illuminated in Matthew 18:11 with Abraham reclining in the kingdom with Isaac and Jacob—his son and grandson. Family reunion! For believers, death brings a joyful reunion with believing family members. What a prospect.[263]

Enns goes on to say "What does it mean that he was 'gathered to his people'? It means Abraham was reunited with Sara and with his family in heaven."[264]

Dr. Arnold Fruchtenbaum, in *The Footsteps of the Messiah*, writes:

Notice that first, the physical death takes place then after death, he is seen as gathered unto his people… They are seen as joining a company of whom they are conscious and who had preceded them. Some interpret this phrase to mean nothing more than being buried in the family cemetery. However, that would not be true of a person like Abraham whose family or clan cemetery was back in Haran.[265]

Many of the people I have worked with in my counseling practice need to know that in eternity there is a continuity of relationships. I need to know there is a continuity of relationship. Randy Alcorn and Paul Enns both do an excellent job in their books on Heaven in showing all the Scriptures to reinforce continuity. And as my dad would say, "It is the nature of God." We grieve now, but we know someday we will be reunited with our loved ones and we will worship God together in a perfect place as we see His perfect being. We are waiting on that day.

Meditate on this verse and others like it. Meditate on the quotes. Write your thoughts and feelings.

---

[263] Paul Enns, *Heaven Revealed* (Chicago, IL: Moody, 2011), 43.

[264] Ibid., 159

[265] Arnold G. Fruchtenbaum, *The Footsteps of the Messiah* (Tustin, CA: Ariel, 2003), 698-699.

DAY 221

I am torn between the two: I desire to depart and be with Christ, which is better by far. (Philippians 1:23, NIV)

I like the way that Greg Laurie and Paul Enns talk about this powerful verse. Greg Laurie writes:

I never fully understood those words... until now. I read that statement from the apostle and say to myself, "Oh sure I'd like to be in Heaven. But then, I'm pretty happy here on earth too." But when you have loved ones on the Other Side—and perhaps someone who has just recently made that journey—then the promise and hope of reuniting in that place brings great joy, and something to look forward to.[266]

Paul Enns writes:

Paul's desire was strong; the word 'desire' stands in the emphatic position. He knew that the moment he left this earthly life, he would be with Christ. That would be 'very much better.' Again Paul's comments are emphatic and strong. There is no comparison between Paul being with Christ in paradise and being on the old earth.[267]

Enns likens this imagery to a ship leaving. When the ship leaves, the people who see it off may cry, but those waiting for it are welcoming it. He goes on to discuss the word *depart*:

'Depart' (analuo) 'means to unloose, to undo. It is used of loosening a ship from its moorings.' It means to lift the anchor and travel to another destination.... When does a crew member on a ship lift an anchor? To depart to a better destination. At death, the believer lifts anchor and leaves for the better destination—heaven.[268]

As you grieve, remember that your loved ones are truly better by far. They have departed this Earth and are with Christ now. Our loved ones were welcomed by Christ Himself, and then probably by those who have gone before. I can imagine Dad greeted Don with open arms. We can hold to the promise that we will be reunited with our loved ones and when we are, it will be better by far. But for now, we pray for strength to do whatever it is God has for us to do while we are waiting on that day.

As you reflect on the verse and the quotes, how do they speak to you?

---

[266] Greg Laurie, *Hope for Hurting Hearts* (Dana Point, CA: Kerygma, 2008), 51.
[267] Paul Enns, *Heaven Revealed* (Chicago, IL: Moody, 2011), 22.
[268] Ibid., 38.

DAY 222

For to me, to live is Christ and to die is gain. (Philippians 1:21, NIV)

J. Sidlow Baxter writes, "There are four big reasons why death is gain to those of us who know and love the Savior. (1) The One to whom it takes us; (2) The place to which is bears us; (3) The state to which it lifts us; (4) The rewards to which it leads us."[269] Death is gain because it takes us to Jesus and that alone is gain. Paul saw with his own eyes a portion of Heaven, and although he couldn't talk about it, clearly he gave us enough to know that it was gain for us all. The awe that we will feel just being in the presence of our Savior and in Heaven will be indescribable. Baxter wrote:

In that transition (I am inclined to think) there will come, all-in-one, such a realization of sinfulness, and such a consciousness of utter salvation from it and a compelling vision of our Savior, as we never knew on earth. It will effect in us such an utter yieldedness to him accompanied by such a renewal of our whole being, that the release and rapture will be instantaneously all infusing.[270]

I don't think I ever realized how much the Bible talks about rewards in Heaven. Looking at all the times the Bible mentions rewards helps reinforce that everything we do matters for eternity. I know I want God to be pleased with my thoughts and my actions. I am in a hurry for Him to come back, but I also want to know that what I do here is what He wants me to do. I want to glorify God until that day He calls me Home.

Baxter lists many of the crowns and rewards that are mentioned in the New Testament. He also writes:

Added to that is the reward of reunion with our own departed loved ones who were near and dear to us in this present world. They will be just the same in their personal identity as when they were here with us.... As we have said earlier there will be neither any fading of identity or blurring of personality. You will always be you. I shall always be I.....Oh, there will be such reunions there!... The coming reunion is one of the tenderer aspects which make death 'gain' to the Christian. Sometimes the waiting days on earth seem too long.[271]

I couldn't agree more. We are waiting on that day!

As you reflect on today's verse and quotes, how do they speak to you?

---

[269] J. Sidlow Baxter, *The Other Side of Death* (Grand Rapids, MI: Kregel, 1987), 100.
[270] Ibid., 106.
[271] Ibid., 110.

DAY 223

Since, then, you have been raised with Christ, set your hearts on things above, where Christ is, seated at the right hand of God. Set your minds on things above, not on earthly things. For you died, and your life is now hidden with Christ in God. (Colossians 3:1-3, NIV)

I have always wondered about Heaven, but now knowing about Heaven becomes even more important to me. My heart and mind are focused on Heaven. Randy Alcorn writes, "The Greek word translated 'set your hearts on' is *zeteo*. So we can understand Paul's admonition in Colossians 3:1 as follows: Diligently, actively, single-mindedly pursue the things above—in a word, Heaven. The verb *zeteo* is in the present tense suggesting an ongoing process."[272]

Not only does the more we focus on Heaven bring us comfort but it also allows us to remember that we need to be getting ready for that day ourselves. As Randy says,

Heaven isn't only our future home. It's our home already, waiting over the next hill. If we really grasp this truth, it will have a profound effect on our holiness.... If we see ourselves in Heaven with Christ, we'll be drawn to worship and serve him here and now, creating ripples in Heaven's waters that will extend outward for eternity.[273]

C.S. Lewis writes, "Aim at Heaven and you will get earth 'thrown in': aim at earth and you will get neither."[274] As Paul Enns points out, "The phrase 'things above' means 'the heavenly world.' It is only as we focus our thoughts on heaven that we will correctly interpret life on earth. It will give us the proper perspective."[275]

We are told to set our hearts on things above and we know that is where we want to spend eternity. Now we have even a bigger part of our hearts there. The more I can stay focused on Heaven and keeping an eternal perspective, the more assurance I feel. I think these verses and these authors sum up having that eternal perspective. We are waiting on that day!

Meditate on today's verses and quotes. Today's thoughts all point us to Heaven, how comforting is that to you?

---

[272] Randy Alcorn, *Heaven* (Carol Stream, IL: Tyndale House, 2004), 21.
[273] Ibid., 193.
[274] C. S. Lewis, *Mere Christianity* (New York, NY: HarperCollins, 1952, 1980), 134.
[275] Paul Enns, *Heaven Revealed* (Chicago, IL: Moody, 2011), 184.

DAY 224 REFLECTION

Looking back over the last week, what speaks to you the most? We are reminded to fix our eyes on the unseen. Our loved ones are in the unseen world; unseen by us but even more real than what we do see. Paul tells us to not grieve like those who have no hope. Why? Because we will be reunited with those we love. We will worship our Lord together in Heaven. We worship now even in our grief, and we worshiped with our loved ones when they were with us. But someday our worship will be perfect because we will actually be in Jesus' presence. We will know Him fully. We are waiting on that day!

We also read where Abraham was gathered to his people. We read where many authors believe that "gathered to his people" is not the burial but the reunion of families, of their people. Paul tells us that Heaven is far better. We are reminded that our loved ones are in a far better place. We long to be with them, but we know we will be when God is ready. Heaven has always been a far better place, but when we have a loved one there before us, it increases our desire even more. We read again that death is gain. We are reminded of the continuity of life and how everything we do here matters for eternity.

We read again to set our heart on things above. This tells us to diligently seek the things above. As Paul Enns says, "It is when we focus our thoughts on Heaven that we correctly interpret life on earth." As you look back over this week there are many verses that speak of the continuity of life and relationships. The verses this week are all good ones to memorize and quote aloud. The verses help us focus on Heaven and eternity. Record your thoughts and feelings. What do you feel like God is laying on your heart this week?

DAY 225

For what is our hope, our joy, or the crown in which we will glory in the presence of our Lord Jesus when he comes? Is it not you? Indeed, you are our glory and joy. (1 Thessalonians 2:19-20, NIV)

Paul was writing to the Thessalonians and was clearly expressing his love for them, but notice that he takes it a step further. Paul says his crown in which "we" will glory in the presence of Jesus are those that he loves. We have read throughout the Bible verses that show a clear continuity of our relationships; this is one more passage that reinforces that truth. Jesus is clearly the presence that is most desired in Heaven as Paul writes, but Paul also tells us that he looks forward to being with those he loves in Heaven.

We know even in our sorrow and pain that Jesus understands. We know that in our grief, we have the hope of the eternal life with Christ. We have the hope of the continuity of our relationships with our loved ones. In the following two quotes, Randy Alcorn's words resonate with me:

On Earth, the closer we draw to Him, the closer we draw to each other. Surely the same will be true in Heaven. What an honor it will be to always know that God chose us for each other on this old Earth so that we might have a foretaste of life with him on the New Earth. People with good marriages are each other's best friends. There's no reason to believe they won't still be best friends in Heaven.[276]

Jesus was closer to John than to any of the other disciples. Jesus was closer to Peter, James and John than to the rest of the twelve, and closer to the twelve than the seventy, and closer to the seventy than to his other followers. He was close to Lazarus and Martha, and closer still to their sister Mary. He was so close to his mother that while he was dying on the cross, he instructed John to care for her after his death. Since Christ was closer to some people than to others, clearly there can't be anything wrong with it.[277]

Our friend Debi, a faithful Christian who has been through much in her life, yet faithfully endures, says, "The crown I want most is to be reunited in Heaven with the ones I love." Paul agreed those loves were a crown. I think we do, too. Our hope is in the presence of Jesus. I feel like this is not my real life that I am in a nightmare; like right now is a parenthesis of my real life and when I see Jesus my real life will resume. I know all of my family will someday be together in Heaven worshiping our Lord and Savior. I am waiting on that day.

As you reflect on the verses and quotes, how do they speak to you the most?

---

[276] Randy Alcorn, *Heaven* (Carol Stream, IL: Tyndale House, 2004), 351.
[277] Ibid., 357.

DAY 226

For now we see only a reflection as in a mirror; then we shall see face to face. Now I know in part; then I shall know fully, even as I am fully known. (1 Corinthians 13:12, NIV)

Why was someone we loved taken from us? My neighbor's twenty-year-old son went Home after a tragic accident. A friend's thirteen-year-old son took his own life. Don was taken so quickly, so full of life and with so much left to give. My Dad suffered with COPD and preached until his last breath. My cousin brutally killed with so much left to give. A friend jogging was struck by a car. A friend's twenty-three-year-old daughter had complications of diabetes. Another friend's baby lived one hour. A Christian grandmother who with her wonderful husband was raising their grandchildren died of cancer. Our pastor of missions died of cancer. A friend's godly wife went Home after a courageous and faith-filled battle with cancer. None of this makes sense to us. Yet, God knows best. Someday I will understand, but for now I trust God.

As I write this, I have over twenty-five families in my prayer journal who are grieving the loss of a loved one. In addition to those, I am also praying for many who I do not know: the families who have lost people in a recent hurricane, a recent earthquake in another country, and those dying every day as martyrs in other countries. I have many in my prayer notes who are battling a terminal illness. The list goes on and on. We live in a fallen world. But fortunately this world is not all there is. This life is temporary. For now we see dimly, but someday we shall see face to face; we know in part, but someday we will know fully and be fully known. As Greg Laurie points out:

Why does God allow torment for some and triumph for others? No one can say this side of heaven. The Bible gives us the account of wicked King Herod who arrested and immediately executed the apostle James—brother of John and a close personal friend of Jesus when He walked on this earth. And like that he was gone.... But why did James die and Peter go free? It's hard to say. Life just doesn't make sense a great deal of the time. But God has His purposes that often remain a mystery to us.[278]

Philip Yancey writes, "After death the two worlds will come together fully. Paul describes it as a kind of maturity or completion of what started on earth."[279] We have to trust Jesus even when nothing makes sense. We look forward to the day we see clearly, just as our loved ones do now. We are waiting on that day!

As you reflect on the verse and thoughts for today, how do they speak to you?

---

[278] Greg Laurie, *Hope for Hurting Hearts* (Dana Point, CA: Kerygma, 2008), 130.
[279] Philip Yancey, *Rumors of Another World* (Grand Rapids, MI: Zondervan, 2003), 186.

DAY 227

Therefore we do not lose heart. Though outwardly we are wasting away, yet inwardly we are being renewed day by day. For our light and momentary troubles are achieving for us an eternal glory that far outweighs them all. (2 Corinthians 4:16-17, NIV)

Nothing seems light and momentary to me right now. I started this book seven months after God called Don Home. I felt the strong impression that God wanted me to write this book. I know that reading, praying, and writing have helped me focus on the eternal perspective, which has comforted me. I am writing this particular devotional twelve months and nine days after God called Don Home. I feel like I have an internal magnet constantly searching for my other half. I have cried every day and I long for the day I am reunited.

Don was an amazing home builder and kept quite busy. But he had decided to also become an insurance adjuster. His background as a builder would help, and with the economy as it is building was up and down. Don had not gone assignment, however. One night as we sat on the deck, he said, "You know, some people are gone six months on this insurance adjusting. I don't think I can be away from you that long." I told him I didn't want to be away from him that long either and maybe that is why he had not been called on by the insurance companies. God had always provided and we were not worried.

I think about that conversation a lot now. I never imagined myself without Don. I still can't and it has been over a year. So light and momentary does not fit. But Paul certainly had not had it light. He had been imprisoned and beaten; even now he faced certain death. So how could he call it light and momentary? Because Paul knew his troubles were earning him eternal glory. He knew this life was not all there is. We must remember that as well. Max Lucado writes:

If we assume this world exists just for pregrave happiness, these atrocities disqualify it from doing so. But what if this earth is the womb? Might these challenges, severe as they may be, serve to prepare us, equip us for the world to come? As Paul wrote, These little troubles are getting us ready for an eternal glory that will make all our troubles seem like nothing (2 Corinthians 4:17, CEV).[280]

I still have deep sorrow and hurt and I long for that day I see Jesus and all of my family is together again in eternity. I know that Don and Dad have witnessed God's eternal glory just as _____has. Someday we will see His Glory and our suffering will seem light and momentary.

Reflect on today's verses and thoughts. What are your thoughts and feelings?

---

[280] Max Lucado, *Fearless* (Nashville, TN: Nelson, 2009), 133.

DAY 228

"Naked I came from my mother's womb, and naked I will depart. The Lord gave and the Lord has taken away; may the name of the Lord be praised." (Job 1:21, NIV) After Job had prayed for his friends, the Lord restored his fortunes and gave him twice as much as he had before. (Job 42:10, NIV)

The first verse was what Job said after he found out he had lost everything, including his seven children. The last verse is at the end of Job. In the past I never understood Job, but I have a newfound respect for him. Job is a book that cuts to your core. Job lost everything and still did not blame God. He asked why. He begged for answers, but he did not turn his back on God. He remained faithful. Reread Job carefully. Philip Yancey does a good job in his book, *Disappointment With God*, covering Job. He points out that the Bible is full of people with questions. We are not the only ones who wonder why. But the Bible is also full of hope and faithfulness. God is faithful and He has an eternal plan. We do not understand things from our limited perspective, but God does.

One thing that always bothered me about Job was that no amount of other children would make up for the ones he lost. I could not get past that thought. So he went through all of that loss and got double returned to him, what good does that do when you have lost a child? I failed to notice one very important detail in the book of Job. Charles Spurgeon points out something very interesting that helps me understand. Spurgeon says:

Did you ever notice, concerning Job's children, that when God gave him twice as much substance as he had before, he gave him only the same number of children as he formerly had? The Lord gave him twice as much gold and twice as much of all sorts of property... Why? Because God regarded his children who had died as being Job's still. They were dead to Job's eyes, but they were visible to Job's faith. God numbered them still as part of Job's family, and if you carefully count up how many children Job had, you will find that he had twice as many in the end as he had in the beginning.[281]

Job would be reunited with his children someday. He could not see them now, but he would be with them again. We too will be reunited with our loved ones. Job was a faithful man of God and was not immune to the trouble of this fallen world, but he remained faithful and God was faithful. We are waiting on that day.

Read the book of Job. As you read these verses and comments, what are your thoughts and feelings?

---

[281] Charles Spurgeon, as cited by Randy Alcorn in *We Shall See God*, (Carol Stream, IL: Tyndale House, 2011), 55.

DAY 229

For it is God who works in you to will and to act in order to fulfill his good purpose. (Philippians 2:13, NIV)

God not only has an eternal plan, but He has a purpose for you. As Asher Intrater points out:

What God created at the beginning of Genesis had in mind what happens at the end of Revelation. The end was planned from the beginning. This can be compared to a building contractor who would not start the construction until the entire plan was already designed by the architect. God's purpose for creation was already planned before He started the creation itself. The end product is determined by the original design.[282]

I like this quote. Since Don was a builder, we have a lot of home designs that he has built through the years. Building is an art that requires talent and planning. God is the Master Builder, the Creator of all of things. He has a divine plan and purpose. God will work in you to fulfill the purpose He has for you. After pointing out the Bible makes no guarantee of long life, Greg Laurie writes:

The Bible tells us that our times are in His hands (Psalm 31:15). It also tells us, in the book of Acts that 'after David had done the will of God in his own generation he died and was buried' (Acts 13:36, NLT). In other words when David's time was up, God said, 'Come home.' We really have nothing to say about the date of our birth, or our death. Then again, we have a lot to say about that space in the middle.[283]

I don't know why some people are taken so young. It does not make sense that a young child has cancer or a baby dies in the crib. It does not make sense that people we love who seem to be in the prime of life are taken. It does not make sense in this fallen world. But we know God does have an eternal plan, and we know someday we will understand how His purpose and plan was fulfilled. We know that if this world was all there was it would be sad and unfair. But God has a purpose and as believers we are a part of that purpose. Our loved ones fulfilled their purpose; it seemed too short to us and we wonder why they are gone so soon. But they are safe in His glorious presence. Each day could be the day Jesus comes back or calls us Home. While we wait for that day, we must continue to seek Him, to be open to His will and His purpose.

As you reflect on today's verse and thoughts, what are your own thoughts?

---

[282] Asher Intrater, *Who Ate Lunch With Abraham?* (Peoria, AZ: Intermedia, 2011), 169.
[283] Greg Laurie, *Hope for Hurting Hearts* (Dana Point, CA: Kerygma, 2008), 131.

DAY 230

Since, then, you have been raised with Christ, set your hearts on things above, where Christ is seated at the right hand of God. Set your minds on things above, not on earthly things. (Colossians 3:1-2, NIV)

William Scroggie, mentioned earlier, was a minister who lived from 1877 to 1958. He wrote *What About Heaven?* when his wife of thirty-nine years went to Heaven. He said, "It is when we confront death close up that we think most deeply of life here and hereafter."[284] He wrote that he has had to say good-bye to his mother, father, and wife, and that experience did not leave him the same.

In the first month after my beloved wife 'passed on,' a number of questions clamoured for an answer. Where is she? What is she doing? What is her state now? Does she still see me and hear me? Is she with and does she know loved ones of hers who have 'passed on' before her? Will she know me when I reach the other side? Does she retain memory of life here? Has she any regrets? If she sees my loneliness, does any degree of sadness touch her spirit? Has she actually seen Christ, the Jesus who died for her, and Whom she loved? These, and such like, are questions pressed in upon the heart only in some overwhelming experience of loss and sorrow. Those whose days and nights have not been haunted by them have not known the sorrows which induce them.[285]

Scroggie writes about not wanting to just have sentiment, but to search the Bible and know what God says. It was very important to him to stay biblically grounded and true despite his pain and what he wanted to believe. I can certainly understand his thinking. I pray continually that anything I think and write will be grounded in God's Word, and not just what I wish to be true. Scroggie states, "Crushing sorrow needs a rational faith to keep it from despair."[286] But through his studies he found the answers he so desperately desired. He longed to see his Savior and to be reunited with his wife. He concludes his book with this:

It may well be that our loved ones are watching us and waiting for us, and this should lead us to hasten our step; and Christ we know is coming to meet us. Wonderful fact! Wonderful truth! Wonderful hope! But if the Lord should tarry, we shall go the way our loved ones have gone, and it will be as wonderful for us as it was for them.[287]

In 1958 William Scroggie went Home and his desire was met. We, too, are waiting on that day. How do these powerful verses and words speak to you?

---

[284] William Scroggie, *What About Heaven?* (London: Pickering & Inglis, 1954), 11.
[285] Ibid., 12.
[286] Ibid., 44.
[287] Ibid., 136-137.

DAY 231 REFLECTION

As you reflect back over the week, what seems to speak to you the most? In a very profound verse we read that Paul's crown in Heaven would be the people he loves. What were your thoughts on the quotes by Randy Alcorn? Relationships matter here on Earth and they continue to matter in Heaven. We are waiting on that day!

We read that we see dimly now, but we will see fully. We have so many questions that most likely we will not understand this side of eternity. But we know someday we will see fully and be fully known. Our loved ones are seeing fully now. We are told to not lose heart; that no matter how bad it seems right now, in light of eternity it will seem like light and momentary troubles. I am waiting on that day. Pain does not seem light or momentary right now, but I take comfort that in light of eternity it will.

We read powerful words in Job. Philip Yancey tells us, "Probably the oldest book in the Bible, Job reads like the most modern. Its extreme portrayal—one man confronting the abyss in a universe that makes no sense—foreshadows the predicament of modern humanity."[288] We read that Job gets back twice as much for his faithfulness; however, he does not get back twice as many children. Some scholars suggest that he still had them; they were just waiting on him in Heaven. I love that thought! It speaks of family reunions. We are waiting on that day!

We read that not only does God have an eternal plan; but that He also has an eternal purpose for each of us. As short as the life of our loved ones may have been, they fulfilled their eternal purpose. We may not see what the purpose was in such a short life, but we will see in eternity. We must also seek Him to fulfill our eternal purpose.

We read one of my favorite passages that tells us to set our hearts and minds on Heaven. We read how many grieving Christians find comfort in focusing on Heaven. William Scroggie was one author that we read. He wrote a number of books and was pastor of several churches in Scotland, New Zealand, the United States, Canada, and England—including Charles Spurgeon's Metropolitan Tabernacle in London, England, during World War II. We can draw comfort from his life and words. I know he rejoiced as He met his Savior. Scroggie was reunited with his wife and his desires met! We have always been told to set our minds on Heaven, but now Heaven is the lifeline that allows us to get through the day. We find comfort in thinking on Heaven. As you read back over the week, record your thoughts and feelings. What does God seem to be laying on your heart this week?

---

[288] Phillip Yancey, *Disappointment With God* (Grand Rapids, MI: Zondervan, 1992), 180.

DAY 232

When the perishable has been clothed with the imperishable, and the mortal with immortality, then the saying that is written will come true: "Death has been swallowed up in victory." "Where, O death, is your victory? Where, O death, is your sting?" (1 Corinthians 15:54-55, NIV)

Death has no victory over the believer. Our hope is in Christ. He satisfied the demand of the law. Paul Helms writes:

But Christ has satisfied the demands of the law, and thus deprived sin of its strength, and death of its sting.... What he [Paul] is saying is that though, in death, men and women seem to be dealt a final blow, this is not so. For the man or woman in Christ there is the prospect of glorious, incorruptible life beyond the grave. And this fact, because it is certain, is the ground of a present triumph and exultation in what God is going to do.[289]

Our believing loved ones went straight into our Father's presence. There is life beyond the grave. God's eternal plan is unfolding and at some point, He will say, "No more," and we will all live on the New Earth in an imperishable body. We will live eternally with our Father. Death hurts us here because we love so deeply. We miss those we love. We miss their physical presence. But we will be with them physically again when the perishable is clothed with the imperishable and the mortal with immortality. Dr. Luke Terveen writes:

The resurrection drains the deadly, poisonous 'sting' of death and its close ally, sin, of their power over us. We shall be finally and completely free at last, thanks to God's victory for us in Jesus.... There is no greater hope than this perfect consummation of our relationship with the Lord.... Though we yet grieve the death of loved ones in Christ and our own future well-being may hold uncertainties, still our grieving and concerns are not like those of people 'who have no hope.'... Our funerals should look forward to the 'homegoing' of our believing loved ones, coloring our sorrows with joy and hope. And the promise of our future resurrection creates a hope-filled eager expectation for that day when Jesus returns and when our relationship with him and all other believers who have gone before us will reach heavenly proportions.[290]

Hold to the eternal hope. This life is not all there is. We are waiting on that day!

Meditate on the verses and the quotes. What are your thoughts and feelings?

---

[289] Paul Helm, *The Last Things: Death, Judgment, Heaven and Hell* (Carlisle, PA: Banner of Truth, 1989), 131.

[290] John Luke Terveen, *Hope for the Brokenhearted* (Colorado Springs, CO: Victor, 2006), 166-167.

DAY 233

And if you address as Father the one who impartially judges according to each one's work, live out the time of your temporary residence here in reverence. (1 Peter 1:17, NET)

Peter repeatedly reminds us that our lives here are temporary. In both 1 and 2 Peter, he uses terms such as alien, strangers, temporary residence, and temporary stay. Peter and Paul both refer to their bodies as tents, temporary dwellings. As C.S. Lewis says, "Our Father refreshes us on the journey with some pleasant inns, but will not encourage us to mistake them for home."[291] Joni Erickson Tada writes:

First Peter is written to people who were suffering. Peter's letter is a practical explanation of where hope can be found and what it looks like to live with hope in a broken world. Chapter 1 roots present hope in the promise of eternity. This chapter also connects present obedience to future hope. In the chapters that follow, Peter keeps connecting practical, everyday living to the hope of eternity.[292]

An eternal perspective allows us to face the overwhelming sorrow and pain. We know this life is temporary. We are on this Earth for a purpose, and our bodies are a temporary residence because our true home, our true residence, is in Heaven, and someday on the New Earth. Our believing loved one's stay was all too temporary for us, but ours is a temporary stay too. We don't know how long it will be before God calls us Home or until He comes back; but either way it will happen! We will see Jesus; we will be reunited with our loved ones. So for now we live out our temporary stay with reverence and obedience.

God will look at our lives and judge our works. As believers, we are saved by grace not works. But our works do count for eternity. As you pray, ask God to show you what He wants you to do as you wait for His coming. Even in pain and sorrow we can serve Jesus. Suffering in this world is inevitable. We are suffering because of the loss of someone we love, but we have hope rooted in eternity. Our stay is temporary. Spend your time wisely, knowing that everything you do counts for eternity. We must remember that there is continuity of our lives, and that we want to hear, "Well done, my good and faithful servant." We are waiting on that day!

As you reflect on this verse and thoughts, ask God how to serve Him now.

---

[291] C.S. Lewis, *The Problem of Pain* (New York, NY: HarperColllins, 1940, 1996), Location 1283.

[292] Joni Eareckson Tada, *Heaven: Your Real Home* (Grand Rapids, MI: Zondervan, 1995), Location 1478.

DAY 234

The Lord is near to the brokenhearted and saves those who are crushed in spirit. (Psalm 34:18, NASB)

My sister Teresa says, "You can prepare for death but you cannot prepare for a broken heart." As therapists, Teresa and I have always dealt with grieving people. We have cried with others and our hearts hurt for them. But we were not prepared for our own broken heart. Many authors whom I read were ministers that had dealt with others' broken hearts but were not prepared for their own broken heart.

The intensity of the pain when your heart is crushed is indescribable to someone else. And although they may hurt for you, as I have for others, my own crushed heart was indescribable to anyone. The pain overwhelms you. You feel isolated and alone, even if you know you are not. The pain is raw and intense. The Bible tells us the Lord is near. We know that Jesus understands; we know He wept and we know He intercedes for us. Your heart is crushed, my heart is crushed, and we will never be the same. But what we do have is hope—hope of eternal life, hope in Christ, and hope in the reunion of our loved ones for eternity. So our faith is what we hold to now. As Charles Stanley writes, "Trusting God in the dark when you doubt, when you do not understand when you are ready to crumble at any moment, is the stamp of true faith. It rests on the faithfulness of God. You can trust Him because He is trustworthy. You can depend on Him because He is dependable."[293]

Our faith rests on the faithfulness of God. He is faithful. No matter what you feel now, God is faithful. Our redeemed loved ones are with Jesus now. We have to always remind ourselves of that truth. We must know that God is faithful. His eternal plan will come to completion. The hope that we have professed is real and true. Our God is in control. We will be with our loved ones again. The nightmare does have an end when we see Jesus and our loved ones. We are a part of God's eternal plan. This life is temporary. Charles Stanley also writes, "You can redeem your suffering, give meaning to it, and rescue it from emptiness by realizing your pain can be used to glorify Jesus."[294] We focus on Heaven and our faith. We also have to remember that we, too, will stand before our Redeemer. Ask Jesus now how you can glorify Him through your pain and sorrow as you wait for that day.

Meditate on this verse and the quotes. What are your thoughts and feelings?

---

[293] Charles Stanley, *Enter His Gates* (Nashville, TN: Nelson, 1998), 88.
[294] Ibid., 92.

DAY 235

Two men, Moses and Elijah, appeared in glorious splendor, talking with Jesus. They spoke about his departure, which he was about to bring to fulfillment at Jerusalem. (Luke 9:30-31, NIV)

All three accounts of the Transfiguration (Mark 7:1-13, Luke 9:28-36, and Matthew 17:1-13) describe the brilliance of Jesus' face and clothing, all describe how the disciples recognized Elijah and Moses, and all describe how in awe the disciples were. Luke tells us that Moses and Elijah were speaking of Christ's departure, which He was about to bring to fulfillment in Jerusalem. There is so much eternal truth in these verses, but two things I want to ponder. One thing to think on is the glorious splendor of Moses and Elijah. We have already talked about how they were recognized; even though the disciples had never known Moses or Elijah, they knew them now. Moses and Elijah appeared in glorious splendor because they reflected the glory of Christ. Randy Alcorn writes, "Since God Himself is consistently portrayed as existing in brilliant light, it shouldn't surprise us to think that in his presence we too will partake of his brightness."[295] It should always be our goal to reflect Christ on this Earth and to show His glory, but it sounds like in Heaven we may literally reflect His glory.

Another thought to ponder is how interesting that Moses and Elijah are discussing current and future events, which would mean they were very much aware of what is going on here on Earth and they knew what was about to happen, which was the unfolding of the eternal plan. This would indicate, at least sometimes, that people in Heaven are aware of what is going on here on Earth, especially, it seems, if it has to do with His eternal plan and salvation.

Moses and Elijah were very real. They had a conversation about what was about to take place and they had glorified bodies. We also know that the disciples were overcome with awe in what they witnessed. If they were overcome with awe, can you imagine what our loved ones are experiencing? I wonder every day what they are experiencing and if they know about what is going on here. If they know when we will join them, how time feels to them, and the list of questions go on and on. I know I miss Dad and Don so much, and the pain is ever-present. It is only through reading about Heaven, God's promises, and His eternal plan that I can find comfort because I know they are with Jesus, just as _____ is with Jesus. We know our loved ones are experiencing inexpressible joy, and we know we will be with them again. I pray we glorify Christ while we are here, knowing that someday we will truly see Christ's glory. We are waiting on that day!

Reflect on these verses. What are your thoughts and feelings?

---

[295] Randy Alcorn, *Heaven* (Carol Stream, IL: Tyndale House, 2004), 293.

DAY 236

While he was speaking, a cloud appeared and covered them, and they were afraid as they entered the cloud. A voice came from the cloud, saying, "This is my Son, whom I have chosen; listen to him." (Luke 9:34-35, NIV)

While Peter was still talking about seeing Jesus, Moses, and Elijah together, a cloud covered them and God spoke. Peter, James, and John were still in awe from what they had witnessed, not sure what to say or think; then a cloud appeared and covered them and a voice says, "This is my Son, whom I have chosen, listen to him." No wonder they were afraid. Matthew 16:6 tells us they fell face down to the ground terrified. But Jesus touched them and said, "Don't be afraid."

The other thing we can take from this verse is that Heaven is closer that we may think. God is ever present. He sent His Son for us and because of Jesus we have eternal life. Even in our pain we can be reminded of Jesus' words and hold to them. He is what gives us hope. As you look at the clouds, be reminded of the nearness of Heaven. Paul Enns writes, "Moses and Elijah, who appeared at the transfiguration are seen as coming from God's presence in heaven, indicated further by God speaking. It is a reminder of the nearness of heaven."[296] I think of all the times clouds are mentioned in the Bible in relation to God. I have always admired and loved the sky and cloud formations. But since God took Don Home, I have become obsessed with the sky and have many pictures in my phone of the clouds. Clouds remind me of the nearness of Heaven.

Notice, too, that even after witnessing the splendor of the Transfiguration, the disciples are not quite prepared when Jesus dies. They are still stricken with grief and overwhelmed with the reality of His absence. So what can all this tell us? I think there are several things we can learn. First, grief is overwhelming. The pain of not having someone you love with you can take your breath away and you can lose your footing so easily. You can go through periods of not remembering what Christ has done for you because you are blinded by the pain, which is why it is even more important to hold to His Word and His promises. We have to remember things that we know to be true. Just like the disciples had to recall these things. Of course they did get to see the resurrected Jesus while on Earth. But because Jesus did rise from the dead and conquer death, we too will see the resurrected Jesus and be reunited with our loved ones. We also learn Heaven is closer than we think! We are waiting on that day.

Reflect on today's verses and thoughts. Truly look at the clouds this week. What are your thoughts and feelings about the nearness of Heaven?

---

[296] Paul Enns, *Heaven Revealed* (Chicago, IL: Moody, 2011), 57.

DAY 237

Teaching them to obey everything I have commanded you. And remember, I am with you always, to the end of the age. (Matthew 28:20, NET)

I asked my 81-year-old mother, who has lived through the homegoing of both her parents; all three of her brothers; my dad, her husband of fifty-nine years; and my husband, who she thinks of and loves as a son, what Scripture brought her comfort in grief. Mom's response was this verse. Jesus was ascending when He said these words. *The Quest Study Bible* has this to say about this verse:

Though physically absent, he remains with believers in a spiritual sense. Those who trust in Jesus will find him with them no matter where they go or what problems they face... the end of the age means until Christ returns again. Then a new era will begin when we shall be with Jesus and see him in his physical form.[297]

Jesus is with us always. He will call us Home someday. Jesus is with us now in our pain. He is with our redeemed loved ones. There are times we may not feel Him, but we hold to what we know is true. Jesus told us He is with us always so we know it is true. When we don't feel Jesus, we say, "I trust you, Jesus, even though I don't feel you." The times of doubt are when we say, "To whom shall I go Lord? You have the words to eternal life." Jesus promised to be with us, and He is faithful and true.

Our redeemed loved ones have seen Jesus face to face now in His physical form. How amazing is that for them? Our loved ones know fully what it is to be "with Him." I try to remind myself of how awesome it is for Don and Dad when I am crying and thinking, "I just want my life back." Our loved ones are where we all long to be—where we will be someday. We are relying on faith and we have this verse and many others to cling to in faith and in our blessed hope.

This verse is a part of what is called the Great Commission. Christ is sending His followers out to spread the word. Jesus knew they would be killed and persecuted for His name. But Jesus also knew that He would indeed be with them through all the persecution and He would receive them into His kingdom. Just as Stephen saw Jesus when he was being stoned, Jesus would be with all of the disciples. No matter what we go through, even death, Jesus is with us. He will lead us Home and be with us physically. Jesus is with us now, too. Sometimes when I pray I just say, "Jesus, Jesus, Jesus." He hears us, He intercedes for us, and He is with us, always. Call his name and trust Him.

Meditate on today's verse and thoughts. Try to imagine yourself in the same room with Jesus. How can you feel more in His presence?

---

[297] *The Quest Study Bible* (Grand Rapids, MI: Zondervan 1994, 2003), 1433.

DAY 238 REFLECTION

Read over the last week. What seems to speak to you? We are reminded that this body is perishable, but we will receive an imperishable and immortal body. Death has no victory over the believer. Our loved ones are with Jesus, and we all wait on that day of the resurrection. We read in 1 Peter that we are in a temporary residence. It gives us hope to remember, despite our suffering, that this life is temporary. We read the Lord is near to the brokenhearted and crushed in spirit. Brokenhearted and crushed certainly describes each of us. We know the Lord is faithful, and He is near. We know Jesus loves us.

We read about the Transfiguration and it reminds us of the glorious splendor of those who see Jesus. What must our loved ones look like in His glory? Moses and Elijah discuss future events, which tell us some in Heaven know what is going on here on Earth. The cloud covering the disciples reminds us that Heaven is near. Peter, James and John have just witnessed Jesus shining like lightning, whiter than bleach, like the sun, and Moses and Elijah in glorious splendor. While trying to take it all in a cloud surrounds them, and they hear the voice of God confirming Jesus is His Son. We see that the disciples, even after witnessing this miraculous event, have a hard time when Jesus is gone. We know grief is overwhelming. We, like the disciples, need to recall those times Jesus has seemed near in the past and what His Word says. We read Jesus telling us He is with us until the end of the age. We read that the end of the age is when He will come back, and then we will live with Him and our loved ones for eternity.

When Don and I would get home in the evening after work and spend time together, we would always ask the other how their day was. I still wonder how his day is; only I don't know how time is counted in Heaven. Is Heaven timeless? There are so many questions. But what I do know is that God is in control. So many of the verses we read this week remind us of the continuity of life and relationships. We are waiting on that day! As you read over the last week, record your thoughts and feelings. What does God seem to be laying on your heart this week?

DAY 239

Call to Me and I will answer you, and I will tell you great and mighty things, which you do not know. (Jeremiah 33:3, NASB)

Don and I were reading the Bible through when God called Don Home. I continued to read the Bible through, and as soon as I finished I started again. I felt compelled to be reading His Word. When I read this verse, it became a memorized verse. Why? Because I was constantly asking God questions about Heaven, about where He was and why I didn't feel Him. I reminded God (not that God needed me to remind Him, but I needed to remind myself what He said) that if I called to Him He would answer. I slowly realized that my answers were coming, not like I wanted them in a booming voice, but in the assurance that can only come from the Holy Spirit.

There are many books available, but not all are good; there are many voices that are not from God. It is difficult at times to navigate through what is from God; we must pray for discernment. But if you are spending time yourself in God's Word and in prayer, then you must trust that what you are hearing is God. Chris Tiegreen, in his devotional book *Experiencing God's Presence*, writes:

The possibility of hearing God's voice with reasonable certainty troubles many Christians. Some are worried it undermines Scripture (which by the way, gives example after example of people hearing God's voice), while others are convinced they can't hear Him speak. In most cases those that haven't heard Him haven't asked questions with expectation that He will answer them. And most haven't sat in His presence for long periods of time and focused their minds on Him. Both practices— asking with expectation and waiting for His voice—are prerequisites of hearing Him consistently........you'll know He has whispered in the depths of your spirit.[298]

My problem was not having expectations, nor was it sitting in His presence. My problem was trusting that what I heard was from God and not my own desires. But what I slowly realized was that I was expecting to hear from Him and I was sitting in His presence and waiting, so maybe that whisper in the depths of my spirit was God and not my own desire. Maybe God was speaking and I was so busy being guarded that I wasn't hearing Him. I don't know where you are in hearing from God. Make sure that you are asking, listening, and waiting for Him to speak. Maybe praying this verse will remind you, as it did me, that God will answer. You may not hear the booming voice, but you may hear a whisper.

Reflect on the verse and quote. Are you hearing God?

---

[298] Chris Tiegreen, *The One Year Experiencing God's Presence Devotional* (Carol Stream, IL: Tyndale, 2011), March 12.

DAY 240

But the Lord is faithful, and he will strengthen you and protect you from the evil one. (2 Thessalonians 3:3, NIV)

During this time of sorrow it is more important than ever that you look to God for your strength. When we are vulnerable the evil one is ready to attack. Recognize the spiritual warfare around you and lean on God. God will strengthen you and protect you from the evil one. The enemy wants you to lose sight of "the hope" that we as believers have. The enemy wants the overwhelming sorrow to crush us and to turn us away from God. But our Lord will strengthen us and protect us. As Charles Stanley points out, "God's plan for redemption did not include lifting the disciples out of their immediate surroundings. The pain and stress of facing life as children of God would never deliver them from the earthly reality of trouble. Jesus made that clear when He said, 'In this world you will have trouble.'"[299]

We are facing much suffering right now. The pain of sorrow is suffering in a most intense way. Now is the time to hold to all the promises we study, to rest in the assurance the battle has been won, and to recognize that each time the pain encompasses you, God is with you even if you do not feel Him. He alone can give you the strength. God will protect you from the evil one. We live in a fallen world and the devil is the prince of this world, the prince of darkness. The devil is the father of lies. Do not allow the lies of doubt and despair to overtake you. Listen to praise songs, hymns, and words of encouragement from the Bible. Recite the verses you memorize to remind you of our blessed hope in Christ. Pray for a hedge of protection around yourself and others that you know are grieving. Our loved ones are safe from the spiritual warfare; they are in the presence of the Lord. We hold to those promises and God's promise to protect us. This is no time to neglect prayer and Bible reading. This is the time you must rely on Him and immerse yourself in God's Word.

Meditate on this verse. How are you relying on God to strengthen you at this time? If you feel like you are not, what would help you to rely on Him more?

---

[299] Charles Stanley, *Enter His Gates* (Nashville, TN: Nelson, 1998), 116.

DAY 241

Now the poor man died and was carried away by the angels to Abraham's bosom; and the rich man also died and was buried. In Hades he lifted up his eyes, being in torment, and saw Abraham far away and Lazarus in his bosom. (Luke 16:22-23, NASB)

When I used this verse before, I quoted the New International Version, and it reads, "Abraham's side." Arnold Fruchtenbaum sheds light on the words "Abraham's Bosom" used in the NASB.

'Abraham's Bosom' is a figure of speech describing a guest at a feast, reclining on the breast of a neighbor. Just as in the Gospel of John, John was reclining at Jesus' bosom at the Feast of Passover; this is what Lazarus was doing in Abraham's Bosom. This is a figure of speech of a guest at a feast, reclining on the breast of his neighbor or his host.... Bosom symbolizes blessedness after death. While Lazarus did not do well when he was living as far as the material world was concerned, after death he was indeed in a state of blessedness.[300]

Of course, in today's time we read those words and it doesn't mean the same thing, but if you look at in the language of the time and the culture it is a beautiful picture of closeness and blessedness. Allow yourself to think about your loved one carried to Heaven by angels. And when she saw Jesus, how amazingly awesome that was for her. Now our loved ones are in fellowship with family members, friends, and other believers that have gone before us. Think of the times that we get together with those we love and share food and fellowship. Times with those we love are times that we feel love and we can be ourselves and know we are completely loved. What we have here on this fallen world with family is a hint of what that will be like in Heaven. Those times will be what our loved ones are already experiencing—a state of blessedness.

According to Fruchtenbaum, Abraham's Bosom is a term a common term in the rabbinic writings; it is another name for *Paradise*, which as we have learned earlier, means "a royal park or a garden."[301] Close your eyes and try to imagine what that Paradise in Jesus' presence is like right now for our loved ones. Our loved ones are truly in a place of wonderment and awe and someday we will join them for an eternity. We are waiting on that day!

Reflect on the terms *Abraham's Bosom* and *Paradise*. Write your thoughts and feelings and how you might imagine Paradise to be.

---

[300] Arnold G. Fruchtenbaum, *The Footsteps of the Messiah* (Tustin, CA: Ariel, 2003), 747.
[301] Ibid., 747.

DAY 242

So is my Word that goes out from my mouth: It will not return to me empty, but will accomplish what I desire and achieve the purpose for which I sent it. (Isaiah 55:11, NIV)

God is sovereign; He is in control and has an eternal plan. When everything is chaotic in your world, when nothing seems in control, hold fast to the fact God is in control. This world is not all there is. This life is temporary. The pain, the chaos, and the sorrow are all temporary. Read all of chapter 55 in Isaiah. The chapter is seen as dual prophecy: the restoration of Israel from exile and the restoration in the coming Messianic Kingdom. God tells us that His ways are higher than ours. His Word goes out and accomplishes what He desires. There is an eternal plan and it will come to fruition. God has promised us an eternity with Him. Our hope is in God. As Mark Hitchcock writes, "Prophecy teaches us that God is sovereign, that He rules from His throne in heaven, that He has a plan, and that His kingdom will ultimately come to this earth."[302]

When grief and sorrow consume us, nothing feels in control. Your world feels unsteady, and you fall into an abyss of pain and sorrow. But we have hope; we have eternal promises; and we have an eternal, Sovereign God who is in control. God's Word will achieve what He desires; His eternal plan will happen. Hold to those promises now. Remind yourself every day, every hour, that God has an eternal plan. This life is temporary. We have a God who knows how everything will come about. We have to trust Him in the darkness and chaos.

When I was a little girl, I remember watching a scary movie with my dad. We were in the living room on the couch, and I grabbed his hand and put it over my eyes. I figured Dad's hands were bigger and stronger than mine, so I was safer. God is big and strong. God is in control. He saw our loved ones Home safely in His presence. He will see us Home in His presence when He is ready.

I had just finished typing this day's devotional when I received an email from the church prayer chain. Someone in our church had had a heart attack and was now in surgery. I immediately prayed for him and his wife. That was the second person in the last two weeks I had prayed for who had had a heart attack, and they were both about Don's age. I prayed immediately, but then I thought, "Why, God, did they get a chance to have surgery and heal and Don didn't?" Immediately, as I prayed this crying, I was reminded of what I had just typed. God is in control. He called Don Home immediately. He gave the other two men more time here. Don and Dad are in His presence. I don't understand why God did it that way, but I trust Him. God is in control.

Read all of Isaiah 55. Journal what brings you the most comfort.

---

302   Mark Hitchcock, *The End* (Carol Stream, IL: Tyndale, 2012), 49.

DAY 243

How long, Lord, must I call for help, but you do not listen?
Or cry out to you, "Violence!" but you do not save? (Habakkuk 1:2, NIV)

There were many days, especially at first, that I feel disconnected to God. I cried out to feel God, to hear Him, and yet it seemed like nothing was there. We know that grief can make God seem far away. We have looked at different verses that show many people throughout the Bible experienced the same feeling that God was far away and that He was not answering them. And yet God allowed all of those times of doubt and lamenting to be recorded in the Bible, so we know He understands. We know God is listening. Just because we do not feel God does not mean He isn't there.

Priscilla Shirer writes about Habakkuk, "Although the prophet expected God to answer, he had two fundamental questions: "How long?" and "Why?"… "We don't know how long Habakkuk had been calling out to God, but he most likely been at it for quite a while, because he was pointing an accusatory finger at God."[303] God answers in verse 5, but He doesn't answer directly. As Priscilla points out, "Instead of responding directly to Habakkuk's complaint, God encouraged him to look around and see what was happening. God basically said, 'I am speaking and I am doing something. You have been looking through the wrong lenses so you just don't hear or see it.'"[304]

Recognize that God speaks to us in different ways. We can't put God in a box. Be open to ways He is speaking to you. Perhaps He is speaking to you through other Christians, through "coincidences," through books and music written when someone else is in pain. Perhaps He speaks to you when a verse seems to leap off the page to you. Maybe He is speaking to you when you see a sunset or sunrise that shouts His majesty. Or perhaps you hear God when in a feeling of a moment of assurance, although elusive, is there. Journal the times you have felt God or thought you felt Him. Hold on to those times. God is working toward His eternal plan. Keep in mind that God is always working for His eternal plan and keep an eternal perspective. Yes, the pain is still there and we hurt, but we also know our life here is temporary and that one day we shall see God. We shall see our loved ones again. Then all we don't understand will make sense. We know God is listening; we have to listen to Him now. We know God has saved us. He is working in our lives and in the world and we shall see Him. We are waiting on that day.

What are your thoughts and feelings on the verse and on the quote?

---

[303] Priscilla Shirer, *Discerning the Voice of God* (Chicago IL: Moody, 2007), 21.
[304] Ibid., 21.

DAY 244

For the revelation awaits an appointed time; it speaks of the end and will not prove false. Though it linger, wait for it; it will certainly come and will not delay. (Habakkuk 2:3, NIV)

The first part of this chapter, we hear Habakkuk say, "I will stand at my watch and station myself on the ramparts. I will look to see what He will say to me" (2:1a). The Lord replies in vs. 3. There are two things for us to note. Habakkuk expected a reply and he waited on that reply. God answered, and when He did, God told Habakkuk, "It may linger, but wait, for it will certainly come and will not delay." God is talking about the fall of Babylon in 539 BC, which is about sixty-six years after this prophecy.

God has told us what will happen and we must wait for it. His Word is true and prophecy is fulfilled. This particular revelation had to do with the fall of Babylon, but we have many revelations through the Bible that tell us about Heaven and about the restoration of the Earth. God's promises for eternal life and living with Him on a restored New Earth are talked about in both the Old Testament and the New Testament. Focusing on those verses and God's Word allows us to have an eternal perspective. God shows us through these prophecies that He is sovereign and that His eternal plan will always come to pass. For those of us hurting, these are the promises to hold to. Mercy Me sings, "How long must I wait to be with you?"[305] Steven Curtis Chapman sings, "I am counting down the days."[306] Waiting…

We find ourselves waiting… waiting for the nightmare to be over and waiting to get our life back. But in reality we are waiting on the final fulfillment of the eternal plan. That time may linger, but it will happen. Hold to those promises and that eternal perspective. God's eternal plan will come to pass. You will see Jesus. This temporary time of pain and sorrow will end when you see Jesus. You will be reunited with your redeemed loved one. We will live on a restored Earth with our loved ones with Jesus our King. The revelation awaits an appointed time. "Wait for it; it will not prove false. It may linger, but it will certainly come." We are waiting on that day!

Meditate on this verse. What are your thoughts and feelings? Do you feel like you are waiting?

---

[305] Mercy Me, "Homesick." *Itunes Original.* MercyMe, 2008.
[306] Steven Curtis Chapman, "See." *Beauty Will Rise.* Sparrow, 2008

DAY 245 REFECTION

Looking back over the last week, what speaks to you? We are reminded to call out to God, and He will tell us great and mighty things that we do not know. We have to call out and then listen. We read that the Lord is faithful and will protect us from the evil one, which speaks to spiritual warfare. We are not told that we will not suffer, only that He will strengthen us and protect us from the evil one. The ultimate protection will be in Jesus' presence where our loved ones are now. We read again how Lazarus is carried to Abraham's bosom and how that represents a guest reclining at a feast—blessedness. We think of the closeness and fellowship with Jesus that our loved ones have now, and that we will have with them when we arrive.

We read in Isaiah that God says He will accomplish what He desires. He has an eternal purpose. God is sovereign. So when I want to cry, "Why didn't you give Don a chance?" "Why was he taken so suddenly with no warning?" I have to hold to God is in control and trust Him. We read how Habakkuk asked, "How long?" and "Why?" We ask the same questions. God allows those questions to be in the Bible because He knows how we feel. We also read in Habakkuk that God lets Habakkuk know that He has an appointed time, and what He says will happen. We are reminded that God is sovereign and has an eternal plan. We wait for the final fulfillment of the eternal plan. It may linger, but it will come. Hold to the eternal perspective. When the pain and sorrow of not having your loved one here threatens to overwhelm you, pray that the Holy Spirit teaches you how to have an eternal perspective. As you reflect back over the week, record your thoughts and feelings. What thoughts from the past week seem to resonate the most with you?

DAY 246

I will show compassion to Jerusalem, to all who live in her ruins. Though her land is a desert, I will make it a garden, like the garden I planted in Eden. Joy and gladness will be there, and songs of praise and thanks to me. (Isaiah 51:3, GNT)

Randy Alcorn writes, "Just as Eden is our backward-looking reference point, the New Earth is our forward-looking reference point. We should expect the New Earth to be like Eden, only better. That's exactly what Scripture promises."[307] Scripture is full of references to restoring the Earth to Eden-like qualities. Even our most beautiful places on Earth are shadows of Eden and shadows of what is to come on the New Earth. Our loved ones are in Heaven now and what they see is glorious. Not only are they in our Lord's presence but they are in Paradise. But our loved ones are also waiting on that day all of Earth will be restored. I would love a glimpse of what our loved ones are seeing now as I know you do, and someday we will.

For now, we look to the Scripture and see those verses that promise the beautiful restoration. Note in this verse that not only will the New Earth be like the Garden of Eden, but there will be songs and praise of thanks to God. As Paul Enns writes, "Paradise will result not only in the restoration of the earth, but it will be a day of joy, thanksgiving, and music. The fall of man through the first Adam demands a restoration of all things by the Last Adam, Jesus Christ."[308] He goes on to say, "The new earth will have Eden everywhere, as earth is restored to Eden-like conditions with peace in every realm."[309]

We will have joy, gladness, and sing songs of praise and thanksgiving to God. There will be peace. We have sorrow and pain now, but someday there will be joy again. We will celebrate God's goodness and His blessings in the New Earth as it is restored once again like Eden. We can only imagine, as we take in the beauty on this Earth now, what it will be like when God restores the Earth. But best of all, we will be with Jesus. There will be joy and gladness again. The pain and sorrow will be gone; we will be reunited with our loved ones never to be separated again. We are waiting on that day!

How does this verse speak to you? Look up other verses that refer to Eden being restored; how does this speak to you?

---

[307] Randy Alcorn, *Heaven* (Carol Stream, IL: Tyndale House, 2004), 244.
[308] Paul Enns, *Heaven Revealed* (Chicago, IL: Moody, 2011), 20.
[309] Ibid., 89.

DAY 247

Because they all saw him and were terrified. Immediately he spoke to them and said, "Take courage! It is I. Don't be afraid." Then he climbed into the boat with them, and the wind died down. They were completely amazed. (Mark 6:50-51, NIV) Read Mark 6:45-52 and Matthew 14:22-33.

A friend, whose thirteen-year-old son tragically took his own life, shared this verse. It was several years after his son's death and a long struggle with God. I asked him how these verses spoke to him. He had heard a sermon that morning on these verses. He said, "Jesus sent them into the boat. Jesus knew I was going into this. In the roughest storms the captains always turn the ships into the storm to meet it straight on. I believe that is what Christ wants us to do. He is watching and ready to help us when we fall."

As I read these verses several things stood out to me. Jesus was watching and He was also praying. Jesus is watching and interceding for us even now. Jesus sees the storm we are in, and He is watching and praying. Jesus tells his disciples and us, "I am here; don't be afraid." Jesus gets in the boat with us. It is hard to imagine Jesus in this boat with us because this boat and storm we are in is heart-wrenching and painful. But at first, the disciples didn't even recognize Jesus was with them. The disciples had just been with Jesus on the shore, and yet they were still terrified in the storm.

Dr. Luke Terveen also writes about these verses. He states, "I can identify with the disciples' struggle in those deep waters on that dark night, a poignant symbol of my own struggle with overwhelming grief in the lonely aftermath of my daughter's death. We wondered whether we were going under, feeling isolated in the midst of the storm."[310] Dr. Terveen points out Jesus' heart was heavy at that time, He knew what had just happened to John the Baptist and He knew His own cross He would bear. But even as He prayed, Jesus kept His eyes on His disciples. And as our friend noted, Jesus sent his disciples on the boat knowing what would happen. But Jesus is still watching and praying.

Dr. Terveen points out in the book of Matthew, Peter is said to have jumped out to meet Jesus but starts to sink when he takes his eyes off of Jesus. Jesus' hand pulls Peter out of the storm. He adds this note: "We must remember that what looks like it is going to be over our heads is already under Jesus' feet."[311]

Jesus stands ready to lift us up and get in the boat with us. Jesus is with us and He is saying, "Don't be afraid; I am here."

Meditate on both passages listed and the quotes; how do they speak to you?

---

[310] John Luke Terveen, *Hope for the Brokenhearted* (Colorado Springs, CO: Victor, 2006), 87.

[311] Ibid., 81.

DAY 248

If we are thrown into the blazing furnace, the God we serve is able to deliver us from it, and he will deliver us from Your Majesty's hand. But even if he does not, we want you to know, Your Majesty that we will not serve your gods or worship the image of gold you have set up. (Daniel 3:17-18, NIV)

Why is this passage in a devotional on grieving? Because of something I heard while I was in a Beth Moore study of Daniel. As Beth Moore was teaching on Daniel 3 and the fiery furnace, she made a comment that is worth sharing now. As you know, God did deliver the men from the fiery furnace. But there were also many times His people were not delivered. Tradition has it that Isaiah was sawed in half. We know most of the disciples died a martyr. Beth Moore points out that God can use the fiery furnace in life three ways. "We can be delivered from the fire... Our faith is built. We can be delivered through the fire... Our faith is refined. We can be delivered by the fire into His arms... Our faith is perfected."[312] I thought of Dad that night as I listened to Beth Moore's study. Dad struggled through the COPD and the collapsed lung. He struggled for breath, but kept preaching, even in the hospital. Dad certainly was in a fiery furnace. God did not deliver him from that furnace. God delivered Dad straight into His arms. Dad's faith was perfected. Don went straight into Jesus' arms. Your redeemed loved one, whether they were delivered by the fire or taken straight through, arrived in our Savior's arms. His or her faith is perfected.

Now we are in a fiery furnace of a different sort. The pain and sorrow of grief is overwhelming. And we feel alone in the furnace surrounded by pain that threatens to consume us. But, as Nebuchadnezzar noticed when he looked in the fiery furnace, the men were not alone. There was an angel of God, perhaps Jesus incarnate, with the men in the furnace. These men were not alone. We are not alone. God will see us through this fire and bring us to Himself. The God you serve will take care of you. Our faith can be strengthened as we rely on Jesus to hold us. It is important that during this time of sorrow, you do hold to Jesus and allow your faith to grow. We want to know that even in pain and sorrow we can glorify our God. We want to continue to serve Jesus. Jesus can use us wherever we are if we rely on Him. And someday we will see Jesus, and know our suffering was all worthwhile. We will understand. The pain and sorrow will be gone, and we will be perfected in our faith. We will be reunited with our loved ones and together praise the God who brought us Home. We are waiting on that day!

As you reflect on today's verses and thoughts, how do they speak to you?

---

[312] Beth Moore, *Daniel Lives of Integrity Words of Prophecy* (Nashville, TN: Lifeway, 2012), 46.

DAY 249

But someone will ask, "How are the dead raised? With what kind of body will they come?" So will it be with the resurrection of the dead. The body that is sown is perishable, it is raised imperishable; it is sown in dishonor, it is raised in glory; it is sown in weakness, it is raised in power. (1 Corinthians 15:35,42,43, NIV)

Our loved ones are witnessing the glories of Heaven. Our loved ones are also waiting on that day when there will be a bodily resurrection. It is important to hold to the comfort that the ones we love are with Jesus in Heaven. But it is also a comfort to think of the day when there will be a bodily resurrection. If we are here when Jesus returns, then we are changed in the twinkling of an eye. If not, we still participate in the bodily resurrection. What does that all mean? Paul Enns writes, "Beyond escaping sickness and disease, our powerful body will never again know physical, emotional or mental pain.... We will have strength, energy, abilities, and use of all facilities in inconceivable dimensions."[313] He also says:

The new body will be a spiritual body. Yet it will also be a fully physical body. Jesus had all the faculties of a material body. There was a physical continuity with His former body, demonstrated in the nail prints in His hands and wound in His side. Further Jesus talked, ate, and functioned in a normal physical way. But the resurrection body will be heightened spiritually.... In this life we are exhorted to 'walk by the Spirit' to be controlled by the Holy Spirit (Gal. 5:16). In the future day when we each receive a resurrection body, we walk according to the Spirit the way God intended for us to walk—it will then be our *normal life.*[314]

Randy Alcorn writes:

Scripture portrays resurrection as involving both fundamental continuity and significant dissimilarity. We dare not minimize these dissimilarities—for our glorification will certainly involve a dramatic and marvelous transformation. But, in my experience, the great majority of Christians have underemphasized continuity. They end up thinking our transformed selves as no longer ourselves, and the transformed Earth as no longer being the Earth.[315]

The continuity of life and relationships is important for us to hold to.

Meditate on the verses and quotes. What are your thoughts and feelings?

---

[313] Paul Enns, *Heaven Revealed* (Chicago, IL: Moody, 2011), 80.

[314] Ibid., 81.

[315] Randy Alcorn, *Heaven* (Carol Stream, IL: Tyndale House, 2004), 124.

DAY 250

I know that my redeemer lives and that in the end he will stand on the earth. And after my skin has been destroyed, yet in my flesh I will see God; I myself will see him with my own eyes—I, and not another.
How my heart yearns within me! (Job 19:25-27, NIV)

When I feel like I can't go another day, I will quote these verses. This passage reminds me of so much. First, our Redeemer lives and He is coming back just as He said He was. These words spoken by Job are amazing. To think all those many years ago, Job is speaking of a bodily resurrection. As Randy Alcorn says, "The anticipation of seeing God face-to-face in our resurrected body is heartfelt and ancient."[316]

This passage also reminds me that I myself will see God with my own eyes—"I and not another, how my heart yearns within me." On those days when pain and sorrow threaten to overtake me, it helps to remind myself of this truth. I will see God and I want to please Him. As Paul Enns points out:

A time will come when all who believe in Him will see Him. In Heaven we will enjoy a unique fellowship that would have been thought utterly impossible. Jesus promises, 'Blessed are the pure in heart for they shall see God' (Matt. 5:8). But this involves more than visual sight. In seeing God, we will know God.... This is beyond our comprehension—to see God and to know God! This will result in a satisfaction that on this present earth is incomprehensible: seeing Him and living in His presence.[317]

Our redeemed loves one have experienced seeing God! When I try to focus on what Don and Dad are experiencing, it helps me not focus on my own pain. I also remind myself that I will see God. I want to know that even in my pain, I glorify Him now. I want to know that even though I don't understand why and even though I don't always feel God, that I trust He is with me and I trust Him. My heart yearns for that day I see Jesus, but until that day comes, I want to be in His will. It is easy in the grief to give up, and there are days I feel defeated and discouraged. I feel like I can't do any of this; the pain is overwhelming and without Don, nothing is the same. But this passage reminds me that because there is continuity, I myself will see God. I have to give an account of my actions; I want to be faithful to His calling. I have to trust Jesus now, and remind myself that I will see Him. But I don't have to remind myself that my heart yearns within me because that is a constant! Come, Lord Jesus. Come. I am waiting on that day!

Meditate on this verse and the devotional. Write your thoughts and feelings.

---

[316] Randy Alcorn, *Heaven* (Carol Stream, IL: Tyndale House, 2004), 175.

[317] Paul Enns, *Heaven Revealed* (Chicago, IL: Moody, 2011), 174.

DAY 251

I am torn between the two: I desire to depart and be with Christ, which is better by far. (Philippians 1:23, NIV)

On Thanksgiving we went to the cemetery, and when we got back I was writing in my journal and crying. I thought of all the Thanksgivings that we spent as a family, and how right about then—after a wonderful meal and fellowship—Dad would have fallen asleep in the recliner and Don would have watched the Dallas Cowboys play. I was hurting because they were not here to join us. But as I wrote in my journal, I realized they weren't missing out on anything. Our family is missing out on them. But Dad and Don are in the presence of God, just as your loved one is. They are not missing out. They are in an awesome place. A place we look forward to going to. This life is temporary. It is hard to be here without our loved ones. Our pain is natural. The pain and sorrow do not leave. But you can find comfort in reminding yourself that Heaven is better by far for our redeemed loved ones.

If we need surgery, we know we will have pain. We tolerate the pain and find comfort in knowing someday healing will happen. So it is with grief; pain is natural. We have pain, but we know our true healing will come in Heaven. We can find comfort now—even in our pain—by focusing on Heaven and where our redeemed loved ones are. Those who have departed and are with Christ are far better than us. As Graham Scroggie wrote, "He is in conscious enjoyment of the Lord's presence."[318] As Randy Alcorn writes, "His mind was being with his Lord Jesus which is the most significant aspect of Heaven."[319] Our loved ones are with Jesus. Alcorn also points out:

Life in the Heaven we go to when we die, where we'll dwell prior to our bodily resurrection is 'better by far' than living here on Earth under the Curse, away from the direct presence of God.... Still, the intermediate or present Heaven is not our final destination. Though it will be a wonderful place, the present Heaven is not the place we are made for—the place God promises to refashion for us to live forever. God's children are destined for life resurrected beings on a resurrected Earth. We must not lose sight of our true destination.[320]

Pain is a natural response to loss, but focusing on the end result allows you to find comfort even in your pain. Our redeemed loved ones are in a far better place, and we will join them. We are waiting on that day!

As you reflect on the verse and quotes for today, how do they speak to you?

---

[318] William Scroggie, *What About Heaven?* (London: Pickering & Inglis, 1954), 5.
[319] Randy Alcorn, *Heaven* (Carol Stream, IL: Tyndale House, 2004), 187.
[320] Ibid., 42.

DAY 252 REFLECTION

Read over the last week. What brings you comfort? We read again of the land being restored to Eden-like conditions and having joy and gladness. We will sing praises and thanks to God with our loved ones. We are waiting on that day! We read how Jesus tells His disciples not to be afraid. Jesus had sent his disciples into the storm. Jesus watched them, prayed for them, and then entered the boat with them. At first, His disciples did not recognize Jesus; they were so afraid of the storm. We can relate as we ride the storm of our life, but Jesus is riding with us. He is never far, even when we can't feel Him or don't recognize Him.

We read how Meshach, Shadrach, and Abednego faced the fiery furnace knowing whether they lived or died that God would deliver them. He would deliver them from it, through or to Him. I thought Beth Moore's words were very true and worth pondering. Can you see how your own loved one was delivered? Can you identify with us being in a fiery furnace?

We read again about the bodily resurrection. We will be raised with power. There is continuity in Heaven. Our bodies will be glorified and be far better, as are our redeemed loved ones'. We read how Job yearned to see his Redeemer. Job anticipated seeing his Redeemer face to face on this Earth. We are reminded we will see Jesus face to face and we must continue to be obedient to serve Him until that day. We read again how Paul looked forward to Heaven because He knew Heaven was far better. We are reminded that our loved ones are not missing out here; we are missing them but they are far better. We know there will be a day we will join them in Heaven, and we will be far better too. We have a true destination to look forward to, even in our pain. As you reflect over the week, record your thoughts and feelings. What thoughts seem to resonate with you the most?

DAY 253

He says, "Be still, and know that I am God; I will be exalted among the nations, I will be exalted in the earth." (Psalm 46:10, NIV)

Being still goes against what we find in the world today. We live in a fast-paced world and we want it all now. Don called our society a microwave society. We are so used to getting things quickly and rushing about that we often lose sight on being still. Don was so good at being still. He would sit outside on our patio to do his devotion most mornings. One morning my sister's dog came for a visit and Don, being the dog lover, was holding her in his lap. I took a picture of Don, his Bible on the table next to him, his glasses laying on his Bible, and the dog loving on him. That's my man. He had such patience. I have pictures of Don on vacations just meditating as he would look across nature scenes. Don knew how to be still and listen to God. I have a harder time with being still, but I am learning.

In this time of sorrow, especially when you don't feel God, it is more important than ever to spend time being still. I have time set aside in the mornings and at night to spend time with God. That is not the only time I spend with God, but those times I have set aside. The time is my time to spend alone with Jesus. I notice as I pray for others and as I spend time thanking God for all He has done, I can gradually feel less alone and more at peace. I often end my time in the evening before I go to sleep listening to the song by Mercy Me, "Word of God Speak." The lyrics and the melody are powerful tools to help me be still.

> Word of God speak
> Would You pour down like rain
> Washing my eyes to see
> Your majesty
> To be still and know
> That You're in this place
> Please let me stay and rest
> In Your holiness
> Word of God speak
>
> I'm finding myself in the midst of You
>
> Beyond the music, beyond the noise
> All that I need is to be with You
> And in the quiet hear Your voice[321]

Reflect on today's thoughts. What times are you being still before God?

---

[321] Mercy Me, "Word of God Speak." *Itunes Original.* MercyMe, 2008.

DAY 254

I know that my redeemer lives and that in the end he will stand on the earth. And after my skin has been destroyed, yet in my flesh I will see God; I myself will see him with my own eyes—I, and not another. How my heart yearns within me! (Job 19:25-27, NIV)

Remember that Job had lost everything, but in it all he did not lose his faith. Job cried out and asked why, but he kept talking to God no matter what. Job endured well-meaning, but not so helpful, friends. In grief you may have experienced those well-meaning, but not so helpful, friends. You may also have those friends and family who just hurt with you; that love you and cry with you and just listen. I hope you have some of those family and friends, like I do, who love you and will cry with you. More than likely, you have experienced both—as I have. No matter what happens, you must hold to your faith and pray.

Pray even when God seems distant; that is what Job did. He kept praying even when things got worse, even when no answer seemed to come. But finally, God spoke. And although God did not give Job an answer to his questions, God spoke and that was enough for Job. I think that we all want to hear that booming voice. I don't hear the booming voice. But the more time I spend with God, the more time I have that peace. Does the assurance of His voice come and go at times? Yes it does. But the assurance and peace do come. Philip Yancey, in *Disappointment with God*, writes:

In any discussion of disappointment with God, heaven is the last word, the most important word of all. Only heaven will finally solve the problem of God's hiddenness. For the first time ever, human beings will be able to look upon God face to face. In the midst of his agony, Job somehow came up with the faith to believe that 'in my flesh I will see God; I myself will see him with my own eyes.' That prophecy will come true not just for Job but for all of us.[322]

We look forward to the day we see God with our own eyes. Then the why's will not seem so important, just as it didn't with Job, because experiencing God will make everything make sense. When you feel like giving up, remember that you will see God in your own flesh. Our redeemed loved ones are seeing God now. Remind yourself of this truth daily. Job eventually died, and his faith would have been even more rewarded on that day. Not only did he see his Redeemer but he was reunited with his children in Heaven. We shall see God!

Reflect on the verses and the quotes. We have read these verses before. Each time there is more to see. Do you have any different insights than before?

---

[322] Phillip Yancey, *Disappointment with God* (Grand Rapids, MI: Zondervan, 1992), 297.

DAY 255

"But now bring me a harpist." While the harpist was playing, the hand of the Lord came on Elisha. (2 Kings 3:15, NIV)

Although I had read the entire book of 2 Kings a number of times, this verse struck me differently the last time I read it. I was struck by how Elisha asked for a musician to play before he answered their questions. He was seeking an answer from God. I was struck because of how much music has comforted me this past year. Musicians such as Mercy Me, Comfort Manyame, Mandisa, Steven Curtis Chapman, Casting Crowns, and Chris Tomlin have drawn me closer to God and comforted me as I listened to their songs. Later, as I was reading Chris Tiegreen's devotional book *Experiencing God's Presence*, I was impressed by what he wrote:

Why did Elisha need a harpist in order to hear from God? Because the Lord's presence can often be experienced in music—or any other creative expression—far more easily than an analytical, deductive approach. The Lord speaks to the heart, or to our right brained intuitive side, more often than to our logical skeptical side. As mathematician Blaise Paschal once said, 'the heart has its reasons that reason cannot know.' God's Spirit seems to connect with us at a creative imaginative level. His power comes upon those who can perceive Him without having to analyze Him.... He stretches us to the point that we must embrace Him intuitively, subjectively, and instinctively. When we're open to that, He opens to us.[323]

This devotional particularly spoke to me since I had had several different people I was close to tell me that I was "analyzing too much." I was crying out to God to feel Him and hear Him, then explaining away anything for fear I heard wrong. Once, when I was writing in my journal, I had the distinct impression that I should listen to the word of the songs. I started writing down the words. The words were directly relating to how I was feeling, and were powerful words of comfort. God uses different ways to speak to us. Music is one of those ways. We know that in Heaven, angels are always singing praises before God's throne. Sometimes we have to just be still and listen. Listening may actually be opening ourselves to different ways God speaks. Pray that you will hear God's voice. God may speak to you through songs, through others, or through His Word. Be open to how God may speak to you. Be still and listen.

Reflect on today's words. What songs have ministered to you? Write some of the words to those songs down and meditate on them. How else have you felt God's presence through other forms of creative expression?

---

[323] Chris Tiegreen, *The One Year Experiencing God's Presence Devotional* (Carol Stream, IL: Tyndale, 2011), July 21.

DAY 256

The time came when the beggar died and the angels carried him to Abraham's side. The rich man also died and was buried. In Hades, where he was in torment, he looked up and saw Abraham far away, with Lazarus by his side. (Luke 16:22-23, NIV)

Read Luke 16: 22-31. Arnold Fruchtenbaum, in *The Footsteps of the Messiah*, agrees with Randy Alcorn that this is not a parable. He wrote, "Though it is frequently called a parable of the Rich Man and Lazarus, this is incorrect. Luke does not say that it is a parable, nor does Jesus begin the story as He often did by saying, 'learn a parable.' Parables do not have names like 'Lazarus' and 'Abraham'."[324] He goes on to explain how Lazarus and the rich man are fully conscious although they have physically died. Paul Enns writes:

He (the rich man) remembered his father's home. He remembered his brothers. He remembered their spiritual need. He remembered his home and the situation in his home. He remembered Lazarus. If those in hell have this knowledge and remembrance of their earthly lives, it is surely true of those in heaven. As the rich man remembered details of his family life, so we too, in heaven will remember both the people in our lives and the details of our lives on earth.... There will be a glorious, happy reunion of loved ones—family and close friends—in heaven. Never to be separated! And we will know each other *better* than we knew each other on earth.[325]

The pain and sadness of the absence of our loved ones and the longing to be with them are natural feelings. But as Christians we have the promise of eternal life with Christ—the promise of Heaven. So while we grieve, we have hope. We know that one day we will be with our loved ones again in the presence of our glorious Lord and Savior.

Verses like these reaffirm the continuity of our lives in all areas. The ideas of soul sleep, of wiping out of relationships, or of unconsciousness are not scriptural. We will have an eternity to worship our Savior in Heaven with our loved ones, never to be separated again. God gave us those relationships on Earth. Thank God for your relationships, and know that you will resume them in Heaven. This life is temporary. We have an eternal Home. Our loved ones got Home before us, but they are aware and waiting for us. They are with Jesus, and are more aware than we are. There will be joy when we see Jesus and become more aware than we ever have. We are waiting on that day!

As you reflect on today's passage and thoughts, how do they speak to you?

---

[324] Arnold G. Fruchtenbaum, *The Footsteps of the Messiah* (Tustin, CA: Ariel, 2003), 702.

[325] Paul Enns, *Heaven Revealed* (Chicago, IL: Moody, 2011), 162.

DAY 257

Command them to do good, to be rich in good deeds, and to be generous and willing to share. In this way they will lay up treasure for themselves as a firm foundation for the coming age, so that they may take hold of the life that is truly life. (1 Timothy 6:18-19, NIV)

These passages are clear indicators that what we do on Earth matters for eternity. These passages are also clear indicators of the continuity of who we are in Heaven. Paul is commanding the hearers to be generous, and in doing so they will lay up treasure for themselves for the coming age. The coming age is usually in reference to the eternal kingdom. Paul tells us we lay up treasure in the coming age and adds "that we may take hold of the life that is truly life." He may have been referring to the fact that if we focus on laying up treasures in Heaven, we will truly live here. Or it seems to me Paul could be saying that the life in the ages to come is truly life.

In verse 12, Paul told Timothy to take hold of the eternal life for which he was called. Our true Home is Heaven; our true life will finally be in fullness in His eternal kingdom. What we do here matters for eternity because our life truly comes to fullness in Heaven. We want to be obedient here and share as much as we can of the Gospel and glorify God. When we do share the Gospel, we encourage others to take hold of the eternal life, the true life. As Joseph Stowell wrote in *Eternity*:

The resurrection of Christ, and His post-resurrection appearances gave the apostles a keen sense of the reality of the world to come. It was this reality that empowered, energized and defined the New Testament church as a force with which this world could not reckon. Because heaven was real to these early believers, the lesser things of this world would not seduce them. They viewed the threat of death as simply the door to all that is better.[326]

Our true Home is Heaven; everything we do while here matters for eternity because our life is truly in Heaven. Our loved ones are in Heaven now; they are truly living. We will join them someday. But for now we also have to heed the command to further His kingdom. All that we do now, even in our sorrow, counts toward eternity. You can pray; you can give to others even when you are hurting. We are still laying up that foundation. We will take hold of that true life when He calls us Home. We are waiting on that day!

Reflect on the verses. What are your thoughts on eternity being true life?

---

[326] Taken from *Eternity*, © 2006 by Joseph M. Stowell, and used by permission of Discovery House Publishers, Grand Rapids, MI. All rights reserved. 27.

DAY 258

And if our hope in Christ is only for this life, we are more to be pitied than anyone in the world. (1 Corinthians 15:19, NLT)

I wake up in the night and quote this verse. When I look around me and become overwhelmed with sorrow, I quote this verse. My hope in Christ is not just for this life. He has blessed me with a wonderful family and a blessed life here, but this life is not all there is. We have an eternity to look forward to. We have an eternity to spend with our redeemed loved ones. We live in a fallen world, and as Joseph Stowell writes:

If this is the only world for us, then misery of a passive pessimism is indeed our lot.… The world around us tends toward unfairness, danger, and disappointment, and ultimately it will leave us unsatisfied and disappointed. It is a world controlled by our adversary. Its intrinsic nature is temporal. Filled with the qualities of our good and loving God, the world to come, on the other hand, is characterized by limitless satisfaction and joy. And the redemptive world within is equipped to be a victorious, first wave expression of our final experience in eternity.[327]

It is so easy to get caught up in the here and now, when in fact our focus should be on eternity all along. An eternal perspective allows us to think forward and heavenward.

Heaven is the only place of full and final healing fulfillment. A heaven-oriented point of view also realizes that at times God permits us to be less than fully healed here. He often desires through our sorrows to accomplish things that could in no other way be accomplished for His glory.[328]

There are times now that the pain and sorrow reach into the very core of my being and create an abyss of pain, but I know that this life is not all there is. I know Dad and Don are realizing a hope that they had prepared for and lived for all of their lives. These two godly, faithful men are now realizing something they could only dream of. And you must realize that for your own loved one. We must rejoice for those we love, even in our pain. If we focus just on our pain—and trust me, that is easy to do because pain shouts at me—then we miss the eternal focus and the remembrance that this life is not all there is. Our hope in Christ is not just for this life.

As you reflect on the verse and quotes, how do they speak to you?

---

[327] Taken from *Eternity,* © 2006 by Joseph M. Stowell, and used by permission of Discovery House Publishers, Grand Rapids, MI. All rights reserved. 21.
[328] Ibid., 99.

DAY 259 REFLECTION

Reflect over the last week. What brings you comfort? Several of the verses we looked at this week are my favorites and those I quote the most often. We read that God tells us to be still and know that He is God. We put this on Don's headstone because he truly took this verse to heart. We are reminded that we must make the time to be still and truly know God. We must make the time to be still.

I never tire of Job 19:25-27. There is so much in these verses, but this week we focused on Job not giving up on prayer and seeking God. We saw that when Job experienced God, it gave Him all the answers he needed. Just to experience God was enough. Job was rewarded for continuing to seek God. We are encouraged to seek Him and to yearn for Him. We shall see God face to face. We are waiting on that day! We read how Elisha called for a harpist. Music continues to bring me comfort as I grieve. As Chris Tiegreen points out that we can become too analytical and music can help us stop and just experience God. Are you being too analytical? What ways are you hearing God? Have you noticed God speaking to you through music?

We read again the account of Lazarus carried to Paradise. We are reminded that the rich man in Hades could remember details about his family and his home. We are reminded how much more will those in Heaven remember. If the man in Hades knew his brothers and still continued to see them as his family, how much more will we in Heaven! Paul Enns points out, "There will be glorious happy reunions of loved ones—family and close friends—in heaven never to be separated!" We feel the pain and sorrow of not having them with us. Our loved ones know the time we are separated will be short compared to eternity. We have the hard part.

We read how we are encouraged to store up treasures in Heaven, and to take hold of our true life. Everything we do here matters for eternity. We must remember that truth. 1 Timothy 6:18-19 speaks clearly of continuity. We continue to store up treasures in Heaven as we wait on the day that we take hold of our true life in our true Home. Another favorite verse reminds me that if our hope in Christ is just for this life, we are to be pitied more than anyone in this world. Joseph Stowell points out that. "The biblical word *hope* comes from the Greek root that means trust."[329] If this life in this fallen world is all there is, we are a miserable lot even if we have had a wonderful life. But this life isn't all there is. 1 Corinthians 15:19 truly helps us have an eternal perspective. We are waiting on that day! As you reflect back over this week of powerful verses, record your thoughts and feelings. What does God seem to be laying on your heart this week?

---

[329] Taken from *Eternity*, © *2006* by Joseph M. Stowell, and used by permission of Discovery House Publishers, Grand Rapids, MI. All rights reserved.50.

DAY 260

So we fix our eyes not on what is seen, but on what is unseen, since what is seen is temporary, but what is unseen is eternal. (2 Corinthians 4:18 NIV)

Although we know the Earth will one day be restored, now in its fallen form, it is temporary. All that we see is temporary. We act as if this world and life is all there is. Even those of us that have big imaginations have trouble with what we don't see. But remembering that there is a whole dimension that we do not see is important. Remembering that this life is temporary is important, because that allows us to stay focused on an eternal perspective.

David had a good grasp of the unseen. In many places in the Psalms we see his ability to focus on the unseen. Psalm 34:7, "The angel of the Lord encamps around those who fear him and He delivers them." We know that angels did deliver David from several attempts on his life. And we also know angels deliver us to Heaven. David seemed very sure of the unseen world. As Philip Yancey writes,

Throughout his life David believed, truly believed, that the spiritual world, although invisible to him, was every bit as real as the "natural" world of swords and spears and caves and thrones. His psalms form a record of conscious effort to reorient his own daily life to the reality of that supernatural world beyond him. Now, centuries later, we can use those very same prayers as steps of faith.[330]

Praying the Psalms can help us reorient ourselves to the unseen. Reading the various accounts of angels and visions of the prophets can remind us of the unseen world. Remembering how Stephen saw Heaven open up, and Paul was taken to a third Heaven are two other examples of a glimpse into the unseen world. We know that Heaven is unseen, but a very real place that God has prepared for us before the beginning of the world; that is an awesome thought.

Knowing that although we cannot see our loved ones, they are more alive than ever can help comfort us. I would love the veil to be pulled back and "see" Heaven, to see what Dad and Don are seeing, to see them with Jesus. But that is not to be. I have to hold to faith and trust that Jesus has everything under control. I have to know that there is an unseen world, and it is not temporary. Heaven is very real and it is forever. In Heaven there will be an end to the pain and sorrow, we will finally see Jesus and the whole unseen realm.

Reflect on the verses mentioned. Read other examples in the Bible of the unseen world. What are your thoughts?

---

[330] Philip Yancey, *Grace Notes* (Grand Rapids, MI: Zondervan, 2009), 381.

DAY 261

A faith and knowledge resting on the hope of eternal life, which God, who does not lie, promised before the beginning of time, and which now at his appointed season he has brought to light through the preaching entrusted to me by the command of God our Savior. (Titus 1:2-3, NIV)

Concerning hope, Joseph Stowell says:

Significantly, the Bible offers a concept of hope that goes beyond the normal English usage. In the twenty-first century, we understand the word *hope* to mean something we desire based on a certain level of expectation. *Webster's New World of the American Language* states that hope is 'a feeling that what is wanted will happen; desire accompanied by expectation.' This definition and the popular usage do not require that the expectation be grounded in reality.[331]

Stowell goes on to say, "Biblical hope is always grounded in realities. It is grounded in a God who is true and whose promises are sure. When we hope in a world to come—heaven beyond—we place our hope in a reality that has already been confirmed."[332] Notice that the hope of eternal life was promised before the beginning of time and is now, as Paul writes, the appointed time in history. God has brought His plan to light. How amazing is that thought? Before the beginning of time, God had everything throughout history planned. All of history is moving towards God's eternal plan. As Philip Yancey writes:

In the Bible, Heaven is not an afterthought optional belief. It is the final justification of all creation, The Bible never belittles human tragedy and disappointment—is any book more painfully honest—but it does add one keyword: temporary. What we feel now, we will not always feel. The time for recreation will come.... The Bible began with that promise in the book of Genesis. And the Bible ends with that same promise, a guarantee of future reality. The end will be a beginning.[333]

The nightmare, pain, and sorrow seem never-ending. The days and nights are a struggle without the one you love. But we have a very real promise, a very real hope based on realities. We will see Jesus and the sorrow and nightmare will be over, never to return. We will be reunited with our loved ones, never again to be separated. We are waiting on that day!

As you meditate on today's verses and quotes, how do they speak to you?

---

[331] Taken from *Eternity*, © *2006* by Joseph M. Stowell, and used by permission of Discovery House Publishers, Grand Rapids, MI. All rights reserved. 47.

[332] Ibid., 48.

[333] Philip Yancey, *Grace Notes* (Grand Rapids, MI: Zondervan, 2009), 141.

DAY 262

Look, I am coming soon! My reward is with me, and I will give to each person according to what they have done. I am the Alpha and the Omega, the First and the Last, the Beginning and the End. (Revelation 22:12-13, NIV)

Jesus is coming soon! I can't wait. On that day the pain and sorrow will be gone. We will see Jesus! We will live with Him in the eternal kingdom; we will be reunited with our loved ones for eternity. Jesus is the Alpha and the Omega, the First and the Last, the Beginning and the End. From the beginning of time there has always been a divine plan that God orchestrated. Philip Yancey writes:

Revelation promises that our longings are not mere fantasies. They will come true. When we wake in the new heaven and the new earth, we will have at last whatever we longed for. Somehow, from all the bad news in a book like Revelation, good news emerges—spectacular Good News. A promise of goodness without a catch in it somewhere. There is a happy ending after all. In the Bible, heaven is not an afterthought or optional belief, It is the final justification of all creation.... John sees heaven as the fulfillment of every Jewish dream: Jerusalem restored, with walls of jasper and streets of gleaming gold. For someone else—say, a refugee in the developing world today—heaven may represent a family reunited, a home abundant with food and fresh drinking water. Heaven stands for fulfillment of every true longing.... For people who feel trapped in pain or in a broken home, in economic misery or in fear—for all those people, for all of us, heaven promises a future time far longer and more substantial than the time we spend on earth, a time of health and wholeness and pleasure and peace.[334]

Jesus is the Beginning and the End. Jesus was before the creation of the world. The divine plan is unfolding as we speak. We long to be in that perfect world. I deal with people's pain every day. And as long as we live in a fallen world, there will be people in pain. But someday pain and sorrow will end and the true beginning will take place. We long to be with those we love. We will be. Jesus is coming soon. We are waiting on that day!

Reflect on the verses and the quotes. What are your thoughts and feelings? What is your longing?

---

[334] Philip Yancey, *Grace Notes* (Grand Rapids, MI: Zondervan, 2009), 141.

DAY 263

For we live by faith, not by sight. (2 Corinthians 5:7, NIV)

We live by faith. When someone we love is called Home, we are left reeling. It is more important than ever to hold to that faith because it is a time when we are under spiritual attack. We are vulnerable and in pain. Our faith can be tested because everything hinges on our faith. Our faith always been important, but when we have someone in Heaven, then the reality hits us. As we read before, C.S. Lewis writes in a *Grief Observed*, "You never know how much you really believe anything until its truth or falsehood becomes a matter of life and death to you."[335] When our world is shaken we have to hold to our faith, but as Beth Moore points out:

Yes we walk by faith, but we stand on fact. The disciples didn't just hope Jesus was the Son of God when they refused to recant to save themselves from martyrdom. They knew He was. They'd seen His miracles. They'd heard Him foretell what would happen. Then they saw Him fulfill it. 'That which was from the beginning, which we have heard, which we have seen with our own eyes, which we have looked at and our hands have touched—this we proclaim concerning the Word of Life.' (1 John 1:11)[336]

In her study of Daniel she quotes statistics and adds:

Twenty-seven percent of the Bible is prophecy, and twenty percent of the books of the Bible are prophetic... a scientist that took 48 Old Testament prophecies fulfilled in the life of Christ and found based on modern science of probability that the 'chance of one man fulfilling all 48 prophecies to be 1 in 10 with 157 zeros. Keep in mind that is only a small slice of hundreds of general prophecies that have already been fulfilled.... God's ability to foretell and fulfill sets the Bible in a class completely by itself. No other text of the world's religions can begin to compete. Reasonable people can believe God and take Him at His Word because God has proved believable.[337]

If you find yourself shaken and doubting, remember these staggering facts. Yes we live by faith and not sight, but we have so much to stand on. Hold fast to those truths now. The Bible is true, your faith is true, and Heaven is true. God is in control.

Reflect on the verse and the quotes. What are your thoughts and feelings?

---

[335] C. S. Lewis, *A Grief Observed* (New York: Harper Collins EBook, 2009), Location 15.
[336] Beth Moore, *Daniel Lives of Integrity Words of Prophecy* (Nashville, TN: Lifeway, 2012), 205.
[337] Ibid., 205

DAY 264

But our citizenship is in heaven. And we eagerly await a Savior from there, the Lord Jesus Christ. (Philippians 3:20, NIV)

There is so much eternal truth in this verse. The moment we receive Christ as our Savior, we become citizens in Heaven. Even though we reside here for now, our true Home is in Heaven. We are all just passing through. In his book *Everything Happens for a Reason*, Paul Enns writes, "Our real citizenship is not in America; it is in heaven—we need to focus on where our real citizenship lies."[338] Greg Laurie writes, "Deep down we know that we were meant for another, better world. When we become Christians, we realize that our citizenship is in heaven and our life comes and goes, whether you live to be nine or ninety.... The truth is, as Christians we are already citizens of heaven. So we long for something more."[339] Joni Erickson writes, "When a Christian realizes his citizenship is in heaven, he begins acting as a responsible citizen of earth. He invests wisely in relationships because he knows they're eternal."[340]

We tend to think this life is it, and then in a flash a part of our life, a huge part of who we are, is suddenly no longer here with us. Our loved ones have gone Home. But the comfort is in knowing we too will go Home. We will someday join them in our eternal Home, our true Home. We eagerly await our Savior from Heaven. Jesus will either call us Home or come and get us all together. But either way, our time on this Earth is temporary because our citizenship is in our eternal Home. We are walking Home together...

C.S. Lewis writes, "I must keep alive in myself the desire for my true country, which I shall not find till after death; I must never let it get snowed under or turned aside; I must make it the main object of life to press on to that other country and to help others do the same."[341] There is a longing for our true Home and it becomes even stronger when those we love go before us. We have the promise of that citizenship and eternal life. We are waiting on that day!

Reflect on the verse and the quotes. What are your thoughts and feelings?

---

[338]   Paul Enns, *Everything Happens For A Reason* (Chicago, IL: Moody, 2012), 219.

[339]   Greg Laurie, *Signs of the Times, Greatly Expanded and Revised* (Dana Point, CA: Kerygma, 2011), Location 3570.

[340]   Joni Eareckson Tada, *Heaven: Your Real Home* (Grand Rapids, MI: Zondervan, 1995), 110.

[341]   C.S. Lewis, *Mere Christianity* (New York, NY: HarperCollins, 1952, 1980), 138.

DAY 265

For the Lord himself will come down from heaven, with a loud command, with the voice of the archangel and with the trumpet call of God, and the dead in Christ will rise first. After that, we who are still alive and are left will be caught up together with them in the clouds to meet the Lord in the air. And so we will be with the Lord forever. Therefore encourage one another with these words. (1 Thessalonians 4:16-18, NIV)

I confess that the more I study prophecy the more knowledge I have in my confusion. Scholars disagree on the specifics of Christ's return. But they all agree Jesus will return. While I can see the different viewpoints and see that there are compelling arguments for each, the thought of the rapture anytime is very appealing. However, I also see validity in those who cite passages to indicate the rapture will be mid-tribulation. Those who believe that the rapture will occur before the tribulation cite this verse as proof.

Regardless of whether the rapture is before the tribulation, mid-tribulation, or after the tribulation, the knowledge that Jesus is returning is still comforting. Paul tells us to comfort each other with these words. Paul knows there is a whole group of people mourning the death of loved ones. Paul tells his friends we will all be together with our Lord forever. If the Lord tarries and we are called Home as our loved ones were, then we will still be together. If Jesus comes while we are alive, then we will be caught up together with our loved ones. Greg Laurie, in *Signs of The Times*, writes:

Perhaps you've recently lost a loved one to death, and you're enduring a time of grief right now. Paul writes this passage in Thessalonians just for you. Remember this, he is saying. You could be going about your business one day, thinking about your departed loved one, and then suddenly, so quickly that it can't be measured with time; you will be seeing that person face to face. Mothers and fathers will be reunited with sons and daughters. Husbands will be reunited with wives and wives with husbands. Children with their parents. Brothers with brothers. Sisters with sisters. Friends with friends. Your sorrow will immediately vanish and be replaced with ecstatic joy. But not only will you yourself be reunited with your loved ones, you will open your eyes in the very presence of Love Himself, the Lord Jesus Christ. That is what will happen in the rapture. I personally long for this so much, as our oldest son Christopher went to be with the Lord in July of 2008. We grieve his loss deeply each and every day. We miss him so very, very much. We long to see him and speak with him. That day is coming for us, and all of us who have had loved ones precede us to heaven.[342]

Amen. We are waiting on that day! How does today's devotion speak to you?

---

[342] Greg Laurie, *Signs of the Times, Greatly Expanded and Revised* (Dana Point, CA: Kerygma, 2011), Location 1431.

DAY 266 REFLECTION

As you read over the last week, what seems to speak to you the most? A favorite verse in 1 Corinthians reminds us to focus not on what is seen but what is unseen. There is an entire unseen dimension. Our loved ones are in the unseen world, but someday we too shall see. I think of Steven Curtis Chapman's song when I read this verse in 1 Corinthians:

> We'll see with our own eyes
> He was always in control
>
> And we'll sing holy, holy, holy is our God
> And we will finally really understand what it means
> So we'll sing holy, holy, holy is our God
> While we're waiting for that day[343]

We read verses that remind us of God's sovereignty and His perfect eternal plan. Our hope is grounded in biblical realities. We read the glorious words that Jesus is coming soon. We are reminded of continuity as Jesus speaks of our rewards. We see a happy ending, a perfect world. We see a reunion with our loved ones to worship Jesus forever. Jesus is the Alpha and the Omega and He will come again. Come, Lord Jesus. Come! We read that we live by faith, not by sight, and are reminded how prophecies help bolster our faith. We know what we believe is true because Jesus is faithful and true. We may see things that are temporary and we may have things happen in our life that don't make sense to us, but we live by faith. We hold to our faith. We read our citizenship is in Heaven, and that helps us focus on a true eternal perspective. We are here on this Earth temporarily; it is not our true Home. Our citizenship is in Heaven, and we eagerly await a Savior from there. Our loved ones have gone before us to their true Home. But we who are left continue to walk Home.

In another favorite verse in 1 Thessalonians, we read about Paul talking to a group who is mourning the loss of loved ones. Paul reminds his friends that they will be with their loved ones again. We will be reunited with our loved ones again, whether we meet them in the sky or God calls us Home. We long for that day the trumpet sounds and we are "caught up together in the clouds to meet the Lord. And so we will be with the Lord forever." We are waiting on that day! As your read back over the week, record your thoughts and feelings. These verses are all so powerful. How did God speak to you this week?

---

[343] Steven Curtis Chapman, "Our God is in Conrol." *Beauty Will Rise*. Sparrow, 2008.

DAY 267

Since, then, you have been raised with Christ, set your hearts on things above, where Christ is, seated at the right hand of God. Set your minds on things above, not on earthly things. (Colossians 3:1-2, NIV)

In *Signs of the Times*, Greg Laurie tells the story of a young boy flying a kite. Although the kite was very high and he could not actually see it, he knew it was there because he felt its tug. Laurie then writes:

In the same way, you and I know there is a heaven because we can feel its tug. It goes back to the earliest days of our childhood. And I will tell you this: When you know someone who is already there, heaven becomes much more important, and much more real.... All of us should be thinking aggressively about heaven.... To 'set your mind' speaks of diligent, active, single-minded investigation—as if you had lost something and were searching for it. That is how we should be looking at heaven. Another way to translate this verse is simply, 'Think heaven.'[344]

We have all wondered about Heaven and knew Heaven was where we wanted to go. Don and I would often talk about Heaven, especially when we were some place beautiful and surrounded by the beauty of nature. Our talk of Heaven increased when Dad went Home. When Don went Home so abruptly, I could not think and I could barely breathe. Even now each day I awake and think, "I am one day closer to Heaven." Laurie is so right; Heaven becomes much more real when someone you love is there. It is not that you did not think Heaven was real before. But when you have people you love in Heaven, people you share a life with on Earth, it is natural to want to be with them. The tug to Heaven becomes stronger. Our investment in Heaven is even more.

If we set our minds on Heaven, if we think Heaven, it should affect every aspect of our life. I realize more than ever that the things in life we allow to bother us are so insignificant if our minds are on Heaven. If our minds are on Heaven, we have a burden for the lost, for the hurting. I am so ready for Jesus to come again. But I also look around at the lost and hurting and have a burden to pray and share Christ. Even in your pain, you can pray for others. We live in a fallen, temporary world. I am so ready for Heaven, but I also want to serve God until He calls me Home. My mind is on Heaven and I can't wait. I am waiting on the day, but in the meantime I must pray and seek Him.

How are you keeping your mind on Heaven? What do you feel led to do? Voice of the Martyrs is a good place to start to pray for others. Visit http://www.persecution.com

---

[344] Greg Laurie, *Signs of the Times, Greatly Expanded and Revised* (Dana Point, CA: Kerygma, 2011), Location 3625.

DAY 268

If our hope in Christ is only for this life, we are more to be pitied than anyone in the world. (1 Corinthians 15:19, NLT)

This life is but a breath. We are all here on this Earth, as it is now, temporarily. We get so caught up in our lives that we think life is all there is. So many times in the Scriptures we are reminded that this life on this fallen world is not permanent. Greg Laurie writes:

It is frustrating because we meet some people who live long lives that are squandered and wasted. And then we see someone with so much promise and ability and gifting die unexpectedly, and we think that is so unfair. That is because we are putting all our thinking into life on earth, and not realizing that life goes on. Death for the believer is *not* the end of life but a continuation of it in another place. You *will* live forever. Don't forget that. Earth is like a stopover.... We're not at our destination yet, but we're on our way.[345]

Life does seem unfair. There are things we cannot explain. Just this week a man dressed in black forced his way into a classroom full of children, opening fire. When the news finally came out, twenty-six people were dead. Twenty of those were children. My heart breaks for those families. The only hope in any situation of pain and suffering is Jesus. Our hope is in the knowledge that this life is not all there is. This life as it is now is temporary. Our hope in Christ is not just for this life. We live in a fallen world and thank God the fallen world is temporary. Thank God there is more in eternity.

This life on Earth is a stopover. I don't know how many times I have said, "I want my life back." I say it before I think and I wake up thinking that. But I must hold to the knowledge that my true life is eternal; my hope is in Christ, not just for this life; my true life is in eternity; and I will see Jesus. I will be with Jesus for eternity. I will be reunited with Don and with Dad. Someday all of our family will realize this eternal destination. The pain and sorrow can completely overwhelm you. The only way to refocus is to think of Heaven and to remember that our hope is in Christ. We know that this life is not all there is. I quote this verse often to help me focus. This life is not all there is. We will be reunited with our loved ones. We will see Jesus and on that day our true life will be *fully* realized. We are waiting on that day!

Meditate on this verse. What are your thoughts about the verse and the quote? Have you found yourself wondering why some people are still here and your loved one is not?

---

[345] Greg Laurie, *Signs of the Times, Greatly Expanded and Revised* (Dana Point, CA: Kerygma, 2011), Location 4130.

DAY 269

For this world is not our permanent home; we are looking forward to a home yet to come. (Hebrews 13:14, NLT)

We are looking forward to a home yet to come. When we stay focused on the eternal perspective, we know this life is temporary. Our true Home is yet to come. Dad was a Methodist minister. After Don and I married, Dad and Mom and my siblings moved several times. I would find myself saying to someone, "We are going home this weekend." I had never lived in that house, but it was home because Dad and Mom were there. You have heard the saying, "Home is where the heart is." As believers, our hearts belong to Jesus. He has saved us. So the minute we receive Him as our Savior, Heaven becomes our true Home.

When you have loved ones in Heaven, it seems even more like Home because another part of our heart is in Heaven. Paul Enns talks about family reunions in Heaven: "We will excitedly greet one another at that glorious reunion with our believing loved ones. The very moment earth's door closes and heaven's door opens—at that very moment—there will be an excited, joyful, and exuberant reunion."[346] He goes on to say, "Reunion with our believing loved ones and friends, together in fellowship with Christ Himself. What a phenomenal prospect! Celebration and fulfilling fellowship with loved ones—ongoing, unending in Christ's kingdom. What could be greater?"[347] Joseph Stowell writes:

There are many reasons our hearts are drawn to our eternal home. Perhaps in heaven we will reunite with a spouse, a child, a parent, or a dear friend. In heaven we will also leave behind the troubles and heartaches of life.… But the compelling attachment of my affections for heaven is the presence of Christ and the promise of an eventual reunion with Him, the lover of my soul.[348]

As long as we are in the presence of Jesus we will be in Heaven and at Home. At the appointed time, He will usher in the New Heaven and the New Earth. Then this restored world does become our permanent Home. We will finally be Home; Home with our God, Home with our loved ones. Home. We are waiting on that day.

What thoughts and feelings does Home bring to you? What are your thoughts and feelings on the quotes and this very powerful verse?

---

[346] Paul Enns, *Heaven Revealed* (Chicago, IL: Moody, 2011), 43.

[347] Ibid., 71.

[348] Taken from *Eternity*, © 2006 by Joseph M. Stowell, and used by permission of Discovery House Publishers, Grand Rapids, MI. All rights reserved. 110.

DAY 270

I say to you that many will come from the east and the west, and will take their places at the feast with Abraham, Isaac and Jacob in the kingdom of Heaven. (Matthew 8:11, NIV)

I repeat Paul Enns's quote about this verse, "His son and grandson. Family reunion! For believers, death brings a joyful reunion with believing family members. What a prospect!"[349] Well-meaning people have said we will be one big family, which I agree. But they go on to say that we will feel the same about everyone. There will be no distinction in relationships. I just can't believe that. Don and I are best friends. If he is Don and I am Ann, then we will have that continuity. I don't know how relationships translate for sure, but I know that God brought us together at a very young age. God gave us the special and unique relationship we have, so I trust God to continue that special relationship in Heaven. I know God blessed me with a wonderful Dad. Dad would say, "Family is the nature of God." Our kids are such a part of who we are; there has to be a continuity of relationships. Parents, children, spouses, siblings, nieces, nephews, grandparents, and close friends all have special bonds. Greg Laurie writes, "But that doesn't mean our relationship will end. God's plan for our lives doesn't stop in heaven, it continues. God doesn't abandon His purposes in heaven. He fulfills them. Therefore, friendships and relationships that have begun on earth will continue in heaven richer than ever."[350]

After stating that his wife Nanci is his best friend and closest sister in Christ, Randy Alcorn states:

Will we become more distant in the new world? Of course not—we'll become closer, I'm convinced. The God who said 'It is not good for man to be alone' (Genesis 2:18) is the giver and blesser of our relationships. Life on this Earth matters. What we do here touches strings that reverberate for all eternity. Nothing will take away from the fact that Nanci and I are marriage partners here and that we invest so much of our lives in each other serving Christ together. I fully expect no one besides God will understand me better on the New Earth, and there's nobody whose company I'll seek and enjoy more than Nanci's.[351]

We are waiting on that day!

Reflect on this verse and quotes. Do you find comfort in continuity?

---

[349] Paul Enns, *Heaven Revealed* (Chicago, IL: Moody, 2011), 43.
[350] Greg Laurie, *Signs of the Times, Greatly Expanded and Revised* (Dana Point, CA: Kerygma, 2011), Location 4286.
[351] Randy Alcorn, *Heaven* (Carol Stream, IL: Tyndale House, 2004), 351.

DAY 271

Jesus said to the thief on the cross, "Truly I tell you, today you will be with me in paradise." (Luke 23:43, NIV)

The minute our believing loved ones drew their last breath here, they were in Paradise. Our loved ones were immediately in the presence of Jesus. We were left not being able to breathe. We were left with heartbreak and sorrow. But if we focus on eternity, we can find comfort. Every day I wonder what Don and Dad are doing. Every day when I open my eyes I think, "How long, Lord"? How long until I can go to Heaven? We don't know the answer to when Jesus will come back, or when He will call us Home. But we do know our believing loved ones are with Jesus right now. We know they are experiencing unspeakable joy. As Joseph Stowell writes:

The joy of Eden and that initial paradise on earth was focused on the relationship of Adam and Eve with the God of the universe. The relationship brought them a fullness of satisfaction and unlimited pleasure in God....When we cross the border and enter His presence, all the darkness of this world will be left behind. He will fill us like we have never been filled with an unhindered relationship with Him. Imagine the unparallel moment when we experience the brilliance of His welcoming presence and the sight of His Son, the crowned King of kings.[352]

Our loved ones are experiencing the brilliance of Jesus' presence. They were welcomed Home by our Lord. When I feel like I can't take another step, I try to think about what Dad and Don are experiencing. I try to remind myself that it is not about me. There is an eternal plan. God was ready for Don and Dad to come Home. I wasn't ready for them to go. But I have an eternity to spend with them. I have to hold to that truth in times of sorrow. I have to remind myself of the joy they are feeling. I think I want them back, but that would not be fair to them. Our loved ones are with Jesus; they are experiencing Heaven. When you are hurting it can be hard to refocus on what those we love are experiencing. Because what we see and feel is the absence of our loved ones. Their absence hurts unbelievably. Even though it is hard to focus on what they might be doing, it is important. Those we love are with Jesus in Heaven. We will join our loved ones in God's timing. We are waiting on that day!

Reflect on the verse and the quotes. What are your thoughts and feelings?

---

[352] Taken from *Eternity*, © *2006* by Joseph M. Stowell, and used by permission of Discovery House Publishers, Grand Rapids, MI. All rights reserved. 110.

DAY 272

I will go to him one day, but he cannot return to me. (2 Samuel 12:23b, NLT)

David said these words when his baby died. I used this verse earlier, quoting Paul Enns and Randy Alcorn. Both held to the belief that this spoke of David knowing he would join his son in Heaven. Why else would he want to go to him? Dr. Arnold Fruchtenbaum, in *Footsteps of the Messiah,* agrees, "Notice the way that David put it; he expected to go to the place where his deceased son was, and expected to see him at that time after death. So David expected to join his son in a conscious way after his own death, and he expressed it in the passage."[353]

As I write this, our nation is in shock and mourning with a small town in Connecticut. A gunman forced his way into an elementary school and twenty children were killed—along with six adults in the school. No one can explain such an atrocity. But in his blog, Greg Laurie writes:

I know from personal experience that the pain of losing a child is a fate worse than death for a parent.... I know God is there ready to bring His comfort to those grieving right now in Connecticut. I know He is here right now to bring comfort to all of us who are heartbroken to hear such news. At times like this we need perspective. An eternal perspective. We need to remember this life on earth is not all there is. There is an afterlife and there earthly wrongs are righted.... There is also a great safety for those beautiful children who I believe are all in heaven right now resting in the arms of Jesus. No harm will come to them again. Jesus said, 'Let the little children come to me, and do not hinder them, for the Kingdom of Heaven belongs to such as these.' (Mat 19:14) And there is comfort available to their parent who is in the deepest valley of pain and grief right now.[354]

Laurie goes on to say that the parents' hope is in Christ, and if they put their trust in Jesus as Savior and Lord they can have the assurance they will see their dear children again. He quotes King David in this verse. David was a man after God's own heart. The fact that David felt confident in seeing God someday is evident in the Psalms and his writings. David also seems to have the confidence that he will go to his baby someday. This is a verse to hold to the heart for the continuity of family and of children being safe in our Father's arms. We are waiting on that day!

As you reflect on this verse and quotes, how do they speak to you?

---

[353] Arnold G. Fruchtenbaum, *The Footsteps of the Messiah* (Tustin, CA: Ariel, 2003), 701.

[354] Greg Laurie, blog.greglaurie.com/ December 14, 2012 Used by permission from Harvest Ministries with Greg Laurie, PO Box 4000, Riverside, CA 92514.

DAY 273 REFLECTION

All of the verses the past week are some of my favorites and focus on Heaven and eternity. We can see the continuity of life and relationships in Heaven as we read these passages. We read again one of my favorite verses that tells us to set our minds on Heaven. Keep an eternal perspective. Our investment in Heaven is even greater now that our loved ones are in Heaven. We read that our hope in Christ is not just for this life. On Day 267 I mentioned Voice of the Martyrs. I found this website from Randy Alcorn's website. I have since become a prayer partner with the VOM. Praying for others is a powerful way to serve and glorify God. As we read about tragedies in this world and we feel our own pain, this verse in Corinthians focuses us back on our hope. Our hope is in Christ and our eternal life; it is not just for this life. When we read these verses we can see that truly we are walking Home!

And as the next verse reminds us so beautifully, "This world is not our home; we are looking for a home yet to come." I love how the New Living Translation is translated in this verse. We are waiting on our true Home. A home is full of family and love. Our true Home is where God is, and where our loved ones now are waiting on us. The verse in Matthew reminds us of the family's place with God. We read about grandfather, son, and grandson. We read about the family feasting together. Randy Alcorn quotes Amy Carmicael, a missionary to India in the early1900's:

Shall we know one another in Heaven? Shall we love and remember? I do not think anyone need wonder this or doubt for a single moment. We are never told we shall, because I expect, it was not necessary, for if we think for a minute we know. Would you be yourself if you did not love and remember?... We are told we shall be like our Lord Jesus. Surely this does not mean in holiness only, but in everything; and does not He know and love and remember? He would not be Himself if He did not, and we should not be ourselves if we did not. [355]

We read about David wanting to go be with his son. Many scholars agree David knew he would see his son again and be with him. We read Greg Laurie's beautiful words to those suffering in the tragedy of losing children. Laurie's affirmation of God's love and family gives us comfort. Family is the nature of God. We find such comfort in knowing there is continuity in Heaven of our relationships and families. And we read about the thief on the cross being with Jesus that very day. We think with thankfulness how in that instant our loved ones left us; they were with Jesus. Most of our passages this week focus on family, continuity, and Heaven as our true Home and destination. As you reflect on these days, record your thoughts and feelings. How is God speaking to you?

---

[355] Amy Charmicael, as cited by Randy Alcorn in *We Shall See God* (Carol Stream, IL: Tyndale House, 2011), 95.

DAY 274

I tell you the truth, those who listen to my message and believe in God who sent me have eternal life. They will never be condemned for their sins, but they have already passed from death into life. (John 5:24, NLT)

The minute we received Christ as our Savior we passed from the consequences of death to life. So although we may die to this life we have a guarantee of eternal life with Christ. Death has no hold on the believer. The pain of those of us left behind is still very real. The absence of our loved one is overwhelmingly painful. We miss our loved ones very much and there are times that pain threatens to overwhelm us. But we know, with an eternal perspective, that they have entered the presence of our Savior and we will someday be reunited with them. We know as believers we have this hope. Anthony Hoekema writes:

What the Bible stresses is that to live apart from God is death, but that fellowship and communion with God is true life. Such true life is already enjoyed by those who believe in Christ. Life in fellowship with God will continue to be enjoyed by believers after death.... It is this kind of existence after death that the Scriptures hold before us as a state to be supremely desired.[356]

Jesus tells us that He is the truth, and He is the way that leads to eternal life. When we receive Jesus we receive eternal life in His presence. "Eternal life is a quality of life that begins when a person believes that Jesus Christ is Lord and trusts in Him alone for salvation. When physical death occurs, those belonging to Christ will continue to live because the life that Christ gives us will never end."[357] As Joseph Stowell states, "Heaven in a real sense, is a continuation of all that was begun on this side, a continuation of the soul that I now have in a body re-engineered for eternity."[358]

Continuity is important in understanding eternity and what it will be like, and in understanding the continuity of relationships. As redeemed people, we already have that promise of eternal life; our loved ones have just gone before us. We, too, will pass into Jesus' very real presence and be with Him and our loved ones for eternity. We are waiting on that day!

Meditate on this verse and the quotes. What are your thoughts and feelings?

---

[356] Anthony A. Hoekema, *The Bible and the Future* (Grand Rapids, MI: Eerdmans, 1979), 90.

[357] *The Quest Study Bible* (Grand Rapids, MI: Zondervan 1994, 2003), 1530.

[358] Taken from *Eternity*, © 2006 by Joseph M. Stowell, and used by permission of Discovery House Publishers, Grand Rapids, MI 49501. All rights reserved. 73.

DAY 275

Now to him who is able to strengthen you according to my gospel and the preaching of Jesus Christ, according to the revelation of the mystery that was kept secret for long ages but has now been disclosed and through the prophetic writings has been made known to all nations, according to the command of the eternal God, to bring about the obedience of faith. (Romans 16:25-26, ESV)

God is eternal and His Word stands. God has an eternal plan, and that plan is unfolding. Jesus' first coming was prophesied, and His second coming is prophesied. How the Messiah was coming the first time was a mystery to the prophets of the Old Testament, but now, as Paul writes, it is revealed and we can see it through the prophecies. And as we read prophecies for the second coming, we can also see how the prophecies are unfolding even now. Philip Yancey compared the Christmas story in the Gospels with Revelation 12. He tells us the Christmas story is the same story, one from an earthly perspective and one from a heavenly perspective. He concludes:

No matter how it appears from our limited perspective, God maintains firm control over all history. Ultimately, even the despots will end up fulfilling the plan mapped out for them by God. Pontius Pilate and his Roman soldiers demonstrated that truth. They thought they were getting rid of Jesus by crucifying him. Instead, they made possible the salvation of the world.[359]

There is much we do not understand. We find it hard to understand death in general, especially when someone we love goes all too soon. It feels like our world is out of control. An eternal perspective tells us that although we do not understand, we trust Jesus. There is an eternal plan and God is in control. Prophecy shows us God's eternal plan was started from before the beginning. This world in its fallen state is temporary; our lives here are temporary. Life is but a vapor. We take hold of the eternal life that the eternal God has planned for those of us who receive Him. Our faith is true and firm. God is able to strengthen us through this sorrow because this life is not all there is and the sorrow will end. We have an eternity to be with Jesus, to understand, to be with our loved ones again. We just have to hold now to that faith despite the chaos and sorrow. Our God is eternal; His plan is eternal. He will strengthen you. Faith... "I trust you, Jesus, even when I don't understand."

Meditate on these verses. What are your thoughts and feelings? What are your thoughts on Philip Yancey's comparison of the Christmas story?

---

[359] Philip Yancey, *Grace Notes* (Grand Rapids, MI: Zondervan, 2009), 405.

DAY 276

Jesus answered, "My kingdom is not of this world. If My kingdom were of this world, then My servants would be fighting so that I would not be handed over to the Jews; but as it is, My kingdom is not of this realm." (John 18:36, NASB)

Jesus was admitting He was the King, but at that time He was not yet establishing His kingdom on the Earth. Jesus was proclaiming His kingdom, though. For now we live in one realm, but there is also an unseen world. Someday these worlds will be one. For now, there is much we accept on faith. What we see is not all there is, and what we see is temporary. But what we do while we are here does matter in the heavenly realm and for eternity. Philip Yancey writes:

Christians share an odd belief in parallel universes. One universe consists of glass and steel and wool clothes and leather briefcases and the smell of freshly ground coffee. The other consists of angels and sinister spiritual forces and somewhere out there places called Heaven and Hell. We palpably inhabit the material world; it takes faith to consider oneself a citizen of the other invisible world.[360]

We know we are citizens of another world. And now someone or more than one person that we love very much is residing in that other realm. Heaven becomes even more real to us even though we still can't see it. So faith becomes even more important, or the sorrow and sadness of not seeing our loved ones will consume us.

Faith is crucial. Without faith it is impossible to please God. Without faith surviving the temporary loss of our loved one is unbearable. Jesus is our King and He rules from Heaven. Jesus has taken our loved ones to live with Him now, but we will someday join them. We have to hold to that eternal truth and to our faith. An eternal perspective helps us remember there is more than we can see. Reading books like Revelation, Daniel, and Ezekiel reminds us of the unseen world. Philip Yancey writes:

In daily life, two parallel histories occur at the same time; one on earth and one in heaven. Revelation, by parting the curtain, allows us to view them together. It leaves the unmistakable impression that to make everyday choices between good and evil, those choices are having an impact on the supernatural universe we cannot see.[361]

Come, Lord Jesus. Come. We are waiting on that day!

Meditate on this verse. What are your thoughts on Philip Yancey's statements?

---

[360] Philip Yancey, *Grace Notes* (Grand Rapids, MI: Zondervan, 2009), 406.
[361] Ibid., 405.

DAY 277

Then Elisha prayed, "O LORD, open his eyes and let him see!" The LORD opened the young man's eyes, and when he looked up, he saw that the hillside around Elisha was filled with horses and chariots of fire. (2 Kings 6:17, NLT)

Elisha asked for a double portion of Elijah's spirit. He had watched Elijah in action and knew Elijah's relationship with God. Elisha was told that if he saw God take Elijah he would receive his request. Elisha stuck with Elijah and watched as God took Elijah Home. 2 Kings 2:11 tells us how Elisha watched as his beloved mentor and friend was taken to Heaven. Paul Enns points out, "The inference is that heaven is near; Elisha saw his master enter heaven. Amid the blaze of fiery light, the windstorm carried Elijah into heaven."[362]

Watching Elijah taken to Heaven allowed Elisha, without a shadow of doubt, to know what to tell his servant when he looked up and saw the invading Syrian army. Elisha prayed that the Lord would open his servant's eyes and let him see. Paul Enns writes, "When the Lord pulls back the curtain, a powerful army was nearby!... They came from another realm, normally unseen to the human eye.... Elisha saw into the realm of heaven."[363] Paul Enns continues by summarizing how witnesses describe Heaven's location:

1. Elisha saw Elijah go up into heaven. 2. Isaiah saw the Lord on His throne. 3. Ezekiel saw into the heavenly throne room. 4. Nebuchadnezzar saw into heaven. 5. Daniel saw into heaven. 6. Stephen saw Jesus standing next to God. 7. Paul heard Jesus speaking from heaven. 8. Peter talked with the Lord. 9. John watches and hears Jesus' triumphant return. 10. Jesus said heaven is near. 11 Jesus watched heaven come near.[364]

What can we learn? Heaven appears to be closer than we may think. Heaven is another realm that we cannot see, but is a true absolute place. Heaven is a place that our redeemed loved ones are right now, a place brimming with activity and beauty, a place where our Lord and Savior reigns. And right now our loved ones are experiencing this beautiful place. We miss them beyond words. But we hold to the eternal perspective. Heaven is real and near. We will join our loved ones, and see for ourselves Jesus' majesty. I pray God opens our eyes to see His glory and feel His presence in our time of sorrow. We are waiting on that day.

Meditate on the verse and the quotes. What are your thoughts and feelings on Heaven being near?

---

[362] Paul Enns, *Heaven Revealed* (Chicago, IL: Moody, 2011), 49.

[363] Ibid., 50.

[364] Ibid., 55.

DAY 278

And this is my prayer: that your love may abound more and more in knowledge and depth of insight, so that you may be able to discern what is best and may be pure and blameless for the day of Christ. (Philippians 1:9-10, NIV)

Sometimes grief feels like we are falling into an abyss of pain and sorrow. The heaviness and emptiness are overwhelming. You often can't feel God, and are desperate to feel His presence. You are not sure where to turn, nothing feels stable, nothing feels normal, and nothing feels real. I keep thinking: this is not my real life; this is a nightmare. This time in our lives is a vulnerable time. You are more sensitive and more alone—and even if you aren't alone you may feel that way. I pray for discernment for you now. I pray for all of us grieving that God gives us discernment, insight, understanding, wisdom, and knowledge. I pray for an eternal perspective and that we feel His presence.

As I read this verse, I realize this is what Paul is praying for his readers. Pray this for yourself. Pray this for others grieving. Keep reading God's Word. Keep praying, even though you don't always feel God or understand. God will answer through His Word, through other believers, through books He has inspired other believers to write, and through many more ways that He can speak. We just have to listen. Pray for discernment and insight as you seek God. Ask God to speak to you, and for you to be open to what and how He speaks. Remember that you can hear God many way. But the most important thing is to keep praying that you will be immersed in His Word and that your love would abound more and more in knowledge and depth of insight.

Quote those Scriptures that keep you in God's Word and remind you of His love and His sovereignty, and those that remind you of Heaven, eternity, and continuity. We will see Jesus, and when we do we must give account for our own lives. We want to hold to that faith now and not waver. We want to know that when we see Jesus, we held to Him even through those times we didn't feel Him; even through those times that nothing seemed real. We want to know that we prayed and received the discernment, insight, and assurance we so desperately needed. Read these words by Mercy Me:

> Please let me stay and rest
> In Your holiness
> Word of God speak[365]

God is faithful.

Reflect on these verses. Set aside time to pray and listen. Journal your answers.

---

[365] Mercy Me, "Word of God Speak." *Itunes Original.* MercyMe, 2008.

DAY 279

I am the Lord, and there is no other; apart from me there is no God. I will strengthen you, though you have not acknowledged me. (Isaiah 45:5, NIV)

I am God, and there is no other; I am God, and there is none like me. (Isaiah 46:9b, NIV)

These verses pretty much sum up God's sovereignty. He is God and there is none like Him. There are many, many days that feel out of control. There are many days that feel too painful to take another step, too hard to keep an eternal perspective, and too hard to just be. Many days I find myself praying, "You are God and there is none like You." Throughout the day and night as I feel everything sinking and feel like it is too much, I pray, "You are God and there is none like You." Praying those words calms me and it reminds me God is in control. Praying those words reminds me that it is not all about how I feel right now; I have to trust God. God has everything under control even when it seems like nothing is in control. He is God and there is none like Him. I will trust Him. Without God I am nothing.

The close relationships that God has given us are because of Him. Without God our relationships would not be the extraordinary relationships that we cherish. I will trust God that what He started here He continues in eternity because He is God and there is none like Him. Max Lucado writes, "You and I may have power but God is power. We may be a lightning bug but God is lightning.... Consider the universe around us. Unlike the potter that takes something and reshapes it, God took nothing and created something."[366] God is eternal. Lucado also writes:

He does not live sequential moments, laid out on a time line, one following the other. His Word is one moment or better stated, momentless. He doesn't view history as a progression of centuries but as a single photo. He captures your life, your entire life in one glance. He sees your birth and burial in one frame.[367]

God is all powerful and all knowing. There is none like Him. When we focus on God's glory, His awesome power, His holiness, His sovereignty, and His love, we know He has everything under control. This time in our life is a short moment in an everlasting life. God loves you. He knows your pain, but He also knows this will all be okay in eternity. He is God and there is none like Him.

Meditate on these verses and quotes. Pray these verses aloud.

---

[366] Max Lucado, "Live Loved" app (Nashville, TN: Nelson, 2011), Day 51.
[367] Ibid., Day 9

DAY 280 REFLECTION

As you read over the last week, what seems to speak to you? We read that as believers we have the promise of eternal life. Our eternal life starts when we receive Christ as our Savior. Death has no hold on us. We read how God's eternal plan is revealed through His prophets. We find comfort as we read how the prophecies unfold and as we see prophecies unfold now. We read about Jesus telling Pilate He is King and that His kingdom was not of this world. It reminds us of the unseen world. We have hope as prophecies unfold and we wait on that day.

We read again how Elisha prayed for his servant's eyes to be opened. The veil was pulled back and he saw the chariots and God's army. The unseen world is amazing with each little glimpse we get. We are reminded of the nearness of Heaven. We read that in our pain and darkness, and in this time of spiritual warfare, that we need to pray for discernment and insight. We need to truly set aside the time to spend with God praying and reading His Word. We are reminded to pray each day for insight and discernment. I think it is also a good idea to write down those times that you feel like God is revealing Himself to you. When you feel a peace or assurance, write those thoughts in your journal.

We read God's own Words that tell us He is God and there is no other. These verses shout of God's sovereignty. When I pray, I always start out with praising God, and I quote this verse: "You are God and there is no other." God is in control. We need to remember and hold to those words when we feel our world completely out of control. God is sovereign and He is in control. As you read back over the week, record your thoughts and feelings. What day's devotional resonates with you the most?

DAY 281

Deep calls to deep in the roar of your waterfalls; all your waves and breakers have swept over me. (Psalm 42:7, NIV)

The forty-second Psalm is a psalm of sorrow and crying out to God. The psalmist talks about his tears being his food. He cries out to God to be heard, and yet he feels alone. That feeling sounds very familiar, doesn't it? This verse, to me, is one that shows how grief feels. You feel at the mercy of the deep water, waves wash over you and threaten to drown you. The emotions of sadness, sorrow, emptiness, darkness, and pain are overwhelming and tumultuous. When I did grief counseling in the past, I would liken it to waves washing over you. But when I was thrown into the grief myself, waterfalls and waves and breakers seem to be very appropriate. I have never been surfing, but as I read Greg Laurie's description, I could more than identify with it. He wrote this in his blog shortly after a friend's young child was called Home.

Grief is like wiping out on a wave. When you are out surfing and get caught in a set, and go over the falls, you lose perspective. You have to roll with it and remember that it won't last all that long, But sometimes, when you're in the whitewater, you lose your perspective. You literally do not know which way is up, or how to get to the surface. This is where your leash comes in. Your leash is attached to your board, which always goes to the surface due to its buoyancy. So you grab your leash and follow it to the surface. The Scripture is like that leash; it gets us 'above the surface,' where we can get a heavenly perspective. Sometimes I get my head above the water and everything is clear. Everything, in a way, almost makes sense for a few moments. I will think, 'The Lord is leading me in His perfect plan. I have a son on earth another son in heaven. I will see him again.' But then the waves of pain and grief and sadness come and I go under again, I will surface and sink again many times in one day—again, again, and again. That is mourning. But we still have hope.[368]

Laurie goes on to quote 1 Thessalonians 4:13-17 to underscore our hope. He then writes, "But we have the hope of seeing again our loved ones who have preceded us to heaven. It will be a wonderful heavenly reunion."[369]

I think Greg's heartfelt and beautiful blog sums up the grief for a Christian so well. I cried as I read this blog because it resonates with me. The waves and the breakers sweep over us, but we do have hope. We are waiting on that day!

Reflect on this verse. Can you identify with the psalmist? What are your thoughts and feelings on Greg Laurie's heartfelt blog?

---

[368] Greg Laurie, blog.greglaurie.com/December 21, 2012. Used by permission from Harvest Ministries with Greg Laurie, PO Box 4000, Riverside, CA 92514.

[369] Ibid., December 21, 2012.

DAY 282

Don't be afraid of suffering for the Lord. Work at telling others the Good News, and fully carry out the ministry God has given you. (2 Timothy 4:5b, NLT)

Paul was encouraging Timothy to persevere in spite of suffering for the Lord. We know that even though we do not currently live in a situation where our suffering is as a result of persecution, we do know we suffer. Suffering is a part of life. Anything that Satan can use against us, he will; and suffering in times of sorrow is a particularly vulnerable time. But if we keep an eternal perspective we also know how this battle ends. We know that God is in control. We know that all of history marches toward the restoration of the Earth and us living with Jesus for eternity. We know that right now our loved ones have been called Home. We also know that we will be with them again.

The hard part is being here without our loved ones. No matter what we focus on, we still miss them. When you are used to being with someone all the time, their absence is painful. Heartache and longing to see our loved ones, feel them, and hear them is always there. But we have the knowledge that this life here and now is not all there is. We know that there is an eternal plan and God is in control. So we suffer now, but someday the suffering will end.

For now, we carry out the ministry God has given us. Because on that day we stand before Jesus, we want to have served Him as He called us to do. I know that right now it is hard to think of anything else, but when we do think eternally we know that it is vital that we carry on the work. I am so ready for Jesus to come back. But I also have a heart for those who do not have the hope that we have. I have had clients come in grieving and they really have no hope in Christ. I cannot imagine going through the pain and sorrow without the hope of eternal life and the knowledge that I will be reunited with my husband and my dad. What we do here still matters for eternity. So even in your sorrow, you can serve Him. As Joseph Stowell writes, "But if we know that what we do for Him here counts for eternity, though the results may be unseen, we continue to steadfastly carry on for Him regardless of our circumstances. A clear view of the other side enables us to persevere on this side." (1 Cor. 15:58)[370]

When someone you love very much is called Home, it changes you and it changes your perspective. Pray for guidance as to how you can carry out the work He has given you while you wait on that day.

Reflect on today's words. What thoughts come to you on serving?

---

[370] Taken from *Eternity*, © 2006 by Joseph M. Stowell, and used by permission of Discovery House Publishers, Grand Rapids, MI 49501 49501. All rights reserved. 9.

DAY 283

But you, dear friends, by building yourselves up in your most holy faith and praying in the Holy Spirit, keep yourself in God's love as you wait for the mercy of our Lord Jesus Christ to bring you to eternal life. (Jude 20, NIV)

As I began writing this, I have found myself writing many times, "I am waiting on that day." Now, as never before, I am waiting on that day, which is why I chose to name this book *For Those of Us Waiting on That Day*. The pain and sorrow of being without the one you love—the one you spent so much time with, the one you have so many experiences with, the one you had so many dreams with—is overwhelming. As I read this verse I thought that this is what we all have to do: hold to our faith and pray as we wait on that day. The comfort in our sorrow is Jesus. Our comfort is in knowing that we have the assurance of eternal life. The comfort is in knowing that in Christ there is no end, that we will be reunited with those we love who have gone Home.

This verse reminds us what to do as we wait: pray and keep ourselves in God's love as we wait for Him to bring us to Heaven. While we wait we pray, read His Word, and listen to music that praises Him. Immerse yourself in His love. It is important to make sure you are spending time in prayer. My prayer blanket has become a special part of my prayer time when I am kneeling on that blanket crying out to God, I can block other things out. But sometimes praying outside, watching the beauty of God's creation, helps me focus on Him. We know the Holy Spirit will intercede for us. Find ways to immerse yourself in His presence. Jesus will bring us into eternal life just as He did our redeemed loved ones. The words to the song reflect this thought of waiting so well:

> And I'm counting down the days
> Until I see it's everything
> He said it would be
> And even better than we would believe
>
> And I'm counting down the days
> Till He says
> "Come with Me"
> And finally
> We'll see[371]

There will be a day when Jesus calls us Home; while we are waiting, we keep ourselves in His presence, seeking Him. We are waiting on that day!

Reflect on this verse. How are you building yourself in your faith?

---

[371] Steven Curtis Chapman, "See." *Beauty Will Rise*. Sparrow, 2008.

DAY 284

Sell your possessions and give to the poor. Provide purses for yourselves that will not wear out, a treasure in heaven that will never fail, where no thief comes near and no moth destroys. For where your treasure is, there your heart will be also. (Luke 12:33-34, NIV)

Jesus tells us to store up treasures in Heaven. These verses, and more like them, are clear statements that what we do in this life matters for eternity. Verses like these are clear statements on continuity. If I am storing up treasures I will remember, my treasures will follow me. I think of what a legacy Dad and Don left as men of God and of faithful family members. Nothing can take away what we store up in eternity. Perhaps even now you can think of ways your loved one stored up treasures. All the worldly riches cannot compare with what Heaven brings.

I have used several verses that talk about rewards and treasures in Heaven because I think it helps us to focus on an eternal perspective. I find comfort in thinking about the continuity of our lives for eternity. Many times families store up treasures together. When we work together to further God's kingdom and serve Him, we are storing up treasures in Heaven. From the youngest to the oldest, we all have a mission. There are things we will understand more fully when we get to Heaven. We may not know all that our lives have touched until we get to Heaven. Greg Laurie writes:

On this side of heaven you and I don't know how it will all play out. When you pray for the work of evangelism, you become invested in it. When you give financially, you become invested in it. When you are kind to someone and help or bless someone in the name of Jesus, you become invested in evangelizing that life.[372]

Someday when we are in Heaven with our loved ones maybe we will be able to see events that we never realized would affect someone, but did. Maybe we will we find out how the money we gave to missions was used. Perhaps we will someday find out how important the prayers were for the people we prayed for. Maybe we will be able to thank those who prayed for us that we didn't know about. All those people who are now helping us are storing treasures in Heaven. We will have a chance to rejoice with each other in Heaven.

Reflect on the verses and the thoughts. Take time to thank God for the people who have helped you in your time of grief and reflect on what you can do.

---

[372] Greg Laurie, *Signs of the Times, Greatly Expanded and Revised* (Dana Point, CA: Kerygma, 2011), Location 4398.

DAY 285

For the Son of Man is going to come in his Father's glory with his angels, and then he will reward each person according to what they have done. (Matthew 16:27, NIV)

Jesus is coming back in full glory with His angels. I cannot wait for that day. We know we will see Jesus; we know He will either call us Home or come back to get us, and we will spend eternity with Him. This verse, like the passage yesterday, reminds us that Jesus will reward us according to what we have done. What we do in this life matters for eternity. We know we are saved by grace, but we also know that we will receive rewards based on what we have done. Dad was a small-town preacher who led many to the Lord. He had a way of being able to visit with anyone and he loved it. We store up treasures in Heaven when we are faithful to what God has called us to do. My Dad also worked as a volunteer fireman at one of his first churches in a small rural town in East Texas. There was a man in the community who had resisted all invitations to church. One night his barn was on fire and the volunteer firemen showed up to put it out. The next Sunday he showed up to church. After welcoming him, one surprised member asked what finally got him there. He said. "Well, when I looked up and the preacher was the first one off the fire truck, I decided I better come to church."

We serve God in many different ways. Don was a part of our church mission trip to New Orleans the summer before God called him Home. Since the trip was to help repair damage done by Hurricane Katrina and to help in the restoring one of the churches in New Orleans, his skills as a builder were needed. Don came back so blessed; and said he received far more than he gave. Don was also the kind of person who was always behind the scenes. Dad and Don would go out of their way to help someone. Both men were faithful men of God, and faithful to their families. Being faithful to your family in the way God has called you is also storing up treasures in Heaven.

Our daughter Melody found comfort in verses like this because she could see her dad and granddad receiving rewards and rejoicing. Our daughter Michelle is preparing for a mission trip as I write this. Maybe you have a child who has gone before you. Jesus loves the children; that is evident in Scripture. No matter how young a life, that life touches someone else; and when that happens, that life invests in eternity. Perhaps you can think of ways your loved one stored up treasures. You can serve God now as you wait to be reunited. When we read the verses that clearly show the continuity of life into eternity, it brings comfort and a resolve that while we wait, we serve. Jesus will come back for us in His glory. While we wait, we can serve.

Reflect on today's verse and thoughts. How are you investing?

DAY 286

"Shout and be glad, O daughter of Zion. For I am coming, and I will live among you," declares the Lord. (Zechariah 2:10, NIV)

God will live among us! How amazing is that thought. Paul Enns writes:

The joy that Adam lost will be restored on the new earth.... The central focus of our joy and gladness in glory will be the presence of the Lord Himself.... The presence of the Lord will create joy and gladness that will be expressed in joyful singing. In His presence we will experience pleasures beyond description, happiness that exceeds anything on this earth.[373]

Many Scriptures that can be applied to the millennium kingdom can also be applied to the New Earth. So many passages throughout the Bible speak of the time that God will dwell with His people and Earth will be perfected. When we read those passages, whether the passage is referring to the millennial rule of Christ on Earth or the New Earth, we know God will dwell among us, and that inspires hope.

We know Jerusalem will be the center of the millennium and it will be the center of the New Earth. God will live among us. Right now God's dwelling is Heaven. Our redeemed loved ones are with Him. We will join them. There will be a day when God's eternal plan culminates in the Heavens and the Earth being fully restored. On that day, there will be gladness. There will be peace. We will live together for eternity. I can't wait to see what the New Earth is like. I can't wait to actually be in God's presence and have Him live among us.

Now we wonder if we understand God's will. We pray and read the Bible. We read books and listen to music. We pray for insight and discernment to know God better, but still, we wonder, did we hear God? Is this my own desire or is this what God wants for me? There are so many things right now we don't understand. We live in this fallen world where things happen that do not make sense. There is violence, death, sin everywhere, and there is so much pain. People ask: "Where is God?" God is with us, but we can't always feel Him. This verse reminds us that there will be a day when God will actually dwell among us. There will be no more wondering if we heard Him; there will be no more pain or sorrow because God will dwell among us. We will know Him. The days of sadness will be over. We will live with our redeemed loved ones on a restored Earth, and best of all, God will live among us. I am waiting on that day!

Reflect on today's verse and thoughts. What do you look forward to the most?

---

[373] Paul Enns, *Heaven Revealed* (Chicago, IL: Moody, 2011), 123.

DAY 287 REFLECTION

Read over the last week. What brings you the most comfort? We read a Psalm of sorrow and heard the psalmist crying out to God. The words are an apt portrayal of grief. Greg Laurie's beautiful blog is an excellent description of grief. We read encouragement in the face of struggles to keep an eternal perspective. As Joseph Stowell writes, "A clear view of the other side enables us to persevere on this side." We read instructions from Jude on how to wait. How appropriate are those words for us at this time? We pray and hold to God while we wait.

We read verses that remind us that what we do here on Earth matters for eternity. God has called you to do something. What did you feel like God had called you to do before your loved one went Home? What can you do now? Pray for guidance to serve Him. You can serve others in different capacities; you can pray, you can give money to missions. What are other ideas? We know to seek Him as to what He wants us to do while we are waiting on that day. The verses we read where Christ tells us to store up treasures in Heaven are clear statements on continuity. When I think of people storing up treasures in Heaven much comes to mind. I know there are people right now who have ministered to me and our family and have stored up treasures in Heaven—those who are praying for us, those who sent cards, and those who came over and cried with me. My friend Penny texted me in the middle of the night because she woke up feeling like she needed to pray for me. I needed that. There were friends who offered to help me in any way, friends who sat and cried with me, friends who went out of their way to move things for me, fix, and repair different things. Our neighbor and my brother-in-law cut the dead trees down for me, and the list goes on. Lanny, our brother-in-law, finished the house Don was building even though he had much to do on his own, and continues to store up treasures as he does so much for us. Our family, who prayed and cried and gave to each other despite their own pain, stored up treasures in Heaven. I want to be clear; when I talk about you serving it isn't busy work. I know that there are many times I can barely breathe or move, especially the first year. Serving takes many forms. Prayer is one of the most important ways you can serve. God may call you to rest in Him for now, but be aware of times you can pray, give or serve in any capacity—no matter how small it may seem at the time.

Christ coming with His angels in glory and rewarding us is another clear statement of continuity. And finally, we read that God is coming and He will live among us. What awesome words and pictures this verse is for us. The verse in Zechariah is a beautiful statement of God's eternal kingdom and the New Earth. We are waiting on that day! What comforts you the most this week?

DAY 288

Very truly I tell you, you will weep and mourn while the world rejoices. You will grieve, but your grief will turn to joy. So with you: Now is your time of grief, but I will see you again and you will rejoice, and no one will take away your joy. (John 16:20-22, NIV)

Today is Christmas Eve, and as I write this my heart is heavy with sorrow and pain. Dad was called Home December 10; that Christmas was a blur. I really don't remember the day at all. Don was called Home November 2; that Christmas was a blur. Tomorrow will be the second Christmas since Don was called Home, the fourth since Dad was. Christmas is hard. Every day is hard, but those special days of family time and remembrance are even harder.

On December 14 of this year, we had a national tragedy when a gunman opened fire in an elementary school, killing twenty-six people, twenty of which were children. My heart hurts for the families and for all of us hurting now. Jesus knew how sorrowful death is for those of us left behind. In today's verse Jesus was preparing His disciples for His own death. Jesus knew His disciples would weep and mourn. The word *weep* is the same word for *loud wailing*, which carries the idea of deep sorrow and its outward expression.[374] The disciples had spent every day with Jesus, and He knew how devastating His absence would be. Even though the disciples were having a hard time understanding what Jesus was telling them, the reality of what He meant will hit them hard. Jesus wanted them to know ahead of time that their grief would turn to joy. They will see each other again and they will rejoice. Our grief will turn to joy.

Jesus knew the disciples would be in deep sorrow, and the hope and comfort He gave them then is the same hope and comfort He gives us now. This life is not all there is. Not only will we see our loved ones again, we will be with them again forever, never to be separated. Jesus was about to change things forever. He is the first fruits of the resurrection. We now go straight to Heaven, and on the determined day there will be a bodily resurrection. We will live together on a restored Earth with our loved ones and with God Himself. No one will take away our joy. There will be no more death and no more separation. Now is our time of grief, but we will see Jesus, we will see our loved ones, and we will rejoice. We are waiting on that day!

Meditate on these verses. If it is a holiday or other special day, pray for extra comfort. My sister started a new tradition of us giving gifts on Christmas in memory of Dad and Don. We put their stocking out and then put something in it to give to their favorite mission or charity. You might start a new tradition of giving to a special mission or group in memory of your loved one.

---

[374] *NIV Study Bible*, Kenneth Barker Ed. (Grand Rapids, MI: Zondervan, 1985), 1628.

DAY 289

On that day living water will flow out from Jerusalem, half to the eastern sea and half to the western sea, in summer and in winter. The Lord will be king over the whole earth. On that day there will be one Lord, and his name the only name. (Zechariah 14:8-9, NIV)

Some see these verses as part of the Millennial Kingdom, some as the restored Earth. Paul Enns seems to sum up the thoughts of several authors I have read:

The glories of the kingdom that Christ will establish at His second coming will persist throughout the millennium and continue for all eternity on the new earth. Scripture provides abundant support that there is continuity between the millennium and the eternal state on the new earth. It will be glorious. It will be heaven revealed![375]

The land will be restored to an Eden-like environment. There will be living water that flows from Jerusalem. The flowing river is described in Ezekiel 47 and Revelation 22. According to several of the books I read water was scarce in and around Israel. So the idea of the living water flowing would be beautiful; just as it is to us.

Picture the most beautiful river you have seen landscaped to perfection. Don and I took a trip to the Smoky Mountains and drove up the beautiful Blue Ridge Parkway. The river that flows beside the parkway is cool and clear. We would often stop and just sit beside the river listening to the sounds it made as it flowed freely over the rocks. If I had to think of one word to sum up that scenery it would be "peaceful." We also liked to go camping in the spring and fall and we always looked for a spot next to a river. When we were kids, Mom and Dad always looked for a spot next to the river to camp. This river will be flowing out of Jerusalem, and will be living water.

There will be peace in the land because all will worship the one true God. As I focus on an eternal perspective, I try to imagine Heaven now with a flowing river. Our loved ones have the constant delight of the beauty of Heaven now. We will all have the New Earth to look forward to as we wait on that day we are reunited with our loved ones to forever worship our Lord. We are waiting on that day!

Reflect on these verses and others we have read on the New Earth. How are you imagining the New Earth? Think now of a river that you have been to and imagine how that might look in Heaven.

---

[375] Paul Enns, *Heaven Revealed* (Chicago, IL: Moody, 2011), 97.

DAY 290

In that day each of you will invite his neighbor to sit under his vine and fig tree, declares the Lord Almighty. (Zechariah 3:10, NIV) Every man will sit under his own vine and under his own fig tree and no one will make them afraid. (Micah 4:4, NIV)

In the New Earth there will be peace and fellowship. The NIV Study Bible refers to this verse as "a proverbial picture of peace, security and contentment."[376] Don and I toured some vineyards in California the summer before God called him Home. Rolling hills of vines were carefully laid out and landscaped. We wondered then if the New Earth would have these rolling hills with beautifully landscaped vineyards. We will find out; maybe Don already knows now. Someday on the New Earth we will invite people over to sit with us in those beautifully landscaped places with no fear of anything—just enjoyment of what the Lord has made. Paul Enns writes:

On the new earth people will enjoy prosperity; the vine and fig tree represent abundance and suggest that believers will have the peaceful environment in which they will enjoy their abundance. They will have time and relaxation with their loved ones, friends, and neighbors to be refreshed from their orchards.... It will be a time of 'peace and prosperity'; it will be a time of restful fellowship in a perfect environment with friends and loved ones. Believers will enjoy the 'good life' in glory.[377]

I do not have trouble imagining our family relaxing under a tree enjoying nature because we have always relaxed in nature in many different places. If we have done that in this fallen world and felt peace and fellowship, can you imagine what that will be like on the New Earth? Our joy will be everlasting. We have an eternity to look forward to sharing with our redeemed loved ones. When we look at all the Scriptures that give us glimpses of the New Earth, we can look around us now and think how beautiful and wonderful times are here. In Heaven that beauty and joy with loved ones will be continued and magnified. Our experiences here are a glimpse of what we will experience in eternity. The sadness now will be over someday. I think that one of the hardest things in grief is not knowing how long the separation will be. We get so overwhelmed with the sadness now of missing our loved one that it is hard to think eternally, but when we do it brings us comfort. We just have to hold to the promise that this life is but a breath. Our reunion will come. The days of sitting under the trees and enjoying each other again will come. We are waiting on that day!

Reflect on these verses and quotes. What images come to your mind?

---

[376] *NIV Study Bible*, Kenneth Barker Ed. (Grand Rapids, MI: Zondervan, 1985), 1410.
[377] Paul Enns, *Heaven Revealed* (Chicago, IL: Moody, 2011), 126.

DAY 291

And from the time John the Baptist began preaching until now, the Kingdom of Heaven has been forcefully advancing, and violent people are attacking it. For before John came, all the prophets and the law of Moses looked forward to this present time. (Matthew 11:12-13, NLT)

Verses like these show us God's eternal plan, which can help us keep an eternal perspective. Jesus had just told the people that none born of women were greater than John the Baptist, but the least in the Kingdom of Heaven is greater than him. Jesus was ushering in the New Covenant. All the prophets and the Law of Moses had been looking for the Messiah and the Messiah was now among them. The prophets knew this day was coming, they just didn't know when or how. We know there is more to come. Jesus will come again, and when Jesus returns He will come as a conqueror; He is the King of kings.

Someday there will be a New Heaven and New Earth. We will live with Jesus for eternity. It is all in the eternal plan, the plan of the ages, and the plan before the beginning of time. God is sovereign. Our time here is but a breath, it is temporary. But we as redeemed believers have an eternal life. We are a part of that Kingdom of Heaven. Scholars differ as to what is meant by "forcefully advancing." Fortunately, we know with the New Covenant that we don't have to force our way into anything, we just have to know Jesus is the son of God, believe that He died for our sins and was resurrected, repent of our sins, and receive Him as our Savior. We are citizens of Heaven. Our redeemed loved ones are citizens of Heaven. Our redeemed loved ones have gone before us, but we will follow because we trust in the One who makes it all possible. We trust in the Eternal God and His plan for the ages.

Grief makes it very hard for us to look beyond the pain of the moment. Even when we keep the eternal perspective, the ache and longing in our hearts are still very real. We long for that day we are reunited with those we love. But our hope is in Christ, and we have the promise that that we will live with Jesus for eternity. We will be reunited because we trust in Jesus. We know our sovereign God has everything under control. We know that God has an eternal plan, and that we as redeemed believers are a part of the plan. The hard part is waiting, but we also know that this time is brief. God's plan unfolds in His timing. We will have an eternity to spend worshiping God with our loved ones. We are waiting on that day!

Reflect on these verses and what they mean. When you look at the big picture and where you are in that picture, what comes to mind?

DAY 292

How long, O Lord will you forget me forever? How long will you hide your face from me? How long must I wrestle with my thoughts and every day have sorrow in my heart?... But I will trust in your unfailing love. (Psalm 13:1,2,5, NIV)

David journaled before the studies of the therapeutic value of journaling was discovered. David also knew the Scriptures and quoted them. So David journaled and quoted Scripture, two things we know help us now. Philip Yancey writes:

Reading David's psalms, with all their emotional peaks and valleys, it may even seem that he writes them as a form of spiritual therapy, a way of talking himself into faith when his spirit and emotions are wavering. Now, centuries later, we can use these very same prayers as steps of faith, a path to lead us from an obsession with ourselves to the actual presence of God.[378]

I have felt like God forgot me, even though I know that is not true. I have felt like God was hiding from me, even though I know in my heart that is not true. But we may still have those thoughts and feelings. I still feel the sorrow in my heart every day even though I no longer feel like God is hiding from me. I still wrestle every day with my thoughts. And if I let myself, I can go back to the "Why did this happen?" and "This isn't fair!" statements. I wrestle because I know I will not have my questions answered, and even if I did, I would still hurt because I am missing Dad and Don every day. I know that although it "feels" unfair, in reality God has been more than fair to me. He has blessed me immeasurably. I can't stop trusting God now. David seemed to wrestle with his thoughts as well. David and other psalmist wrote their feeling as they wrestled. They wavered at times, but they trusted God.

A client brought me a picture of a headstone. Apparently the family had experienced a tornado that that took the life of their precious son. These words are inscribed on the headstone, "He is Sovereign and mightily in control of the slightest and greatest events in your life. When you study His Word and come to know the beauty of His sovereignty you will then be able to relax and glorify God in your trust." What beautiful words in these parents' grief. When a tragedy occurs we can either blame God or accept His sovereignty, and even though we don't understand, we trust Him. These parents seem to be accepting His sovereignty and trusting God with their powerful words and testimony.

Reflect on today's verses and thoughts. What are your thoughts and feelings?

---

[378] Philip Yancey and Brenda Quinn, *Meet The Bible, A Panorama of God's Word in 366 Daily Readings and Reflections* (Grand Rapids, MI: Zondervan, 2000), 218.

DAY 293

As they were walking along and talking together, suddenly a chariot of fire and horses of fire appeared and separated the two of them, and Elijah went up to Heaven in a whirlwind." Elisha saw this and cried out, "My father! My father! The chariots and horsemen of Israel! And Elisha saw him no more. (2 Kings 2:11-12a, NIV)

In order to get the full weight of these verses, you need to also read 2 Kings 2:1-18. In the first part of the passage, note that apparently all the prophets around knew God was taking Elijah that day. Two separate groups told Elisha that, and his response was essentially the same to both: "Yes, I know, and I don't want to talk about it." I think that thought is amazing, because we know that the spirit of the Lord was with Elisha. Elisha loved Elijah, and even though he knew the Lord was taking him that day and that Elijah would be with the Lord, he didn't want to talk about it. He knew, most likely, that he would miss him very much. Elijah was his mentor and they were close. Elisha had learned so much from Elijah, and he just didn't want to think about losing him.

Elisha gets to actually watch Elijah taken up to Heaven. Can you imagine how exciting that would have been? I think that even though the loss would still be extremely sad, he would have to have felt comfort in watching him be taken to Heaven. I know I wish I had seen the angels take Don and Dad to Heaven, and even though I would still be hurting now, the memory of them carried away would always be with me. But I have to remember that angels did take Dad and Don to Heaven, just like angels took your loved one to Heaven, even if we didn't see it happen. The journey Home is a part of the unseen world.

Watching Elijah go to Heaven made such an impression on Elisha that later, when surrounded by an army and his servant was worried, Elisha nonchalantly says, "Don't be afraid; those who are with us are more than those who are with them" (2 Kings 6:16). And then Elisha prayed that God would open his servant's eyes. His servant was then able to see the horses and chariots. Watching those horses and chariots take his friend Home made a huge impression on Elisha, one that stayed with him and strengthened him. We do not get to see the unseen world. But the unseen realm is there nonetheless. Heaven may be closer than we think. But regardless of how close, Heaven is a real place, and our redeemed loved ones are there now. Our loved ones were carried to Heaven, and though we would have loved to see their journey, we can know where they are and we can trust they are with our Lord. Though we, like Elisha, don't want to think about being here without our loved ones, we know we will be reunited with them because we know where they are. We are waiting on that day!

Read 2 Kings 2:1-18. As you reflect on the verses, what are your thoughts?

DAY 294 REFLECTION

Read back over the week. What seems to speak to you the most? We read how Jesus told us that we will grieve, but that our grief will turn to joy. We know every day is hard, especially those special days and anniversaries, but we have the promise of Jesus that our grief will turn to joy. Our nightmare will end the day we see Jesus. He is coming back as King of kings and Lord of lords. We will see Him and we will be reunited with our loved ones and have an eternity to worship Him together. We are waiting on that day!

We read several verses on the New Earth. The New Earth will be restored to Eden-like conditions. We read about the living waters. We can picture the most beautiful and picturesque river we have ever seen, and it is nothing compared to what God has in store for us in Heaven. We ponder our loved ones now, and what they must be experiencing. We read about vineyards and olive groves representing peace, prosperity, and contentment. We think of glimpses we may see now, but what is awaiting us is phenomenal. We have all of what is described in the Bible to look forward to seeing. We have the reunion of our loved ones to look forward to! We are waiting on that day!

We read of the eternal plan. The law, the prophets, and Moses all looked forward to the coming day of the Messiah. Jesus came and established the New Covenant. He will come again and restore the land. How awesome is that thought? We read in the Psalms how David cried out to God in his sorrow, how he did not feel God. We may be able to relate, but then we read what David wrote: "I will trust in your unfailing love." We are reminded how we too must trust in God's unfailing love. We see how David all those years ago found comfort in writing his feelings. If you have not been journaling and memorizing scripture, try doing that for a week and see if it helps comfort you.

Finally, we read about Elisha not wanting to face the loss of Elijah, his beloved friend and mentor. Elisha got to experience something I am sure we would all love to experience, and it changed his life forever. Although Elisha grieved, he was assured of where his loved one was. We have assurance too. Reading of Elisha's faith can strengthen ours. As you read over the last week, record your thoughts and feelings. What brings you the most comfort this week?

DAY 295

The Lord is good, a refuge in times of trouble. He cares for those who trust in him, but with an overwhelming flood he will make an end of Nineveh; he will pursue his foes into the realm of darkness. Look, there on the mountains, the feet of one who brings good news, who proclaims peace! Celebrate your festivals, Judah, and fulfill your vows. No more will the wicked invade you; they will be completely destroyed. (Nahum 1:7,8,15, NIV)

In the book *Meet the Bible*, Philip Yancey points out that Nahum's prophecy was against Assyria, which had been the world's most powerful empire for two hundred years. Who could believe his prophecy against them?

Nahum delivers the prophecies sometime around 700 B.C. In 612 B.C. Ninevah, the Assyrian stronghold fell to the Babylonians and Persians. Over time a carpet of grass will cover the pile of rubble marking what has been the greatest city of its time. Years later, both Alexander the Great and Napoleon will camp nearby, with no clue that a city has ever been there. Like all biblical prophets, Nahum sees beyond the intimidating forces of history. He knows that behind the rise and fall of empires an even greater force is at work, determining the ultimate outcome. Though God's justice may seem slow, nothing can finally escape it.[379]

Grief is all-consuming; your world is torn apart and nothing feels right or stable. Prophecy has a way of forcing you to look at the big picture and God's ultimate plans. Not just prophecy yet to be fulfilled, but also prophecy that has been fulfilled. Prophecy allows us to hold to God's sovereignty and an eternal plan. Our lives and our believing loved one's lives are all a part of that remarkable plan. Sorrow hurts now, and being apart from our loved ones feels unbearable. But there is comfort in looking through an eternal lens. Although our world has been torn apart for now, there is still an eternal world and an eternal plan. We look at history and see how God has unfolded events just as He said He would. God doesn't get in a hurry, but His timing is perfect. God is in control.

Without our loved ones, the days seem so long; but remember that we will have an eternity to be with them. Read the prophets of old and notice how God worked in history. God is still working in our lives, there is more to be fulfilled, and ultimately we will be in eternity with God. We will be with our loved ones again praising God for all eternity. We are waiting on that day!

Read Nahum 1:1-15 and note that all God said would happen did happen, even in a time it would not have seemed possible. Write how you have seen Him fulfill a plan in your life in the past.

---

[379] Philip Yancey and Brenda Quinn, *Meet The Bible, A Panorama of God's Word in 366 Daily Readings and Reflections* (Grand Rapids, MI: Zondervan, 2000), 303-304.

DAY 296

After six days Jesus took with him Peter, James and John the brother of James, and led them up a high mountain by themselves. There he was transfigured before them. His face shone like the sun, and his clothes became as white as the light. Just then there appeared before them Moses and Elijah, talking with Jesus. (Matthew 17:1-3, NIV)

Jesus took those disciples that He seemed closest to and led them to a high mountain. There Jesus was transfigured before them. Mathew says Jesus' clothes became as white as the light. Mark says, "Dazzling white, whiter than anyone in the world can bleach them" (Mark 9:3). Luke says, "The appearance of his face changed, and his clothes became as a flash of lightning" (Luke 9:29). Clearly the Transfiguration was glorious and hard to describe in terms of how brilliant the light was. Peter, James, and John walked up a mountain with Jesus and were alone with Him, and not only observed His splendor but saw Moses and Elijah. Luke says they appeared in "glorious splendor." Something huge and awesome happened. The Transfiguration gave us a glimpse of what our glorified bodies might look like. The minute our loved ones crossed into Heaven, they saw this glorious light of Jesus that defies description. Our loved ones most likely became bright as they reflect God's glory. Even now as we hurt and yearn to have them with us, they are experiencing that phenomenon.

Also notice that although there is no way that Peter, James, and John would have ever met Moses and Elijah; and although there were not pictures in those days to compare likenesses, the disciples knew who they were! That recognition is a clear statement of continuity and recognition of each other in Heaven. We won't just recognize each other; if there is continuity of individuals and personalities, then there will be continuity of relationships. Paul Enns writes:

It means there is an identification with the past. We will recognize one another. There is a continuity with the past. The bodies we had on the old earth will be recognizable in heaven. The ones we loved in those special bodies on earth will be the ones we will see, know and love in even greater dimension in heaven.[380]

The pain of grief and sorrow are very real and intense. The moments of comfort can come, though, as we meditate on these words. I think that is why the sun is so captivating; the brightness our loved ones are experiencing is like the sun— the brilliance that is hard for our authors to put into words. Our loved ones are experiencing awesome splendor with Jesus. We are waiting on that day.

Meditate on these verses. How can you imagine our loved one in splendor?

---

[380] Paul Enns, *Heaven Revealed* (Chicago, IL: Moody, 2011), 162.

DAY 297

About eight days after Jesus said this; he took Peter, John and James with him and went up onto a mountain to pray. As he was praying, the appearance of his face changed, and his clothes became as bright as a flash of lightning. Two men, Moses and Elijah, appeared in glorious splendor, talking with Jesus. (Luke 9:28-30, NIV)

The Transfiguration is so full of hope and awe that it is worth looking at again and again, and taking in what different authors have to say. We find a record of the Transfiguration in Matthew 17:1-13, Mark 9:2-12, and Luke 9:28-36. Asher Intrater, in his remarkable book *Who Ate Lunch With Abraham?* writes at length what he feels we can learn from these verses. I want to share two of those thoughts. He writes:

In the New Covenant Scriptures, the general pattern is that Yeshua appears in His earthly form in the Gospels, and in His heavenly form in the book of Revelation. The only instance in which He is transformed into His glorified body in the Gospels is on the Mount of Transfiguration. He was glorified on the Mount of Transfiguration for the purpose of teaching us: 1. That He has a glorified, divine form. 2. That is how we and He will look in the world to come...[381]

The Transfiguration was certainly a part of the eternal plan. I don't know what the significance was for Jesus Himself, but the experience obviously served as a huge time of growth for the disciples, and ultimately for us, because in reading the story we can find such comfort and a glimpse into what our loved one is seeing. The minute our loved ones drew their last breath they were in the glorious splendor of God. They were able to see Jesus in all of His splendor and brightness. Our loved ones are not limited by the human eyes that we are limited by here on Earth. They are transformed and now reflect God's glory in a very real way. Paul Enns uses the verses on the Transfiguration as one of many to underscore the continuity of our earthly bodies and personalities.

Scripture is clear: There is a continuity of this earthly personality and body with the personality and body that we will have in the resurrection on the new earth. That has many applications. We will continue the relationships with the people we loved on this earth. The fellowship will be enormous—but we won't be limited by time constraints![382]

Read all the verses on the Transfiguration, remembering the different devotions and quotes. What about the Transfiguration brings you the most comfort?

---

[381]   Asher Intrater, *Who Ate Lunch With Abraham* (Peoria, AZ: Intermedia, 2011), Location 3130.

[382]   Paul Enns, *Heaven Revealed* (Chicago, IL: Moody, 2011), 138.

DAY 298

"You have said so," Jesus replied. "But I say to all of you: From now on you will see the Son of Man sitting at the right hand of the Mighty One and coming on the clouds of heaven." (Matthew 26:64, NIV)

These words Jesus spoke were actually said about the Messiah in the book of Daniel. Daniel 7:13 tells us that in Daniel's vision he sees, "one like the son of man coming with the clouds of heaven." Isn't prophecy amazing? In this chapter Jesus has been taken before the court and in an attempt to frame Him, false witnesses were produced and spoke lies, but Jesus didn't say anything. Then the high priest said, "I charge you under oath by the living God; tell us if you are the Christ, the Son of God." And verse 64 is Jesus' response. To paraphrase Jesus, He basically tells them, "Yes, I am, and this is how you are going to see me when I come again." Jesus lets them know He will be at the right hand of God and they will see Him on the clouds of Heaven. In that moment they grab Jesus to crucify Him. But we know that all that happened in that moment was part of the eternal plan.

We know that Jesus willingly gave His life for our sins. We know that His death and resurrection gives us eternal life. We, as redeemed believers, have that hope of eternal life. Our loved ones have gone before us. We will join them. Jesus will send His angels for us and bring us Home as He did our loved ones, or we will be here when Jesus returns to take us Home at the end of the age. But either way, as redeemed believers we will see Jesus. We will be reunited with our loved ones, and we will have a glorious reunion. Jesus' coming has been a part of the eternal plan since the beginning of the ages.

I have mentioned several times my obsession with the sky and clouds since Don and Dad went Home. Each time I gaze at the sky, I think Jesus will come back on the clouds; the clouds remind me of the nearness of Heaven and the hope of His return. 1 Thessalonians 4:16-17 tells us that we will be caught up in the clouds together with our resurrected loved ones to meet the Lord in the air and be with Him forever. In His Olivet Discourse in Matthew 24, Jesus tells us that we will see the Son of man coming on the clouds of the sky with power and great glory. God covered the disciples with a cloud when He spoke to them after the Transfiguration. Moses was covered by a cloud. God led the Israelites by cloud during the exodus. The clouds speak of God's majesty, His glory, and His closeness. There are days when the sun is brightly shining and the cloud formations are tremendous. On those days I see awe inspiring skies filled with the brightness of the sun peeking through majestic clouds, I am reminded of Jesus' return. I am waiting on that day!

Reflect on these and the many other verses that refer to the clouds and Jesus' return. Journal your thoughts and feelings.

DAY 299

Do not be anxious about anything, but in every situation, by prayer and petition, with thanksgiving, present your requests to God. And the peace of God, which transcends all understanding, will guard your hearts and your minds in Christ Jesus. (Philippians 4:6-7, NIV)

This passage has been a favorite to quote for many years. I have always tended toward worry, and God gave me this passage a long time ago. These verses have been a constant reminder to pray through my anxieties. When Don went Home so suddenly, my anxiety ran rampant. I would quote this passage, but often it didn't seem to give me the comfort it had before. I guess I was not feeling that peace. My world seemed anything but peaceful. My world was completely dark, chaotic, and full of anxiety. I slowly started to feel some peace as I spent more and more time in prayer and in His Word. I can honestly say that God has taken away my anxiety and replaced it with His peace.

Even though I have quoted this passage many times, there was something I had actually never noticed. As I was reading a devotional by Greg Laurie, I was struck by his words. Laurie was writing about the legitimate questions we have when we have loss or heartache. And he wisely pointed out that even if we did have the troubling questions answered, we wouldn't be satisfied. But then he quotes this verse and wrote, "The Bible doesn't promise us a peace that necessarily gives understanding, but it promises a peace that *passes* human understanding."[383] Then Greg Laurie quoted a letter he had received from Warren Wiersbe after Greg's son went to Heaven. He wrote, "As God's children we live on promises not on explanations. And you know as well as I do the promises of God."[384] His words are so true.

There is so much I do not understand, and I am sure you have so many questions yourself. I do believe there are many things we will not have answered this side of Heaven. I think that on the day we see Jesus, the nightmare will be over and we will understand fully. Everything will make sense because we will be in the presence of Jesus. So what now? By prayer and petition with thanksgiving we present our requests to God. I am eternally grateful for the love that Don and I have, for the parents I have and the love they have shown and taught, for our children, and for our family. God has blessed us. Although now I hurt beyond words, I know I will be with my family in eternity praising God. I know I may not understand, but I will trust Jesus and He will guard my heart and my mind with a peace that passes understanding.

Meditate on today's verses and thoughts. What are your thoughts and feelings?

---

[383] Greg Laurie, *Daily Hope for Hurting Hearts* (Dana Point, CA: Kerygma, 2010), 37.
[384] Ibid., 37.

DAY 300

For God so loved the world that he gave his one and only Son, that whoever believes in him shall not perish but have eternal life. For God did not send his Son into the world to condemn the world, but to save the world through him. (John 3:16-17, NIV)

This Scripture passage is probably one of the most memorized, if not the most memorized, passages in the Bible. As simple as this verse is to memorize, it is indeed a deep theological verse. In his book *The 3:16 Promise: He loves,* Max Lucado calls this verse the "Hope Diamond" of the Bible. He goes on to suggest, "Each word is a safe deposit box of jewels. Read it again, slowly and aloud, and note the word that snatches your attention."[385] So as we read this verse and ponder it, we know that God loves us so much that He gave His one and only Son, Jesus. Those of us who believe in Jesus and receive Him as our Savior have eternal life. Jesus has saved us. Our believing loved ones have not perished. They are no longer with us, but they will be some day. Because we have believed in Jesus Christ, we are all promised eternal life. As a Christian, you know that on a cognitive level. You have probably quoted this verse many times. But now that you are in the depths of grief, you have to hold to these words with all of your heart. This is the hope that sets us apart as Christians. Max Lucado sums it up, "He loves. He gave. We believe. We live."[386]

We know we have eternal life through Jesus Christ; because of this truth we know we will be with our loved ones again. We may not feel God at times in the dark hours of our grief, but we can hold to the promises we know are true. We have quoted this passage and we have always believed it, and the truth of the verse does not change just because we hurt now.

The pain overwhelms me. But when I hold to the promises I have always believed to be true, I find comfort. I think that when the intense pain of sorrow and grief grip your very being, it is easy to lose sight of those promises. At times we may mistake the pain and sorrow for God's absence. The pain is there and we cannot nor should we avoid it. Instead, we must draw near to God and hold to those promises we have always believed. We claimed John 3:16 the day we received Christ as our Savior. These verses are not an empty promise. The words are the very promise of life; eternal life. Our believing loved ones have stepped into the presence of our Savior, who died to make eternal life possible. Eternal life means "for eternity." We have an eternity to spend with Jesus and with our loved ones. Don't let the familiarity of this verse diminish its power.

Meditate on today's devotion. What are other familiar verses help you now?

---

[385] Max Lucado, *The 3:16 Promise* (Nashville, TN: Nelson, 2007), Location 23.
[386] Ibid., Location 18.

DAY 301 REFLECTION

Read over the last week. What speaks to you? We read a prophecy that at the time would have seemed impossible and improbable. But events happened just as God said they would. We are reminded to step back and look at the bigger picture, the eternal plan, and God's sovereignty. God is timeless and nothing is impossible for Him. There is comfort in reminding ourselves that God is still in control. There are prophecies yet to be fulfilled, some of which we have witnessed unfolding. We know Jesus will come back, and all things will be restored because God said it would happen.

We read about the Transfiguration twice. We read how amazing it was for Peter, James, and John to see Jesus with Moses and Elijah. The event seemed to defy description. We are reminded that the disciples recognized Moses and Elijah, even though they would never have met them or seen their likeness. What a clear statement of continuity. These verses show identification with the past that speaks of continuity of personality, relationships, and people. Imagine your loved one transformed and in splendor. How awesome is that thought? The thought of Don and Dad in glorious splendor is comforting. To know that our loved ones see Jesus in all His glory is awesome. To hold to the fact that we, too, will be in that glory ourselves someday brings great comfort. The Transfiguration also speaks mightily of the eternal plan and God's purpose.

We read that the peace of God transcends understanding, and will guard our hearts and minds in Him. We don't understand what has happened to us, and if we allow it the anxiety can overcome us. But we do not have to understand; we only need to trust Jesus to guard our hearts and minds and give us the peace we so desperately desire. We will understand some day, but for now we must hold to Jesus. Pray Jesus guards your heart and mind in Him. And finally, we read the familiar but powerful words of John 3:16. God loves us so much He gave His only Son that we might have eternal life. Because of Jesus' sacrifice, our loved ones are with Him now and we will join them at the appointed time. That thought brings us to our knees in gratitude. We will live in eternity with our loved ones, worshiping Jesus. We are waiting on that day. As you reflect over the week, record your thoughts and feelings.

DAY 302

Therefore, since we are surrounded by such a huge crowd of witnesses to the life of faith, let us strip off every weight that slows us down, especially the sin that so easily trips us up. And let us run with endurance the race God has set before us. We do this by keeping our eyes on Jesus, the champion who initiates and perfects our faith. (Hebrews 12:1, NLT)

I was riding on the icy roads with my eighteen-year-old nephew, Carson. He was doing a good job driving. I was reminded how the winter before God called Don Home, he had taught Carson to drive on the ice. Ice storms are rare in Texas, so not many of us like to drive on icy roads. Don was the one who would get us all around; he always had a four-wheel drive and knew how to drive on the ice and snow. Don decided that year that our nephew needed to know how to drive on the ice and had taken him out to teach him. They returned laughing because apparently the lesson included doughnuts in a vacant parking lot. As we pulled into the drive this icy season, Carson asked what the Bible said about our loved ones able to see us. I told him about this verse and some others that suggest it might be possible. Carson said, "Sometimes I have the feeling that Uncle Don and Granddad can see me, like now as I was driving it was almost like I knew Uncle Don was watching and approving, and I felt that way when I was scuba diving. I also felt that way about Granddad when I was shooting hoops and doing the yard. I just wasn't sure if that was okay or in the Bible." I understand that feeling of wanting to make sure something is from the Bible. I also think that these verses could indicate there are times that maybe they do watch and cheer us. Obviously, Christ is the center of our loved ones' attention, not us, but is it possible that they are praying for us and at times can see? Greg Laurie writes:

Another way to look at these men and women aren't simply to give us a template to follow, but are actually observing us and taking note of our progress in our faith. They are the "clouds of witnesses" watching us and cheering us on, if you will. Is that the case? Are there heavenly grandstands where people monitor the progress of loved ones living out their lives on earth? It wouldn't surprise me at all, but I don't know. But I do know this much: we are in the race of our life on earth, and we don't know how long it will last. And I know for certain Jesus is watching me, turn for turn, step for step.[387]

There is a lot we don't know, but we do know that we are running a race and we must keep our eyes on Jesus until we cross the finish line. We are waiting on that day!

What are your thoughts and feelings on the verse and the text?

---

[387] Greg Laurie, *Daily Hope for Hurting Hearts* (Dana Point, CA: Kerygma, 2010), 56.

DAY 303

They serve in a system of worship that is only a copy, a shadow of the real one in heaven. For when Moses was getting ready to build the Tabernacle, God gave him this warning: "Be sure that you make everything according to the pattern I have shown you here on the mountain." (Hebrews 8:5, NLT)

Paul Enns writes that an elderly man asked him if we would know each other in Heaven. The man was worried about this very thing since he and his wife were getting on in years. Paul's response was, "Think of the words. Heaven. Earth. Heaven is always better, in every realm, in every dimension.... You and I cannot think of a single realm or phase of living in which life would be poorer in heaven."[388] Enns goes on to list health, knowledge, relationships all much better. Enns writes:

Yes, we will know one another, better and in a more intense loving relationship than we ever had on earth. What a phenomenal, encouraging thought. Meanwhile life continues for us on this present earth. Yet we are told life for you and me is a shadow of what it will be in heaven. Hebrews 8:5 reminds us that these earthly things serve as ' a copy and shadow of the heavenly things.' The writer refers to the Old Testament worship system as being only a shadow of real worship as it will one day be in glory. This application, however, can extend to every realm of living on this earth. [389]

Because we "see" Earth, it is often our first thought of what is real; other things, then, must be a shadow of what is real. But Heaven was first and Heaven is where God lives. Heaven is where He has prepared a place for us. The Earth is under the curse and yet it is still beautiful. God was very specific to Moses. This verse says God gave him a warning, "Be sure that you make everything according to the pattern I have shown you here on the mountain." God is the Creator. He created everything in intricate detail. God gave specifics on the tabernacle and on the temple. These things we see are a copy—a shadow of the reality of Heaven.

My sister sent a picture of something she had seen in a book, a beautiful scene from a place we have never been. She said, "With places this pretty on earth, can you imagine how beautiful Heaven will be?" Our redeemed loved ones are right now enjoying the real thing. Don always had such an appreciation for the beauty of nature. On the days I look beyond the intense pain, I can imagine him thinking, "Ann, hurry up so I can show you around; you can't imagine how beautiful it is." I am waiting on that day!

What are your thoughts and feelings on the verse and the text?

---

[388] Paul Enns, *Heaven Revealed* (Chicago, IL: Moody, 2011), 14.
[389] Ibid., 15.

DAY 304

Indeed he was ill, and almost died. But God had mercy on him, and not on him only but also on me, to spare me sorrow upon sorrow. (Philippians 2:27, NIV)

I pondered using this verse because at first glance, when you are grieving it is easy to say, "Well, God didn't have mercy on my loved one and didn't spare me sorrow upon sorrow. Where were you, God?" But when we take a step back, we can remember that the friend Paul is writing about did eventually die. And so did Paul after suffering. So for that time in God's eternal plan, God was not ready for Paul's friend Epaphroditus to go to Heaven. It was not his time, and God was glorified in the process of healing him. God does heal sometimes, and He is glorified; His eternal plan is still in place. There are also times when God chooses to call His children Home; His eternal plan is still in place.

What struck me about this verse is Paul's reaction to almost losing his friend. Paul, who said he would rather go be with Christ right now because Heaven is far better. Paul was ready to go be with Jesus; it is evident in so much of what he wrote. But he would have been sorrowful to lose his friend. I have never been afraid to die because I knew I would go to Heaven. As Christians, we need to be ready at any time to go Home. I was and am ready, now more than ever. But even though I knew God could call us Home at any time, I was not prepared for Don to go so suddenly. I think that is what Paul is saying.

Paul knew it would be better for Epaphroditus to go to Heaven; he has said so himself. But Paul also loved his friend and it would be very hard to not have him there in the flesh. So even if you have strong faith and theology, when you don't have the person you love with you physically it hurts beyond words. The pain is like an abyss and it is intense. It is, as Paul says, sorrow upon sorrow. The one who goes Home is in perfect love and peace so there is no sorrow, but those of us left behind feel like we died too. We don't feel alive and yet we are alive. So we feel the deep pain and sorrow constantly; and when we don't feel God, we feel even more dead inside. Sorrow and pain might cause us to lose sight of the perfection our loved one is in. So what do we do? We do what Paul would have done had Epaphroditius died: we remember whose we are and the promises we have always believed. In the chapter before this one, Paul writes: "To live is Christ; to die is gain." He says in the chapter after this one: "Our citizenship is in Heaven." When a loved one goes Home it is normal to have sorrow upon sorrow. But Jesus knows our heart; He knows our pain. The Bible continually reminds us that this life on this fallen world is not all there is; this world is not our home. You will be with your loved one again for eternity. Our loved ones are more than okay now; they are where we want to be and will be: in the presence of our Savior. We are waiting on that day!

As you reflect on the verse and text, what are your thoughts?

DAY 305

He who testifies to these things says, "Yes, I am coming soon." Amen. Come Lord Jesus. (Revelation 22:20, NIV)

"Come, Lord Jesus. Come." These words take on new meaning. The world around us seems to be falling apart. Yes, when our loved ones were called Home our world fell apart, but the rest of the world seems to be in chaos too. It is hard to look at the news and not wonder, "How much longer, Lord?" The book of Revelation gives us hope and promise. As I have mentioned earlier, in the past I have been intimidated by the book of Revelation. But the more I read and study Revelation, the more I realize the message is one of promise and hope. Prophecy speaks loudly of God's eternal plan, His sovereignty, and the hope of our future with Him. Brenda Quinn writes about death: "It will feel like waking up from a dream rather than falling asleep. Everything we've learned of God in this life will take on striking new dimension. It will appear as vivid as the images we find in Revelation, yet without confusion or unfamiliarity."[390] She goes on to say:

The book of Revelation is the flag God waves at the end of the Bible, motioning us to the exciting finish of his story. Don't miss this, he alerts us. This is what you have been waiting for, the goal of the Book, the culmination of all you've invested in the life you're living. ...This life is vital for me because it is the life I'll carry into eternity. God has prepared something fantastic and wondrous, and for those who know him the future is not a bit scary.[391]

John had just seen incredible visions and at times was on his face in awe and fear. Now, at the end of Revelation, he can say with excitement, "Come, Lord Jesus." Revelation is full of blessings and full of promise. Revelation can be scary for the lost, which is the reason we must keep our eyes on Jesus and make sure we continue to pray and witness to the lost. The words of Jesus will come to pass just like the other prophecies. And as Brenda Quinn points out, "Revelation is like a flag God is waving to us.' Every day I wake up hoping today is the day, but I also know I have to continue to pray, give and witness. We are one day closer to Heaven each day we wake up. Our loved ones are in Heaven; they are witnessing the promise now and soon we will join them. In the meantime, we say, "Come, Lord Jesus. Come." We are waiting on that day!

What are your thoughts and feelings on the verse and the quotes? Are you able to see Revelation as a waving flag?

---

[390] Philip Yancey and Brenda Quinn, *Meet The Bible, A Panorama of God's Word in 366 Daily Readings and Reflections* (Grand Rapids, MI: Zondervan, 2000), 686.
[391] Ibid., 686.

DAY 306

To have faith is to be sure of the things we hope for, to be certain of the things we cannot see. (Hebrews 11:1, GNT)

Every day I pray that I will feel God and that I will have the assurance of His presence and the assurance of the continuity of relationships in Heaven. There are days when I have more assurance and days that seem dark. I know regardless of how I feel that God is good, that He is sovereign, and that He has an eternal plan. I know I trust God even when I don't feel Him. I know there are days I feel that certainty, and days that I feel isolated. But by faith I know that I am sure of what I hope for and certain of things I don't see. I remind myself of this and quote this verse. Mark Buchanan writes:

Faith is nothing if there is nothing beyond earth. It is nothing if this world is enough. Ultimately, faith is hope in the city that Jesus' blood secured for us, that He is preparing for us, and where He is now seated at the right hand of God awaiting us—the place where on *that day* and on all days after we will see Him face-to-face. Faith without deeds is dead, but faith without heaven is dead too.[392]

Faith without Heaven is what? It is empty, especially if you have someone who is no longer with you. When a loved one goes Home and you can't visibly see him, you can lose sight of the promises if you are not careful to hold to Jesus. We cannot see our loved ones. I want to be in Don's arms and there is nothing that can replace that longing. I have to trust that the same God I have trusted in all my life is the same God who has eternity securely in place. God is sovereign, and He is in control. We cannot see Heaven, but we know we have glimpses of it in the Bible. We cannot fathom eternity, but we know it is true because God says it is. We hold to our faith. And when the questions come, we remember that it is through faith we believe. As Mark Buchanan writes, "There is ultimately only one way. Through faith. By being certain of things unseen."[393]

Our believing loved ones are in Heaven because they had faith. We have to have the faith that we will be with them in Heaven. Faith means taking one day at a time, one minute at a time, but it means we have faith that God is who He said He is, and His Word is true. We are sure of what we hope for, and we are certain of what we cannot see. God has our loved ones with Him in His presence. We hurt and we want to be with our Lord and with our loved ones. But we wait and we serve Jesus with faith. We are waiting on that day, but we wait in faith.

Reflect on today's devotion. How are you holding to your faith?

---

[392] Mark Buchanan, *Things Unseen* (Sisters, OR: Multnomah, 2002), Location 1666.
[393] Ibid., Location 1688.

DAY 307

Therefore we do not lose heart. Though outwardly we are wasting away, yet inwardly we are being renewed day by day. For our light and momentary troubles are achieving for us an eternal glory that far outweighs them all. (2 Corinthians 4:16-17, NIV)

These verses remind us that this life on Earth as it is now is temporary. This life and troubles are momentary compared to eternity. Mark Buchanan writes:

This is one of the most remarkable declarations in the Bible. Paul is claiming two things here, both staggering in their implications. The first thing Paul claims is that trouble in this life is nothing compared with the glory in the next life. What we will know and what we will be and what we will have in heaven make anything and everything on earth as light as a cotton spore and as brief as a shooting star…Here is the meat of it: There is nothing that you experience—good or bad—in this world that either has more substance or is longer in duration than the glory of heaven. Everything on earth is fleeting.[394]

Buchanan goes on to say that to talk about how the death of his father was not easy to bear unless he compares it to what's coming. Buchanan writes, "Every day we move closer to *that day*, when life—life in all its fullness, life without taint or shadow, life innocent of sorrow—swallows up death"[395] "The second thing that Paul claims is even more remarkable. He says that trouble in this life actually achieves for us an eternal weight of glory. The Greek word for achieve is *katergazomai*. It means to make possible, to fashion, to work out for us."[396]

Our loved ones seem to be gone way too soon. I am sure this is even more if you are grieving a precious child. There is so much we don't understand. Whatever we are experiencing is momentary compared to eternity. We have an eternity to spend with our loved ones. We will see the glory of Christ. Our loved ones have seen the glory of Christ. They have been received in Jesus' presence; their job here done. We still have work to do and when Jesus is ready, we will come into His presence. We will be reunited with our loved ones. The eternal glory will outweigh this pain and sorrow. Suffering and sorrow do not seem momentary and light, and will not until that day we step into Jesus' glorious presence. Then we will fully understand. For now we trust Jesus, we draw near to Him; we obey Him while we wait on that day.

Meditate on today's verse and thoughts. How does comparing our suffering to a moment when compared to eternity help your perspective?

---

[394] Mark Buchanan, *Things Unseen* (Sisters, OR: Multnomah, 2002), Location 2145.
[395] Ibid., Location 2167.
[396] Ibid., Location 2173.

DAY 308 REFLECTION

Read over the last week. What stands out to you? We read again about the huge cloud of witnesses. Randy Alcorn writes that the race marked before us creates the "mental picture of the Greek competitions, which were watched intently by throngs of engrossed fans sitting high up in the ancient stadiums."[397] William Scroggie writes, "It may mean the saints are now beholding the saints of earth as the spectators in an amphitheater witnessed the contest below."[398] We know the center focus of Heaven is our Lord, that all else pales in comparison. But we also know there is a possibility that our loved ones may at times see us and possibly even intercede for us. We also know we are in a race, and we must continue despite the pain. After Dad went Home, we joined the fight for life stair climb for the American Lung Association. We climbed 56 flights. Don finished before me. He was waiting on me as I crossed the finish line. I try to imagine that he and Dad will be waiting on me to cross the finish line into Heaven. We strive to finish the race and to please God.

We read again the words that the Earth is a copy of Heaven. Greg Laurie writes:

Heaven is the real deal, the eternal dwelling place. Earth is the copy, the temporary dwelling place. When you see that sunset or that panoramic view of God's finest expressed in nature and the beauty of it and it just takes your breath away, remember that is just a glimpse of the real thing awaiting you in heaven.[399]

We read how Paul, who we know was eager to go to Heaven, would have been sorrowful had his friend died. Our faith doesn't keep us from sorrow, but our faith gives us the hope of eternity. We read the beautiful words in Revelation, "I am coming soon." We remember that John had seen much sorrow himself. His brother James was one of the first to be martyred; Peter was his former business partner and had also been one of the three in the inner circle with John and his brother James. They were all in Heaven—along with the other apostles and most likely other family members. He found comfort in what Jesus revealed to Him. We can find comfort in Revelation. Come, Lord Jesus. Come.

We read how important our faith is. Faith can be hard when you are hurting and you can't see the one you love. But your faith is what allows you to know that your loved one is safe and that you will join him even if you can't see or hear him now. Our faith reaffirms that what we do not see is eternal. We read again about the light and momentary troubles. We know this nightmare will end, and in light of eternity it will be a brief span. We are waiting on that day! As you read over the past week, what speaks to you the most?

---

[397] Randy Alcorn, *Heaven* (Carol Stream, IL: Tyndale House, 2004), 70.

[398] William Scroggie, *What About Heaven?* (London: Pickering & Inglis, 1954), 68.

[399] Greg Laurie, *Daily Hope for Hurting Hearts* (Dana Point, CA: Kerygma, 2010), 49.

DAY 309

For we live by faith, not by sight. (2 Corinthians 5:7, NIV)

When you are grieving, living by faith becomes even more important than ever. You cannot see the one you love. You cannot hear his voice or feel his arms. You cannot see her smile or hear her laugh. Your faith is absolutely necessary for survival. Grief feels like you are walking in the dark when you can't see anything, but you trust that Someone is guiding you. Walking in faith can be hard to do, period; but when you are in deep pain and sorrow it is the only way you can walk. As Paul Enns writes:

We don't have the big picture. Our vision is too nearsighted. We see only our own needs, and our bodies and emotions cry out for a pain-free life, for tranquility. But God is dealing with the larger picture; He has purposes that we cannot begin to fathom. There is a purpose that far surpasses our comprehension, and we must walk by faith, not sight. We must trust that an all-wise, all-good God is doing what is right and what is best. Yes there is a reason.[400]

We will have that pain-free life and tranquility someday, but not on this fallen world and not in this temporary condition. The perfect, pain-free and tranquil life will come in Heaven and then we will see fully.

You have heard the saying, "I will believe it when I see it." That statement would indicate what we see is real and what we don't see isn't. Faith is exactly the opposite. The New Living Translation version of this verse reads "For we live by believing and not by seeing." We are visual people, but with faith we believe first and know the seeing will come later. Certainly that type of faith seems easier if nothing feels at stake. But when someone you love is no longer with you, everything is at stake. Chris Tiegreen writes, "Those that see the many enemies are not focused on the reality. They are only focused on the visible. They have forgotten a foundational principle of the spiritual life; the visible and the real are two vastly different things."[401]

We have to remember that our faith is based not on sight, but on what we believe and know to be true. It is easy to get knocked off balance and question our faith, especially when we want to see with all of our heart. Our loved ones are seeing fully what we long to see and what we will see. We have to cling to our faith by believing even though we can't see. We are waiting on that day.

Reflect on today's devotional. How are you living by faith and not by sight?

---

[400] Paul Enns, *Everything Happens For A Reason* (Chicago, IL: Moody, 2012), Location 1581.

[401] Chris Tiegreen, *The One Year Walk With God* Devotional (Carol Stream, IL: Tyndale, 2004), Location 660.

DAY 310

For me, to live is Christ and to die is gain. (Philippians 1:21, NIV)

In his book *Everything Happens for a Reason*, Paul Enns writes about God's sovereignty and His goodness. Enns agrees that we cannot explain many things that God permits, and an early death of a loved one is one of those things.

Whether a family member or close friend dies early or after a long, full life, there is a real loss. There is a pain of separation, with the earthly loss of a loved one. The sorrow and grief in losing a loved one is an unparalleled earthly experience. This side of heaven we will never see the loved again.[402]

Without an eternal perspective death is the ultimate bad that can happen. "What is the worst thing that can happen?" we ask. Death would be the answer. Paul states, however, that to die is gain. As Paul Enns points out:

When we consider the 'bad things' happening to God's people, certainly death is the ultimate 'bad thing,' from a human perspective. Yet let's remember that from a biblical perspective it is not loss but gain for the believer...The believer who has lived for Christ finds death to be gain.... For the believer, death is profitable because it continues the life of fellowship with Christ. Moreover we will see Christ in all His glory—the One who gave Himself for us. If we recognize that our departed loved one is with Christ, basking in Christ's presence, seeing Him face to face and worshiping Him, it will comfort us in our sorrow.[403]

I pray every day that God teaches me to have a true eternal perspective. There is sadness in the pain of separation even though we know the separation is temporary. There is sadness in not having our loved one with us right now. Our loved ones' absence screams from every direction and we long to have them with us. The pain of separation can consume our every thought; but when we hold to an eternal perspective we can find comfort. Yes, it hurts now, but our loved ones have gained and our loss is only temporary. Our sadness and pain, though intense, is temporary. Take comfort in knowing that the minute your loved one breathed her last breath here, she gained so much by immediately being in the presence of Christ. We will join them at the appointed time. As we wait on that day, we hold to the eternal perspective that for those who live in Christ, to die is gain.

Reflect on today's verse and text. What are your thoughts and feelings?

---

[402] Paul Enns, *Everything Happens For A Reason* (Chicago, IL: Moody, 2012), Location 2540.
[403] Ibid., Location 2546.

DAY 311

God has set eternity in the hearts of men. (Ecclesiastes 3:11, NIV)

Deep down, there is always a whisper of, "There must be more," or a whisper of, "Someday..." I have been blessed beyond measure, and my life has been one of joy and contentment. But even then, at times I would find myself thinking, "Wait till the weekend," or "When things slow down..." But really, we know that things really don't slow down, and when the weekend is good it still goes away. We have something in our hearts that knows there is more than this life. There is eternal life in Christ; there is eternity. Max Lucado discusses being homesick in his book *Safe in the Shepherd's Arms*. He tells the story of a time he was in college, lost and homesick. He equates our longing for eternity to homesickness. He goes on to say he knows some feel far away from home:

Ever since your husband died, your child was buried.... The twist and turns of life have a way of reminding us—we aren't home here. This is not our homeland. We aren't fluent in the language of disease and death. The culture confuses the heart, the noise disrupts our sleep, and we feel far from home. And you know what? That's OK. You have an eternal address fixed in your mind. God has 'set eternity in the hearts of men.' Deep down you know you are not home yet.[404]

Max Lucado calls this time on Earth "short-term housing." We long to live in the house of the Lord forever, and we will. That desire is exactly what this verse means. Eternity is set in our hearts. We will live in the house of the Lord forever. Lucado goes on to say:

Though our eyes are fixed on heaven, for some of us the journey has been long.... Some of you have bid farewell to life-long partners. You have been robbed of life-long dreams... you are tired. It is hard to see the City in the midst of the storms... the road seems long. Remember that God never said the journey would be easy, but he did say the arrival would be worthwhile.[405]

There are many days when I feel so weary and tired. I am broken and I miss my life as I know it. But I know that this time is short even though it feels long right now. I know God has set eternity in my heart. There is more—much more—coming. We will someday step into Jesus' presence just as our loved ones have. We will be reunited with our loved ones; we will worship God for eternity. We will arrive at the destination of Home. We are waiting on that day!

Reflect on today's devotion. How do you feel eternity in your heart?

---

[404] Max Lucado, *Safe in the Shepherds Arm* (Nashville, TN: Countryman, 2002), 59.
[405] Ibid., 114.

DAY 312

For God so loved the world that he gave his one and only Son, that whoever believes in him shall not perish but have eternal life. (John 3:16 NIV)

My sister Teresa and I have always worked with grief in our counseling practice, but it has become of special interest since our own grief is so deep. We have made it a practice to ask those Christians that are grieving to share what verses brought them comfort. One mother, whose son was killed in a car accident ten years ago, quoted John 3:16. She said these were verses she knew, and she quoted them to constantly remind herself that God loves her. Another verse she quoted that also brought her comfort was Psalm 23:4. Both passages remind her that she is not alone. God has not abandoned her. She knows God is carrying her through this grief. At times when she faltered she would quote these verses. She found comfort in reminding herself of God's love, and that He came to the world to save us and give us eternal life.

She paused as she said, "These verses remind me that God knows what it is like to give a son." The pain in her eyes was still very real after ten years. God could understand her pain in giving up her own son. She knows that she will once again be with her son, just as we know that because of Jesus paying the ultimate price, we too have eternal life. We will once again be with our believing loved ones. The pain doesn't go away, but the comfort found in God's Word gives us the hope of eternity. In his book *If God is Good*, Randy Alcorn writes:

A grieving father asked, 'Where was God when my son died?' A friend answered, 'The same place he was when his Son died.' Despite the statement's power, it's not entirely accurate. For God turned away from his Son when he died. Why? So he would not have to turn away when the grieving man's son died. The man and his son can enjoy eternity together in a world without suffering and death because God's Son died for them.[406]

Alcorn goes on to say: "Many people imagine that though God once suffered on the cross, he's now remote and distant from suffering. Not so! After his ascension, Jesus says to the Pharisee on the Damascus road, 'Saul, Saul why do you persecute *me*?' (Acts 9:4)"[407] Christ suffers with us when we suffer. Jesus knows our pain, but He has promised us this life is not all there is. We have eternal life through Jesus. Like this mother, I find great comfort in those words in John 3:16. We will spend eternity with our Savior, and we will worship Him together with our loved ones. We are waiting on that day!

Reflect on these verses and quotes. What are your thoughts and feelings?

---

[406] Randy Alcorn, *If God Is Good: Faith in the Midst of Suffering and Evil* (Colorado Springs, CO: Multnomah Books, 2009), 216-217.

[407] Ibid., 217.

DAY 313

But he said to me, "My grace is sufficient for you, for my power is made perfect in weakness." Therefore I will boast all the more gladly about my weaknesses, so that Christ's power may rest on me. (2 Corinthians 12:9, NIV)

Several months after God called Don Home, I found out one of our huskies had diabetes. I began the regimen of insulin every twelve hours. Oddly the routine gave me consistency at a time I had none. I may not could breathe or think, but I knew every twelve hours that Dakota would get a shot. Eleven months later she was stable and actually doing well. I came home for lunch and she and her sister Aspen ran to greet me and I was thinking how far she had come; three hours later I returned to watch her draw her last few breaths. I was devastated. Of course, memories of how Don and I had found the dogs at a rescue place, memories of how we had both cried when our other dogs had been killed in an accident, memories and the absence of Don here now to hold me. It was a difficult night.

My friend Penny, who has been by my side and cried with me, texted me the next day and said, "I am so sorry. I know how comforting your dogs are to you. I don't know what to say." Then she added. "His grace is sufficient…" She was right. Since the night God called Don Home, it has been God's grace that has held me. I am weak, but He is strong. I can't do this but God's grace is sufficient. Randy Alcorn writes, "God is sovereign, and whether he heals your body now or waits until the resurrection to heal you, he desires to achieve his own good purpose in you."[408] Alcorn also tells us,

Janet Willis told me she sometimes used to think, I want to stay close to God so nothing bad happens. When her van crashed on a Wisconsin freeway and six of her children died, she drew close to God because she needed him. Now he became not a means to preen harm, but for her to survive. We need only read Scripture, look around us, or live long enough in order to learn that *trusting God doesn't ward off all evil and suffering.* He never said it would.[409]

God does say His grace is sufficient and He will never leave us. I have never felt as weak as I do now. Grief saps every bit of energy from you; it saps the life out of you. But in our weakness His power is made perfect. God is all powerful. His grace is sufficient. We will have an eternity with our loved ones to praise Him.

As you reflect on this verse, journal how you feel God carrying you now.

---

[408] Randy Alcorn, *If God Is Good: Faith in the Midst of Suffering and Evil* (Colorado Springs, CO: Multnomah Books, 2009), 284.
[409] Ibid., 38.

DAY 314

For God saved us and called us to live a holy life. He did this, not because we deserved it, but because that was his plan from before the beginning of time—to show us his grace through Christ Jesus. And now he has made all of this plain to us by the appearing of Christ Jesus, our Savior. He broke the power of death and illuminated the way to life and immortality through the Good News. (2 Timothy 1:9-10, NLT)

It is easy, under the crushing pain and heaviness of grief, to see only this moment in time. We do have to take one day a time; we do have to focus on holding on to Jesus each moment of the day. It also helps to remember that our view of time is not God's view. In his book *If God is Good*, Randy Alcorn writes, "Too many people, Christians included, view the Christian faith in bits and pieces. We should see it as a holistic worldview, a large scale belief system based on the unfolding of redemptive history."[410] Alcorn goes on to say:

God's redemptive plan was not an ad-lib response to unanticipated events. From before the very beginning, God knew the very worst. And the very best it would one day bring. How could God give us grace before our lives began even before the universe itself existed? Only because God knew and determined in advance the work of Christ for us on the cross. God wrote the script of the unfolding drama of redemption long before Satan, demons, Adam and Eve—and you and I—took the stage. And from the beginning he knew that the utterly spectacular ending would make the dark middle worth it.[411]

The pain from grief is all-consuming, and in grief it easy to lose sight of the eternal plan. These verses beautifully depict the eternal plan. Of course, the pain is still there, but when we focus on the eternal plan, and as Randy says, "the spectacular ending," it brings us comfort and hope. This world is not all there is. Our focus is on Heaven and eternal life.

Christ broke the power of death over believers. We have immortality through the Good News of Jesus Christ. One day at a time we move through the fog of grief, but there will be spectacular ending. We know the ending even though we don't know or understand the events now. We have to trust that God is sovereign; His eternal plan will not be thwarted. Jesus broke the power of death for believers. We know we will be reunited with our loved ones to worship our Savior in eternity. God has an eternal plan. We are waiting on that day!

As you meditate on today's verses and thoughts, how do they speak to you?

---

[410] Randy Alcorn, *If God Is Good: Faith in the Midst of Suffering and Evil* (Colorado Springs, CO: Multnomah Books, 2009), 159.

[411] Ibid., 189.

DAY 315 REFLECTION

As you read over the last week, what speaks to you? We read again that we live by faith, not by sight. We are visual people, and we are keenly aware that we can't see our loved ones. We long to hear our loved one's voice, feel his touch, see her face. We must remember that there is an unseen world that is eternal. We live by faith. We can't see Jesus, but He is with us. We can't see Heaven, but it is real. We can't see our loved ones, but they are more alive than ever. We read that to live is Christ and to die is gain. In grief it is normal, expected, and okay to be very sad and in pain, but remember the pain and sadness are temporary; we will see Jesus. If we have an earthly perspective, death is the ultimate bad thing. But we must keep the eternal perspective, and the eternal perspective tells us death is gain.

We read that God has set eternity in our hearts. We are homesick for Heaven. We know there is more coming, and we are waiting on that day. We read again the beloved words of John 3:16, and we are reminded that everything goes back to the cross and the love of Jesus. We read that God's grace is sufficient for our needs. In our weakness, God's power is made perfect. We can't walk this journey on our own; we are not strong enough. It is only in God's grace that we can know we will be with Him someday.

We read that Jesus broke the power of death in a plan that has been since before the beginning of time. We can't just view life in bits and pieces or the here and now, but we must view life through an eternal lens. There is an eternal plan, and as a result of the plan Jesus broke the power of death. Our loved ones are with Jesus and we will join them for an eternity. We are waiting on that day! Record your thoughts and feelings as you look back over the last week. What do you feel like God is laying on your heart this week?

DAY 316

When Jesus rose early on the first day of the week, he appeared first to Mary Magdalene, out of whom he had driven seven demons. She went and told those who had been with him and who were mourning and weeping. When they heard that Jesus was alive and that she had seen him, they did not believe it. (Mark 16:9-11, NIV)

There are several nuggets to look at in these verses. One thing that we note is that Jesus seems to have clearly picked the ones He appears to and the order in which He appeared to them. Jesus seemed to appear to those first that He was closest to here on Earth. He knew their hearts were hurting. Jesus had told them they would grieve and their hearts would hurt.

Notice, too, that before Jesus appeared to the others, Mary ran to tell them. What were the other disciples doing? They were mourning and weeping. Jesus had promised them He would be back. He had told them He would suffer and die. But still they were overcome with pain and sorrow. As we well know, it is hard to hold on to what we believe and know when the pain and sorrow overwhelm us. Jesus understands this. He appeared to His followers and their sorrow turned to joy. But before He appeared to them, they grieved deeply. Notice, too, they didn't even believe what Mary told them. They were too overcome with the pain and sorrow. People tend to skip over this part of the story and get to the part where the disciples become mighty preachers, which was crucial to the spread of the Gospel. But it is important as well to note they were weeping and mourning. Grief is a dark time for all of us. But remember that Jesus knows your heart and He loves you. Your mourning will turn to joy.

Randy Alcorn tells of a man named Randy Butler, who he met when Butler took Alcorn's class on Heaven. The man's eighteen-year-old son had died a few months prior to him taking the class. Butler told Alcorn for weeks after his son Kevin's death he would cry out to God each morning:

I asked God, 'What were you thinking?' God answered, 'I was thinking of what I experienced with my son.' Every time God spoke to me He took me back to the cross. I didn't want to go cross. I wanted my son back. There is a silence and a darkness of the soul. That is where my journey took me. All roads lead to the cross.[412]

Jesus rose and He is alive. Our mourning will turn to joy on that day we see Jesus. We will worship Jesus with our loved ones. We are waiting on that day!

Reflect on today's devotion. How does going back to the cross help you now?

---

[412] Randy Alcorn, *If God Is Good: Faith in the Midst of Suffering and Evil* (Colorado Springs, CO: Multnomah Books, 2009), 189.

DAY 317

But we are looking forward to the new heavens and new earth he has promised, a world filled with God's righteousness. (2 Peter 3:13, NLT)

As long as we live in this fallen world we will have heartache. The days I feel like I can't go on and the pain seems overwhelming, the inevitable "I don't understand, God" hits me. And I beg for understanding. God does not owe me an explanation. But what He does seem to bring me back to is the eternal plan. He brings me to the plan for the redemption of people, and the redemption of the Heavens and the Earth. And on that day the restored world will be filled with God's righteousness. I pray continually that God teaches me how to have an eternal perspective.

When we look forward to the New Heaven and the New Earth, we hold that promise of eternity in our hearts. Randy Alcorn writes:

Though the Lord exiled us from Eden because of our evil, that place remains forever embedded in our hearts. We feel homesick for Eden. We long for what the first man and woman enjoyed, a perfect beautiful Earth with free and untainted relationships with God and each other. Every effort at human progress has tried to regain what we lost in the Fall. Our friends John and Ann watched helplessly as their eighteen-month old son, Gary, died. Ann says, 'In that moment our life was shattered. My big question was how could God love me and allow this? If he could have stopped it, why didn't he? Nothing could take away the pain, but John and Ann faced a choice concerning their perspective. Ann says, 'even though we still have questions, we've decided to dwell on what we know to be true. I see Heaven in a whole new light. After all, my treasure is there. I look forward to joining him. I can't wait to see him, hug him, hold him, and spend eternity with him.'... We can look forward to the eternal future, to the joys— including the joys of reunion—that God has promised await us.[413]

There will continue to be evil and suffering as long as we live in this fallen world. But this world as it is now is not all there is. We look forward to the New Heaven and the New Earth and in doing so hold to that eternal plan. The eternal perspective will be the only way we see through the darkness that now envelopes us. We know Jesus loves us; we know He has a world planned for His children that will be filled with His righteousness. We will be reunited with our loved ones in a perfect world, no longer under the curse. We will be with God. We are waiting on that day!

Reflect on today's devotion. Thinking about the New Heavens and the New Earth helps me focus on the eternal plan. How does it help you?

---

[413] Randy Alcorn, *If God Is Good: Faith in the Midst of Suffering and Evil* (Colorado Springs, CO: Multnomah Books, 2009), 212.

DAY 318

Dear friends, do not be surprised at the painful trial you are suffering, as though something strange were happening to you. But rejoice that you participate in the sufferings of Christ, so that you may be overjoyed when his glory is revealed. (1 Peter 4:12-13, NIV)

As I mentioned many times, grief ushers in a time of spiritual warfare. When we hold to Christ in these times of sufferings, we allow Him to work in our suffering. Someday Jesus' glory will be revealed for all to see as we see Him face to face. But for now we do go through suffering and trials. And certainly what you are going through now is a trial. We have to choose to be faithful to our God, who is faithful to us. You may have watched your loved one suffer. I know watching Dad struggle to breathe was a sword piercing my heart. But I also watched Dad praise God in his suffering. Dad was amazing. And I know when he stepped into our Lord's presence, Dad was overjoyed to see Jesus.

In his book *If God is Good*, Randy Alcorn talks about the prosperity gospel and how it can be harmful. I agree with him very much because when we believe those teachings and then suffering happens, which it will, then we can easily feel like God let us down—or worse, disbelieve everything. Peter is obviously telling us in these verses not to be surprised. Suffering will happen, so to think we won't suffer is a myth. Randy Alcorn writes, "We overrate health and underrate holiness. When hard times come people should lose their faith in false doctrines, not in God. If you are a Christian, God will deliver you from eternal suffering, and even now he will give you joyful foretaste of living in his presence. That's his promise."[414] It is a dark time when we are grieving—and Satan will attack. One way he attacks is to create doubt. Grief is a tumultuous time of pain and sorrow. The pain is always present, but we have an ever-present help in Christ. Cling to Jesus' promises now. Stand faithful because He is faithful. Alcorn says it well:

If you are God's child, then your suffering cannot outlast your lifetime. And since life continues after death, your suffering can last only the tiniest fraction of your true eternal lifetime. Rest in this knowledge. He offers you comfort before death and—one day—rescue by death or his return, whichever comes first.[415]

We are waiting on that day! Reflect on the verses and the quotes. Do you think you have somehow felt that as a Christian, you wouldn't suffer?

---

[414] Randy Alcorn, *If God Is Good:Faith in the Midst of Suffering and Evil* (Colorado Springs, CO: Multnomah Books, 2009), 202.

[415] Ibid., 385.

DAY 319

I am torn between the two: I desire to depart and be with Christ, which is better by far. (Philippians 1:23, NIV)

Paul has seen paradise and knows that it is better by far. Paul knew that immediately on his departure from this Earth, he would be with Christ and that was Paul's desire. Paul also loved the people he was with and wanted all of them to know Christ. Paul wanted to spread the Gospel. He wanted his friends to make that journey into eternity too, so he was torn. But Paul knew to be with Christ was better by far.

We lose sight of Heaven being better by far. I keep reminding myself every day that Don and Dad are better by far. I am not better right now for sure. All of our family grieve and mourn the absence of Dad and Don. Our family is so close that when one of us hurts, we all hurt; when one of us rejoices, we all rejoice. So while we know Dad and Don are rejoicing, and we want to rejoice with them, our own pain screams at us. We can be comforted when we try to focus on verses like this, though. Our loved ones are better by far. We will join them one day when God is ready. Randy Alcorn writes:

For the Christian, death is not the end of the adventure but a doorway to a world where dreams and adventures forever expand. No matter how bad the present, an eternity with Christ in Heaven will be incomparably better. So if God thinks the whole thing is worth it—and we know it will be worth it to us once we reach Heaven—then why not affirm by faith even in the midst of suffering that it is worth it now?[416]

We must remember that no matter what our loved ones went through before they went Home, now they are better by far. Alcorn quotes Emmanuel Ndikumana, who said, "You Americans have a strange attitude towards death; you act as if it is the end."[417] At the time, Emmanuel was a nineteen-year-old in Burundi who had the chance to flee his country upon learning someone wanted to kill him for what he was doing in his work for God. The young man stayed and even survived a murder attempt; he wasn't afraid to die. Grief hurts so badly it is hard to see beyond this moment in pain. But not only is death not the end, death is, as Paul says, what we desire. Because when we depart we are with Christ, which is better by far. Our loved ones are with Christ. We must remind ourselves daily that our loved ones are better by far, and we will join them someday. We are waiting on that day!

Reflect on today's verse and devotional. What are your thoughts?

---

[416] Randy Alcorn, *If God Is Good: Faith in the Midst of Suffering and Evil* (Colorado Springs, CO: Multnomah Books, 2009), 465.

[417] Ibid., 202.

DAY 320

And we know that in all things God works for the good of those who love him, who have been called according to his purpose. (Romans 8:28, NIV)

I will be honest: I didn't want to write this verse at first. I kept thinking, "How is losing Dad and Don good?" How can this be worked out for good? There isn't good in losing someone. But if you read this Scripture carefully it doesn't say that all things will be good for those who love Him. This verse tells us that God works all things for good. We know God works for our good and we have been called to His purpose. God's purpose, though, is rooted in eternity.

There is a divine plan and it is not all about the here and now. Those things that God is working for us will be finally realized in eternity. We may not see how things have worked out for good in this lifetime. Philip Yancey writes, "Not until history has run its course will we understand how all things work together for good. Faith means believing in advance what will only make sense in reverse."[418]

We ask, "Why?" thousands of times. The question of why can't always be answered right now, but we can trust that God has a purpose, and as believers we are a part of that purpose. Someday we will see how all things worked for good. For now, we have to trust God.

I love how Philip Yancey defines faith: "Believing in advance what makes sense in reverse." Right now you do not understand how your pain and your loved one's absence can be good. We must hold to the truth that someday we will know how—and not only will it be good, everything will be perfect. Time marches on, people live and people die, but God's purpose is absolute and He is bringing His plan into fruition. As believers we are a part of that eternal plan. Someday everything will make sense, and someday we will see just how good God will make everything. We are waiting on that day!

How does this verse speak to you? What are your thoughts and feelings on Philip Yancey's definition of faith? What are your thoughts on viewing this verse through an eternal lens?

---

[418] Phillip Yancey, *Disappointment with God* (Grand Rapids, MI: Zondervan, 1992), 224.

DAY 321

You guide me with your counsel, and afterward you will take me into glory.
(Psalm 73:24, NIV)

As we seek God, He will guide us; we may not understand why things happen
this side of eternity, but we hold to God's promises and trust Him. And God,
as the psalmist says, will take us into His glory. The following quotes from
Everything Happens For A Reason by Paul Enns are powerful.

Sometimes we will never see or understand the reason for tragedy. ...Did my
grandmother ever fathom the divine reason why she buried nine of her ten children
and was twice widowed? Probably not. Believers who watch their loved ones
experience enormous pain in sickness, lingering for months of severe suffering
before dying—can they understand God's purpose for their suffering? Probably
not. At such times we must rest in the assurance that God is all wise and all good.
There is a sovereign plan behind all of the events of life, including the bad things,
the tragedies that occur.[419]

God's sovereign control and guidance provides comfort and peace to the believer.
We are promised, 'with your counsel You will guide me, and afterward receive me to
your glory.' This promise is explicit and comprehensive; God's sovereign guidance
covers all of life. Through life and through the hallway of death, ushering us home
into His presence—God's sovereign wisdom will guide us.[420]

Our comfort comes in knowing God is guiding us through life, and best of all
He takes us into His glory. Whatever our loved ones faced here, they were taken
from the suffering into God's glory, and that is where they are right now.

My wonderful brother-in-law, Lanny, just had his precious mother,
Cleo, taken to God's glory—but not before a night of suffering from painful
pneumonia and laboring to breathe. Lanny suffered watching his mother suffer,
just like we suffered watching Dad struggle to breathe. But as painful as their
suffering was, we know they are now with Jesus. If our loved ones could tell
us, they would say, "The suffering was only for a moment, and God has me
now." They can't tell us now, but we do have God's Word and we have to hold
His Word. In the midst of our suffering, we must hold to God's promises. God
will guide us and afterward He will bring us into His glory. In God's glory—in
Heaven—we will be reunited with our loved ones and the suffering will be no
more. We are waiting on that day!

As you reflect on the verse and Paul Enns' words, what are your thoughts?

---

[419] Paul Enns, *Everything Happens For A Reason* (Chicago, IL: Moody, 2012), Location 548.
[420] Ibid., Location 617.

DAY 322 REFLECTION

Read over the last week. What brings you comfort? We noticed that Jesus appeared first to those He was closest to, which speaks of continuity of relationships. We read that Jesus appeared to Mary and she ran to tell the others, but they were so overwhelmed with grief and sorrow they didn't believe her. We know how debilitating grief is. We know that even though Jesus had told His disciples what would happen, they were not prepared for the sorrow. We saw the disciples' mourning turned to joy—just as ours will when we see Jesus. We read the heartfelt words of a father asking, "What were you thinking?" And we see his answer leads back to the cross. I was unable to put the entire quote on the page because margin constraints. But Randy Alcorn's words with this quote is well worth reading, "When you feel God's silence, or think him absent, look at Christ, the lamb... silent before the shearers (Acts 8:32, NLT). He shouts to us without opening his mouth: 'I do care. Don't you see the blood, bruises, and scars? Whatever you may think, never doubt that I care for you."[421]

Peter reminds us to look forward to a New Heaven and a New Earth. We are reminded that as long as we live on this fallen Earth we will have heartache, but someday there will be a world filled with God's righteousness. We are waiting on that day! We read that we will have trials and suffer. Then, we read Randy Alcorn's words reminding us: "Your suffering can only last the tiniest fraction of your true eternal life." Ponder these words of Randy Alcorn: "All healing in this world is temporary. Resurrection healing will be permanent. For that our hearts should overflow with praise to our gracious God."[422]

We read again Paul's words that Heaven is far better. We read that all things work together for good, and we see this verse is for those called according to His purpose—His eternal purpose. As Philip Yancey writes, "Not until history has run its course will we understand how all things work together for good." And finally, we read that God will guide us and bring us into His glory. Bring me Home, Lord. We find comfort and peace in those words. Record your thoughts and feelings for this week. What brings you the most comfort and peace this week?

---

[421] Randy Alcorn, If God is Good Faith in the Midst of Suffering and Evil, (Colorado Springs, CO: Multnomah Books, 2009), 189.
[422] Ibid., 381.

DAY 323

So Peter arose and went with them. When he arrived, they brought him into the upper room; and all the widows stood beside him, weeping and showing all the tunics and garments that Dorcas used to make while she was with them. (Acts 9:39, NASB)

Verse 36 tells us that Dorcas (also called Tabitha) was a disciple who was well-loved and was always doing good and helping the poor. She became sick and died. The disciples asked Peter to come. When Peter arrived, he found the widows who had been with Dorcas crying and showing Peter all that Dorcas had done. My sister said, "Did you notice that in Acts the grieving widows need to talk about their friend who died?" You read this chapter and might miss that part. Of course, the focus on the chapter is that Peter raised Dorcas from the dead. But we know that Dorcas did eventually die just like everyone healed in the Bible. But we also need to notice the grief of these women for their good friend. They are all believers and have faith, but they are in deep sorrow.

Everyone who grieves needs to have the significance of their loved one seen by others. I know that as a therapist, and I truly know that as one who grieves. These ladies loved Dorcas, and they wanted to talk about their love for her, what their relationship was like, and all the wonderful things she had made. The need to talk in grief is not only normal; it is an important part of grief. It is so hard to watch others go on as if life were back to normal. You want to scream, "Stop! Can't you see that life is not normal; that everything is not okay?" Go ahead and talk about the wonderful life that you love and celebrate. Thank God for the wonderful memories and times that you had with the one you love. It is important to share your thoughts, feelings, and memories for yourself and for others. The last thing you want is to have your loved one seemingly fade out and for everyone to act as if he or she had never existed. You want your loved one to stay important and he or she will. No one can take those things from you. Remember, our loved ones are more alive than ever.

Your faith does not protect you from pain, but it does give you the blessed hope that you will be with your loved one again. So hold to that hope and allow yourself to grieve. If everyone seems to be tiptoeing around you and not talking about your loved one, then you speak out. I had people tell me they didn't mean to make me cry when they said something about Don or Dad. I would always reply, "You didn't make me cry. My tears are ever-present; if not openly, they are inwardly." I love it when someone talks about a special memory of Dad or Don. You need to be able to talk about your loved one. But best of all, you will be close to your loved one again in a very real way. We will have an eternity to spend with our loved ones praising God together. We are waiting on that day!

Reflect on today's devotion. Does talking help you in your own grief?

DAY 324

For bodily discipline is only of little profit, but godliness is profitable for all things, since it holds promise for the present life and also for the life to come. (1 Timothy 4:8, NASB)

Paul tells us that bodily discipline is important, and then he goes on to make another statement that is a clear statement of continuity. "Godliness is profitable for all things, since it holds promise for the present life and also for the life to come." This verse shows what we do on Earth matters for eternity. There are many things that do not make sense in this fallen world, unless we have an eternal perspective. Verses like this affirm that eternal perspective. We find comfort when we remember that our time here is temporary, that our life is just a breath, and that there is an eternity to come. Because we know that the life to come is far better, we can look forward to that life eternal and not be stuck in the whys of now. In his book *Eternal Perspectives,* Randy Alcorn writes, "The people who change lives are the ones that point us away from the world's short-term perspective to God's long-term perspective. Life on Earth is a dot, a brief window of opportunity; life in Heaven (and ultimately the New Earth) is a line going out from that dot for eternity. If we are smart we'll live not for the dot but for the line."[423]

We are to strive for godliness because it will profit us now and in the life to come. There is continuity in this life to the next. Our loved ones are reaping parts of that reward even now. I think about Dad and Don, and although we were not ready for them to leave, they had lived each day for God and were ready spiritually. They had been faithful to what God had given them. If you are grieving a child, it is hard to understand why someone young is taken. But we know every life is precious to Jesus. Even the youngest life touches others and all have ripples in eternity. Verses that affirm continuity allow us to know we will be with our loves ones again. You will hold your child again. Pain and sorrow are real, but our faith is real too. When we hold to the eternal perspective and continuity, we can find comfort in being reunited with our loved ones in the life to come. We can purpose to draw close to God so that others see our godliness. We look forward to our life in eternity. We are waiting on that day!

As you reflect on this verse, what are your thoughts?

---

[423] Randy Alcorn in *Eternal Perspectives: A Collection of Quotation on Heaven, The New Earth, and Life After Death* (Carol Stream, IL: Tyndale House, 2012), 473.

DAY 325

Then he said to them, "My soul is overwhelmed with sorrow to the point of death. Stay here and keep watch with me." (Matthew 26:38, NIV)

There are many times in my sorrow I have felt that my soul was overwhelmed to the point of death. The deep pain and emptiness from sorrow makes you feel like you cannot go on, that surely your heart cannot go on beating. Jesus knew that overwhelming sorrow. Nancy Guthrie writes:

What a relief it was to know that Jesus understands what it is like to feel like sorrow is pressing the life out of you. He understands the lump in your throat, the heaviness in your chest, the sick feeling in your stomach.... His sorrow was so intense that he had a physical reaction to it.... Jesus is not a distant deity who knows nothing about the pain of disappointment and death.[424]

Guthrie goes on to encourage us to allow these words of Jesus to draw us closer to Him. Like Nancy Guthrie, I found that holding to Jesus in my sorrow, spending time with Him in prayer, and crying out to Him was the only way to make it through the next moment in time. Even in those moments Jesus seems far away, He is with you. The intensity of the pain can make you feel that you are alone, that God does not care. Jesus knew what it was like to feel alone. His disciples could not stay awake even after Jesus tells them He is sorrowful to the point of death. Jesus even felt God withdraw Himself as He cried, "Why have you forsaken me?"

Sorrow is all-consuming and it crushes us from all sides. There are many tims you may feel like you can't breathe and that you cannot go another step. Jesus understands. Guthrie points out, "Even though it had been his plan since the foundation of the world to give himself as a sacrifice for sin, Jesus was standing at the precipice, staring into the cavernous darkness of death itself. And he was alone. Desperately alone."[425] It is because of Jesus' sacrifice we know we will see Him one day. As we look into the cavern of emptiness that we feel without our loved ones, we know where our loved ones are. We know we will be with them again. We know this because Jesus faced that darkest moment of sorrow, and went to the cross because of His love for us. Jesus overcame death so that we will live. Death is not the end; the sorrow will turn to joy on the day we see Jesus. We have an eternity to praise Jesus with our loved ones.

Meditate on these words of Jesus. How does it reflect your own feelings?

---

[424] Nancy Guthrie, *Hearing Jesus Speak into Your Sorrow* (Carol Stream, IL: Tyndale, 2009), 4-5.
[425] Ibid., 7.

DAY 326

I have told you all this so that you may have peace in me. Here on earth you will have many trials and sorrows. But take heart, because I have overcome the world. (John 16:33, NLT)

Despite the preaching of those who teach health and prosperity, Jesus plainly tells us we will have many trials and sorrows. God does often bless us with health and prosperity, but it is not the point of the Gospel. Jesus was preparing His disciples for what was about to take place. Jesus will choose to die on the cross for our sins, and He will be resurrected. Satan will be defeated; death will be defeated. We who receive Christ will receive eternal life. Jesus has overcome the world. This life on this Earth is not all there is; there is more, much more. Jesus wanted His disciples to remember His words, and in His words find peace despite all the sorrow and trials they would face. Jesus' followers must hold to His words. He has overcome the world, and we must hold to Jesus' words now.

The sorrow consumes us, but this world in the fallen state is not all there is. Nancy Guthrie writes, "But for now we live in an in-between time, in which suffering is an ongoing reality as we await the healing to come when Christ ushers in the new heaven and new earth."[426] She goes on to say, "God's primary purpose in the here and now is not to rid us of sickness and pain but to purify us and empower us to place all of our hopes in his promises, trusting that one day they will become the reality we will know fully and enjoy forever."[427]

Of the eleven disciples left after Judas betrayed Christ, all but one died a violent death. Jesus knew what awaited His disciples. Jesus knew that there would be chaos, and that He was soon to die on the cross. Jesus knew what the events would look like and feel like to His disciples. Jesus knew all of this, and yet He says, "I tell you this so that you may have peace in me. You will have many trials and sorrows. But take heart, because I have overcome the world."

In your sorrow and pain now, you still have those words of Jesus. We have His promise, and with Jesus' promise is the promise of eternity and eternal peace. We will live with Jesus, and that peace will never be taken from us. Our loved ones have gone Home to be with Jesus now. Those of us left behind miss them beyond words. We long to be with our loved ones. Nothing seems to make sense. But Jesus has overcome the world. We can take heart in that eternal truth; we can hold to that promise. We will live with Jesus on a restored Earth because He has overcome this world. We are waiting on that day!

Meditate on this verse. How can you allow these words to bring you comfort?

---

[426] Nancy Guthrie, *Hearing Jesus Speak into Your Sorrow* (Carol Stream, IL: Tyndale, 2009), 31.
[427] Ibid., 32.

DAY 327

These trials will show that your faith is genuine. It is being tested as fire tests and purifies gold—though your faith is far more precious than mere gold. So when your faith remains strong through many trials, it will bring you much praise and glory and honor on the day when Jesus Christ is revealed to the whole world. (1 Peter 1:7, NLT)

Peter writes much about the trials and sufferings in this world. He encourages his readers to look Heavenward. John Piper says this about suffering:

All experiences of suffering in the path of Christian obedience, whether from persecution or sickness or accident, have this in common: They all threaten our faith in the goodness of God and tempt us to leave the path of obedience. Therefore, every triumph of faith and all perseverance in obedience are testimonies to the goodness of God and the preciousness of Christ—whether the enemy is sickness, Satan, sin or sabotage.[428]

How we respond to suffering can purify and strengthen us. How we respond to suffering can glorify God. Grief is a time when we can find ourselves wanting to shut down completely or perhaps become angry and bitter, but it is a time that we must hold on to Jesus. Peter is telling us that when we hold to Jesus even in our pain and suffering we are building our faith. Peter reminds us that Jesus is coming back; everything is going to make sense someday, even though right now much does not make sense. Nancy Guthrie writes:

How do you display the glory of God? You reflect his character. Instead of demanding an answer, you decide to trust him, recognizing that your circumstances provide an unparalleled opportunity to glorify God just by your trust in his unseen purpose. Trusting God when the miracle does not come, when the urgent prayer gets no answer, when there is only darkness—this is the kind of faith God values perhaps most of all. This is the kind of faith that can only be developed and displayed in the midst of difficult circumstances; this is the kind of faith that cannot be shaken because it is the result of having been shaken.[429]

One day you will be reunited with your loved one. You will see Jesus face to face, and you will know holding to your faith through all the pain, holding to Jesus when you didn't understand, was worth it all. We are waiting on that day!

As you meditate on the verse and quotes, how do they speak to you?

---

[428] John Piper, *Desiring God Revised Edition*, (Colorado Springs, CO: Multnomah, 2011), 257.

[429] Nancy Guthrie, *Holding On to Hope: A Pathway Through Suffering to the Heart of God*, (Wheaton, IL: Tyndale, 2002), Location 402.

DAY 328

The Lord says, "I will rescue those who love me. I will protect those who trust in my name. When they call on me, I will answer; I will be with them in trouble. I will rescue and honor them. (Psalm 91:14-15, NLT)

Someone shared the ninety-first Psalm with me shortly after Don went Home. As I read the Psalm, I wondered how was I to find comfort in a verse on protection when God did not protect Don? Or Dad? I wrestled with this Psalm. A year later I was reading Nancy Guthrie's book *Hearing Jesus Speak in Your Sorrow.* Apparently she wrestled with the same thing that I had, and she came to much the same conclusion I have as I study His Word. After wrestling with the verses that talk about God's protection and at a low point in her grief, she writes:

My solid confidence in the integrity of God's Word told me that there must be something foundational that I did not understand for it to appear to me that this passage was not true. I wanted to figure out how the scriptural promises apply—not only to me, but also to the missionary who is raped, the Chinese pastor who is imprisoned, the godly mother of three who succumbs to cancer. I figured if I could come to an understanding of what God's promises of protection mean, then there would be a breakthrough for me in my understanding of God and in my experience of loss.[430]

What she discovered was that Jesus was clear about the persecution we would have, and that we will die. Jesus even says, "Don't be afraid of those who want to kill you. They can only kill the body; they cannot touch your soul. Fear only God, who can destroy both soul and body in hell" (Matthew 10:28). What is important to Jesus is our soul and eternity. Guthrie continues:

But when we look at Jesus' life and violent death, when we consider the lives and deaths of his disciples, and when we listen to what Jesus said over and over again about how we will receive rewards for enduring persecution for his sake, it becomes obvious that here is something more important to Jesus than our bodily comfort and safety. While He cares deeply for us and the physical pain we experience, he cares far more about our spiritual conditions.[431]

As you reflect on these verses and Nancy Guthrie's insightful words, what are your thoughts and feelings? Have you wrestled with verses like these?

---

[430] Nancy Guthrie, *Hearing Jesus Speak into Your Sorrow* (Carol Stream, IL: Tyndale, 2009), 58.
[431] Ibid., 60.

DAY 329 REFLECTION

Read over the last week. What seems to bring you the most comfort? We read how friends and loved ones of Dorcas were crying and wanting to talk about her. We are reminded in our own grief how important those memories are, and how we want our loved one to be remembered. This need to talk about our loved one is a normal part of grief. We read how godliness is of profit in this life and in the life to come. This verse in 1 Timothy is a clear statement of continuity, and a reminder that what we do on Earth matters for eternity. We ponder our own need to continue in godliness as we grieve our loved ones. Randy Alcorn quotes Isaac Watts:

When we mourn the death of friends who were prepared for an early summons, let their preparation be our support. Blessed be God they were not found sleeping! While we drop our tears upon the grave of any young Christian who was awake and alive to God, that blessedness which Christ himself pronounces upon them, is a sweet cordial to mingle with our bitter sorrows...[432]

As we read this quote, we are reminded our own loved ones are with Jesus and even the youngest life here impacts eternity. We read how Jesus was overwhelmed with sorrow even unto death. You may be feeling sorrowful unto death. Jesus felt alone. You may be feeling alone. This verse in Matthew reminds us that Jesus understands our sorrow, our pain, and our feeling alone. We can trust Him. Jesus tells us we will have sorrow, but He also tells us we have His peace. We can have peace because Jesus has overcome the world. Just these words are amazing to me, Jesus has overcome the world.

We read Peter telling us we will face trials, but in the trials our faith will be shown as genuine. We are in the trial of our life, and we are reminded that our faith must remain firm and that we will be rewarded. God knows our heart and He knows our pain. We will someday see Jesus face to face and feel His glory. We must remain faithful. We read the psalmist saying that God will rescue us, and we may wonder, "How can that be?" Then we read Nancy Guthrie's words reminding us how Jesus told us that we will have sorrows and trials. What Jesus appears to be most concerned with is our spiritual rescue. God's idea of rescue will be for our eternity. I truly like Guthrie's words about faith, "This is the kind of faith that cannot be shaken because it is the result of having been shaken." We trust Jesus as we hold to Him while we are waiting on that day. Record your thoughts and feelings as you reflect over the last week. What resonates with you the most?

---

[432] Isaac Watts, as cited by Randy Alcorn in *Eternal Perspectives: A Collection of Quotation on Heaven, The New Earth, and Life After Death* (Carol Stream, IL: Tyndale House, 2012), 469.

DAY 330

While Jesus was here on earth, he offered prayers and pleadings, with a loud cry and tears, to the one who could rescue him from death. And God heard his prayers because of his deep reverence for God. Even though Jesus was God's Son, he learned obedience from the things he suffered. In this way, God qualified him as a perfect High Priest, and he became the source of eternal salvation for all those who obey him. (Hebrews 5:7-9, NLT)

Jesus understands our pain. Jesus suffered and cried out to God, and God heard Him. But Jesus voluntarily went to the cross for our sins. This passage shows Jesus' understanding of our pain and suffering. Although Jesus was fully God, He became human to take on our sins. Because Jesus took our place on the cross, we have salvation. Our loved ones are in His presence even now and we will be too someday. Jesus, as High Priest, intercedes for us as He understands our pain and sorrow. Nancy Guthrie tells us that in the lowest part of her grief she was struggling to harmonize the power of God with the compassion of God, and then she came across Hebrews 5:7-9.

I think that is the wall that those of us who believe in God's sovereignty run into eventually. And when we feel its full force, it hurts. We think, God, if you are powerful enough to have done things differently, why didn't you? How can I accept your comfort and believe you want to heal my broken heart when you could have kept me from experiencing this sorrow in the first place? If you'd only given me what I wanted, neither of us would have to be sad.[433]

It helps me to know that Jesus doesn't dismiss suffering and sorrow by suggesting that it doesn't matter or that it should hurt. He too cried hot tears.... Somehow it helped me to know that Jesus wrestled with God's plan for his life— and his death— even as he submitted to it, because I, too, have wrestled with God's plan for my life even as I have sought to submit to it.[434]

We do not have a Savior who dismisses our pain. Indeed Jesus understands our struggle. We will have an eternity to understand, but for now we know God's eternal plan is in place. We live in a temporary place on our journey to our eternal Home.

What are your thoughts on the verses? Have you run into this "wall" as Nancy Guthrie stated? Journal your feelings on the wall you have run into.

---

[433] Nancy Guthrie, *Hearing Jesus Speak into Your Sorrow* (Carol Stream, IL: Tyndale, 2009), 12.

[434] Ibid., 17.

DAY 331

The righteous perish, and no one takes it to heart; the devout are taken away, and no one understands that the righteous are taken away to be spared from evil. Those who walk uprightly enter into peace; they find rest as they lie in death. (Isaiah 57:1-2, NIV)

I wrote earlier how our daughter, Michelle, had found comfort in these words of Isaiah. Nancy Guthrie also found comfort in Isaiah when her two children went Home. She writes how she had wanted to watch her daughter grow up and be friends in her old age. But she also knew she didn't want her daughter to have a life of pain. Guthrie's profound words:

I don't believe it is a tragedy that Hope had the opportunity to be spared from evil and pain of this life and instead be in the presence of God.... That is what I believe. It is not necessarily how I *feel*, but my belief does make a difference in how I feel.... There is no tragedy in being ushered quickly from this life to the next when that next life is spent in the presence of God. There is nothing to fear. The only real tragedy is a life that ends without the hope of eternal life in the presence of God.... Do you find yourself yearning for heaven in the midst of your sorrow or difficulty? Perhaps that is a part of the purpose in your pain- a new perspective, a proper perspective, about life on this earth and the life after.[435]

I like the way she says, "This is what I believe. It is not necessarily how I feel." I think that statement took a lot of honesty. During this time of intense pain and sorrow our feelings can be so deep and intense that we lose sight of what we believe. We must then purpose to stay in God's Word, to remind ourselves what we believe. State those things you believe even if you are not "feeling" the words at the time. We don't understand why our loved ones are taken. Death does not make sense in our limited ability to understand. Guthrie continues:

Our task is not to decipher exactly how all of life's pieces fit and what they all mean but to remain faithful and obedient to God, who knows all mysteries. That is the kind of faith that is pleasing to God—a faith that is determined to trust him when he has not answered all the questions, when we have not heard the voice from the whirlwind.[436]

We can't make sense of the loss, but we have to trust God has everything under control. We will stay faithful as we wait on that day.

As you reflect on the verses and the quotes, how do they speak to you?

---

[435] Nancy Guthrie, *Holding On to Hope: A pathway through suffering to the heart of God* (Wheaton, IL: Tyndale, 2002), Location 438.
[436] Ibid., Location 531.

DAY 332

Don't be afraid! I am the First and the Last. I am the living one. I died, but look—I am alive forever and ever! And I hold the keys of death and the grave. (Revelation 1:17-18, NLT)

Jesus is in control; He holds the keys to death. We have already read in Psalm 139:16 all our days are numbered before were born. We saw other Scriptures that affirm God has an appointed time for us to join Him. Jesus Himself tells us He holds the keys. He says, "Don't be afraid." Our believing loved ones went Home when it was their time. We were not ready, but would we ever be?

My dream was that Don and I would go together while sleeping in our old age. The summer before Don went Home we were in our yard enjoying a beautiful summer day. We were talking about Heaven and death. Our daughter Melody said, "As hard as it would be to lose you both, I know it would be better if you went together. I can't imagine one of you without the other." But God is in control and He knows what He is doing, I have to trust God, and know that this life is not all there is. We have an eternity to understand. For now we trust Jesus.

Nancy Guthrie writes how she was struggling with just wanting her daughter to be with them a little longer. She knew she would have to let her go, but she wanted the days to stretch out. Her friend Anne Graham Lotz called her and said, "The purpose for Hope's life will be completely accomplished in the number of days that God gives her." She had also just read a quote from Joseph Bayly, who lost three children—one at eighteen days old, another at five years of age from leukemia, and a third at eighteen years old in a sledding accident.

I read that Bayly was once asked how he would feel if a cure were found for leukemia shortly after his son died of the disease. His response was something like this: 'My son lived exactly the number of days God had determined for him. No cure or lack thereof could have added to or shortened his life.'.… It soothed my fear about the reality of death closing in on us. My growing confidence that God was in control of Hope's life and death gave me peace.[437]

It is hard for us to understand how our loved ones' purpose could be filled when we had so many more plans for them. I don't have the answer, but I know that Jesus holds the keys and I have to trust Him. I know I will have an eternity with my loved ones worshiping God because Jesus has conquered death and holds the keys. I am waiting on that day!

How do today's powerful verses and quotes speak to you?

---

[437] Nancy Guthrie, *Hearing Jesus Speak into Your Sorrow* (Carol Stream, IL: Tyndale, 2009), 138-139.

DAY 333

Fight the good fight of the faith. Take hold of the eternal life to which you were called when you made your good confession in the presence of many witnesses. (1 Timothy 6:12, NIV)

As believers we are promised eternal life. Our loved ones have entered into that realm of eternal life. Our loved ones are with Jesus. We are the ones who are facing the sorrow and the pain. And the sorrow and the pain can seem overwhelming. There are days you may think, "Okay, God; what do you want me to do?" Then there are days you may think, "I can't do this; I can't handle another day." The truth is you cannot do any of this grieving on your own. We have to take hold of Jesus and hold on to Him. We have to fight the good fight of faith until Jesus calls us Home.

How can you glorify God even in your pain? How can you take hold of the eternal life to which you were called? Only through the grace of God and seeking Him constantly for what He wants in your life can we fight that fight. And grief is a fight. Spiritual warfare is immense—especially for those who are grieving. You are at you most vulnerable right now. You may not feel God, and that can usher in doubts. Or perhaps the doubts are no longer there, but you still battle with hearing God like you want to hear Him. You may want to feel Him in a supernatural way, see the burning bush, or see the handwriting on the wall. But instead, God seems to answer in subtle ways that still leave you wondering. But then we go back to the words of Paul, "Take hold of the eternal life to which you were called when you made your good confession in the presence of many witnesses." As a believer, you made that confession when you received Christ as your Savior. Jesus has not changed. Our circumstances have changed. Our life has changed, but we have the promise of eternal life, just as our believing loved ones have. Our loved ones are with Jesus.

We must now continue the fight, and living does feels like a fight right now. It feels like a fight just to make it through the day. It feels like a fight to hold to your faith when you feel attacked. But you are not alone. Continue to pray and read God's Word. Continue to ask what God wants for you. You may wonder how you can serve Jesus when you can't make it through the day. You can pray for others and you can encourage others—even in your own grief. Ask Jesus how you can serve Him. Jesus may call you to rest in Him first, but eventually He will open the door in some way. Even in rest though, we hold to Him, because we are resting in Him by praying and being in His Word. Take hold of the promise of God. We shall see Jesus and we shall be reunited with those we love. We are waiting on that day!

How does this verse speak to you? Describe how you feel grief is a fight. What are ways you can be serving God even now?

DAY 334

And I will make a covenant of peace with them, an everlasting covenant. I will give them their land and increase their numbers, and I will put my Temple among them forever. I will make my home among them. I will be their God, and they will be my people. (Ezekiel 37:26-27, NLT)

The land has always been a part of the promise for Israel. As Asher Intrater points out, "The return of the Jewish people to the land of Israel since the end of the nineteenth century is not just a matter of history or politics. It is an issue of covenant and prophecy."[438] Jesus will come back, just as He ascended, on the Mount of Olives in Israel. Israel will stand as a nation because God has His hand on Israel, and He has a covenant with the Israelites. As Christians, our beliefs are rooted in Judaism. Prophecy has been and is being fulfilled today. Prophecy unfolding is all part of God's eternal plan.

Many scholars see these verses as a prophecy describing the millennium. But as Paul Enns points out, "These words cannot be restricted or limited to a thousand years.... Christ's kingdom will continue on the new, renovated earth"[439] Forever is not limited. God says in that time, He will make His Home among us and it will be everlasting peace. No longer will we be in a fallen world but a world where God dwells among us. We all long for a day of peace. We cry unfair now because we long for that perfect world. We will have that perfect world when God dwells among us.

When the pain threatens to overwhelm you, when the roller coaster of emotion consumes you, focus on this eternal truth. God's eternal plan is unfolding before our eyes. In God's perfect timing all redeemed believers will live again on the New Earth. We go immediately to live with God when He calls us Home, but someday we will all live together on the New Earth. God will dwell among us, and we will have everlasting peace. Forever is forever. Someday we will have the peace we long for now. We will be reunited with our loved ones and live on a restored Earth. We are waiting on that day!

What are your thoughts and feelings on these verses? What are your thoughts and feelings on the quotes? What brings you the most assurance in the verses and the quotes?

(For more perspectives on the land and Israel, visit www.reviveisrael.org.)

---

438 Asher Intrater, *Who Ate Lunch With Abraham?* (Peoria, AZ: Intermedia, 2011), 155.
439 Paul Enns, *Heaven Revealed* (Chicago, IL: Moody, 2011), 62.

DAY 335

And we believers also groan, even though we have the Holy Spirit within us as a foretaste of future glory, for we long for our bodies to be released from sin and suffering. We, too, wait with eager hope for the day when God will give us our full rights as his adopted children, including the new bodies he has promised us. (Romans 8:23, NLT)

Paul was looking forward to the day when we receive our full rights as God's adopted children, and when we receive new bodies and are released from sin and suffering. All the first-century believers looked forward to the day they would go to Heaven. That is why so many early believers willingly died for their faith. They knew this world was temporary. The first followers of Jesus knew there was something far better coming. Paul says we "groan"; this isn't just saying Heaven is going to be good; this is knowing, wanting, and desiring to be in Heaven. This statement is looking forward to the day of eternal glory when we will live with Jesus forever. In our western culture we have gotten so used to life here that we tend to think this life is all there is. Nancy Guthrie writes:

There is coming a day when death and disease will be healed for good. That is our sure hope in the midst of sorrow. But for now we live in an in-between time, in which suffering is an ongoing reality as we await the healing to come when Christ ushers in the new heaven and the new earth. Paul describes the frustration we feel living in the here and now as we wait for that day.... The day is coming when the healing ministry of Jesus will come to full fruition, His healing will be pervasive and plentiful... and it will be eternal. Until then, we 'wait with eager hope' for that day.[440]

Paul groaned for the day of restoration. We live in a fallen world full of sin and suffering. But we as believers have the eager hope for the day when God gives us our full rights as His children. Since we have loved ones who are already in Heaven, we look forward to Heaven even more. The reality of Heaven and future glory hit you when someone you love goes before you. Suddenly Heaven is not a distant thought but a reality. And you do groan for the day of restoration. With the loss of a loved one we fully begin to understand just how temporary life here is. But as believers we have the promise of eternity. We can look forward to that day of restoration even in our pain because we know the pain will end when we see Jesus. We know we will have an eternity to spend with our loved ones in the presence of our Lord. We groan for that day.

What are your thoughts and feelings on the verse? Can you identify with the groaning for that day? What are your thoughts on Nancy Guthrie's statements?

---

[440] Nancy Guthrie, *Hearing Jesus Speak into Your Sorrow* (Carol Stream, IL: Tyndale, 2009), 31-32.

DAY 336 REFLECTION

Looking back over the last week, what seems to speak to you the most? We read how even though Jesus willingly went to the cross, even though He knew the plan since before the beginning of time, He still pleaded with God over the plan. We read how Nancy Guthrie told us she struggled with God's plan for her life and found comfort in Jesus' struggle. We recognize our struggle with God over His plans in our lives right now. We read again how the righteous sometimes perish young and Nancy Guthrie's words, "There is no tragedy in being ushered quickly from this life to the next when it is spent in the presence of God." Her words are deep and profound. As we think about our loved ones we hold to beautiful sight of them being in the presence of God. You will be reunited with your precious loved one, whether a child, spouse, parent, sibling, grandparent, grandchild, close relative, or friend. I also found these words of Nancy Guthrie's to be insightful, "Perhaps that is a part of the purpose in your pain- a new perspective, a proper perspective, about life on this earth and the life after." What are your thoughts on these words? We certainly do have a new perspective don't we?

Jesus tells us He is the first and the last and that He holds the keys to death and the grave. There is comfort and peace in Jesus' words. Our loved ones joined Jesus on the day when He called them Home. Jesus is in control. He is sovereign and Jesus holds all in His hands. Jesus holds our loved ones now. We read that we are to fight the good fight and take hold of eternal life. We are certainly in a fight, and we must keep an eternal perspective as we fight the fight. We read the beautiful words in Ezekiel of an everlasting covenant, and that God will live among us forever. The words *everlasting* and *forever* are powerful and speak of the New Earth and our eternity with Jesus and with our loved ones. We are waiting on that day.

And finally, we read that Paul reminded us to wait with an eager hope for our eternal life. We are reminded of the temporary nature of this life. Nancy Guthrie writes:

What we really want from him is to give us everything he has promised us here and now. We think that physical life on the earth—the length of it and the quality of it—is of ultimate importance. We have a hard time grasping the significance and the reality of the life to come.[441]

We are all waiting as never before. We await the healing, the reunion, the rest from spiritual warfare, and the presence of our Lord in the New Earth. We are waiting on that day! How is God speaking to you this week?

---

[441] Nancy Guthrie, *Hearing Jesus Speak into Your Sorrow* (Carol Stream, IL: Tyndale, 2009), 37.

DAY 337

Your kingdom come. Your will be done, On earth as it is in heaven. (Matthew 6:10, NIV)

Jesus was teaching His disciples how to pray and His words were powerful. I pray these words of Jesus all the time. When I am not sure what to pray, I pray, "Your kingdom come. Your will be done on Earth as it is in Heaven." The New Living Translation says, "May your kingdom come soon. May your will be done on earth as it is in heaven." We are all waiting on Jesus' kingdom to come to Earth. On that day we will be on the New Heaven and the New Earth, and His will will be done on Earth as it is in Heaven. Isn't that what we all want?

There will be a day when His kingdom comes to Earth in its fullness. Right now we live in a fallen world, but we are citizens of His kingdom. Our believing loved ones have been called to Heaven and are in His presence. All of us, as believers, will be in Heaven someday. Right now in Heaven, in God's presence, all is in His perfect will. There is no sin, no pain, no death, no suffering. But because we live in a fallen world, we still experience all those things. But there will be a day His kingdom fully comes to Earth and His will will be done on Earth as it is now in Heaven. Heaven will come to Earth and the perfect will of God will reign.

Jesus teaches us to pray, "Your kingdom come." We look forward to the day when we will be in His presence. There will be no more death, no more mourning, no more pain, and no more suffering. Warren Weirsbe writes:

There was a time when heaven and earth existed in perfect harmony and God would survey his creation and call it very good. Indeed in the beginning everything in creation was working in beautiful harmony because only one will was operating in the universe, and that was the perfect will of God.... The rebellion of Satan and the disobedience of Adam and Eve brought division and conflict between heaven and earth... God in his grace seeks to bring heaven and earth together and he will never change his plan. He bridged the gulf between heaven and earth by sending three gifts to our rebellious planet; his inspired Word, his beloved Son, and the Holy Spirit.[442]

God's plan is eternal, and He will come again. We pray His kingdom comes soon. And someday, someday maybe soon, we will see God's perfect will. God's kingdom will be firmly established on Earth as it is in Heaven. And we will be with Him forever. We are waiting on that day!

You have most likely prayed the Lord's Prayer many times. What do these words mean to you now?

---

[442] Warren Wiersbe, *On Earth as It Is In Heaven* (Grand Rapids, MI: Baker, 2010), 77.

DAY 338

"Look! How good and how pleasant it is when brothers live together! It is like fine oil poured on the head which flows down the beard—Aaron's beard, and then flows down his garments. It is like the dew of Hermon, which flows down upon the hills of Zion. Indeed that is where the Lord has decreed a blessing will be available—eternal life." (Psalm 133:1-3, NET)

I like the way the New English Translation separates the ending like a "grand finale"—eternal life. And isn't it the grand finale? Only this grand finale is not the end; it is just the beginning. Other translations read "life forever," "life everlasting," and "life forevermore." Yes we are blessed here on Earth, but our true blessing is in Heaven. *Our blessing is eternal life.*

Also note the first verse: "How pleasant it is when brothers live together." David is exalting the family and family unity. Some commentaries referred to this as the family and extended family; others as the nation of Israel. But the nation of Israel was and is a huge extended family. God created the family; our families are a blessing. Your loved one is a blessing. However short or long her life was here, she was and is a blessing.

We miss our loved one unbelievably. We want our life back. The pain and sorrow can seem unbearable. While nothing stops the pain, we can find solace in the promise that we, as believers, have the blessing of eternal life. We will be reunited with our loved ones. The true blessing will come in Heaven. In her book *Holding on to Hope*, Nancy Guthrie talks about how older hymns are more about Heaven, and she points out that we don't see that as much now:

We don't really yearn for heaven—because we're so comfortable right here. We tend to think this life on earth is all there is, and we certainly live that way much of the time. God wants to radically alter that perspective. He wants us to live with an eternal perspective, putting life on this earth in its proper place and living in anticipation of an eternity in his presence.[443]

Even when we sing songs of Heaven, I think we may skim over the words, not allowing the majesty of the promises to dwell within us. David did not have the words of Jesus; he did not live under the New Covenant, but even he knew the true blessing from God for believers is eternal life. Hold on to the promise of the blessing of eternal life. We will be reunited with our loved ones in eternity. What a blessing! We are waiting on that day!

Meditate on these verses. Read some old hymns, note the emphasis on Heaven.

---

[443] Nancy Guthrie, *Holding On to Hope: A Pathway Through Suffering to the Heart of God*, (Wheaton, IL: Tyndale, 2002), Location 425.

DAY 339

Jesus said to her, "I am the resurrection and the life; he who believes in Me will live even if he dies." (John 11:25, NASB)

As I have mentioned, this verse is one I quote often, it refocuses me and reminds me Don and Dad are with Jesus. Yes, I know that as a believer. But when the trauma of losing someone on this Earth hits you, the sheer magnitude of the pain and the intensity of the loss sends you reeling. If you can't see your loved ones, hear them, or hold them, grief can begin to suffocate you. Quoting Scripture reminds you of what you believe. And, yes, sometimes you have to remind yourself of those things you have always believed. Nothing seems real; life can't be real, or so it seems.

Nancy Guthrie writes, "But most of us would have to admit that resurrection can seem very far away—far away in the future and far away from the reality of our deep longing to be with the people we love here and now. It can seem like a theological Band-Aid that just doesn't stop the hurt."[444] She goes on to point out that Martha knew about the resurrection but hurt at that moment just as we do. But what we have to remember is Jesus' victory over death is now. When Jesus returns and we have the bodily resurrection, then we will all live together on the New Earth. We look forward to that day! But because we know Jesus conquered death we know that our loved ones wait with Him for that day.

Our loved ones are not with us now because they are with Jesus. As believers we have that promise, and even though it seems so far away, we will one day be with our loved ones again and will have an eternity to worship Jesus with them. We have no idea when our time to go Home will be. Within the course of a couple of weeks I was praying for two new families. A church member's granddaughter was born on a Monday morning and went Home to be with Jesus Monday night. A few days after hearing this sad news, I had a new client grieving the loss of a precious baby who lived one hour. Death is hard to understand. These families looked forward to rejoicing in the birth of a new family member, and instead mourned the life they did not see grow up. Nothing will stop that pain or mourning, but they can take comfort in the knowledge that the child is in the arms of Jesus, and they will someday hold that child. They can take comfort in knowing Jesus knew their babies even before the babies were born, and that He has them now. Jesus is the resurrection and the life and we will live. We are waiting on that day!

Meditate on this verse. Allow the power to sink in. Remind yourself often of these words. Our loved ones are alive now as we all wait the resurrection.

---

[444] Nancy Guthrie, *Hearing Jesus Speak into Your Sorrow* (Carol Stream, IL: Tyndale, 2009), 124.

DAY 340

May he strengthen your hearts so that you will be blameless and holy in the presence of our God and Father when our Lord Jesus comes with all his holy ones. (1 Thessalonians 3:13, NIV)

The New American Standard Bible translates the last part of this verse as, "The coming of our Lord with all His saints." Our believing loved ones are now with Jesus. According to most of the commentaries I read, our believing loved ones are the saints and the holy ones spoken of in this verse. This verse is a prayer for those Paul wrote to at that time—and for us. Paul prays for our hearts to be strengthened while we wait for the appearance of the Lord Jesus. When your heart is broken it needs a lot of strengthening. I know my heart will never be the same. My heart has been shattered into a million pieces and even though my heart beats, it is not whole. But I know my heart will be whole again someday. I know that on that day I see Jesus my heart will be healed. For now my prayer is for enough strength to serve Jesus until He calls me Home.

I have read many Christian authors who wrote out of the pain of a loved one going to Heaven before them. All of them talk about their broken heart and pain. But they all have hope because they know their loved one is with Jesus and they will be reunited with them someday. The brokenness of the heart is inescapable. When I have counseled with those who come in with grief, I have to tell them the pain doesn't go away. Their heart is broken. As one author had stated, "When she left, she took a part of my heart with her."

I have words laminated with pictures depicting different emotions in my office. Our daughter Melody drew them for me several years ago when I was a school counselor. One of the pictures has no word attached to it; it was just a picture of a puzzle with one piece missing and the missing piece set to the side. I worked with a young girl whose mother had passed away. As she looked at the picture of the puzzle with the missing piece, she indicated that she felt that way. I asked her what that meant to her. She said, "My mom is missing and a part of me is missing." I cried with her. That is how we all feel, isn't it? Our pain is real; a part of us is missing. But we do have hope and comfort.

Not only are our believing loved ones with Jesus now, they will accompany Him as He comes back. And we will be with them and with Jesus forever. We can pray our heart is strengthened to get through the day because we know we will be with our loved ones again. The separation is hard because we don't know how long we will be separated or when we will be reunited. But that is where we trust God and hold to Him as we serve Him here. We are strengthened to do God's will and to be holy and blameless for the day Jesus comes. We are waiting on that day!

Meditate on the verse and the words. What are your thoughts and feelings?

DAY 341

And to grant relief to you who are afflicted as well as to us, when the Lord Jesus is revealed from heaven with his mighty angels. When he comes on that day to be glorified in his saints, and to be marveled at among all who have believed, because our testimony to you was believed. (2 Thessalonians 1:7,10, ESV)

In the context of this verse, Paul is encouraging those who are being persecuted and letting them know that relief will come when Jesus comes. Verses 8 and 9 have to do with the punishment for those who do not believe. But Paul goes on to write about God in His glory and believers seeing God's glory someday. What struck me when I read this passage was the word *relief.* Not just relief for those persecuted, but relief for us all. Relief from the fallen world; relief from the overwhelming pain and sorrow we feel now. The Lord Jesus will reveal Himself and on that day the world will know Jesus is indeed who He said He was. On the day when Jesus comes back we will find relief from the pain. We will see Jesus and we will be reunited with our loved ones.

A grieving friend said, "I would not wish this pain on anyone, even my worst enemy." He was talking about the pain that he was feeling as he mourned the loss of his beloved wife. The pain can suck the very life out of you, and it is all you can do to walk and breathe. But relief will be ours again on the day we see Jesus. And we know we will. Jesus will come back and reveal Himself to the whole world. Or we may see Him as He gently call us Home; but we will see Jesus. What sets us apart as believers is the knowledge that we will see Jesus. On that day we see Jesus, relief will come not just in the absence of pain, but in the curing of the sorrow that causes the pain. There will be no more sorrow.

Paul is also letting his readers know that because they believed, they will be counted as those saints to marvel at Jesus' coming. His encouragement is to bolster their faith in a time of tribulation and persecution. We too need our faith encouraged. It is faith that allows us to hold to that hope, but sometimes that faith can flounder. The pain, the separation from our loved ones, and not knowing how long we will have to wait can take its toll; and when it does, we can waver at times. We think we can't find God because we don't feel Him. Just as those in Paul's time needed reminding of their hope and to hold on to their faith, we do too. As believers, we must hold on to the faith we know is true. The promise that relief will come and that that this life is temporary is a real promise. We do not know when, but we know we will see Jesus and we will have an eternity to marvel in His glory. We will have relief from the pain and sorrow because there will be no more sorrow. We will be with Jesus and our loved ones. The day will come; we are waiting on that day.

Meditate on these verses. What are your thoughts and feelings on relief coming?

DAY 342

However, as it is written: "What no eye has seen, what no ear has heard, and what no human mind has conceived"—the things God has prepared for those who love him. (1 Corinthians 2:9, NIV)

This verse is quoting Isaiah 64:4, and Paul is writing about those mysteries that God has revealed—His plan for redemption. I think it is fitting to relate this verse to Heaven as well because, after all, His ultimate plan is the restoration of all things and the New Heaven and New Earth. His plan is for us to live with Him for eternity on the New Earth.

God has given us glimpses through the Scriptures of what Heaven will be like, many of which we have looked at in this book. God speaks throughout the Scriptures of His eternal plan and redemption. So although we may not be able to truly comprehend all that God has in store, we know enough to know, as Don would say, "Whatever it is will be good." And as my Dad would say, "We know the nature of God." We know what God has given us here on Earth. We also know that Earth is a shadow of what is to come. So with eager anticipation we can await the day we see what God has prepared. Anthony Hoekema writes, "Though, to be sure, there is continuity between the present world and the world to come, the glory of the world to come will far outshine the glory of the present world."[445] He goes on to quote today's verse and write, "All we know is that it shall be wonderful, beyond our highest imaginings."[446]

Our loved ones no longer wonder what God has prepared for us; they are seeing it with their own eyes even as they wait on the New Earth. I love Steven Curtis Chapman's song "See":

> And I'm counting down the days
> Until I see it's everything
> He said it would be
> And even better than we would believe
>
> And I'm counting down the days
> Till He says
> "Come with Me"
> And finally
> We'll see[447]

And we will see; we are waiting on that day! What are your thoughts?

---

[445] Anthony A. Hoekema, *The Bible and the Future* (Grand Rapids, MI: Eerdmans, 1979), 75.

[446] Ibid., 252.

[447] Steven Curtis Chapman, "See." *Beauty Will Rise*. Sparrow, 2008.

DAY 343 REFLECTION

As you read over the last week, what seems to speak to you the most? We read the familiar words from the Lord's Prayer, "Your kingdom come, Your will be done, on Earth as it is in Heaven." We are waiting on the kingdom to come, where our King Jesus will rule. We will live in perfect harmony with our loved ones and in Jesus' glorious presence. We are waiting on that day! We read David exalting harmony among family and community and how that pleases God. And we read that the reward is eternal life. The grand climax of this life for believers is eternal life with the Lord.

Jesus reminds us that He is the resurrection and the life and we live in Him even though we die. We are comforted in that knowledge because we know our loved ones are with Him now. Nancy Guthrie offers a very good thought on this John 11:25.

Those who believe in Jesus know that when physical death comes, as it does for each one of us, our bodies may be buried, but our souls go immediately into the presence of God. We also know that God will not leave our dead bodies in the earth forever. When he returns, he will reunite our soul with our bodies, changing them into glorified, perfected resurrection bodies like his own. While our physical bodies may be on a steady march toward death, in reality we are drawing ever closer into life as it was meant to be, in bodies fit for a new heaven and a new earth, where we will be together forever with the one we love most—Jesus himself.[448]

We read several verses that encouraged us to hold on to Jesus to strengthen our faith. We read a prayer for our hearts to be strengthened so we can serve Jesus while waiting on that day. Paul tells us relief will come when Jesus comes. On that day we will have relief from our pain and from the fallen world. We find strength and encouragement in Paul's words. We wait on the relief!

We read that God has prepared something so wonderful for us it is hard to conceive. The verse in 1 Corinthians speaks of God's eternal plan and love. We find comfort in knowing our loved ones now know what God has prepared. We know we will fully know someday. We are waiting on that day! Record your thoughts and feelings as you reflect on the past week. What speaks to you the most this week?

---

[448] Nancy Guthrie, *Hearing Jesus Speak into Your Sorrow* (Carol Stream, IL: Tyndale, 2009), 127.

DAY 344

Let me hear in the morning of your steadfast love, for in you I trust. Make me know the way I should go, for to you I lift up my soul. (Psalm 143:8, ESV)

When you are grieving, the pain is constant and every day is hard. Every moment is hard. But there are times that are even harder. Of course, holidays and special days are harder. The times you would normally be spending with your loved one are hard. Perhaps you had a special time you talked to your loved one. Nights can seem long and painful. Mornings are hard as well. When you wake up, the reality of being without the one you love hits you; the reality that it is not just a nightmare that you can wake up from in this lifetime.

Although I had studied the Psalms and read them numerous times, as I read this verse written on the bottom of my journal it stood out to me. I began to pray this at night. It seems at times I feel under attack while I sleep, so sleep doesn't come easy. When I do sleep it is often restless or filled with fitful dreams. Psalm 143 is powerful. David was crying out to God because he did not feel or hear Him. David asked God not to hide from him and then utters these words in verse 8. I know that feeling of wanting to hear God and to feel His love surround me. I know the feeling of wanting to know what God wants me to do, and giving it all to Him because I am utterly broken. Although I am sad and the absence of Don is painful, I want to hear from God and to be reminded of His steadfast love. And I want to have the assurance each morning of God's love and of the promise of eternity; to know that the separation is temporary, that we will one day worship God together again in eternity.

Earlier in the Psalms, David says, "I remember the days of old; I meditate on all that you have done; I ponder the work of your hands. I stretch out my hands to you; my soul thirsts for you like a parched land." So as I lay in bed at night, I pray this verse and remember the days of old, meditating on all that God has done for me, and pondering the work of God's hands. Each day when I wake up, I know that day is one day closer to Heaven, and is one more day to serve God here as I wait for that day. Jesus holds our loved ones; His love is steadfast. We trust in Jesus as we wait for that day.

Meditate on this verse. If nights and mornings are hard for you, pray this verse and meditate on what God has done and will do. What better way to fall asleep than to quote Scriptures and pray? If another time is hard, find those verses that help you through the time, but above all, remember that God's love is steadfast and we must trust Him.

DAY 345

Then I heard a voice from heaven say, "Write this: Blessed are the dead who die in the Lord from now on." "Yes," says the Spirit, "they will rest from their labor, for their deeds will follow them." (Revelation 14:13, NIV)

Scholars are varied on how they view "Blessed are the dead who die in the Lord from now on." Many Premillennialists who think the church is raptured prior to the tribulation believe this refers to the saints who die during the tribulation. Many Amilliennialists who think the tribulation started with Christ's resurrection and continues to worsen until His second coming believe this refers to all believers who have died. Some with other approaches believe this refers to those who die under the New Covenant. In the *New American Commentary*, the commentator, a Premilliennialist, states that this verse describes those who attempt to live for Christ during the tribulation. However, he goes on to say, "That these are the ones who are primarily in view in the text is indicated by the words, 'from now on.' Nevertheless, surely the promise to them at that specific time is also applicable to all believers who die in the Lord."[449] The first time I read this verse, I felt that it was about our believing loved ones too. Our believing loved ones were called Home under the New Covenant. Their death, while painful for us, is blessed for them.

Another important truth to take from this verse is "their deeds will follow them." This is a clear statement of continuity of the person, their personality, their work for the Lord, and with that, their relationships. Our loved ones have received rest from this world. Paige Patterson writes:

The rest of Heaven is not to be portrayed as a passive 'cloud potato' existence of inactive slumber but rather as the cessation of the difficulties associated with life on the earth and a new and exciting order with the contributions made to the kingdom of God on earth following as their reward.[450]

No longer do our loved ones have to deal with the difficulties of this world. Our loved ones are blessed because they are with Jesus. We must continue our deeds that will follow us until the day Jesus calls us Home. We will be with Jesus and with our loved ones in Heaven. We will rest from the labors of this world and worship Jesus together for eternity. We are waiting on that day!

Meditate on this verse. What does it mean to you? What are your thoughts on the different views?

---

[449] Paige Patterson, *The New American Commentary: Revelation* (Nashville, TN: B&H, 2012), 295.
[450] Ibid., 25.

DAY 346

While they were still talking about this, Jesus himself stood among them and said to them, "Peace be with you." He said to them, "Why are you troubled, and why do doubts rise in your minds? (Luke 24:36,38, NIV)

I was reading this verse and so much struck me. This is days after the crucifixion. The disciples and followers were in intense pain when Mary Magdalene said she had seen Jesus alive; Peter then said he had seen Jesus alive. The group was together talking about all that Peter and Mary had said when Jesus appeared to them all and said, "Peace be with you." Peace is what we want, isn't it? The peace in knowing that our loved one is with Jesus, that this separation is temporary, that we will be reunited, and there is a continuity in relationships. Peace that God is in control, and despite how we feel right now, that He loves us. Peace that everything will all be okay in eternity. Peace that everything we ever believed is still true and that Jesus has indeed risen. Peace is what we want right now.

The next thing that strikes me is how He picks up with all His disciples just as things had been. Jesus met them in their needs. Beth Moore points out in her study of James how the brother of Jesus, who had not believed that Jesus was the Messiah, needed to see his risen brother and he was one Jesus appeared to. Peter, who had denied Christ, needed to see Him and He appeared to Peter. Mary, who had stayed so faithful, saw Him first.[451]

Greg Laurie wrote on his blog on April 1 that is was a hard day for his family because it was his son Christopher's birthday. And though he knows his son is with Jesus, he misses him greatly. Those special days cut even deeper, but as Greg Laurie points out:

We miss him with all of our hearts and of course think about him every day. But we believe that God will one day restore all things. By that I mean relationships that were cut short this side of heaven will continue later. After Jesus was crucified and then rose three days later, He effectively picked up where he last left off with His disciples. I believe we will do the same with our son.[452]

Jesus picked up where He left off in His relationships. We will do the same. And then we note Jesus asked, "Why do doubts rise in your minds?" He understands, but He wants us to trust Him—even in our doubts. Pray for that peace and assurance. Hold to the promises of our Lord.

Meditate on these verses; how do they speak to you? What peace do you need?

---

[451] Beth Moore, *James Mercy Triumphs* (Nashville, TN: Lifeway 2012), video.

[452] Greg Laurie, blog.greglaurie.com/April 2, 2013. Used by permission from Harvest Ministries with Greg Laurie, PO Box 4000, Riverside, CA 92514.

DAY 347

The Lord, the Mighty One, is God, and he has spoken; he has summoned all humanity from where the sun rises to where it sets. Then let the heavens proclaim his justice, for God himself will be the judge. Interlude Then call on me when you are in trouble, and I will rescue you, and you will give me glory. (Psalm 50:1,6,15, NLT)

Psalm 50 is about God's sovereignty. God assures us He is in control. Our rescue may be in Heaven, but He is in control and His people are in His care. In his book *It's Not About Me*, Max Lucado writes about a couple who were missionaries. One day while celebrating their anniversary, they were taken hostage by militants and in a barrage of gunfire she was shot and he was killed. It does not seem fair, does it? Max asks the question and then answers it: God is sovereign. The missionaries glorified God in their life and death. Lucado recounts his father's painful struggle with ALS and his faithfulness to God through the pain of the horrible disease. He talked about how his Dad's sickness glorified God. As I read his words I thought of my own dad as he lay in the hospital witnessing for Christ with his last breath and how God was glorified in his sickness. Max gives an account of a friend who had cancer and was dying. Friends had told this friend that if his faith was strong enough, he would be healed. Max told him, "Maybe it's not about you. Your hospital room is a showcase for your Maker. Your faith in the face of suffering cranks up the volume of God's song." He goes on to say his friend was relieved. "Seeing his sickness in the scope of God's sovereign plan gave his condition a sense of dignity. He was a missionary in the cancer ward."[453]

I don't know why bad things happen. I don't pretend to understand. But I do believe God is sovereign. If we hold to an eternal plan, and if we hold to the fact this life is not all there is, then we can be comforted. It is not about me; it is not about this brief time on Earth. It is the plan of the ages and God's glory that will bring all His followers into eternity to be with Him forever. It is about God. Whatever your circumstance, however painful life is, there is a day when everything will be okay. We will be with Jesus; we will see how our lives and how history played out. We will know how our suffering and our loved one's suffering glorified God and furthered His kingdom. For now we have to trust God. He is God; He is sovereign. For now we trust that we will be reunited with our loved ones and worship God in eternity. We are waiting on that day!

Read all of Psalm 50. What are your thoughts on the chapter and on the selected verses? What are your thoughts on Max Lucado's words?

---

[453] Max Lucado, *It's Not About Me* (Nashville, TN: Nelson, 2004), 126.

DAY 348

Lord, hear my prayer, listen to my cry for mercy; in your faithfulness and righteousness come to my relief. The enemy pursues me, he crushes me to the ground; he makes me dwell in the darkness like those long dead. So my spirit grows faint within me; my heart within me is dismayed. I remember the days of long ago; I meditate on all your works and consider what your hands have done. I spread out my hands to you; I thirst for you like a parched land. (Psalm 143:1,3-6, NIV)

Read all of Psalm 143. The enemy in our case is death and the spiritual warfare that ensues with death. Not only are we overcome with the pain of being separated from our loved ones, God can seem far away. And that is when the enemy strikes. Our spirit grows faint within us. What does David do? He remembers the days of long ago; he meditates on all God's works and considers what God's hands have done. Then David spreads out his hands to God and says, "I thirst for you like a parched land." Our desire to feel God right now is like thirsting in a parched land. God is the only one who can give us the assurances and the comfort that we so desperately need.

In the next verse, David cries out, "Answer me quickly, Lord; my spirit fails." He begs God, "Do not hide your face from me or I will go down to the pit." Do you feel like God is hiding His face from you? I did. This is where we call out to God, like we are thirsting in a parched land. There is no way around the pain of someone we love being taken away from us. We have no idea how long we will be separated and their absence is everywhere. There is hope, though. I can handle the pain if I know everything will be okay in the end. And in this case, the ending is not even an ending; eternal life with Jesus is just the beginning. We must rely on God even when you don't feel Him. Like David, we spend time with God. David spread his hands out to God. But note what else he did: David remembered the days of long ago. David meditated on God's work. Chris Tiegreen writes, "If we once were convinced of God's goodness, then we ought to remain convinced through difficult times. The best way to do that is to remember.... Choose to remember what God did in the past."[454]

When the sorrow overwhelms you, remembering your blessings can be difficult. But in those times of sorrow, remembering the blessings are even more important. The same God who has always been there for us no matter how difficult life became is with us now. So we cry out to God and we continually remember the works of His hands; we remember His steadfast love.

Meditate on the verses. Journal the works of God's hands in your past.

---

[454] Chris Tiegreen, *The One Year Experiencing God's Presence Devotional* (Carol Stream, IL: Tyndale, 2011), June 26.

DAY 349

Those who have insight will shine brightly like the brightness of the expanse of heaven, and those who lead the many to righteousness, like the stars forever and ever. (Daniel 12:3, NASB)

In the first two verses of Daniel 12, Daniel is given a description of the last days. I encourage you to read the whole chapter. Verse two is a clear reference to the bodily resurrection. Verse three is a description of those who are righteous. Daniel has seen amazing visions, many which came true with amazing accuracy and many that are yet to be fulfilled. We know that because the first ones have been fulfilled, we can have confidence that the rest of Daniel's prophecies will be fulfilled just as accurately. In the book of Revelation, John had amazing visions which can be connected to Daniel. Together the two books give us an awesome glimpse of what the future holds. This verse in Daniel is a clear statement of how important what we do on Earth is for eternity. We also have a clear indication of God's eternal plan. Daniel had these visions long before they took place, and some of his visions are yet to happen. Many of those yet to happen were seen by John as well.

Today's verse is so important to all of us, especially as we grieve. This verse reaffirms everlasting life. Our loved ones are in Heaven; they live now because they have everlasting life. This verse also reaffirms the continuity of life from here to Heaven. Daniel is being told about eternal rewards, he is being told that what we do here on Earth follows us into eternity. If what we do here on Earth follows us, there is certainly continuity. Daniel also helps us to remember that we must continue to work to serve God even in our grief. Even when you have no strength to move, you can pray for others. When you are interceding, you are serving; you are helping to lead others to our Lord. Chris Tiegreen writes:

Righteousness is a gift from a holy heaven to an infected race. It comes from outside of ourselves, available only through faith in its Giver. Those who are wise will tell others about this gift. Those who want to shine will know the Source of light and will be completely preoccupied with Him. [455]

We make investments in eternity when we seek God and obey Him. Our loved ones have entered into His presence; they are shining now. While we wait on that day, we can look for ways to serve God—even in our grief. We have a promise from the Ancient of Days.

Meditate on these verses. How are you investing in eternity?

---

[455]   Chris Tiegreen, *The One Year Walk With God Devotional* (Carol Stream, IL: Tyndale, 2004), Location 2164.

DAY 350 REFLECTION

As you read over the last week, what brings you comfort? We read the psalmist cries out to God for the morning to bring word of His steadfast love. We read the powerful words in Revelation that a voice from Heaven tells John to write these words, "Blessed are the dead who die in the Lord from now on." As I read those words, they resonate with me. Our loved ones are blessed now because they are with Jesus. We also read in that same verse that our deeds will follow us, a clear statement of continuity.

We read that Jesus tells His disciples, "Peace be with you," and asks why doubts are troubling them. When we read this in context we see the disciples were pretty much where we are in grieving, and we find comfort in Jesus' words. Peace is what we crave. We read Greg Laurie's thoughts that just as Jesus picked up life with His disciples; we will pick up where we left off with our loved ones. We are waiting on that day!

We read two powerful Psalms. We see a clear statement of God's sovereignty. God has an eternal plan; He is sovereign. We must hold to that as David did. We read David's heartfelt plea as he is surrounded by the enemy. We are surrounded by the enemy now. We are encouraged to seek God—to thirst for God. We must trust and rely on Him as we consider all He has done for us.

And, finally, we read a clear reference to the resurrection in Daniel. We read a clear reference to the continuity of life. And we are encouraged to invest in eternity as we wait for the day of our Lord and the reunion with our loved ones. We are waiting on that day! Record your thoughts and feelings as you read back over the last week. What seems to speak to you most this week?

DAY 351

For I know whom I have believed and I am convinced that He is able to guard what I have entrusted to Him until that day. Retain the standard of sound words which you have heard from me, in the faith and love which are in Christ Jesus. (2 Timothy 1:12-13, NASB)

I read several commentaries on these verses because as I read them, I was struck by Paul's resolve. We know "that day" is the day Jesus will come back. We can say we know what we believe, but Paul takes it a step further and says, "I know whom I have believed in." And because he does, Paul is convinced that Jesus will guard what Paul has entrusted to Him until that day. Paul is in prison, and he is reminding Timothy of God's eternal plan and encouraging him. Paul has suffered through a lot, but can still say, "I am convinced because I know whom I believe in."

One commentator pointed out that Paul had entrusted everything to God that was precious to him. And while reading this, I thought of how Don and I had entrusted our marriage and our children to Him. My parents had entrusted our family to God. Our family and relationships are precious to us and to Christ. We entrust our lives to Jesus. So like Paul, we know whom we believe in and we know God is able to guard that which we have entrusted to Him. If you have a child that you are grieving this temporary separation from, you can trust God with your child. Whomever you are grieving at this moment in time, you can trust that God has your loved one. I can trust that God has Don and Dad. We can all know that our believing loved ones are with our Savior, and we can be convinced that God will guard those we have entrusted to Him until that day.

Of course, our loved ones are God's anyway. He loves them even more than we do. But God also knows how much we love them. God knows we have entrusted that relationship to Him. Our God is in control. We know God and we know He will guard all we have entrusted to Him until that day.

What is that day? That day is the day we are all looking forward to, that day we are with Jesus in Heaven forever. And on that day we will all be reunited with our loved ones in the most perfect place. We will see fully; we realize the eternal plan and how everything fits together. In the meantime, as Paul says, "We retain the standard of sound words which we know are from God." Paul reminds Timothy that we hear these words in faith and love, which are in Christ Jesus. When the pain encompasses you, remind yourself that God is able to guard that which we have entrusted to Him until that day. We look forward to that day, we hold to God until that day, we stay in the Word, and we stay convinced because we know Him. We are waiting on that day!

Meditate on these verses. What have you entrusted to God?

DAY 352

As for you, go your way till the end. You will rest, and then at the end of the days you will rise to receive your allotted inheritance. (Daniel 12:13, NIV)

Daniel had just been given amazing prophecies, and he was understandably confused. Daniel 12:8 says, "I heard but I did not understand. So I asked, 'My lord, what will the outcome of all this be?'" The response in verse 9 was, "Go your way, Daniel, because the words are rolled up and sealed until the time of the end." Daniel was highly esteemed, and God was basically telling Him to keep doing what he was doing, then he would rest, but at the end of the days he would rise to receive his allotted inheritance. "The end of the days" is the bodily resurrection when Jesus returns. Daniel didn't have to understand all the visions right then; he couldn't. But he could continue to obey and follow God. On that day of resurrection, Daniel would rise and receive his allotted inheritance—his rewards. This is a clear statement of continuity, of the resurrection, and of rewards.

Randy Alcorn writes, "Inheritance typically involves not just money but also land, a place lived on and managed by human beings. After our bodily resurrection, we will receive a physical inheritance. The New Earth is the ultimate Promised Land, the eternal Holy Land in which all God's people will dwell."[456] And, "What's allotted to Daniel will be his, not mine or yours."[457]

Our loved ones have completed their days, and although we don't understand why their days have to be so short to us, we know they are with our Lord and we trust Him. We know we, too, will be with Jesus when He calls us Home. As believers, we will all be a part of the bodily resurrection. We know there is continuity—that we will be ourselves; we will have to be in order to receive our inheritance. I don't know everything our inheritance will include, but we know for sure we inherit eternal life. We can also make assumptions based on what we else we know. I know that everything God has given me is good. He has blessed us beyond measure. Besides salvation, the most precious treasure that God has given me is my family. The love for each other and for God has always been what our family wanted most. God has given you your loved one and your relationship with those you love. We can trust that whatever God has planned for us in eternity is wonderful. Our inheritance most likely will include those things that God has already given us that He delights in. We will know someday. For now, like Daniel, we seek to serve God until He calls us Home. We are waiting on that day!

Meditate on this verse. What are your thoughts on your inheritance?

---

[456] Randy Alcorn, *Heaven* (Carol Stream, IL: Tyndale House, 2004), 211.
[457] Ibid., 370.

DAY 353

All whose names have not been written in the Lamb's book of life, the Lamb who was slain from the creation of the world. This calls for patient endurance and faithfulness on the part of God's people. (Revelation 13:8b,10b, NIV)

Most authors who are futurists see this verse as referring to the tribulation. Those whose names are not written in the Lamb's Book of Life will worship the beast. Those who are here, and whose names are written in the Book of Life, must be patient and endure faithfully because they will be persecuted, many unto death. Authors who take different approaches interpret this verse in many different ways. Regardless of what approach you hold, I think one thing for those of us who are grieving to focus on are the words "before the creation of the world." The eternal plan for the Lamb to be slain, for people to be saved, and for all history to come to a climatic end was all known before the creation of the world. Paige Patterson writes, "The Book of Life is related then to the Lamb, whose program of death and resurrection on behalf of the objects of his love was known before the actual creation of the world. The text then confirms a plan and a purpose of God in all these things."[458]

Although the last part of verse 10 is most likely talking about those going through the tribulation, endurance and faithfulness are stressed throughout the Scriptures. So I think for us to hold to this verse in our time of sorrow and grieving is applicable. We are going through the most difficult time of our lives. The pain and sorrow are relentless. Doubt and spiritual warfare threaten us. What must we do? Patiently endure and be faithful. We have to trust that God is in control—that He has an eternal plan. We trust that what we have always believed is true. We trust that our believing loved ones are safely with our Lord and we will be reunited with them. Paige Patterson writes on these verses:

In any age two things essential for Christ's followers in persecution, and even martyrdom, are endurance coupled with faith. Faith in the purposes and promises of God makes endurance possible. Endurance, on the other hand, is the sure, visible outworking of the inner faith that provided the impetus for obedience to God even under intractable circumstances.[459]

Our circumstances right now are overwhelming painful. But we will hold to the promises of our Lord while we are waiting on that day.

Meditate on these verses and the quotes. Can you see the connection with the eternal plan and the faithfulness and endurance we need now?

---

[458] Paige Patterson, *The New American Commentary: Revelation* (Nashville, TN: B&H, 2012), 278.
[459] Ibid., 279.

DAY 354

The LORD God planted a garden toward the east, in Eden. (Genesis 2:8b, NASB)

Then he showed me a river of the water of life, clear as crystal, coming from the throne of God and of the Lamb. (Revelation 22:1, NASB)

I have read many authors who point out that the Bible begins with the Garden of Eden and ends with The New Garden, the New Jerusalem coming down as the New Heaven and The New Earth begin. The Bible begins with Paradise being lost because of sin, but it ends with Paradise regained in the New Earth. In *In Light of Eternity*, Randy Alcorn writes: "The Bible begins with God casting men out of the garden and ends with God welcoming them into a garden city.... Man's tears in Genesis 3 are wiped away by God in Revelation 21. Paradise Lost becomes Paradise Regained. More than that—Paradise Magnified."[460]

Other authors had similar thoughts. We have the Bible that unfolds God's eternal plan and we see it start to finish, or rather start to a new beginning. We can easily get wrapped up in this world as the whole of our life. But we who are grieving become even more aware of the reality that this life is not all there is. We can find comfort in looking forward to the restoration of all things. We can understand that although we hurt now, this life is temporary.

One day all will be made right. We have an eternity to explore the Paradise God has planned for us. Our loved ones wait now with our Lord in Heaven; they are already in Paradise but more is yet to come. We will all be together as we behold the New Jerusalem coming down from Heaven as we begin the New Heaven and the New Earth. Pain and sorrow are always present in grief, but because we have the promises of God for the restoration of all things, we know that someday there will be no more pain and sorrow. We know we will be reunited with those we love. We know we will see our Savior and the Paradise He has planned since before the beginning of the world. Holding on to those promises is what gives us comfort and hope. We will one day see the Paradise ourselves. Where Revelation ends, life starts on the New Heavens and the New Earth. We can read it throughout the entire Bible; we know it is God's eternal plan. We are waiting on that day!

Read Genesis 2 and Revelation 21-22. What are your thoughts on the beginning and the end of the Bible? How does seeing the whole picture reinforce the eternal plan?

---

[460] Randy Alcorn, *In Light of Eternity* (Colorado springs, CO: Waterbrook, 1999), 149.

DAY 355

This is eternal life, that they may know You, the only true God, and Jesus Christ whom You have sent. (John 17:3, NASB)

Grief is ongoing as you take one day at a time. As I constantly seek to be with God, He seems to bring different things in my path. There are times I read one author, and if that author quotes another I will look the author up they quote and read his or her works. But sometimes I "stumble" upon authors. Through one of those "stumbles" I discovered Greg Laurie's book and then his website "Harvest Time," and then I began to receive his devotionals. I also received his wife Cathe's blogs from time to time.

One day as I was working on this book and crying with my own pain, I received a blog that had some very powerful thoughts I am sharing here. Cathe was talking about attending a funeral of a dear friend's five-year-old child. These are some of the words in her blog:

I know the Scriptures; I do not have any doubt Lenya is alive and we will see her again. But all I could think at that moment was: No, no, no.... This is so wrong, so not fair. This beautiful family, this godly couple, this child so adorable, full of energy and delightful personality, shouldn't have to go through this. Some things cannot be explained to satisfy grief. Amen. We must learn to live in this fallen world through difficult and frightening circumstances. Even Jesus' followers are not exempt from all of the tragic entanglements of its fallenness. As I write this, I'm transported back to many painful and empty places I walked in my own unexpected journey through grief. How hard are all those "firsts" that mark such a loss. The first week, the first month, the first trip to the grocery store, crying in the aisles like a baby as I passed by his favorite foods. That first Mother's Day, Father's Day, Fourth of July... and for me one of the most painful: standing beside Christopher's young wife, Brittany, as she gave birth to his daughter Lucy. We cry out, "Why did you take them, so young, so talented, so needed, so irreplaceable? Why them... not me?" We can only wait for heaven's answer one day, and meanwhile grip tightly onto God's promises like a drowning person—because without them, without Him, we will drown. As there is no going back, only forward, what do we do now with this new reality? I heard the story of a certain man who, after the death of his beloved wife, went to his minister with the question, "What does God have left for me now that she is gone?" To this the minister quietly and firmly replied, "To know and love God still."[461]

As I read her words, I was moved to tears. How true that we hold to Jesus or we will drown. How true that we continue to know and love God as we have before. We hold to Jesus as we wait on that day.

Meditate on the verse and Cathe's heartfelt blog; how do they speak to you?

---

[461] Cathe Laurie, www.harvest.org/virtue/cathes-notes.html?p=8711.

DAY 356

He will wipe every tear from their eyes. There will be no more death' or mourning or crying or pain, for the old order of things has passed away." He who was seated on the throne said, "I am making everything new!" Then he said, "Write this down, for these words are trustworthy and true. (Revelation 21:4-5, NIV)

Quoting Scriptures as I fall asleep helps me. One night about sixteen months after Don went Home, I was lying in bed crying and quoting Scriptures to fall asleep. As I quoted this much loved verse, something stuck out to me that had not before. I have often found comfort in the words, "no more death." Death will be over, the last enemy to be conquered. And I have comfort in God wiping away my tears. But for some reason as I quoted this passage this particular evening, it hit me just how much God does see our mourning and how deeply He must care that we mourn. God chose the word *mourn* along with death, crying, and pain. We cry and have pain over many things; certainly death is one of those. But mourning is most closely associated with death. God knows how much we love our loved ones. He is the one who gave us those wonderful relationships to begin with. So for God to specifically say there will be no more mourning underscores how He sees and feels that deep loss with us. I find comfort in the fact that God does understand how hard separation is for us.

Some people seem to think that as Christians, knowing that our loved ones are in Heaven should allow us to rejoice for them and just move on. And we do rejoice that they are with our Lord. However, even finding comfort in knowing our loved ones are in Heaven and rejoicing does not take the pain away from not having them with us. Knowing does not stop you from missing your loved one—from aching to be with the one you love. We don't know how long it will be before we are with our loved ones again. So as I quoted this verse in the dark, it seemed profound to realize that God knows all of that. God knows that I am thankful for all the days He gave me with Dad and Don. God knows I find comfort in Don and Dad being with Him. God knows I long for the day I will be with them again. God also knows I hurt deeply at them not being here so much so He includes mourning in His "no more" list.

John had experienced his share of mourning and pain. John was exiled and alone. His brother had been the first disciple martyred. John had lived through or would live through all the disciples, his closest friends, being killed. John needed to hear that there would be no more death and mourning, just like we do. God will wipe away every tear and He will abolish death and mourning. We will be with Him and our loved ones on the New Earth; that, my friend, is trustworthy and true. I am waiting on that day!

Meditate on these verses. Does seeing the word *mourning* listed speak to you?

DAY 357 REFLECTION

As you read over the last week, what seems to speak to you? We read that Paul writes, "I know whom I have believed and He is able to keep that which we have entrusted to Him." We are reminded that we have entrusted our loved ones to God. God has our loved ones and we can trust Him.

We read the words to Daniel that he would live his days, and at the end of them he would receive his inheritance. These amazing words to a faithful servant of God are a clear statement of continuity and the resurrection, and are a clear statement of the investment in eternity that encourages us to serve God until He calls us Home. In Revelation, we read of the Book of Life and the words that speak of the eternal plan. We also are reminded that we must pray for faithful endurance as we are waiting. As we read verses that remind us of the eternal plan and of the suffering on this fallen world, we know there is more. In the *New American Commentary of Revelation* Paige Patterson writes:

But this underscores what the Scriptures teach, namely, that the life of this earth is transitory and unpredictable, but God's children will someday experience a life that is bound by neither the transitory nor the unpredictable. And this life is the only life whose possession ultimately matters.[462]

We read that the Bible begins with the Garden of Eden and ends with the New Garden of Eden and the New Jerusalem. These verses are an awesome picture of the eternal plan and the restoration of all things.

We read how God sent us His Son that we might have eternal life, and we are reminded of His faithfulness. We must trust God even in our pain. Cathe Laurie's heartfelt words can resonate with all of us. And, finally, we read the amazing words again in Revelation that there will be no more death and no more mourning, and we heard the awesome promise that this statement is trustworthy and true. We are waiting on that day! Record your thoughts and feelings as you reflect over the week. What does God seem to be laying on your heart this week?

---

[462] Paige Patterson, *The New American Commentary: Revelation* (Nashville, TN: B&H, 2012), 278.

DAY 358

After you have suffered for a little while, the God of all grace, who called you to His eternal glory in Christ, will Himself perfect, confirm, strengthen and establish you. To Him be dominion forever and ever. Amen. (1 Peter 5:10-11, NASB)

Peter was encouraging believers. He told them in the previous chapter, "The end of all things is near." Peter was reminding his fellow believers that it is not just about this Earth. God has called them to eternal glory in Christ. We may suffer here and it may seem endless at times, but this life is not long when compared to the eternal life we have been promised. You and I are suffering now and there are times when the pain seems endless. Perhaps you have thought, "I can't do another day of this." God has called us to an eternal glory and someday we will enter into that glory just as our loved ones have. For now, we remind ourselves that no matter how long the suffering is here, compared to eternity it will not be that long. Christ will perfect us and establish us with Him, just as He has our believing loved ones.

Peter knew pain and suffering; he knew loss. Peter knew he would die soon, but he also knew that he had the promise of Christ's eternal glory. Peter knew that all the suffering would be worthwhile. He knew that the time here would seem like a "little while" compared to eternity. I know that concept might be hard to fathom; it is for me. I keep thinking, "How long, Lord?" How long before you come back and make everything perfect? How long before we are reunited with our loved ones? How long before we see You, Jesus?

When you go through surgery, the pain afterward can be intense and you are impatient to be restored. But you also know that you will be healed. Usually, the recuperation time seems long as you are going through it, but in retrospect, compared to the rest of your life, the time is short. Someday, from eternity we will see how short this time of separation and sorrow was, even though it certainly doesn't feel like it right now. Peter knew this life would not be long as he encouraged other believers. Randy Alcorn writes:

Devastation and tragedy feel just as real for those with faith as they do for those who have none. But knowledge that others have suffered and learned to trust God anyway gives the faithful strength to keep going. Because they do not place their hope for health and abundance and secure relationships in this life but in an eternal life to come, believers' hope remains firm regardless of what happens.[463]

Reflect on the verses. How can you hold to the "little while," even though it seems endless?

---

[463] Randy Alcorn, *90 Days of God's Goodness* (Colorado Springs, CO: Multnomah, 2011), 19.

DAY 359

So do not fear, for I am with you; do not be dismayed, for I am your God. I will strengthen you and help you. I will uphold you with my righteous right hand. For I am the LORD, your God, who takes hold of your right hand and says to you, Do not fear; I will help you. (Isaiah 41:10,13, NIV)

Grief brings dismay and anxiety. When your world falls apart and God seems far away, your world can be very scary. But God is not far away. God tells us He is with us, His right hand holds us. Thinking of God holding my hand with His hand is comforting, and although there are many times I have wondered where He was, I come back to knowing God is with me. God has Don and Dad with Him in Heaven, they are more than okay. God has _____. God holds me, even if I don't always feel Him, just as God has you even, though you may not feel Him. God is sovereign; He has an eternal plan and His plan will not be thwarted. I have to trust God despite how I feel and what my circumstances look like. God will lead us into eternity and the wonderful eternal life He has planned for us. We just have to trust Him now.

When my mother was young, her mother had gone Home to be with the Lord suddenly. Shortly afterward, her father contracted tuberculosis and was sick. My mother was alone with her sick Dad and a terrible storm came up. She was still grieving the loss of her mother, whom she was very close to, and was now grieving the sickness of her Dad, whom she was also very close to. As the storm pounded the windows and Mother's fear increased, she heard a voice say, "Do not be afraid, for God will take care of you." I never tire of hearing Mom tell of that encounter. And I never saw my mother afraid in a storm. My mother knew no matter what was going on outside she would be okay. Her faith sustained her.

Most of us don't get the opportunity to hear an audible voice, but God still speaks to us in ways that let us know He is with us. During grief, hearing God seems harder though. And for me, when I do think I hear Him, if I am not careful, I will doubt that what I heard or felt was God. I have to keep reminding myself that God holds my hand, He is with me, and I trust Him. Hold to the faith you know is real, despite how things feel at times. God holds our loved ones next to Him now; they finally do hear Him and see Him. We trust God is with us even now, holding our hands, as we serve Him and wait on that day when we finally see Him. We are waiting on that day!

Meditate on this verse. What are your thoughts and feelings? When you truly take time to reflect on God holding you with His hands, what are your thoughts?

DAY 360

And if our hope in Christ is only for this life, we are more to be pitied than anyone in the world. (1 Corinthians 15:19, NLT)

I love 1 Corinthians 15:19 and as I have said before, I quote it often. We have to hold to this verse as we grieve; otherwise, we are consumed by the grief. Although the grief is ever-present and can be consuming, we have this hope. We have the hope of knowing that this life in the fallen world is not all there is.

God has blessed us tremendously with the loved ones He gave us, even if for a short time here. We have to remember this life is not all there is. In *90 Days of God's Goodness*, Randy Alcorn writes:

Resurrection, and what it means to live forever in the presence of our God, is—or should be—what we live for.... The resurrection means the best parts will carry over to the next, with none of the bad.... Without this eternal perspective, we assume that people that die young, who have handicaps, who suffer poor health, who don't get married, who don't have children, or who don't have this or that will miss out on the best life has to offer. But the theology underlying those assumptions presumes that our present Earth, bodies cultures, relationships and lives are all there is—or that they will somehow overshadow or negate those of the New Earth. The stronger our concept of God and Heaven, the more we understand how Heaven will bring far more compensation for our present sufferings.[464]

The day-to-day process of being without those we love is very painful. The pain can center our attention on the moment. While nothing takes away the pain, knowing that the suffering is temporary because we have an eternity waiting for us can bring us comfort. We hold to the eternal truth in this verse: that our true hope in Christ is not just for this life. This truth allows us to think eternally, and not just focus on the pain and the absence of our loved ones.

There is a coming day when these bodies will be resurrected and we will live forever on the New Earth. Our hope in Christ is a promise that the best is yet to come. The wonderful memories and times we had with our loved ones are glimpses of what we will have in eternity. We look forward to the day when this hope is realized. Our hope in Christ is not just for this life. Because of this hope we know that we will live with Christ forever. We know we will be reunited with our believing loved ones. We are waiting on that day!

Reflect on this verse and the quote by Randy Alcorn. What are your thoughts and feelings?

---

[464] Randy Alcorn, *90 Days of God's Goodness* (Colorado Springs, CO: Multnomah, 2011), 129.

DAY 361

Let us hold unswervingly to the hope we profess, for he who promised is faithful. (Hebrews 10:23, NIV)

I quote this verse in Hebrews as I go to sleep and during the night. Holding on to the hope that we profess is important. Paul writes in Ephesians 1:18, "I pray also that the eyes of your heart may be enlightened in order that you may know the hope to which he has called you." "Hope has an objective quality of certainty. It is the assurance of eternal life guaranteed by the present possession of the Holy Spirit."[465] Our hope is based on our faith, our certainty of the assurance of eternal life. God is faithful and we must hold to that hope even when everything around us seems hopeless.

As believers, our eternity is guaranteed. Our believing loved ones are with Jesus now as we read this; they are with Him in glory. We have the most difficult tasking of being here without our loved ones. But we are only temporarily separated from them. Because we have the hope of eternal life, the promise of eternal life, the certainty of eternal life we will enter into Jesus' presence and be with Him and our loved ones forever. Randy Alcorn writes:

Hope is a much stronger word in the Bible than it is for most of us today. The hope of deliverance and resurrection is based solidly on the promise of an almighty truth-telling, covenant-keeping God who never fails and is never thwarted, who *always* keeps his promises. Whenever we hope for what God has promised, we don't wish for a possibility; we anticipate a certainty.... Hope points to the light at the end of life's tunnel. It not only makes the tunnel endurable, it fills the heart with anticipation of what's at the other end; a world alive, fresh, beautiful and without pain, suffering, or war. A world without disease, without accident, without tragedy. A world without dictators or madmen, a world ruled by the only One worthy of ruling.[466]

The hope that we profess is what we hold to now. Pain and sorrow can sidetrack us, but we must hold unswervingly to the eternal hope. God is faithful, and He has promised eternal life for those who believe. Despite what you feel, despite the pain, God is faithful. We will someday see Jesus and realize fully the hope that we have professed and that we hold to now. And on the day we see Jesus, everything will make sense; there will be no more pain or sorrow. We will be with Jesus. We will be reunited with our loved ones and we will be in Paradise. We are waiting on that day!

Say this verse out loud and meditate on the meaning of hope.

---

[465] *NIV Study Bible*, Kenneth Barker, Ed. (Grand Rapids, MI: Zondervan, 1985), 1792.

[466] Randy Alcorn, *90 Days of God's Goodness* (Colorado Springs, CO: Multnomah, 2011), 269.

DAY 362

And He will send forth His angels with a great trumpet and they will gather together His elect from the four winds, from one end of the sky to the other. (Matthew 24:31, NASB)

For the Lord Himself will descend from heaven with a shout, with the voice of the archangel and with the trumpet of God, and the dead in Christ will rise first. (1 Thessalonians 4:16, NASB)

I heard Chris Tomlin's song "I will Rise" shortly after Dad went Home. This beautiful song always brings tears to my eyes. I could picture Dad as we watched him take his last breath in the hospital and imagine him rising to Heaven to be with Jesus, no more pain, no more struggling to breathe. After God called Don Home, I was listening to the song again and realized even more what the words meant. The song speaks to all of us. There is a day we will hear His call.

> And I will rise when He calls my name
> No more sorrow, no more pain
> I will rise on eagles' wings
> Before my God fall on my knees
> And rise
> I will rise
>
> There's a day that's drawing near
> When this darkness breaks to light
> And the shadows disappear
> And my faith shall be my eyes
>
> Jesus has overcome
> And the grave is overwhelmed
> The victory is won
> He is risen from the dead[467]

We will see Jesus. The victory is won. Jesus defeated death and the grave is overwhelmed. The song is powerful because the message is powerful. Our loved ones heard their name called and they are with Jesus. We will someday hear that call. The darkness will break to light and we shall rise to see Jesus. We will fall on our knees at His majesty. We have an eternity to worship Jesus. Our loved ones just got there before us. We are waiting on that day!

Read and listen to the powerful words of this song. Meditate on the verse.

---

[467] Chris Tomlin, "*I Will Rise*," *Hello Love*, Sparrow, 2006.

DAY 363

But Stephen, full of the Holy Spirit, gazed steadily into heaven and saw the glory of God, and he saw Jesus standing in the place of honor at God's right hand. And he told them, "Look, I see the heavens opened and the Son of Man standing in the place of honor at God's right hand!" As they stoned him, Stephen prayed, "Lord Jesus, receive my spirit." (Acts 7:55-56,59, NLT)

These verses are so powerful to read and to try to envision. Our loved ones saw Heaven open and saw the glory of God. They saw Jesus standing at God's right hand. This alone can bring comfort. But as pointed out earlier, we still grieve. Even those standing near Stephen and heard his exclamation grieved the loss of their friend's presence with them. We know it is okay to grieve, but we have hope and so our grieving is different. How? The difference does not mean there is less pain. The difference means we know this life is not all there is. The difference means we know where our loved ones are and we know we will be reunited with them someday. I think again of Chris Tomlin's song "I Will Rise." He sings, "I will rise when He calls my name."[468] We will have a bodily resurrection and rise when Jesus comes back. But we will also rise to meet Jesus when He calls our name, whenever that may be. When our days are fulfilled on this Earth, Jesus calls us Home. Although the time we have our loved ones with us is never enough for us here, it is within the time-frame of God.

Some things we will not understand this side of eternity. Why was Stephen stoned and James martyred so early in their ministry? Their purpose was fulfilled. Stephen saw Heaven open and Jesus stand to meet him. We grieve, and understandably so; but our loved ones were received into God's presence. The heavenly realm is so hard to wrap our brains around, but we need to meditate on this truth and picture our own loved ones in Jesus' presence.

We found a picture of Dad speaking at a church in the background on the wall was Jesus with His arms outstretched. The way Dad was standing in the picture looked like he was standing in Jesus' arms. I had never noticed that until after Dad went Home. But when Dad went Home he was truly in Jesus' presence. My friend Terry found comfort in songs when her precious daughter, Beth, was taken Home. She sent me a song on YouTube. One of the pictures in the song was Jesus hugging a man, welcoming him Home. I wept as I tried to imagine Don, and how amazing his Homegoing was for him. Our loved ones saw Heaven open up and Jesus met them. From the smallest baby to the oldest parent, from the most peaceful departing to the most violent, Jesus met our loved ones. Jesus will meet us on the day He calls us Home.

Meditate on these verses. Try to imagine Jesus meeting your loved one.

---

[468] Chris Tomlin, "I Will Rise," Hello Love, Sparrow, 2006.

DAY 364 REFLECTION

As you read over the last week, what brings you comfort? We read Peter encouraging believers, reminding them that they will suffer; but God's grace will give them strength and establish them as He calls them to eternal life. We read the comforting words that God holds us in His hands. God says, "Do not fear." We know we can trust God to see us through and call us Home.

We read again that our hope in Christ is not just for this life—words we need to remember to keep an eternal perspective. Randy Alcorn reminds us that, "Heaven will bring far more compensation for our present suffering." This life is not all there is. We have an eternity to look forward to being with our loved ones. We read that we must hold unswervingly to the hope we profess. We know our hope is a certainty based on the promises of God.

We read the beautiful and amazing words that Jesus will descend on the clouds and call His people to Him. We read the verses in Acts telling us that Stephen saw the Heavens open, and Jesus was standing to greet him. We know that whether we are here when Jesus descends on the clouds to call us Home, or whether Jesus calls our name and we go Home as our loved ones did, Jesus will greet us. What an awesome picture to think of Jesus greeting our loved ones from the youngest to the oldest.

I did not plan the devotionals this way, but this is our last reflection—with one day left over. Fittingly, the last devotional is one that brings us hope for eternity and Jesus' return. The angel said to me, "These words are trustworthy and true." (Revelation 22:6a, NIV) The angel tells John several times that the Words are true. We believe them and we hold to those words.

The last few pages are a poem written by our friend Dillon Enderby. He wrote the poem in honor of Don and me on our first anniversary apart. The words are a balm to my spirit as I read them. The words resonate with me and bring me comfort each time I read them; to me the words had to be inspired by God. I hope you find comfort in them as well. Record your thoughts and feelings of the last week. There is nothing magical about getting through the first year of grief. The pain still continues and you still miss the one you love. But you do have hope; hope that rests in the knowledge that you will be together again with your loved one. You know that you will have an eternity to worship Jesus with your loved one. We are waiting on that day as we walk Home together. As you reflect, what is God laying on your heart now?

DAY 365

He who was seated on the throne said, "I am making everything new!" Then He said, "Write this down for these words are trustworthy and true" (Revelation 21:5, NIV)

Look, I am coming soon! My reward is with me, and I will give to each person according to what they have done. I am the Alpha and the Omega, the First and the Last, the Beginning and the End. He who testifies to these things says, "Yes, I am coming soon." Amen. Come, Lord Jesus. The grace of the Lord Jesus be with God's people. Amen. (Revelation 22:12-13,20-21, NIV)

I think these are great verses to end the year of devotions. When I wrote these last verses, it had been eighteen months since Don went Home; and nearly three and half years since Dad went Home. Today, after an additional 20 months of praying, editing and reworks, I am close to finishing. I grieve deeply. I miss Dad and Don more than words can describe. Each day I hurt. When I go to bed at night, I am keenly aware of Don's absence, and when I wake in the morning I feel his side of the bed as if somehow Don will be there. And every moment is filled with memories of our wonderful life. At every family meal, both men are deeply missed. Every day we check on Mom, Dad's presence is missing. I am thankful that God started my life with a godly father. I am thankful that God gave me a godly husband, and for the richly blessed life God gave us. I am blessed beyond measure. I hurt now beyond measure. But I know there will be a day when all will be restored. God is faithful and true. His words are trustworthy and true. I know that I must cling to Jesus and trust His words. Although the pain and sorrow continue deeply, God has given me a peace and assurance of His love, of Heaven, of eternity, and of the continuity of life and of relationships. I continue each day to cling to Jesus and to try to keep an eternal perspective as I journey Home.

The words in these verses are so powerful. These verses speak of God's eternal plan, of His faithfulness, and of our need to trust Him. An eternal perspective is necessary as we continue this journey. Jesus is the Alpha and Omega. Jesus is the First and the Last. From the beginning of time God has unfolded the eternal plan that will result in all things restored. Jesus promises rewards in these verses and it remind us that all we do here on this Earth matters for eternity. The word *Amen* is used twice in these verses. Amen means "let it be so." We hear Jesus' grace is with us and He is coming soon. When Jesus returns, we will have a New Heaven and New Earth, a new body, but we will be ourselves and our loved ones will be themselves. We will be reunited with our loved ones in eternity to worship and live with Jesus. We look for that day because Jesus promises He will come soon. I am waiting on that day! Come, Lord Jesus. Come. Amen and amen.

BOND UNBROKEN

Their bond – a fusion of whole souls – constructed on the eternal Foundation.
A lifetime in the making – each brick and stone laid with the mortar of
genuine intent and self sacrifice.

So much self given away in its making, the connection shared
Is unlike any other – in form, in radiance, in anatomy, in majesty.
the virility of its luster plain to everyone.

Decades given to its building, it strengthened with each passing moment,
Each of them giving fully, and each receiving more in return
than had been given away.

Definitive synergy.

A relationship unquestionably sublime, yet perfectly real.
A marriage deeply spiritual, yet supremely practical as it flourished in
each day's moments, no matter how mundane.

A oneness fully seated in Heaven, yet fully blossoming on Earth.
An immense and inarguable testament to the power of its Creator,

Blessed immeasurably by Him in return.

A bond of perfect substance, stalwart and unchanging.
An illumination of incalculable radiance, brilliant and powerful –
Giving them both light and warmth on their journey together.

Then without warning, a cloud passes before the sun.
Only a wisp of matter for a glimmer of a moment.

But for that moment of shade and shadow,
The light appears to lessen in radiance, and heart takes a shock of pain
rarely known in the world.

Her Earthen eyes, subject to the temporal illusions of darkening –
Fallen and incomplete enough to be fooled by the fleeting tricks of mortality
strain through their own tears to see again
all the brilliance they had known and lived whole-heartedly
within for so many joyous years.

And with the tears flow questions and uncertainty.
She knows the Truth, but the shade is so heavy –
      and it fills up the seemingly countless moments
      once saturated with the words, touch, comfort, and safety
      of the tangible presence of her one and only –
Then, now, and forever her soul mate.

Where is the assurance that had so infused the decades past?
Where is the affirmation that had so enriched the life she knew?
      She wants that life to return –
      She misses her love.

Then speaks the Word – the Word made flesh

DEAREST ONE, IT IS NOT THE SHADE THAT IS REAL –
NOR ARE THE SHADOWS,
      NOR THE MIST OF THE CLOUD.

EARTHLY EYES BEHOLD VISIONS COLORED BY
      BLINDED SPACE, MEANINGLESS TIME,
      AND THE REMNANTS OF A FALL FROM PERFECTION.

BUT HEAVEN LOOKS DOWN TO SEE WHAT IS REAL –
      WHAT IS ETERNAL AND TRUE – NO MATTER HOW THINGS
      SEEM TO THOSE STILL ON EARTH,

AND WHAT IS REAL IS THAT WHICH WILL LAST FOREVER.
      WHAT IS REAL IS CRADLED IN THE ARMS OF ETERNITY.
      WHAT IS REAL IS THE SUM OF LIFE AND LOVE AND
      EXPERIENCE WHICH FINDS ITS SOURCE IN THE FATHER –

THE MAKER OF TRUTH,

THE AUTHOR OF ETERNITY.

Then moves the Word – the Word made flesh

For a moment, He bridges a gap, Spirit coming to her side,
His presence overwhelming with peace and calm and understanding.
Even without words, He assures her –
      He too has felt the pain and loss and loneliness
      that can only be found by the heartbroken on Earth. then speaking
      again – *SWEET CHILD, KNOW THIS –*

THE SHADOW IN YOUR LIFE WILL NOT LAST –
  CANNOT LAST.
IT WILL PASS AWAY WITH ALL THINGS WHICH
  ARE NOT FROM ME.
FOR THE LIGHT BEHIND THE CLOUDS IS ALL ETERNITY,
  MAGNIFICENT AND GLORIOUS,
ONLY THAT WHICH SHARES ETERNITY'S POWER
  CAN WITHSTAND ITS FORCE.
ONLY THAT WHICH IS BUILT ON MY OWN POWER
  WILL BE CALLED "FOREVER."
AND YOUR LOVE, YOUR BOND, WITH THE ONE
  FOR WHOM YOU WERE MADE
FLOWS DEEP AND RICH
  WITH THAT POWER.

IT IS A JEWEL MOST PRECIOUS ON EARTH, AND
  REJOICED OF IN HEAVEN,
AN EARTHLY LOVE – YET THE NEAREST POSSIBLE
  REFLECTION OF HEAVENLY LOVE.
IT IS TODAY, AS YESTERDAY, AND AS IT WILL BE
  WHEN ALL TIME PASSES AWAY
A BOND OF PERFECT STRENGTH AND BEAUTY –
  IT IS, NOW AND FOREVER,

A BOND UNBROKEN. ~~

Bond Unbroken was written for me in honor of Don and me by our friend Dillon Enderby. He gave it to me on Don's and my first anniversary apart June 15, 2012. It is used with his permission.

Printed in the United States
By Bookmasters